CHEADLE'S JOURNAL

Assiniboine's   Milton   Our Party Across the Mountains.   Battenotte   Assiniboine's
son   (*From a Photograph.*)   the Assiniboine   wife
                                    Cheadle

CHEADLE'S JOURNAL

OF

TRIP ACROSS CANADA
1862-1863

by WALTER B. CHEADLE

With Introduction and Notes by
A. G. DOUGHTY and GUSTAVE LANCTOT

M. G. HURTIG LTD.
Booksellers & Publishers
EDMONTON

PRINTED IN JAPAN

INTRODUCTION TO THE NEW EDITION

In 1865 there was published in London one of the most popular British travel books of the late nineteenth century, *The North-West Passage by Land. Being the Narrative of an Expedition from the Atlantic to the Pacific, Undertaken with the View of Exploring a Route Across the Continent to British Columbia Through British Territory by one of the Northern Passes of the Rocky Mountains.* Appearing as joint authors on the title page were William Fitzwilliam, Viscount Milton (1839-77), and Dr. Walter Butler Cheadle (1835-1910). That the book was written by Cheadle had been known for some time, but was fully confirmed in 1931 by the publication in Canada of *Cheadle's Journal of Trip Across Canada 1862-63*, a detailed diary upon which the earlier work was based.

Appealing to the interests of an increasing number of imperial-minded Englishmen, *The North-West Passage by Land* combined an account of an adventurous journey with a plea for a policy of empire development by opening the Canadian West to settlement and the establishment of a transcontinental commercial system from Atlantic to Pacific. Cheadle's *Journal*, with more candour, admits that "we were a mere party of pleasure." It is this candour, and much greater intimate detail concerning the circumstances of life and travel in the Northwest and British Columbia in the last years of the fur trade era, which gives Cheadle's work its unique value as an historical document.

The dependence of the white man on the Indians of British North America for guidance through the hostile wilderness and help in time of need, is more frequently reported by Cheadle than in any other nineteenth century traveller's narrative. Hudson's Bay Company policy sustained a state of good will between whites and Indians, evidenced by the fact that no British subject was exposed to hostility and molestation. Yet south of the border army posts and well-armed cavalry units

were deemed necessary for the protection of American fron-
tiersmen.

Cheadle's *Journal* also documents another aspect of Indian-
white relationships—the increasing demoralization of Indian
life produced by the impact of European culture. The craving
for alcohol was only the most obvious evidence of this malaise
in native society. It was one of the most frustrating problems
which Cheadle faced in maintaining morale during the harsh
winter of 1862-63, spent in a primitive log cabin some eighty
miles north or northwest of Fort Carleton. The exact location
of these winter quarters at "La Belle Prairie" has not been
determined, but it was situated on one of the many lakes
beyond the Shell River, and the doctor devotes some fifty pages
to this episode in the journey. It was during this winter that the
essential qualities of the two travellers were clearly revealed.
Cheadle became the real leader of the expedition, demonstrat-
ing the determination and capacity for conciliating the Indian
and Métis guides which were almost completely lacking in his
companion, and without which the expedition would have
foundered before reaching the Rockies. The qualities of the
twenty-three-year-old Milton—indolent, temperamental and hot
blooded—can be only partially excused by his youth. Moreover,
as they proceeded west he was frequently afflicted by bouts of
illness, adding to Cheadle's already heavy responsibilities.

That Milton and Cheadle were not the first to explore the
route from Fort Edmonton to Kamloops is well established
today by historical evidence, but was not fully understood by
the two travellers. The difficult trail from Lac Ste. Anne to Brulé
Lake and Jasper House, which the motorist follows from Edmonton to Jasper National Park, was originally an Indian hunting
path over which H. J. Moberly took the first pack train in the
1850s. In 1859 Lord Southesk had used this trail to reach the
Embarras River. The route up the Athabasca and the Miette
to the Fraser and Tête Jaune Cache and the North Thompson,
thence downstream to Kamloops, was pioneered by one of the
parties of Canadian emigrants known as the Overlanders of '62.
This particular party was assisted to the upper reaches of the

Thompson by the famous guide André Cardinal. The reader should note that Cheadle usually refers to this group as Americans, confusing them with a few wandering American miners making their way to the Cariboo country down the Fraser River, a route chosen by some other Overlanders.

The comic relief of the account of this arduous journey begins at Fort Edmonton, where Milton and Cheadle befriended a destitute Irish schoolmaster and adventurer, designated as "Mr. O'B" in the various editions of *The North-West Passage by Land*. Egotistical, arrogant and ungrateful, he had quickly worn out his various hosts and travelling companions in his efforts to reach Victoria from the Red River Settlement. Referred to by them as O'Byrne, or O'Beirne, his true identity has been established by the recent research of Mr. Tommy Tweed as Eugene Francis O'Beirne, who was about fifty-two years old when he inflicted himself on the good people of Western Canada. A tenderfoot in wilderness travel, O'Beirne survived through the forbearance of Milton and Cheadle. At Kamloops they sent him on his way, having received no acknowledgement of the gratitude he owed the two young men. In a later edition of *The North-West Passage by Land* it is reported that Mr. O'B. proceeded from Victoria to Australia "where, upon occasion, he enlivens the bush fireside by an account of hairbreadth escapes during 'that terrible journey across the Rocky Mountains.'" Some readers were inclined to think that he was a mythical character—a conclusion which would have amazed the people he encountered during his wanderings. The reaction of his two companions to the naming of a peak in the Yellowhead Pass by the Canadian Board of Geographic Names can be easily imagined, though doubtless they would be relieved to know that Mount O'Beirne cannot be seen from Mount Milton and Mount Cheadle in the valley of the upper Thompson.

The journey down the Thompson was the worst part of the expedition's experiences. After abandoning rafting as too dangerous, they cut their way with one small axe through the deadfall and bush along the side of the valley, with the Assiniboine and his wife and boy leading much of the way. Constantly short of food, they resorted to killing two of their horses for meat. On emerging from the lower canyon they encountered Shushwap Indians with whom they traded for food, and arrived at Kamloops on August 29th, six weeks and some one hundred and eighty miles after their departure from Tête Jaune Cache.

Despite their recent harrowing experiences Milton and Cheadle were determined to see more of the Pacific colony, proceeding northward via Harrison Lake and the Fraser by steamboat, stage and on foot. The *Journal* provides a detailed account of this six week's trip which brought them to the limits of the Cariboo gold-producing region at Williams Creek. Cheadle's account of mining techniques and the character of the miners is an important source for this early phase of British Columbia history.

After leaving Victoria in late December the travellers proceeded by ship to Panama, crossing the isthmus to the east side where they found a vessel proceeding to New York. Here they boarded the ship which landed them in England in March 1864.

Fate decreed a striking disparity in the later careers of Milton and Cheadle, with the former dying at the early age of thirty-eight, and the latter steadily advancing to distinction in the world of medicine in London. His abilities were many and varied, including hospital administration, lecturing, and productive research in children's diseases. Despite professional opposition he was a pioneer in supporting the rights of women to full equality in medical education, and was one of the first to lecture to the London School of Medicine for Women.

The first edition of Cheadle's *Journal* was prepared for publication by A. G. Doughty and Gustave Lanctot of the Public Archives of Canada, with explanatory notes which have been retained for this new edition.

LEWIS H. THOMAS

University of Alberta
Edmonton
August 1969

INTRODUCTION.

This is the journal of the first transcanadian tourist. Before him others either on business, exploration or duty, had crossed overland from Eastern Canada to British Columbia. But Walter Butler Cheadle was the first to traverse the whole country from the St. Lawrence to the Pacific simply "for pleasure", for the sheer enjoyment of seeing new lands, hunting the buffalo and visiting the gold regions of Cariboo. He was then twenty-seven years of age, in the prime of his manhood, a sturdy son of Old England and a former Cambridge oarsman. This may explain his adventurous propensities, to which the reader is indebted for a faithful narrative of the primitive conditions and extraordinary hardships which attended a transcontinental trip through the mountainous solitudes of Western Canada, — conditions and hardships which were faced with indomitable courage, and inexhaustible endurance. For one must remember that in 1862 the Prairie and Pacific provinces were really a wild West, a country without roads or settlements, and deserted with the exception of distant fur-trading posts and occasional roaming Indians.

The author, Walter Butler Cheadle, with his companion, Lord Milton, left Liverpool in June 1862 and reached Quebec on the 2nd of July. By boat they proceeded at once to Toronto, visiting Niagara Falls, and then by railway through Detroit and Chicago to La Crosse, on the Mississippi. Here, they boarded a steamer which conveyed them to St. Paul, whence a journey by rail brought them to St. Anthony. From that place, they travelled by stage to Georgetown on the Red River. Here they took to the canoe and reached Fort Garry on the 7th of August.

Soon the actual difficulties of the journey began. Equipping themselves with necessary food, arms and utensils, they purchased horses, secured reliable half-breed guides and left Fort Garry on August 23rd for the prairies. Their first stop was at Fort Ellice on the Assiniboine and their next at Fort Carlton, on the North Saskatchewan, which they reached on the 26th of September.

The season was now well advanced and therefore Cheadle and Milton went into winter quarters near White Fish Lake, at a place called Jolie or Belle Prairie, about eighty miles from Carlton, where they remained till the 3rd of April 1863. On that date, they returned to Carlton. Securing new guides and provisions they made preparations for the most difficult task of their journey, the crossing of the Rockies. Three days later, they started on their daring enterprise, stopping at Fort Pitt and later at Fort Edmonton, posts of the Hudson's Bay Company on the North Saskatchewan. On the 3rd of June, the party left Edmonton heading for the Rockies, having decided to cross the mountains by way of the Yellowhead Pass, at that time a very little known route.

Here they faced an exceedingly arduous part of the trip. With a weak party and no experience of local mountain conditions, they reached Jasper House on June 29th and Yellowhead Pass, July 17th. Difficulties soon increased. Well-nigh impassable routes along the Thompson river owing to steep rocky hills, close forests and fallen timber, delayed their advance. A diminishing quantity of food, scarcity of game, the subsequent loss of provisions, instruments and horses, added to their hardships and privations, and reduced them to the necessity of killing their pack-horses to save the party from starvation. But thanks to an indomitable spirit and the resource of their French half-breed guide, they finally reached Kamloops on August 28th. But their condition was pitiable. Their clothes were in tatters, their faces were gaunt and haggard, and their bodies in a state of almost complete exhaustion from exposure, fatigue and lack of nourishment.

At Kamloops the travellers re-victualled and proceeded to New-Westminster and Victoria. Now they carried out the last part of their programme, by taking a trip by boat and stage to the gold regions of the Cariboo as far as Richfield. Returning to Victoria, they spent a day at San Juan Island, at that time a bone of contention between England and the United States. On the 20th of December, Cheadle and Milton sailed for San Francisco and from there to New York where they took passage on board the *China*. They landed at Liverpool on the 5th of March 1864, after nearly two years of absence.

After their return, they published in their joint names an account of their travels under the following title: *The North-West Passage by Land. Being the narrative of an expedition*

TRIP ACROSS CANADA

from the Atlantic to the Pacific, undertaken with the view of exploring a route across the continent to British Columbia through British territory by one of the northern passes in the Rocky Mountains. By Viscount Milton, F.R.G.S., F.G.S., etc., and W. B. Cheadle, M.A., M.D. Cantab., F.R.G.S. London, Cassell, Petter, and Galpin, Ludgate Hill, E.C. (1865). The book, a good-sized volume of 397 pages, with 23 full-page illustrations and 2 maps, met with instant success. It soon ran through eight editions. A ninth and last edition appeared in 1891.

In spite of the two names on the cover it was well known the book had been written by Cheadle. A comparison with his *Journal* will make it quite evident. The book is simply the journal abbreviated, re-arranged and changed from its daily entries into a more systematic and logical account and turned, thanks to explanations and comments, into the ordinary palatable form of travel narrative for general consumption. But, on the other hand, it is shorn of the immediate subjectivity and spontaneity of daily notations; it lacks the intensely dramatic element of the actual hardships, anxiety and the experience recorded day after day; it misses also the spice of opinion and criticism of things and persons, which the diary exhibits with open and undiluted frankness. In the diary, names are given in full; for instance, one of the travellers' companions, designated under the anagram of Treemiss, recovers in the *Journal* his real name of Messiter. Many such facts and statements not incorporated in the book, are to be found in the *Journal*. Besides many informative pages relating to British Columbia have been entirely left out of the finished narrative, as well as the account of the trip from Victoria to New York and Liverpool.

Such is the great superiority of the *Journal*. In some measure, by the presence of considerable unused material and a different recording of information, it is almost a new work, the documentary value of which cannot be exaggerated. Written from day to day under all kinds of conditions it, naturally and fortunately, does not bother with style nor composition. But crammed with incidental details, it is a mine of interesting observations, accurate descriptions and vivid pen-pictures, interspersed with a rich vein of humour, simplicity and sportsmanship. It is a book that no lover of the West can ignore.

It is to be remarked that in the title of the book, the tourist trip of the authors is raised to the dignity of an exploration. To it is ascribed a purpose of greater importance, probably as bearing a larger public appeal. Such a claim is not quite substantiated either by the *Journal* or by the facts recorded in it. It is evidently an afterthought, which does not detract from the merits of the excursionists. Indeed it might be interesting to read the *Preface* to their narrative, as it constitutes a remarkable illustration of the economic ideas of the period concerning the future of Canada and her part in developing imperial trade with the Far East. Here follow the essential parts of their introduction:

"The following pages contain the narrative of an Expedition across the Continent of North America, through the Hudson's Bay Territories, into British Columbia, by one of the northern passes in the Rocky Mountains. The Expedition was undertaken with the design of discovering the most direct route through British territory to the gold regions of Cariboo, and exploring the unknown country on the western flank of the Rocky Mountains, in the neighbourhood of the sources of the north branch of the Thompson River.

"The Authors have been anxious to give a faithful account of their travels and adventures amongst the prairies, forests, and mountains of the Far West, and have studiously endeavoured to preserve the greatest accuracy in describing countries previously little known. But one of the principal objects they have had in view has been to draw attention to the vast importance of establishing a highway from the Atlantic to the Pacific through the British possessions; not only as establishing a connection between the different English colonies in North America, but also as affording a means of more rapid and direct communication with China and Japan. Another advantage which would follow — no less important than the preceding — would be the opening out and colonisation of the magnificent regions of the Red River and Saskatchewan, where 65,000 square miles of a country of unsurpassed fertility, and abounding in mineral wealth, lies isolated from the world, neglected, almost unknown, although destined at no distant period perhaps, to become one of the most valuable possessions of the British Crown.

"The idea of a route across the northern part of the Continent is not a new one. The project was entertained by the early French settlers in Canada, and led to the discovery of the

Rocky Mountains. It has since been revived and ably advocated by Professor Hind and others, hitherto without success.

"The favourite scheme of geographers in this country for the last three centuries has been the discovery of a North-West Passage by sea, as the shortest route to the rich Countries of the East. The discovery has been made, but in a commercial point of view it has proved valueless. We have attempted to show that the original idea of the French Canadians was the right one, and that the true North-West Passage is by land, along the fertile belt of the Saskatchewan, leading through British Columbia to the splendid harbour of Esquimalt, and the great coal-fields of Vancouver Island, which offer every advantage for the protection and supply of a merchant fleet trading thence to India, China, and Japan."

With their intelligent estimate of Canadian conditions, the above quotations well deserve reproduction. For there is no doubt that Cheadle's *North-West Passage by Land* played an important part in directing Great Britain's attention to Canada, the abundant agricultural possibilities of the West and the mineral resources of British Columbia. One might even say that it created an atmosphere most favorable to the proposals of Confederation. It is also worth while noting that the Grand Trunk Pacific, in adopting the Yellow Head Pass for its road through the Rockies, followed the track of Cheadle and his companions. All these considerations but serve to enhance the value of the present *Journal*.

Of the author, a biographical notice should find its place here.

Walter Butler Cheadle was born at Colne, in Lancashire, on October 15, 1835. His father, the Reverend James Cheadle, who had been thirteenth wrangler at Cambridge in 1831, was then vicar of Christ-Church at Colne. His mother was Eliza, daughter of John Butler of Ruddington, Nottinghamshire. When Walter was six years old, his father became vicar at Bingley, Yorkshire. The young Cheadle went to the grammar School of the little town and proved himself assiduous and successful in his class work. In 1855, his father sent him to his old Cambridge University as a scholar of Gonville and Caius College, where he distinguished himself both in sports and studies. In 1859, he experienced a great disappointment, when, being selected to row in the University eight against Oxford, he was prevented by a family bereavement from taking part in the great race and securing his full blue. The same year, he obtained his B. A. He began the study of medicine at Cambridge, completing it at St. George's Hospital, London, in 1861, when he took his M.B. degree.

In the following year, 1862, Cheadle, who had made the acquaintance of William Fitzwilliam, Viscount Milton, his junior by four years, started with him for Canada. Being absent nearly two years the two adventurous travellers did not return till 1864.

After writing a narrative of his voyage, Cheadle returned to his medical profession. In 1865 he became physician to the Western General Dispensary, London, and was elected a member of the Royal College of Surgeons. The same year, he took his degree of M.A. and M.D. at Cambridge. The next year, he married Anne Murgatroyd of Bankfield, near Bingley in Yorkshire. Meeting with great success in his career, he was appointed in 1867 assistant physician to St. Mary's Hospital, and in 1869 to the Hospital for Sick Children. In 1870, he was made a fellow of the Royal College of Physicians. Dean of St. Mary's medical school, from 1869 to 1873, he took a great interest in its welfare, contributing to the foundation of scholarships and promoting the success of its athletic clubs. In 1898, he endowed a Cheadle prize and a gold medal for an essay on clinical medicine, donating for the purpose a sum of of over $5000. Later he donated the Cheadle cot at the Children's Hospital in memory of his wife. In 1884, he contracted a second marriage with Emily Mausel, of Rothbury, Northumberland. Dr. Cheadle died on the 25th of March 1910 at 19 Portsman Square, London, and was buried in Ocklinge cemetery at Eastbourne.

A physically strong man, Cheadle was tall and of heavy build. In politics he was a radical. In his profession, his practice lay mainly among children and his chief writings are devoted to children's health and ailments. In face of much professional opposition, he stood among the early supporters of women's claims to a right to practice medicine. He was one of the first professors to lecture at the London School of Medicine for women. His second wife predeceased him, but four sons by his first wife survived him.

In the publishing of Cheadle's journal, the editors had

chiefly in mind a volume that would appeal to the general public. They have adhered to the only sound principle of following the manuscript as faithfully as possible. A few deviations were allowed in the case of well-known names but otherwise variations in spelling have been maintained as in the original. Punctuation, often omitted by the author, was introduced when necessary to facilitate the understanding of the narrative. Words inserted to complete the text are printed between square brackets. The addition of two maps showing Cheadle's route, has obviated the necessity of a series of foot-notes giving geographical information. The illustrations which are from sketches taken on the spot by the travellers are reproduced from the printed book. They constitute documents of great retrospective interest. For the sake of convenience all notes have been placed in an Appendix, at the end of the volume.

The original manuscript of Cheadle's *Journal*, a copy of which is in the Canadian Archives, is the property of W. W. Cheadle, Esq., of Bridge Road, Grays, Essex. For the readiness with which he acquiesced in the publication of such a valuable contribution to Western Canadian history, the editors wish to express to him their highest appreciation.

CHEADLE'S
JOURNAL OF TRIP ACROSS CANADA.
1862-1863

Sailed in *Anglo-Saxon* from Liverpool
to Quebec, Thursday, June 19th, 1862.

Montreal Ocean Steamship Co.

RULES

Breakfast	8.30
Luncheon	12
Dinner	4
Tea	7 — *Supper only to order*

Lights in Saloon out at 11 — In Cabins at 11.30.

Thursday, June 19th.—Sailed at 5, only 25 Cabin passengers as yet. Weather very drizzling on leaving in the
tender but soon became fine though cloudy.

Had the temerity to smoke 2 pipes immediately on the
ship's getting under way. About 6 o'clock 3 little devils found
stowed away amongst the coals, hauled out, ship brought to,
& boat from a pilot vessel signalled to come alongside, when
they were quickly sent over the side with a bag of biscuits
from the Captain. They did not appear at all disconcerted
at being discovered, but went away grinning, one waving a
biscuit in farewell. Smoked more pipes, & then retired to our
berths about 11.

Friday, June 20th.—At Londonderry took on board 200
Emigrants. About 100 were from Liverpool. On turning out
about 8.30 found the sea little rough. After breakfasting on ham
& eggs went on deck to smoke a pipe, but feeling a little squeamish desisted & retired to berth for a couple of hours. Sea much
worse on returning to deck, but found still water off Moville
where we arrived about 12, having to wait until 6 for passengers
& mails. There at anchor enjoyed a very good dinner, at tea
most passengers made their appearance. Amongst them we

15

have, (in two cabins) 2 Romish bishops (Quebec[1] & Kingston)[2] on their return from Rome where they have been assisting at the Canonization of the Japanese martyrs, & glory in the possession of a silver medal apiece presented to them by the Pope for their eminent services on the occasion. One (he of Quebec) a 'round fat oily man of God' who greatly affects a meerschaum pipe & blows his cloud with much complacency. The other a very tall emaciated party with extremely long coat & puritanical expression of countenance jabbers French in a thin squeaky querulous voice, one smokes, the other snuffs, one feasts, the other fasts. We have one Irishman on his way to seek his fortune in Canada. Fresh coloured, blue eyed, golden bearded fellow; like Mark Tapley always jolly, full of spirits, always poking fun at some one, & going into fits of laughter at the slightest provocation, & telling wonderful stories of Australian life of which he had 5 years experience. Native Corroborees & so forth. One man a great sweep, a bragging fellow, says he has been an officer in the army, don't believe him, says he never felt fear, & can drink against anyone, never sea-sick. He became such a nuisance that we induced two of the passengers to treat him with whiskey bought at Moville, when he rapidly got drunk & tumbled about the deck, eventually subsiding quietly into his cabin. Weather blowing stormy very.

Saturday, June 21st.—A gale of wind, & heavy sea during the night & still continuing. Turned out to breakfast. Lord Milton wisely taking his repast in his berth. I got through a little breakfast but had to bolt downstairs, was sick & expected to have to endure frightful tortures, but recovered in a few minutes. Hardly anyone at table. Felt seedy & spent most of the day in my berth. Weather not improving.

Sunday, June 22nd.—Certainly one of the longest days I ever passed. Did not turn out till evening & found only the Irishman & one or two more. Delighted to find our drunken friend has suffered horribly, & vows he will not taste drink again during the voyage! he has become very subdued. Lord M. did not turn out at all. Felt myself very headachy & squeamish & stuck to dry toast & coffee; great distaste for food being the principal discomfort.

Monday, June 23rd—Turned out towards 11, & shortly

after Lord M. put in his first appearance for 2 days. Both felt very uncertain. No catastrophe however occurred. Still very rough wind dead ahead the vessel pitching tremendously, being very lightly laden—cargo tea. Everyone appears to have suffered & several passengers who have crossed the Atlantic several times agree that they never suffered so much before; therefore I may congratulate myself upon my good fortune in my first long voyage. We begin to make the acquaintance of some of our fellow sufferers. We find a Mr. Messiter, a tall fine young fellow, Etonian & Oxonian, who has been suffering from prairie fever for last 5 years & is now on his way to enjoy what he has so long looked forward to, viz., hunting the buffalo & grisly bear in the neighbourhood of the Rocky Mountains. He has been awfully ill & looks very woebegone, having eaten nothing since Saturday. He goes out prepared with arms & ingenious appliances of all kinds to alleviate the discomforts of a wild life. 5 rifles, 3 revolvers & a gun! Gloves! Musquito nets, strychnine, rifle shells for the 'grislys', &c., &c. What he will do with all his fixins I can't imagine. A jolly young fellow. Another pleasant agreeable fellow in Mr. Gamble, an officer about to rejoin his regiment at Halifax. He too has been 'in profundis'. Have not made 200 miles in 24 hours except the first. Prospect of another bad night, but we regard it with more calmness. Take the precaution however of having our meals in the passage, or on deck.

Tuesday, June 24th.—The gale moderated a little, very rough during the night, wind dead ahead. Have seen several pieces of wood floating past & the Captain says there must have been a very severe storm ahead of us, judging from the sea which is much more agitated than even the gale at noon would account for. Lord M. & myself quite lively, & after much hesitation ventured to sit down in the saloon to dine, & without evil result or unpleasantness. Have been equal to a pipe *every* day. Today made the acquaintance of a Yankee, a Mr. Gray of Missouri. A great talker, but less prejudiced against 'Britishers', & of larger mind than the majority of his fellow countrymen. We have badgered him about the slave question & the present condition of the Cession pretty considerably, but he makes a good fight & replies with perfect good humour. He is a complete Yankee in appearance, tall, thin, clean shaven cheeks & chin, light moustache, long face, eyes near set & quick, wears a drab wide-awake set jauntily on the side of his head. His American twang is not very strong tho' very perceptible, & he speaks good English. Although born & bred in a slave state he is an Abolitionist & strong Unionist. Yet hating & despising the niggers most cordially. Says they are not human beings. No argument however except that we don't know what animals they are. Had him extensively about General Butler's villainous proclamation to the woman at New Orleans. This he could not defend, merely saying that it was foolishly worded & misunderstood, his meaning being that they should be imprisoned, & not necessarily in the New Orleans Spinning House, or otherwise be treated as prostitutes. Admits that our railroads & mutton chops lick the American, but we have nothing to compare to Buckwheat cakes, & green corn, &c. Lord M. allowed to him that the American women are the most beautiful in the world. A fine afternoon, making good way with light wind ahead; fine red sunset.

Wednesday, June 25th.—Fine bright morning; have made 270 miles in last 24 hours. Everybody reappeared at meal times. Shovel-board introduced, very slow game & most of us dreadfully bored. Much annoyed with the cabin steward who pertinaciously persists in calling me for breakfast. Have however given strict orders to be left to sleep as long as possible, for the day is tedious enough. A pious old lady sits with her daughter at the Captain's (our) table, thinks it very wrong of the Queen to have accepted the present of a sideboard from the Pope. Notwithstanding a lucid explanation she womanlike stuck to her point & was utterly unable to see any difference between his Temporal & Spiritual position. As we are on deck smoking pipes & enjoying the first fine day, an old gentleman in a battered white hat came up & sat down to read. The Purser, a jolly Irishman, immediately came across from the bridge & accosted him with, "Well Colonel, I hope you are all right again." — "All right, sir," said the Colonel, (Col. Gugy)[3] "I am *frightfully* ill. I have suffered horribly. I am thoroughly ashamed of myself & I shall never hold up my head again." — "What have you been doing, my dear sir," cried the Purser, "there can be nothing in sea-sickness to be ashamed of." — "I tell you Sir," replied the Colonel, "it is the most demoralising thing a man can go through, it is degrading to lie on one's belly on the floor, with one's head over a basin; to be the slave of one's squeamish stomach, & a disgusting beast in the face of the company. No Sir. I shall never hold up my head again amongst my fellowmen." This all said with such earnestness & sincerity that we were compelled to burst out laughing. We hear that he is a great Politician & a man of some note in Quebec.

Thursday, June 26th.—A fine morning. Wind S. W. so that we are able to hoist our canvas again. About 1 o'clock the Captain, whilst talking with us on deck suddenly exclaimed: "By Jove, there's the wreck of a vessel." After some little time we discovered a small object on the horizon, which by the help of glasses we made out to be the hull of a ship, dismasted & no one on board & almost directly in our course. The Captain's surmise that there had been a tremendous storm ahead of us is therefore probably correct. He guessed her 3 miles distant & as we took 18 minutes to reach her he would be about right. We altered our course a little N. so as to pass under her stern which was towards us, & at about 2 yds. distance read her name 'Ruby'. She was completely waterlogged, the waves which were not very high washing over her. Probably laden with timber or casks or she would not have floated. The masts (2, a schooner) had evidently been cut away, & her sides down to the level of the deck were broken up so that only the skeleton beams were left. The bowsprit was carried away, & the boats had either been the refuge of the crew, or washed away & the men on board drowned. They had evidently made a good struggle for life, but from the dreadfully battered state of the hull it would seem doubtful whether the boats could live in such a sea as there must have been. The bits of wood we saw floating past a few days ago might be part of the *Ruby.* We met with her about 10 miles west of Lat. 51° 15', Long. 40° 50', but as there was a strong west wind blowing & had been throughout the week would probably be some few hundred miles in front of us. It appeared quite recent from the freshness of the cut & broken wood of the ship. Resumed shovel-board but soon tired. Played whist in the evening. Wind getting up fast & quite a gale before we turned in about 12. Phosphorescence of the sea. Crest of each wave breaking in light. Wake of the ship a path of light brilliant scintillations; thought at first there were lights at the stern.

Friday, June 27th.—Rain & fog. Very strong head wind W. N. W. but fortunately allows canvas to be hoisted which steadied us amazingly. All ennuyéed: backgammon, chess &

cards most of the day. Our Yankee got upon religious matter this evening; says his parents were staunch Presbyterians but he himself aint much of a hand at going to church. Guesses that "most that go don't go to worship but might just as well call & leave their cards on the Communion table! !" Towards evening the wind & sea began to go down, the fog however getting denser & the whistle having to be sounded every few minutes. Very cold. During the morning the screw shaft became heated, the hose was laid on, & everything soon right again.

Saturday, June 28th.—Awoke about 6 by the stopping of the screw. Got up & looked out but could see no cause, hoped to see an iceberg. On going on deck found that we had passed very close to one. Fog dense. Wind slight W. Whistle sounding at short intervals & frequently we proceed at half speed. Stopped the engines about 12 to take soundings. could not find bottom with 130 fathoms. Very cold & raw. Now in the region of ice & about 100 miles from Cape Race. Only 195 miles in last 24 hours. 1886 in all. Great caution used, 2 lookouts in the bows, two officers on the bridge, & generally the Captain also who is very diligent. He had the *Canadian* when she was lost, struck on a piece of ice wh[ich] was under water & not seen. Shock so slight that he standing on the bridge did not perceive it. Keel torn out so that she filled rapidly, about 40 lost. Stop the engines every few hours to sound. Off the Banks of Newfoundland.

Sunday, June 29th.—Heard a great whistling before getting up. Find that we passed a steamer very close. Fog very dense until about 9 a.m. when the sun struggled out & we resumed full speed & are making about 11 knots. Like the Captain much, a good straightforward bluff seaman. Went to service in saloon at 10.30. About 80 saloon & steerage passengers present. Captain G. read prayers with very great expression, far better than most parsons. Morning prayers without Litany or Communion Service. 2 hymns. Last night gentleman who became so objectionable on the 2nd day of our voyage again had a good soak & became very uproarious, singing scraps of songs, doing the double shuffle & talking very large. Lord M. & Messiter treated him to beer in the hope of ridding the Company of a nuisance by rendering him incapable. The Purser however stopped his grog. About 9 he was walking about in the saloon & with a paper to his tail "Please kick me" & inveighing against the Purser, vowing he would serve him out, get him dismissed from his situation, cut his throat &c., &c., & swearing tremendously. He persuaded us to try & get him a bottle of beer but the steward said no, so that he went to bed without. The Irishman & he in the 'shuttle' singing to a select party of steerage & saloon passengers. This morning he is subdued, has hot coppers & a headache, & renews his vow not to touch intoxicating liquors again! His wrath has evaporated. 4 p.m., a fine afternoon, sunny & favourable N. W. wind so that we have a chance of seeing Quebec on Wednesday morning. Numbers of bets laid about being in by noon on that day. 168 miles from 12 yesterday to 12 today.

During service the two bishops retired to their cabins. I presume to pray for our benighted souls. It was observable that on Friday the lank one (he of Kingston) fasted diligently. The corpulent one of Quebec sustained the weakness of the flesh by 4 good meals. About 3, passed St. Pierre, an island in possession of the French for fishing purposes.

Monday, June 30th.—On rising 8.30 a.m. found a beautiful bright sunny morning, very clear atmosphere, passing Cape Race just at the entrance of the Gulf of St. Lawrence. The cape consists of low bluffs with patches of snow upon them at various places. Sea very calm & blue. Numerous fishing boats in sight. Last night Lord M., myself, the Doctor & others who joined in at times had a 2 hours argument as to the right of the south to secede from the Union (with Mr. Gray the Yankee). He contended against 3 or 4 of us with admirable temper, & great ingenuity, of course the thing remained at the conclusion where we began. Mr. Gray contended that a state's joining the union was final; that although the Constitution said not a word on the matter (except in that part relating to the army stating that it was to be "employed for the resistance of invasion & the suppression of rebellion") yet it was implied in every sentence, & all acts of Government that the agreement was that the majority should rule. A state could secede only with the consent of the rest, or of a majority (represented by the Government). He asked whether Scotland would be allowed to separate, or whether that would be considered rebellion on her part. But we could not admit that a parallel case, stated that the state of Louisiana actually belonged to Union Government by purchase, & that most others had been partly bought by it. On another question asserted that the Irish to a man would fight against England in case of war. Did not understand that Romanism was the cause of that. Several Englishmen (to his own knowledge) had taken the oath of allegiance to the union, were now serving in the states' army & would stick by their new colours in case of war with Great Britain. Our idea of the States wanting Canada a mistake. No wish for it. Desire of conquest in a southerly direction (Mexico, &c.). Feel perfectly well & lively but still no appetite. 3 p.m. just passing the "bird islands", where large numbers of eggs are collected, belong to Admiral Coffin who makes nothing of them. Messiter agrees to go to the Saskatchewan with us.

Tuesday, July 1st.—Heavy rain during the night. Dull but fair on rising. Passing between Anticosti & Gaspe, about 12 & have fairly entered the mouth of the St. Lawrence. Yesterday afternoon had a lesson from the Captain in the use of the sextant, artificial horizon, &c. Discovered that an unfortunate man in the steerage had been robbed of the whole of his money except 5 or 6 shillings. We got the Purser to investigate the story, & subsequently Mr. Gray, Lord M., Mr. Messiter & myself examined the man. He is a rough strong dirty fellow, not at all like a professional swindler. The story he told was this. He arrived in Liverpool on Wednesday the 18th, the day before the ship sailed. Spent the night with his wife at a Mrs. Garraty's who keeps a lodging house in Union St. He is a Staffordshire miner. On Thursday, having bid goodbye to his wife & supplied her with £20, he had 16 sovereigns left which he placed in a leathern purse given him by his wife. About ½ an hour before the tender sailed he & a "mate" of his who is coming out in another ship the 'John Bell' fell into conversation with a sort of a gentleman on board the tender, who asked them if they were about to sail for Canada & on their replying in the affirmative said it was a fine place to settle in if a man had some £20 when he landed, & "I suppose you'll have about that." they said they should have something but not much; Well said the "gentleman sort of a man," I had only 30 shillings when I landed there, & now I've an estate there worth £700 or £800, wife & children. He then said they had better go & have a glass with him before leaving the old country & they accordingly went to a liquor vault & had 3 pennorths' of gin apiece for which the stranger paid. At this place the miner drew out his purse & changed one of his 16 sovereigns in order to have change on board ship.

On leaving the pothouse the stranger felt hungry & asked them if they would not like something to eat. They could do half a pound of mutton chops or steak, & he gave the miner 1/6 to go and buy some. On his returning with his mate they could not find the man. Thought they had mistaken the place & as they had no time to spare returned to the tender expecting the man to turn up there. However they saw no more of him. When off Moville the man took out his purse whilst in his berth which was dark & counted over 15 pieces. He did not again look at them until yesterday when he wished to change one for silver ready when he should land. To his dismay he found 15 counterfeits. Lord M., Messiter, Gray & myself were all convinced of the man's truthfulness & Lord M. & Gray commenced getting subscriptions for the unfortunate man. On tackling the Colonel however he was met with a long oration on the advantages of getting the man employment in Quebec rather than giving him money & this he undertook to do. Stating at the same time his conviction that the man was an impostor (without having seen or examined the fellow). This rather shook Gray, & there was some hesitation in proceeding with the subscription. It seemed to be however the wish of the passengers generally to give the man some money & to give all an opportunity of seeing the man & hearing his story, he was invited into the saloon to relate what he had told us before. The Colonel put two or three questions to him, failed to elicit anything to shake the man's story, & then rising from his seat said in a loud angry voice, "It's all a lie. I don't believe a word of it; & I cannot help saying a most barefaced attempt at imposture." There was a general outcry against him thus vituperating the poor fellow whom we had invited to come, & who had never made any application for assistance to any one, & feeling set strongly in the miner's favour & against the Colonel who retired from the meeting to express to the ladies his pity for our credulity. Having further rigidly cross-examined him & examined a witness as to what had taken place since his coming on board, finding the tale hang perfectly well together, & considering that he deserved some assistance, Lord M. went round with his hat & collected £7 for him. The Colonel & the two priests refusing to give, twas placed in charge of the Purser to be handed to him on landing. The Colonel now much at a discount. Northern lights rather fine.

Wednesday, July 2nd.—The purser gave the £7 to the

miner who cried like child. Last night Mr. Shaw (The Commercial) proposed & all supported (except the Colonel) the proposition of signing a round robin to thank Captain Graham for his great kindness & courtesy to all on board. This was done. At 8.30 in the evening we arrived at Father Point, 168 miles from Quebec & took the pilot on board. The scenery along the first part of the St. Lawrence is wild & barren, low ranges of hills covered with pine, with white wooden fisherman's huts along the shore. Further up the country becomes much more fertile. The houses larger, white, & on turning out this morning the view was beautiful, 7 or 8 miles from Quebec & a beautiful sunny morning. Arrived at 9.15. The promontory on which the citadel stands seems to shut in the river; on one side runs the St. Lawrence, on the other the River St. Charles. We passed the falls of St. Montmorency on the right about 7 miles from Quebec. The City of Quebec is built round the base & up the sides of the bluff, some streets very steep. Country round & on banks pretty, well wooded & studded with very clean white villas. Town itself poor, lower town streets very narrow, dirty & ill paved with planks, others with rough boulders. Likely to be run over, carriages approach so noiselessly on wood. Houses built of wood, clinker fashion, painted white with bright green Venetian shutters, which in the brilliant sunlight look very gay; others of white brick, rubble or stucco. Bothered to death to hire calashes, which resemble broken-down gentlemens' cabs. Names seem nearly all French & Irish. French seems the prevalent language. Advertisements & bills in both. Went with Gray, Rosenberg, Lord M., & McFaddle to see the plains of Abraham. Understood the plan of the battle perfectly from plan at hotel. Saw the Monument where Wolfe fell, raised by British Army. Farther on the plains one to both him & Montcalm. Quebec considered impregnable but taken & retaken 4 times.[4] Solitary young lady on arrival not met by expected lover. Half frantic & telegraphing. Expectant lover too late at the wharf but at last found her at Russell's Hotel. Married in an hour. Travelled to Montreal with us. Parted with the Yankee & Rosenberg with regret.. Both gave us their address & obtained ours. Gray very pressing for us to visit him if we came to St. Louis. Promised. Rosenberg told Lord M. & myself with air of mystery that he was the man who chartered the *Mary*

Wright which arrived in Liverpool, a short time ago having run the blockade at Charleston.[5] Made $50,000 by it, has now chartered her back from Nassau (West Indies) with arms &c., which he sends on there from England. Going to meet her at Charleston if he can pass the lines. Came by Quebec to avoid observation. Made us promise not to tell Gray. Weather hot & bright, a good summer's day in England. No rain for 7 weeks. Worst summer for drought for long time. A man came into the room where Lord M. was unpacking, seized a 'portable scrip' & wanted to trade. On Lord M.'s refusing, he walked off with it & said if he could not fix the price it was not his fault. Afterwards came & apologized. Did not know to whom he was speaking, &c., &c., & offered to present 5lbs. of tobacco. Accepted. Had a mint Julep. Very hot. Billiards & bed.

Thursday, July 3rd.—Have a fearful cold. Corn Cake very good. Writing letters & filling up log. Messiter buying fur, nicknacks, &c. Start for Montreal at 5 p.m. Messiter took a calash to see plains of Abraham. Extremely hot, bright & clear. The journey from Quebec to Montreal, 168 miles, almost entirely thro' forest, principally pine. Very fine for a few miles after leaving Quebec, hills well wooded, & rocky streams. After that, country very flat. Trees by the track burnt. Here & there new clearings, burning stumps, &c. Very dusty. Peculiar cars. Strange company (2 ladies of Craig St.), Victoria Bridge, 2 miles, close to Town. Arrived at St. Lawrence at 12 midnight. Good house. Very full & busy. Lord Monck holding review. Full of officers. Bought a sextant for £6, before leaving Quebec.

Friday, July 4th.—Montreal decked with flags, &c., in honour of the Governor. Very superior to Quebec. Houses mostly good brick & stone. Green shutters as at Quebec. Streets broader but not good. Country mostly flat, enclosed. Brandy squash & mint julep. Guns altered. Bought powder & caps, &c. In the afternoon Messiter 2 miles chivy after his dog. Feed pretty good but too much hurry & very bad waiters, mostly Irish. Contrary to expectation see more English names & less French than at Quebec. Bothered with currency, York shillings, dimes, &c. Bar system. Liquors high, 1/- a bottle of beer, &c. In the evening called on Captain Graham of *Anglo Saxon*, found he was staying with Mr. Edmonston, one of the owner's firm. Took a car, stupid driver took us to Allan's (senior partner), went on to Edmonstons, found Captain G. out; returned at ½ past 10; ran him to Earth. Mr. Edmonston very screwed, takes great interest in Indians & dilated upon the game of La Crosse & told us that a grand match was to be played between the Caughnawagha Indians & Montreal Club tomorrow. He referee for Indians; much repetition. Thorough Scotchman in appearance & conversation very hospitable. Gave us two bottles champagne. Very good. Invited Captain G. to breakfast at 10.

Saturday, July 5th.—Very hot & close. Completing our preparations. Captain G. to breakfast. Then went down to the ship with Lord M. to take the sextant for examination by Captain G. Turned out to be about 20 m. wrong, the Captain very kindly corrected it for us, & gave us a lesson in navigation & use of the sextant. Found Mr. Edmonston there again. Explained to me all about La Crosse, having evidently quite forgotten last night's conversation. Bye the Bye, sir, have you ever heard of the game of La Crosse? Played by the Indians, &c. Bade adieu to the Captain & promised to acquaint him of our safe return if it came off. Messiter, meantime purchased 8 months old Newfoundland pup for £4. Celebrated breed. Started at 5 p.m. for Cornwall about 80 miles, thence by steamer to Toronto. Very hot & dusty. Yankee very irate because no filter. Messiter asking him what was the matter, he fired up at me & said he could tell by his look that he meant to make fun of him, &c., neither he nor any other man should, &c. Fire flies alias "lightning bugs" very beautiful. Land almost all enclosed, posts and rails, flat & apparently not very fertile. Arrived at Cornwall at 10 p.m. Told us at the station that the boat was gone. Sent boys to fetch waggon for baggage to wharf, i.e. loose planks laid on 4 wheels, sent luggage on & walked. Got there about 11.30. Steamer arrived about 12, 12 miles Canal & locks to avoid rapids. 3-decked steamer, long saloon. Danish emigrants lying all ways asleep on lower deck. Captain says great many going to west now.
Had supper & turned in. Double berthed cabins & larger berths than on board ocean steamers.

Sunday, July 6th.—All day up the St. Lawrence. The Thousand Islands, like those on Derwentwater, of rock cropping out covered with trees. Banks low, well wooded, timber not very large. Expect to be in Toronto at 8 tomorrow morning. Met a fellow passenger on *Anglo Saxon*, the Canadian. He tells us

we have two Corpses on board, one an M. P. & the other a
Swedish emigrant. At Kingston at 7 p.m. (The M. P. Wm.
Hamilton Merritt, one of the members of the original Canadian
Upper House (?).[6]

Met Morris on landing. Stop at Toronto.

Monday, July 7th.—Arrived at Toronto about 9.30 a.m. Fine
weather, very warm. Passed up Lake Ontario during the night.
Had breakfast on steamer & then landed. Crowd of cabmen
bullying you to engage, & rival Hotel porters. Patronised
Rossin House, a good, large Hotel. Nigger waiters. Curious
effect of black hands waiting at table. Peculiar walk of
negroes, very leisurely, moving the body round on its axis
at each step. Special tone of voice. At 1 p.m. took steamer
for Lewiston, thence by rail to Niagara & on to the Clifton
House. Arrive at 5. First view of the falls disappointing.
After a time Horseshoe fall very fine, especially from the edge,
place of Blondin's ascent. River enters Ontario between high
wooded cliffs. Rail from Lewiston along the edge of American side. Suspension bridge & first view of falls. Moose
hair work & bead do. at Bazaar. On the Lewiston steamer
a gentleman with smooth-shaven face, light moustache, white
hat with knowing look & bland smile on his countenance,
accosted Messiter & myself with a remark on the heat of the
weather or something of the kind, & speedily placed himself in
the most intimate terms. Sorry he had not a card, but shewed
us his case silver mounted, & with his name & address, Captain
Hutchinson of Guelph. Asked us to come over to a nice
little place of his about 50 miles from Toronto & have some
woodcock shooting. Turned the conversation on to Lord M.
& speedily introduced himself to him also. Asked us to go
to the bar & taste Canadian whiskey. Introduced us to a
Major Kane (?) of the Canadian Rifles with great ceremony.
Wonderful stories of his deeds at the Cape. Killed two Caffres.
Peculiar Caffre dress, &c. American ladies—style to address
them. Damns the Yankees. If they knew he was over on
their side the water would mob him, &c. Stuck to us like a
leech. Went to Clifton House. Introduced Lord M. to General Napier, Commanding Officer. Two pretty daughters,
one engaged to Aide-de-Camp. Walked out up to the head of
the fall (Horseshoe). Saw largest wild cat in the world.
Museum containing little but a stuffed juvenile donkey. Messiter

& self having headaches, & Lord M. having been before, did not go under the falls. Returned & had tea-dinner at Clifton House. Wood-strawberries very good. Don't like system of feeding, viz. small portion on little dish for each person. After, visited Bazaar. Messiter invested large sums in Moose hair work. Some very beautiful. Captain H. followed us continually, discoursed again on the freedom of manner of American ladies. Induced us to go into drawing room & instructed us to face the ladies boldly & we should find they liked it; made our best toilette which was a very seedy one. Found party of ladies & gentlemen round the piano. Hushed on our entrance. They almost immediately turned out of the windows on to the verandah (shaded balcony going round two sides). Finding it no go adjourned to Billiard room & played with Messiter till 12.30. Walking round verandah discovered thro' open window a black gentleman & white lady in a private sitting room! Turned in to bed.

(Before leaving Toronto tried to change B. P. bills for gold. Bank required a reference. Tried to find young Gamble. Met with G. senior, a barrister who kindly proved our identity. Good looking gentlemanly old boy. Young G. met us at boat going to Niagara. Tried to persuade him to go with us, promised to meet us on our return next day.)

Tuesday, July 8th.—Turned out at 7.45 to catch 8.15 train. Tremendous hurry. All rather seedy & sleepy. Lord M.'s adventure with the boots the night before. Captain H. appeared at breakfast. Went in bus with us, & tacked himself on to us in the car & boat. Told us of a spectacle he saw on coming out of his room. Had a comfortable sleep on board steamer. Captain H. inveighs against smoking. Rode one horse 100 miles between sunrise & sunset at the Cape with despatches for Sir H. Smith. Did not understand a question of Sir Henry's & answered irrelevantly. Sir H. d—s his s—l to h—l with great violence. All over in a moment & "brandy & water, my dear fellow". Found Gamble waiting for us at the wharf. The Captain follows us to Rossin House having first given his arm to a young lady on to the boat with great elegance. Liquors us up again, bids an affectionate farewell & renews his invitation. Play at Billiards. Captain reappears & liquors us up again. Offered to initiate us into the mysteries of Toronto; didn't see it. (Lord M. caught him at the bar with two other fellows talking very large about his friends Lord M., Messiter & myself. "Capital fellows, got

devilish intimate with them," &c. Asked if he had been over-
heard). Captain at length bids a final adieu. Gamble takes
us to lunch with his people. The horror on being taken into a
room full of ladies, having a fortnight's beard & seedy appearance. Mrs. G. jolly, like a 45 year old. Mrs. T., young sister,
nice looking. 30 year old cousin sets into Messiter, furious
talking match. Switzerland, falls, &c., all very pleasant. Go
to see Osgood Hall Law Courts opened by P. of W. Very
fine building. Then with Gamble across the lake to an island
to bathe, fine shelving sand, water very cold. Roll in the
sand to warm ourselves. Return & dine at 6.30. Start for
Detroit at 11.15. (The Gambles don't know the Captain,
dropped his h'es. Not sure whether he is a sharper, or merely
an impertinent fool.) Toronto a good wide-streeted town.
Each house with its garden & plenty of trees. 60,000 inhabitants.

Wednesday, July 9th.—Arrived in Detroit at 8.15. Cross
by ferry-boat. Bad breakfast on board for $1½. Custom's
officer wants 30 p.c. duty on value of guns, &c., begins on
Messiter's big case at last. Miss our train forward to Chicago
by the delay. Messiter very indignant. Taken at last to head
Customs officer who was very civil & gives us a pass through
to Fort Garry to our great relief for $1 on our taking oath
we were passing through there. On leaving Toronto telegraphed to Hamilton for berths in sleeping car. Turned in
about one. All others already bedded. Messiter passed on
to ladies' compartment. Two ladies & a gentleman in one
opposite. Like ships berths, only much wider, no sheets, rug;
don't undress completely; very comfortable night's rest;
washing & toilet conveniences; the young couple married at
Quebec on board the train. Go to Biddle House, Jefferson
Ave. Regular Yankees now. Sallow faces, large straw hats,
clean shaven cheeks & moustaches, or beards. Nasal twang
& "that's so", "I guess", used universally for "I suppose"
Detroit a large straggling place; wide streets.

Thursday, July 10th.—Left Detroit at 8 p.m. on Wednesday & got sleeping cars for which we paid $1. Charged
enormously for extra luggage, $2½ for mine. $1 per 100
extra & refused to allow more than $4.87 for sovereign,
actual exchange, $5.35. Turned in about 11. Ladies & gentle-
men very promiscuous. Ladies don't keep their division
curtain down but watch the gentlemen dressing with great

satisfaction. Went to Briggs House at Chicago, where we arrived at 8.15. A very good Hotel & Lord M. welcomed with satisfaction, the waiter talking to him as if he had been his own brother. Hamburger, the wizard, introduces himself to Lord M. & requests his patronage. Find his handkerchief in my pocket, &c. Go to Exchange office & get $5.35 for English sovereigns. Great dearth of small change & consequent difficulties, seems to be quite usual to be unable to give change, for the man at the bar gave us a glass of beer rather than change a dollar note! General rudeness of the people; push past without begging pardon, &c. Shopmen serve you as if they were doing a favour. Bought 5 lbs. powder & 3,000 French caps, &c., 1 dram strychnine (for which paid 4 doll. per 1 dram). Messiter bought 2 double guns for $7 each, to trade with. Spent considerable time in searching for some one to correct the new sextant & last found a Mr. Bradley in some business in Chicago; an amateur observer who takes the city time, & who very kindly offered to do all he could for us, went to his house, 271 Ontario St., which our Cabby had great difficulty in finding. Told Cabby he might wait if he liked to take the chance of a fare back, but we shouldn't pay him for his time. From Mr. Bradley got Greenwich time & Lat. Longitude of St. Paul. Found our Cab waiting & drove to the Hotel. Cabby wanted $2½ for his time; refused; said he would make us; ascertained true fare to be $1.50 which just as we were starting for the train he gladly took (.50 a mile, & .25 for second passenger!). Bustled off to station & there they charged us the usual $ for every 100 lbs. over the first. Very high (£3) for the 2 dogs. Train very full. Conductor very surly, had to stand about until some of the passengers landed. This part of the journey on the Chicago & North Western R. to Minnesota Junction, leaving Chicago at 9 p.m. on Thursday & arriving at Minnesota junction at 5 a.m. Friday; got sleeping cars for .50 at 11 p.m. & turned out at M. Junction at 4.30 thinking it a great nuisance. Took the train at 5.30 from M. Junction to La Crosse where we arrived about noon on Friday. Having stayed 20 minutes at Portage "City" for breakfast. Find I have lost my best pipe & 6 oz. of tobacco. Did Herr Hamburger take it?

Conductor in train between Minnesota junction & La Crosse very anxious to know if England would interpose between North & South. Said we thought not at present. He guessed that England would lose a lot by going to war with the Yankees, &c., along the Canadian line.

Friday, July 11th.—Found that the steamer did not start until 9.30 p.m. Intensely hot. Most powerful sun we have yet experienced. The line yesterday from M. Junction by Milwaukee & La Crosse R. R. passes thro' very pretty country. Wooded hills, & occasionally rather fine cliffs. Plenty of water. Cleared land, very well farmed. Plenty of wheat, dead ripe. Seems the finest country we have yet passed thro' by far. Went thro' the only tunnel I have yet noticed. Only about ¼ mile long, very low & narrow, cut thro' solid rock. At station close to this saw first Indians in paint, one rather fine face, good Roman nose & well-shaped head.

At La Crosse having 9 hours to wait, we borrowed a boat from the Captain of the steamer (Mr. McClellan) & some rods (i.e. bamboos with a piece of lead & a hook on string). From the R. Station we essayed to fish, but in a few minutes we found it too hot & rowed slowly up the "Father of waters" to a sandy island & bathed. The water brown, generally not more than 3 or 4 feet deep. Holes here & there rather deep water very warm & bathing delightful. Stayed in wading & swimming in different directions for 1½ hours. The bottom very sandy, continually shifting, the sand rolling over & covering the feet very quickly. The river very pleasant scenery. Channels branching off continually round wooded islands, &c. While bathing saw a small boy & a nigger in boats fishing with dead bait. Had caught a considerable number of catfish, bass, & some pike, all from 1 to 7 or 8 lbs. Came back to steamer about 6 & had tea. Most of these nigger waiters only quadroons or octoroons apparently. Many of them very European faces & heads, the hair & complexion only telling a tale; one played a guitar & sang pretty well during the evening. Turned in at 11.30, having discovered to our great horror that breakfast is at 6.30! Decided that Wisconsin is the prettiest state we have seen.

Saturday, July 12th.—Up at 7 to breakfast. Beautiful morning; sun not so bright as yesterday; there being a little haze. A gentleman on board remarked to me that it was a very dull day, & on my dissenting said that it was very seldom they had one so bad in this part. It was a bright glorious summer day for England! The scenery as we pass along very pretty, winding Mississippi. Channels deviating

round islands covered with trees, backwaters &c., & fine
rounded hills, partly bare & green, or covered with timber.

About 10 a.m. entered Lake Pepin, a small lake 7 or 8
miles long & about ½ one broad, similar scenery; about ½ way
up is the Maiden's Rock, a small cliff over the lake & on the
Wisconsin side opposite Clare City about which there is a
legend that an Indian girl leaped over to avoid a hated marriage enforced by her family. Saw several large fish in the
lake from the steamer, & some of apparently 10 or twenty lbs.
rising. Rather struck by the amount of swearing, a favourite
oath being 'by Jesus Christ' 'God Almighty'. I secured a
smoke from an urchin of some 12 years who sold papers in
the train to us [at] La Crosse. Arrived at St. Paul about 10,
& paid $1.50 for baggage transporting. The International, a
large Hotel, very comfortable. The Proprietor & waiters shook
hands with Lord M., welcoming him very cordially.

Sunday, July 13th.—Turned out about 10 & after breakfast
enquired & found the mail from here started on Monday 14th
for Georgetown, but the steamer not until the 28th from there
leaving us 3 or 4 days there. We decided therefore to go on
to Georgetown at once, & from there to Fort Garry by canoe
sending our luggage forward. Then ensued a furious unpacking & repacking, preparing arms & ammunition, kettles &
pans, &c. Bought 4 lbs. of strong tobacco at .50 a lb. At
work all day & a tremendous grind to get it ready at 8 for
Burbank & Co., the State people who charged us 20 dollars
for our passage to Georgetown, 390 miles, & 17 dollars for my
luggage to Fort Garry, 500 miles further. Went to Burbank's office in evening to settle about it amid the most magnificent lightning I ever saw, finer than that I saw near Hands-
worth in Mr. H.'s company. One or two tremendous bursts
of thunder. Train starts tomorrow at 5.30 a.m. to St. Antony,
thence go by Mail Coach to Georgetown. Tried to take an
observation at noon but found the sun's altitude too great for
an artificial horizon, the sextants not being large enough.
Wrote to Eliza & Lady Q. having written at Quebec to my
Mother, & at Toronto to Sam & Lady F. Got $5.25 for gold
at a Tobacconists Shop, they refusing at the bureau to give
more than $4.90.

Monday, July 14th.—Last night about 11, Lord M. came
in rather excited having just discovered he had only $30 in-
stead of $68, the proper exchange for the £13 at Mr. Hart's.
The money had been placed in the firebag on his belt which had

been taken off & laid on the bed after coming in. After much discussion & calling Mr. Blote the proprietor of the Hotel out of bed, we decided that the money had been stolen out of the house, recollecting also that Lord M. had only received $63 we all having made the mistake of $5 in the calculation. Turned out & roused up Hart's brother at the shop who went to Hart who was said to be ill (this was about 1 a.m.). He sent word, too ill to get up but would count his money in the morning & forward balance if correct. Could make nothing of the scrub missing $30. Turned in about 2 a.m. & turned out again about 4. Lord M. not having notes enough to pay the bill had a great row with bureau clerk who refused to give more than $4.90 per £1. At last paid it under protest, the clerk agreeing to send $5.25 if he could get it afterwards. Kept the train waiting. At St. Antony took bus to town. Glimpse of falls. Good town. Great resort of Southerners; none now & place half ruined. Falls like great weir. Quantity of lumber. 70 miles crowded in Mail Coach to St. Cloud, 5 outside, 8 & 4 children inside, two dogs on the roof, self inside, Lord M. & Messiter on box; stifling heat. Smell of babies & incessant crying. The Yankee ladies, Miss Julia Daly over again, incessant talking, shewed me Confederate States note for 15 cents! To talk Yankee accent every word the opposite of English & with "I guess" "now" & "kinder" & nasal twang you are complete. Talked with two Yankees about intervention. Very anxious to know whether England was likely to interfere. America would rise to a man. Liked England better now than she used to do & liking on the increase. Thought very highly of P. of Wales who seems to have made an extremely favourable impression. All spoke in terms of great admiration for Queen & Prince Consort. Could not understand why England favoured South. Insisted like all I have talked with that the real question the North were fighting for was abolition. Told them we didn't swallow that in England. Awfully tiresome ride. German women jabbering & slapping squalling German babies. Yankee women chattering like magpies. Musquitoes very irritating; spotted some hundreds. Journey thro' park-like scenery, stay at St. Cloud. Lie on the floor as objecting to bed fellows. Buy bacon, kettle, &c., for canoe journey at Burbank's store & turn in.

Tuesday, July 15th.—Leave St. Cloud (pronounced as spelt) at 6. Thro' fine mixed brush & prairie land to Sauk Centre, 65 [miles] in spring-waggon which is great improvement on Coach. Find to our horror that German woman & brats go on to Fort Abercrombie. Squalling, &c., continued. Lord M. swears considerably as also the rest. Musquitoes for ever, begin to get on to the prairies. Clearwater about 6 p.m.; pretty place. Fine teams of cream & roan ponies to Sauk Centre where we arrive about 7, and stay the night. (Left the dogs at St. Cloud; follow in next stage as they were always tumbling off the roof yesterday & hanging by their necks). Messiter, Lord M. & myself went to river to look for ducks; found none & Lord M. tired went back. Messiter & self went forward to a lake & found two which we killed but could not get owing to treacherous bog; nearly worried by musquitoes. Return & bed, one on the floor.

Wednesday, July 16th.—Leave Sauk Centre about 6. Lord M. buys Rover for 20 dollars. Women weep at parting with him & the man gives us many injunctions to "take care of the little fellow." Over Prairie land becoming more & more extensive & thro' Alexandrian woods; hope to see bear; shoot a turkey buzzard. Get out about 4 miles from Pomme de Terre & shoot 2 flappers which turn out too small for use, a wood duck & large mallard. Messiter strips & fetches them out. Several wild geese; can't get a shot. Plenty of ducks but darkness came on & we had to give up. Almost worried by musquitoes in bed-room. Messiter does not get a wink. Face & hands swollen up, in morning. I escape any swelling or marks. Fare only pork & eggs, dried apples; coffee or tea, milk, no beer or spirits. The Santa Cruz; comes in very useful & keg leaks fast. Messiter loses powder flask when wading after ducks.

Thursday, July 17th.—Leave Pome de Terre about 7. Messiter & self walk on. Finds he has left fishing basket & all effects for canoe expedition; swears; see flock of ducks on pond close to road. I kill two & Messiter one. Wet to the knees. Rover retrieves them well. Go on to Fort Abercrombie. Get out last 3 miles & walk. Get Prairie hen & plover. Rover spoils sport by chivying them as hard as he can tear. Go on towards Georgetown by mistake. Meet a man on horseback with seedy double barrel, trumpery, ornamented Hunting Knife, screwy horse, Mexican saddle & wooden stirrups! Ask the way & return. Tells us he is one of a party travelling for health. Americans. Pass their camp by side of Gully. Hail the ferry. Miscalled Fort, slovenly soldiers. Water-melon. Guard refuse to go to war. Musquitoes for ever.

TRIP ACROSS CANADA

Friday, July 18th.—Have our ducks which are very good. Leave about 8 for Georgetown, 50 miles. Stop for a dinner at 12 at a Norwegian's who speaks English like a native. Shoot our first American pigeon. Pretty bird, long forked tail, looks like a small pheasant on a tree. Mail stops for us to shoot a pheasant; bag a brace of young ones; arrive at Georgetown about 4 p.m. A few wooden houses on banks of Red River; much better place than Abercrombie. A company of soldiers stationed on account of threats of Sioux & Sotabs. Indians complain justly of non-payment for wood cut for Fort Garry steamer. Half breeds have killed 4 Elk within a few miles today. See them bringing the meat home in carts, came on a band of about 22 & could have killed more, but would not waste meat. Buy 1 birch bark canoe for $6 & hire another for $2½. Man asks $5 a day to go with us to Ft. Garry.[7] Offer 1 for journey there, & ½ dollar for return; can't agree, leave it awhile & expect he will come to terms. Long talk after tea with Mrs. Lull's sister nice looking regular "Yankee gal".

Saturday, July 19th.—Fine weather throughout. Try to buy moccasins, wants $1 a pair. Horrible old hag dressing Elk meat. Sleighing dogs like wolves desire to devour Rover. Get more kicks than halfpence. Mr. Murray's store. Very hot, few musquitoes. War party of Sioux within a few miles. Half breed saw them skulking & ran for it. —Mixed soldiers at Fort.— Uncle Sam's boy & Messiter.

Sunday July 20th.—Bought our canoe & hired another from half-breeds. $6 & $2.50. Engaged a drunken half-breed, but first rate hunter, to go with us to Fort Garry for 1-50 per day. Try the canoes, rather crank but get on well. First lesson in washing 2 pair socks & 4 pocket handkerchiefs. Lord M. 2 trousers, &c. Cast bullets & prepare tins, &c., buy necessaries. Lord M. goes 2 miles on horseback to buy whiskey. Man gives short quart; remonstrances. Fellow keeps keg & talks of prosecuting for libel. Messiter sets out for it with one of American hunters, but turned back by thunderstorm which is splendid. Wrote log. Mail arrived at 6 with the rest of our luggage which was hauled straight to Murray's store & unpacked again. Pertinacious Columbian Emigrant half-breed asks 1½ dollars per day & provisions for return, refuse, the man goes to consult his squaw. Race two Yankees in dug-out, licked. They talk of going to Fort Garry by canoe. I tell awful stories of Indian barbarities on the river to funk them from it. It evidently produces an effect; Messiter backs me up.

Monday, July 21st.—Up at 5 to complete preparations. Pemmican, flour, grease, salt, &c. Frying pan, soup kettle. basin, coffee pot. Lord M. goes in small canoe alone which he bought, Messiter & self in larger one. Good-bye to Mr. & Mrs. Lull. Take 1 gun, 1 lb. powder each, 20 lbs. of shot between us, 12 revolver & 20 gun bullets. Jolly feeling of independence quietly paddling along with all our traps. Halfbreed sits on the bank smoking quietly & making no sign, we therefore start without him. Lord M. & self turn up shirt sleeves, skin burnt. I take warning & turn them down, Lord M. persists. See plenty of ducks. Kill a couple, stay to dine, endeavour to cook duck on stick, failure. Tremendously hot. Canoes as steady as a rock. We go much faster than Lord M. Start again after 3 hours rest. Camp just at sundown, dark directly, great bother preparing supper &c. everything already wet with dew, had to go on to open prairie. Take out canoes. Most uncomfortable place. Mosquitoes dreadfully fierce, piercing thro' trousers & coat, all out of temper & first nights camping exceedingly disagreeable, turn in to sleep but little; reckon to have done 25 miles.

Tuesday, July 22nd.—Get up at sunrise after very wakeful night. Bitten to death, hands & face much swollen. Messiter much disfigured, Lord M's arms very red & sore, Messiter's back, hair gone to grief. Lord M. with red handkerchief over head &c. set out again about 8, very hot, kill 3 or 4 ducks & a goose, canoe leaks, have to stop in about an hour to pitch, put her in, still leaks, take her out, & do it over again, still leaks, find the place & tar for the third time, effectual cure, go on for another hour, & then stay for dinner. Pemmican utterly condemned by Messiter & self as chips & tallow, start again about 4, camp at 6 not liking our late hours of yesterday. Bitten again. Hear a shot, expect our Yankee friends. Fried goose & ducks. Pleasant camping place with plenty of shade & wood, break axe handle, turn in, done 7 or 8 miles only.

Wednesday, July 23rd.—Lord M.'s arms covered with large blisters & tremendously swollen, unfit to paddle, take him in tow. very hard work, the wind holding her, my arms very red & sore, mosquitoes as usual. See fewer ducks & geese, wish for half-breed to do some of our work. Camp before sundown. Banks very monotonous & muddy, stream gets wider, very tortuous, belt of wood along banks or open prairie, do about 25 miles.

Thursday, July 24th.—Pitch our canoe again which leaks abominably. Start very late & stop again for dinner in about an hour. Agree to stay till about 7 & then go all night. Find fresh tracks of an elk & young one, follow them for some distance & find where they have just laid down, but lose them entirely before long. Messiter will talk. Paddle all night, rather dark, starlight, Lord M. goes to sleep in canoe towed behind, dreadfully monotonous work, look out in vain for elk at daybreak, go on till 4.30 when neither could keep eyes open (both had nodded whilst paddling): turn in to first landing place under a cliff formed by a landslip, banks knee deep in mud.

Friday, July 25th.—Breakfast, very wet with dew. Messiter feeling wakeful after hunts for deer, Lord M. & self make a slant & turn in to sleep, fearfully hot, the cliff just facing the sun & sheltered from the wind, sleep for about 3 hours, dine, & start about 5, all very languid & idle; hardly able to load canoes Horrible tempers. Find M. & Lord M. squabble dreadfully. 5 ducks killed yesterday stink already! Paddle on for about 2 hours & then turn in. Pleasant camping ground under small tree, tempers improve, still little sleep for musquitoes, hear two shots. Have passed a few rapids, wonder whether they are Goose Rapids & where Frog's Point is which we were told was only 45 miles by land & calculate we have done 90.

Saturday, July 26th.—Start about 11 after a better night's rest & agree not to stop for dinner, shoot some rapids, & let Lord M. loose; he nearly comes to grief upon a large rock in the middle & while we watch him are suddenly whisked close to another; vigourous paddling just saves from that, but we find ourselves almost immediately aground, jump out, swear at one another, & the canoe floats off, get in again each abusing the other. Messiter in the bows, shoot several small rapids, see about 20 geese ahead, give chase, they land & I get ashore about a yard deep in mud to beat the bushes, 2 come out, Messiter kills one & I the other. Lord M. follows mine up. Float down stream & I & Messiter try for more but without success. Paddle on for about ¼ mile, & to our delight see a trail on the banks, oxen & men, shoot a goose; see the steamer "International" hauling up the rapids. Lord M.'s canoe on board. Wait on the bank. Captain tells us to come on board, go up to the side of the steamer & wheel set agoing at the same time, the stream terrific, nearly whirled under it, Milton nearly swamped, also by steamer, just saved being swamped by most frantic paddling & sheering away & shooting down the rapids which carry us down in a moment, both very angry. Rover carried down in attempting to follow. Try to stem the rapids & fail. Two passengers push off from steamer in Lord M.'s canoe & come to our aid; one gets into ours & I take his place in the other; by holding on to the bank, bumping the bottom against the stones, & the most frantic paddling we, after some ¼ of an hour succeed in getting up again to the boat (some 100 yards) but *only just*. Passenger treats us to cheroots & brandy & water. Can't buy any spirits on board, but get pork, flour & biscuits. Dine on board, start again with minds at ease! Steamer does not expect to reach Georgetown & will probably catch us on way back to Fort Garry in 3 or 4 days. Find we have done about 113 miles, and are still about 3 from Frogs' Point! Paddle on quietly, shoot a few ducks, & camp early in a snug place among small birches. Messiter constructs such a luxurious tent of our two sheets that we sleep like tops & do not wake till 10.

Sunday, July 27th.—Take it very quietly writing up log, cleaning guns, &c., until 4. (Lord M. very slow traveller). Fearfully hot and all languid. Lord M. wanting to pitch his canoe, clean his gun, wash white ducks, &c. We decided to remain in our pleasant little camp until Monday, keeping watches at night in order to turn out in good time for a start in the morning. I took to fishing with frogs (which are as abundant as in the plague of Egypt) & a stick & caught gold-eyes as fast as I could throw in. The river seemed alive with them; caught about 15 & then desisted; these we split open & smoked over the fire for future provision. Lord M. chose the 1st watch from 10 to 12; Messiter the 2nd, from 12 to 2, & I the 3rd from 2 to 4. Armed to the teeth, Messiter thought he heard Indians, & nearly fired at Rover. In my watch in which day broke heard lowing something like that of cattle but more like a horn, in two directions, apparently about ½ mile off.

Monday, July 28th.—Tempted to call the others but refrained lest I should be objurgated if the sounds were not those of elk. Called them up at 4 & a start effected at 7. Saw a few geese & ducks, all very wild; about 12, some oxen, men & carts on the banks for Pembina. Men said they were going on the fall hunt which relieved our minds. Despair of a dinner of fresh meat & just about to land at 1 p.m. when 3 ducks get up close, I spot one. Messiter another at about 70 yards, with No. 3 Eley, wire cartridge; cooked & ate them immediately. All went into the shade to sleep. [On the way took a shot with ball at a splendid eagle size of a turkey about 50 yards off, missed, but hit him hard with second barrel No. 5, as he passed about 30 yards off; marked him down, pulled in & went after him; put him up but could not get a shot for trees. Messiter sent a ball after him flying 100 yards off, of course, without effect.] Left Messiter & Lord M. sleeping, I finding it too hot, wrote up log, baled canoe, caught a few goldeyes, & then at 5 turned them out & all started again for about 2 hours when we camped amongst some small aspens. Banks very muddy. Just before landing a duck (blue winged teal) flew straight at us. I shot at him coming, Lord M. directly after but Messiter wiped both our eyes at a cross shot. Heard the whippoorwill for the first time. Squabbled about cooking bread, each stating his way was best. Great labour cutting wood with only a bill-hook, the axe having broken; constructed tent as before, & turned in about 11. Saw marks of large herd of elk close to our camp a day or two old.

Tuesday, July 29th.—Slept till 11. Got up & baked bread & fried fish for breakfast, lolled about. Sun intensely hot & musquitoes troublesome. Intend to stay till tomorrow to look after the elk this evening. Monotony of river. Traces of fire, storms & floods in trees torn up, broken down & carried into heaps. Many half burnt.

Wednesday, July 30th.—Set out about 5 yesterday evening with Lord M. for a small elk hunt, leaving Messiter to look after the camp. Went thro' the belt of timber which covers the banks & followed the edge of it on the prairie for about 3 miles. Saw a little old sign, but nothing fresh. Sat down, had a pipe, & returned nearly worried by musquitoes which were in a perfect cloud. Hit off the point where we left the wood exactly & found Messiter with the camp in order, & supper ready. He was just about to fire off his gun as it was getting dark; not much surprised at our non-success, but had hoped for at least some prairie hens. I turned in about 10, leaving Lord M. & Messiter in a very warm argument as to the rights of and injuries done to the Indians. This morning set out at 11 intending to make a long day of it. Just before setting out the Columbian emigrant, whom we met at George-town appeared in a dug-out. Found that he had only left that place on Saturday! & calculated that he had done about 130 miles; passed the steamer aground somewhere in Goose rapids & was told she would not start back for a week altho' not going on to Georgetown. After we had paddled for half an hour we overtook him, he very kindly offered some butter, having left our fat behind, & filled one of our cups with it. We in return gave him a fishing line of which he stood in need & some shot. Went on till about 5 doing some 18 or 20 miles & killed a goose & some duck, then pitched Lord M.'s canoe which had begun to leak, & baked a large amount of bread in the frying pan for night & day's provision, intending to go on during night & most of next day with but little rest. Started at 9. *Very monotonous.* Darkness increasing. Thunder & lightning about 11. Continued to increase; about one the storm became terrific & lasted about 2 hours, the rain in sheets, thunder & lightning the most fearful any of us ever beheld. We were evidently in the very focus of the storm, the light-ning completely blinding us & almost continuous, hissing & playing about us, roaring like a furnace; the thunder with most awful crash being at the same instant. Lord M. came & held on by our canoe & I steered for a long time by help of the lightning. We all sat still, huddled up in our own wraps in the drenching rain, & letting the boats drift where they would. The longest night I ever passed & the most uncomfortable, the canoes being half full of water, & all soaked most tho-roughly. I shivered so that I could hardly speak; at daybreak the storm suddenly abated & then quickly ceased & we landed in most miserable plight on a muddy bank, then lay down to sleep in our wet clothes amongst the long soaking grass; could not light a fire. All vowed to have no more night work. The paper & matches soaked. No fire to be got. Lord M. went to sleep almost instantly, but Messiter very kindly by my advice roused him up & gave him a dry flannel shirt.

Thursday, July 31st.—Awakened about 11. (Messiter's watch stopped; had to guess at time.) Nearly dried by the sun, but feeling very chawed up. Messiter also turned out & endeavoured to get a fire by firing rag from a gun tinder, &c., but could not manage a flame; gave up in despair after working at it for an hour & set to work to clean guns & re-volvers which were in a mass of rust, & turned out all our things into the sun to dry which fortunately came out very hot. At 1 our Columbian friend again appeared; he had managed to keep everything dry except caps with which we supplied him. He in return supplied matches & we soon had a fire; told us we had passed some half breed huts about 6 miles off, & that they had two good canoes, & were willing to go with anyone. Messiter & I therefore called Lord M. & after dinner set out in his little canoe to see if we could not get a better than our leaky one, & also a man to assist & go along with us. After paddling some 9 miles up stream (awful hard work) & finding nothing but a deserted Sauteux camp, we returned much disappointed. Shot two ducks but they escaped us & we returned to supper & found Lord M. with everything ready. No fresh meat now for two days. Turned in about 10.

Friday, August 1st.—Fine hot day. Cleaning up & tarring canoes. Lord M. finishes his by dark. I try to catch fish but only get one small goldeye which I present to Lord M. No fresh meat, frying pan handle breaks off & we have to use cleft stick. Break the bill hook. Little pork; a few lbs of flour. Turn in intending to start after tarring our canoe in the morning.

Saturday, August 2nd.—Awakened about 4 by distant thunder. Quickly grew into a storm almost as terrible as the one of Thursday, but in daylight having laid our waterproofs with the opening up hill, the water got in & soaked our beds, the rain being tremendously heavy. About 9, the storm subsided & we turned out very soaked & miserable, having, however, managed to keep powder & matches dry. No dry things. "Lend me a hand to wring my trousers," was the order of the day. Thanks to the Columbian's gift were enabled to get a fire which did not, however, burn very brightly; managed however to boil some coffee & fry some pork, a small portion of which & some little flour being all our provision. Made a stalk after a duck up the creek, but only get a long shot; made good practice with ball, only 2 inches off her. Set into pitching canoe using remnant of two cambric handkerchiefs; during this I providently set a fishing line with piece of pork & tied to a stick. To our delight find large fish on which turns out to be a 9 or 10 lb. pike in very fine condition & a most acceptable addition to our stock, 1 lb. pork, 2 lbs. flour, ¼ lb. tea, do. coffee, and a tablespoonfull of vile Georgetown whiskey. To our intense disgust rain again came on about 5 & we left our boat & enveloped ourselves in waterproofs; fire went out; wet night. Water gets into waterproofs—wretched night.

Sunday, August 3rd.—Lent Messiter my dry blanket last night as all his were wet & consequently wet & starved to death. Heard elk all round lowing within a few hundred yards at daybreak. Load with ball & set out after them leaving the other two to sleep. Follow the sounds up wind along the river bank. I approached with the greatest caution, listening & moving on without noise—when I heard a bellow apparently within 20 yards of me but could see nothing; it was down wind & as all sounds ceased I presume that they passed me coming from the water & getting down wind scented me & bolted. I found the tracks but could not catch a sight of the animals. Return much disappointed at having missed so good a chance, make the fire, call the others. Finish canoe, start at 1. Can't see a duck or goose—only tail of pike & two cakes left. Messiter despondent. Calculate 4 or 5 days more may bring us to Pembina. Fearfully hungry. I throw a line out of the boat & catch two goldeyes viewed by all with eager anticipation of supper—only one cake can be allowed in addition—no ducks—no geese—camp at sundown—small supper but comfortable tent—bone of pork left at last camping place.

Monday, August 4th.—Messiter up first about 7. Remains of pike & small piece of our last cake for breakfast. I save some of mine for the long day & chance of not seeing game. On—on—on—paddle—paddle—paddle—nothing to be seen until noon; awfully empty, especially Messiter who ate his allowance first. Lord M. then wishes to stop—shoot a half grown duck without mercy. Persuade Lord M. to struggle on. About 4 see some geese; a yell of delight & furious chase, although before pulling very languidly & hardly speaking a word. Kill 3; soon after I shoot a duck. Land at wooding place to empty small canoe. Signs of recent presence of some one but not since the rain (fresh cut wood, &c.); cannot see a hut. Lord M. wishes to stay. Persuade again to go on. Soon come upon a lot of ducks, kill 6 & two more geese. Fine supply not before needed; go on till 5. Light a fire as quickly as possible & then set to work plucking geese & ducks; make a roaring fire & roast them on sticks. Lord M. & M. eat a goose apiece & I 3 ducks. Nothing to them but Harvey sauce & salt—no bread or vegetables but manage to stay our stomachs. Make up the fire, pluck ducks for breakfast; pipes & bed under tent. Messiter very anxious for steamer.

TRIP ACROSS CANADA

Tuesday, August 5th.—Awakened about 5 by steamer sound, jump up & call the others. Messiter turns over with an 'all right' but on perfectly understanding the fact jumped up in frantic delight. Lord M. & self much more philosophical. Call out to the Captain who had already caught sight of canoes, stop & take on board us & all traps. Expected we had got to Fort Garry. *Such* a breakfast—*wonderful!* do. dinner, do. tea. Cleaned guns & pistols; my revolver full of rust & one spring broken which is not to be mended at Fort Garry. Good wash & luxury of clean clothes. Find all luggage safe on board, & Druid & Sailor in good condition. Dress Lord M.'s foot with splinter in it.

Wednesday, August 6th.—Arrive at Pembina about 11; 2 or 3 houses. Half breeds & huts. Find our half breed of whom we hired the large canoe & who had come by land with mails. Wants 5 dollars for return of canoe to Georgetown; offer $2\frac{1}{2}$ for which it can return by steamer; takes it & chuckles over bargain tremendously. All day rewriting pencilled log & finishing. In splendid health & very jolly. Appetites but little abated. Steward thankful for ducks & geese as they are rather short of provisions.

Thursday, August 7th.—Came a tremendous crack against a rock yesterday evening & broke one of the binding chains; can be easily repaired; stick fast innumerable times. Lord M.'s legs very much inflamed from the effects of the sun & covered with small boils. Dressed them with Moss's ointment & recommended rest. Pil. Col. Coqr. Quinine & Port after. This morning stuck fast for an hour on two rocks, stem & stern. Messiter sick in the night from over eating after the fast, Lord M. & myself both have dyspepsia from same cause. Arrived at Fort Garry about 2. The Fort very superior to Abercrombie or Georgetown; good stone wall enclosure flanked by round towers; port holes glazed; offices, store & governor's house inside—2 Yorkshiremen on board steamer, Wakefield & Barnsley, one knew Bingley—(Bradford man at Fort Abercrombie). La Ronde[8] comes on board; prepossessing appearance; delighted to see Lord M. again; decide to camp in tent near his house. Luggage across in ferry boat. La Ronde ready to go with Lord M. anywhere. Asks after Thompson. Fall hunt does not go for a month. La Ronde killed 40 cows in spring hunt from which he has just returned. After tea turn in. Madame & Misses La Ronde; too late to call on McTavish.[9] Fort at junction of Assiniboine

& Red Rivers. Good white houses. Settlement 20 or 30 miles along River. Nunnery. Hudson's Bay store always full; pretty good port & sherry; Lord M.'s leg worse; order perfect rest & cold water bandage; quinine & port wine.

Friday, August 8th.—Breakfast in La Ronde's house. Lord M. with numerous boils, leg worse. After pipe go to Fort & deliver introduction to McTavish: very civil. Prescribe for his servant with Eng. Cholera. Mr. Smith introduces himself. Executive Officer. Takes me in his light cart to see a patient 3 miles off. Call at Post Office, Printing Office, & office of The "Nor-wester". No letters. Find Archdeacon Hunter there, introduced. Promise to call on the Bishop.[10] Mr. Smith drives against a post, & with his daughter tumbles out under the wheel. I remain in cart, not hurt. Drive on to Mr. Preedon's. Son got abscess in kidney. Old boy very hospitable; cold roast beef; delicious; left England at 13. A chief Factor of H. B. C., knows Saskatchewan, killed 6 grisly bears. Canoe party arrange canoes round, & light fire in centre. Grisly jumps boats, & fire & carries off a man like a baby in arms. Another hearing his cries jumps up & sees what takes place. Calls out; he cannot fire for fear of hitting other. Bear hearing drops one & rushes at 2nd man, [who] wounds him mortally, but seized by bear & dreadfully bitten in arm. Indian near who was blinded & scalp torn over eyes by stroke of grisly's paw. Buffaloes. Go up to them very quick, raised tail, & forward course without looking round, signs of mischief, &c., &c. Port wine & pipe with Dr. Bird who comes up, then walk back, overtaken by thunderstorm & drenched. Resolve to go a month's hunt in plains at once, then return here & start for Saskatchewan. Things at Fort stores dear & Messiter frantic with many preparations & packings. Half breeds & drunken Indians. Tom-tom going all night.

Saturday, August 9th.—Prepare for first short expedition. Messiter & I take dug-out down river, bring 28 lbs of lead, &c. back—very hard work—swear at one another. Box mending 5/-. See patient at Fort. Chalk & opium. Go to bed early. Thunderstorm comes on, brilliant lightning & heavy rain; none of us can sleep; get up & smoke; long argument with Messiter on use of "damn it"; discuss trip; conclude we have not time for first; to ask La Ronde if we can get running on way to Saskatchewan, & in that case start for there at once. La Ronde promised to look at horses at Church.

Sunday, August 10th.—Not up until about 10. Cathedral 4 miles off across Assiniboine. Dressed Lord M.'s boils, foot, & whitlow. Went to Fort for linseed meal, found patient nearly well. McTavish treated us to beer & cheroots & gave us loaf of bread for food & poultices; nice change after bain. Wrote log & idled about all afternoon. In evening, half breed brought Runner for Messiter to look at—white legged, white faced, low shouldered, low legged, stilting pony of 14 hands—has reputation of first-rate runner. La Ronde says he is "très bon" for buffalo. Wants £30. Messiter after much bargaining gives £27. Devilish little to look at for the money. Large travelling saddle nearly hides him.

Monday, August 11th.—Went to the Fort after breakfast. Messiter already there & purchased a horse for £30, having given £1 to be off his bargain of last evening. The best-looking animal we have seen & goes pretty freely, but La Ronde says he is no use after the first mile, being very short-winded, & also keeps his flesh badly. Tried the horse recommended to me by La Ronde, a strong looking beast some 14.2, with one rather crooked foreleg, but warranted sound & to go up to buffalo well & stand fire; goes pretty well though rather sluggish; gave £20 for him & think I have a good bargain. See my patients who are all improving satisfactorily, make out a list of necessaries at the Fort Store, & return to tea & bed; ordered 3 cwt. flour, 1 cwt. pemmican, 8 gals. rum, 20 lbs. tobacco, 22 lbs. powder, 56 lbs. shot, 32 ball, 1 blanket, 1 buffalo robe, 20 lbs. tea, 10 lbs. coffee, 14 lbs. salt, 3 lbs. pepper, 2 yds. duffle, 1 pr. beaverteen trousers. Also of Madame La Ronde 12 pr. moccasins, 1 cariboo skin hunting shirt, 1 pr. moose skin breeches & leggings.

Tuesday, August 12th.—After breakfast another horse brought for Messiter to look at, a good sized well-made horse, rather lean & long-backed, but the best goer we have seen; very hard-mouthed. Want £30 for him. Messiter offers 25 which they eventually take. Then to the store & make agreements with La Ronde & Voudrie,[11] £12 a month to the first, & £30 in advance to leave with his family. £4 a month to the second & £8 of it in advance. After return have a fierce argument with Messiter, as to salvation of savages; who ended by using very ungentlemanly language, for which he soon after apologized & all right again. Take to letter writing.

Wednesday, August 13th.—Messiter slept last night in his own little tent, & alas! took his musquito net with him. Lord M. & myself consequently spent a very unhappy night tormented by musquitoes. I did not get off until daybreak, & then obliged to wrap my head in a flannel shirt so that I was nearly stifled. The enemy however succeeded in taking advantage of my unconsciousness & I awoke itching & swollen from a hundred bites on my face & hands. Spent the morning in drawing up agreements with the men, & getting them signed. La Ronde brought Jean Baptiste Vital, one who had been out with Palliser, & in whose hunting, guiding & fighting powers he had so much confidence that he agreed if we would only take him at the £6 a month which he required, he himself (La Ronde) would take £11 per month instead of £12 as we first agreed with him. So settled. In the afternoon had a patient with chronic bronchitis. My deficient French very awkward. Messiter casts bullets, Lord M. arranges his boxes & makes Kinnikinnic, I made up medicine, write log & letters.

Thursday, August 14th.—Last night made a small fire in a hole in the ground inside the tent; when it had burnt up well, placed sods over; filled the tent with smoke & kept in till morning, effectually settling the musquitoes. This morning tried to take an observation at noon but found the sun still too high for an artificial horizon. Went to the Fort, had a cigar & glass of beer with McTavish & a Mr. Griffin, a Hudson's Bay man I fancy, who had been over the Rocky Mountains into Columbia. He recommended the lower pass to Columbia River, too far south of Cariboo for us. Bought another skin for breeches—saw two patients—returned to dinner & after smoked a pipe over Shakespeare. Black flies made their appearance. A fire lighted for the horses. Messiter makes bullets, Lord M. buys cart-horse for £7, & makes up leaf tobacco bought at Chicago. Found that the Bishop had left cards at the Fort for Lord M. & myself.

Friday, August *15th.*—Saw patients, packed boxes, cleaned gun & pistols until dinner. After that got up in last clean collar, black coat & waistcoat, hobnail boots & clean shirt to call on Bishop. Lord M. in cords & boots, our most respectable costume. Walked to the fort, called on McTavish & borrowed 2 horses on which we rode to the palace, a little square white house well furnished, untidy garden like all others. Bishop & sister plain homely people, very kind; stayed tea; talked over English news. Heard of Archdeacon Mackenzie's death. Report of Prince of Wales passing by this route to Columbia. Returned home after dark.

Saturday, August 16th.—Fetched to view body of man found dead & supposed killed by horse he had gone to fetch from prairie. Small lacerated wound on left temple, large discoloration of crown of head. Found lying forward. Then to the Fort & Bannatyne's. Bought harness. Looked over list at Fort store, returned to dinner. After, Lord M. went to Fort store to arrange list, Messiter took my saddle to Driver's store to exchange for Indian pad. I made revolver bullets. Got 35/- & pad for saddle. Messiter offers 15/- & his robe for the one I got at Fort in the morning; decline.

Sunday, August 17th.—Fetched after breakfast, to see youth of 17 across river in epileptic fit, had them for 5 years. Thread worms; prescribe accordingly. Messiter starts on Jack for church. I remain to write letters & log, having no clean linen.

Messiter returns unshrived, having arrived two hours too soon & finding it too hot to wait.

Monday, August 18.—Find Lord Dunmore, Col. & Cap. Cowper & Cap. Thynne at the Fort, intent on going with McKay to South Saskatchewan for buffalo & grisly bear. Introduced. Settle with Bannatyne & buy horse for £9. fetch away carts. Look over list at store. Find my horse very sluggish & stumbling, but La Ronde gives him so good a character that I resolve to keep him. Lord M. buys 'La Grande Rouge'. Messiter falls in love with Vital's bay.

Tuesday, August 19th.—Load our carts & settle bill at Fort store. La Ronde gets screwed & tells me in confidence that when he said something about my carts, Lord M. said "Damn the Doctor's carts," which he thought very wrong & it his duty to tell me. Very silly, laughing at nothing & very confidential. The Bishop sends note inviting us to dine tomorrow; accept. Pack boxes.

Wednesday, August 20th.—Go to the store as usual in morning, see patients &c. Lord M. packing. In the evening to the Bishop's. Lord M. returning from store keeps us waiting;

late to dinner. Bishop & sister very hospitable. Meet Dunmore & party, only other guest Mr. Black, new judge. Turkey, veal, & beef, 2 bottles port. Stay rather late. Lord M. sits with Miss La Ronde until 1 a.m. fixing hunting shirt.

Thursday, August 21st.—Transfer things across river to carts. Egg Lord M. on; severely chaffed at Fort; all ready by night to start myself, Messiter also. Patients. Camp W. of Assiniboine. Post letters to Tylor.

Friday, August 22nd.—Very anxious to be off. English Cholera. Other party off at 4. a.m.. Lord M. all day packing. Look on, take Pulv. Cretu cum Opio & smoke. Lord M. finds he requires another cart. Messiter tells me capital punishment abolished in settlement, last murderer condemned to 10 months imprisonment. Petition got up & sentence commuted to 3 months. Worked at harness-making & potted much money during term.

Saturday, August 23rd.—Up at 7. Breakfast. Bill. Go to Fort to McTavish for change for it, grants it as personal favour but complains of Lord M's. abuse of Company. I make the best of it. Go to dinner ready to set sail immediately after. Shall we ever? P. M. goes to Fort & explains to McTavish that he has misunderstood him; all right. Find the carts ready & *start!* ! at 4. 9 miles to Sturgeon creek, camp there. Called in to see Mr. Rowand. Albuminaria anusacea. Stout man. Pretty, white, wood house picked out with green. Garden. Best place we have seen at Red River Settlement. New feeling riding alongside caravan.

Sunday, August 24th.—Find that one of Messiter's oxen has bolted in the night. Send Voudrie to Fort on horseback to seek him in pouring rain. There having been thunder, lightning & heavy rain nearly all night, about noon it cleared up. Voudrie returned without tidings of missing ox. Bruneau[12] sent off on grey. Go & look for ducks with La Ronde up the creek; kill a couple. Dine; tremendously hot; go & bathe, kill ducks. Messiter exchanges oxen for horses on the chance of the other turning up. Bruneau returns without any tidings, at dark.

Monday August 25th.—Messiter gets two little horses for oxen and £2, the man to find the missing one; if not found M. to give another on return from Saskatchewan; about 7 miles & then stay for dinner; lots of ducks. M. & I kill about 6. On a few miles & camp close to Romish Chapel & River Assiniboine.

La Ronde gets permission to go to a wedding. Call on the judge who treats us to very good brandy & water.

Tuesday, August 26th.—Up about 7. La Ronde comes in very screwed, goes off again. Get carts ready. La Ronde comes back almost helpless, goes to sleep in mud. Ready; find he is fast asleep in a lodge; leave him & his horse & set off. Messiter very wroth. Travel about 4 miles & then turn off to see wedding party; get raisin, pasty, beef & tea. Great number of guests. Two fiddlers; dance a cross between lancers & quadrille; much double shuffle. Bride very pretty, pensive-looking. Lord M. dances. Messiter & I decline. Get former away with difficulty from his amusement, Voudrie who introduced us being cousin of the bride swearing there was no water for 15 miles & that we must camp there till next day as the horses were done! Find the men at the Fort ½ mile further on; all say no more to be done that day. Lot of drunken half breeds collect round us & insist on treating us to corn whisky. Messiter very angry. We call on Mr. Lane, Co's officer at the Fort, to inquire the truth. He says road by the river good & shorter. English half breed says not; determine to go on to get away from place. La Ronde turns up very misty just after we start; penitent. Rover missing. M. goes back. Shortly after Milton & La Ronde turn back to wedding party, ostensibly to seek Rover. M. meets them & returns. Rover comes up directly after. We go on, find roads very bad & camp after about 5 miles. Milton & La Ronde turn up at dusk. On the way in the morning, Milton & Messiter quarrel tremendously & threaten to fight. I ride between & expostulate, quieten down.

Wednesday, August 27th.—La Ronde rather sulky in the morning, penitent. Travel about 10 miles; camp by swamp near a few houses. Exchange a stone of flour for butter & eggs with half breed; finding carts too heavy. Long hot journey; no water for 14 miles; swamps full of ducks; difficult to get near, the water being dried up except towards centre; after heavy trashing through mud & reeds for some 4 miles I get two ducks; the rest don't turn out.

Thursday, August 28th.—Another long hot journey to camping place by swamp for dinner. Milton & I turn in to a house near to ask for milk. Find old Scotch woman & granddaughter very kind; give us good bread & milk. Descendant of Black Douglas & therefore fraternises with Milton. Want us to stay all night & promise to give us linen not used since left Scotland 26 years ago; obliged to decline. Only just migrated from Canada. Come up Red River with 200 Columbian emigrants. Request Captain Noble to haul down Stars & Stripes & hoist Union Jack; declines. Next morning dishcloth flying instead at Pembina; run down American flag & hoist British with grand salute of firearms—&c. Old woman much delighted. Very pleased to see us; only 7 whites in that part of settlement; good furniture & 2 looking glasses; saw face for first time for a week; appearance not prepossessing. Went forward about 2 miles & camped near fort. Went out & shot ducks in evening. A number of Sauteux crowded round camp & supped with us on invitation. 50 miles from Fort Garry; 64 way we came.

Friday, August 29th.—Left at 7 & after doing some 14 miles camped near a swamp, dined off pemmican with Worcester sauce, & then moved on 2 miles to another swamp & stopped for night. Vital will ride. Chain of swamps & many ducks. Messiter & I go out. I kill 5 & lose all; Messiter brings home 3. At dark Voudrie fancied he heard Indians prowling round. Drive in the horses close to camp, iron hobbles for Tom & La Grande Rouge, La Ronde loads with ball, & watches. No more heard. In Indian territory, after leaving the last Fort (Portage), & have seen the last of houses for many a long day.

Saturday, August 30th.—Made a good start at 6.30. Did about 10 miles before dinner. Camped at swamp. Milton kills 3 prairie chickens on the way, & I spot a duck. On again through an undulating country with scattered copses of white poplar, red willow, & wild roses. Gentianella. Very pretty camp on a little wooded stream with delicious clear water, a great treat after the strong nauseous swamp water previously. Write up log. A long discussion whether it is Saturday or Sunday, decided by La Ronde in favour of former. Cook ham for Sunday dinner. Milton makes Pembina jam.

Sunday, August 31st.—About 12 miles forward to Pine Creek, through undulating prairie & scrubs. The men set good example after dinner by adjourning to prayers. On way to Pine Creek, in the morning passed half-breed's grave with rude cross at the head. Also buffalo skull memento of La Ronde's success when driving Company's train 5 years before when he killed 3, all they met. After dining, forward some 10 miles to a very pretty lake, up some height & surrounded by trees, a very jolly camping ground. On way in afternoon all expostulated with Vital concerning his continually riding in the cart, which the other two did not. Very surly, would not understand that we did not wish him to walk all day but occasionally. Said he had agreed to ride only. We said never made any such arrangement. In the evening have a shot at some teal, very wild. Vital very surlily smoking & assisting the others very little. I observe him arranging his bag, & it crosses my mind that he may bolt but say nothing, thinking it unlikely as we are so far from settlements & he don't like pedestrian exercise. Retire, after mushroom supper.

Monday, September 1st.—Just awake when Voudrie comes to the tent & informs us that Vital 'est parti.' Hardly surprised but much vexed. La Ronde very indignant & calls him thief, stating that he will have his month & half wages in advance back from him & take it as part of his own pay. In the night Messiter, having nightmare from mushrooms, jumped up under the impression that Indians were in the tent, rushed out shouting & seizes Voudrie (in shirt only). La Ronde sleeping under cart jumps up & breaks head against bottom of cart; general turn out. Messiter chaffed by all. Starts off, the men joking greatly at Vital's expense; La Ronde saying that he believed his experience with Palliser had funked him from any more acquaintance with Blackfeet, & the others that he had never rested since he left, being extremely anxious to return to his Indian wife. Just before noon, having accomplished 14 miles, we met a train from Carlton. The head man returned with us to camping ground near a swamp, & bore back a letter from La Ronde to his 'cher père', acquainting him with Vital's rascally conduct & with a postscript, inserted by the express desire of Bruneau & Voudrie, to the effect that they were very well, & much pleased with their masters. Gave the man some rum for his trouble, & La Ronde went back with him to see if he could induce a man to leave the train & supply Vital's place. We proceeded forward about 7 or 8 miles & encamped by a swamp. La Ronde turned up just before dusk bringing with him a lou- tish lad of 18,[13] the only one he could get, they being very reluc- tant to turn back when so near Red River after a long absence. £5 a month the lowest terms. At dark another train turned up & camped close to us. Presently the head man came over with a letter from Lord Dunmore to Milton saying he was laid up with jaundice, would be glad of my advice, & would wait our arrival there. I came to the conclusion that it would be only right to set out at once on horseback, ahead of the carts, to his assistance. I communicated my design to Milton, & Messiter immediately volunteered to accompany me. Lord M. finding I was bent on going ahead said he would go also, & we all resolved to start early next morning. La Ronde told us there was plenty of water on the road, & that we might do it in two days, fast travelling, whereas the carts would take at least 4.

Tuesday, September 2nd.—Took necessary medicines, & set out with Messiter about 9; sacks tied behind the saddle containing blanket, coffee pot, & cup. Milton remained behind, not having equipped so rapidly, & intending to ride fast & overtake us, he carrying on his saddle tea, salt, rum. We had two cakes of galette each, trusting to our guns for fresh meat. After about 2 miles, Messiter's sack persisting & swinging over to one side & nearly pulling the pad off, he returned for his English saddle, & I continued at a foot's pace. Came upon a large covey of prairie chickens sunning themselves on a mound; killed 3; but having no dog only found one; further on came upon a large number of snipe & killed one with each barrel; could not do much execution with No.2 shot. Messiter here joined me & fired 7 or 8 barrels, but the snipe being in smaller flocks, he only got one, much to his disgust. About 5 or 7 miles on, Lord M. came up at a gallop fully equipped with cavalry saddle & all appurtenances. Forward at about 4 miles an hour until camped near a swamp & cooked snipe which were delicious, & I & Messiter made a vow to devote ourselves to them for the future. Killed 4 ducks after dinner & proceeded. At sundown camped near a large swamp with smaller ones near, enfarged the horses & cooked ducks for supper. Lord M. had forgotten his galette which made rather short commons. After, I felt uneasy about the horses & persuaded Messiter to go with me to look after them & drive them up near the camp. Looked in vain for some time, but after following the road back for about a mile, I descried them, Tom & the Grey without hobbles & mine & Darius with them on the point of coming off. Collared mine & Darius & then had a chivy of half a mile before we could get hold of Tom & the Grey. At last returned with them safe to camp. Milton in bed & given us up, hobbled them all afresh *very tight* & turned them beyond us so that we were between them & the road in a narrow space with the lake on one side, & thick trees on the other. About half an hour after we turned in they made a rush, I jumped out of bed & turned them back. Shortly after they made another rush & succeeded in getting past, & I left them to their own devices. Calculate to have done 27 miles.

TRIP ACROSS CANADA

Wednesday, September 3rd.—Turned out about 5, found the horses near, hobbles all right. Had rum & water, ham & galette with Messiter, Milton waiting behind to light a fire & boil his favourite beverage; rather disgusted we did not likewise, but too intent on going ahead, from 6 to 12, & then camp for dinner, Milton overtaking us about 1½ hours previous. Messiter uses up his powder & shot at ducks. I have about 8 charges left. Dine at swamp & proceed about 2. Calculate we did 15 miles before dinner; on, shooting prairie chickens, to the Shoal Lake & camp there on a small hill near a wood covered with marks of old camp fires, the skulls of numberless ducks & geese. The Shoal Lake very pretty, hills covered with trees around, beach sandy, water clear & good. A flock of geese came past us & I killed one, distance 68 yards, shot No. 3. Wanted a supper & just obtained it in time. In the night, rain came on & it became very cold. Milton jumped up & seized some wood which he took to bed with him for morning fire. Covered 38 miles.

Thursday, September 4th.—On awaking just after daybreak found my waterproof had leaked a little & we were rather wet; very cold & raw morning; turned the other two out who were very reluctant to show a leg. Messiter & I fetched horses to water. Milton busy getting a fire. Messiter & I had a little rum & water with goose, no galette. Didn't wait for tea but started immediately about 7 leaving Milton to follow, & he caught us up in about 2 hours. Found fresh signs of waggons & horses, & my Indian horse (Bucephalus) began to snuff the air, prick his ears, & evince an alacrity to go forward quite unusual to him. Finding the sign grow fresher, we went forward at a gallop & soon came in sight of about 20 waggons, caught them & found they were bound for Fort Ellis.[14] Asked for some galette but they had none. One man gave me some pemmican as we were out of food, and nearly ammunition. Went on slowly with them till they camped, when we cooked our geese & ducks & boiled our tea at their fire, a motherly looking party kindly making us some bain. They told us we might reach Fort Ellis that night if we travelled quick. Hurried off, & cantered ahead over some respectable hills, through Bird-tail Creek & another, & at about ½ hour before sundown descried the Assiniboine, & a building on the opposite side of the valley on the hill which we took to be the fort. On arriving at the river we descried a scow moored on the opposite side. According to La Ronde's directions fired two shots, waited some time, but no one from the fort. At last 2 half breeds came up on our side of the river, one volunteered to wade over & fetch the scow, which he did; it proved half full of water, the logs which covered the bottom floating about. Messiter got in with his 2 horses; aground; push off; immediately sinks at one end & goes to the bottom, not very deep. Messiter & his horses floundering about amongst floating logs & big stones. Messiter frantic, horses becoming frightened & unmanageable. At last get them back to shore, Milton & I looking on from the bank. Decided to try where the man had waded across; crept with horses along a shelving bank about 50 yards down & crossed. Messiter first with his 2 got into deep mud & nearly missed the Grey. Milton & I taking warning crept along water's edge, plunging into a few deep holes, & at last all scrambled up perpendicular bank & got on to the track again which we followed along the valley for a mile & then turned very steep stony path which our horses scrambled up with some difficulty; found the building was a new fort now building, the old one being still about 1½ mile further, as some freemen informed us whose lodges we passed. Arrive at Fort; gates closed. Make a great hullabaloo. Doors open; drunken Indian, with only breechcloth on, immediately seizes my hand with friendly shake. The Factor Mr. Mackay appears without shoes or stockings. He had gone to bed having no candles made & just before been aroused by drunken Indian. Provide us with dried meat & galette & makes us beds on floor with blanket from store. Find Dunmore & party had left 3 days before. A note from him to Milton stating he was better & had resolved to risk it. Rather provoking to us after our forced marches to his relief. Turn in tired & sleepy, having ridden some 40 to 45 miles.

Friday, September 5th.—Did not appear at breakfast until 9, then took a turn towards new Fort to see that & view some Indian & half-breed lodges. Making pemmican. Half-breeds just driven in from Fall hunt by Sioux who killed one man, two women & a boy, surprising them whilst cutting firewood. The half breeds however rallied and drove off Sioux, killing one, whose quiver, bow and arrows they showed us. After dinner to a new lodge beyond Fort; go in & smoke. Nicely painted on outside with number of men killed & seen killed by owner & brother. Milton takes a great fancy to the lodge. In the next lodge a man groaning & much hurt about head in drunken squabble. At night the train we passed arrived, our lady friend turning out to be Mrs. Mackay.

Saturday, September 6th.—Get up rather late & spend the day in idling about. Clean guns. Indians & squaws come into Fort, especially about meal times & squat in corner. Mackay kind in giving food & tobacco. Says he makes many bad debts with them, lends them carts & horses often for plain hunt. Many drunk. Company abolished liquor traffic except at Fort Garry; but many private traders with alcohol & water. Blind Assiniboine & wife sings war song on death of Sioux. At dusk La Ronde arrives. Two carts had broken down, & had to buy axles with rum. Carts had gone forward between Assiniboine & Capelle Rivers. Turn in.

Sunday, September 7th.—In the morning ride over to camp with the horses which were becoming very thin with bad pasturage. Get money &c. to pay for my new wheels which are required. Return towards evening, get new wheels, very good for 35s. Milton takes a plated Calumet & gun to bargain for lodge. Indian agrees to sell for Calumet, & a cart-cover to shelter family until he can make new lodge. Wish to settle with Mr. Mackay, but he wishes us to stay another night, not liking Sunday traffic; agreed.

Monday, September 8th.—Remember, strangely enough, that it is a birthday! — Moody all day, & thoughts of Bingley & my poor Father.
Ride off with Messiter after breakfast to camp, leaving Milton to await La Ronde whom we were to send with horses for lodge. Old Rouge strayed away; expect to find him returned to camp. Find carts have gone forward. On the way Messiter & I argue about weights on each horse. He loses temper & calls me a fool. I set into him very coolly & demonstrate the ungentlemanliness of his language; excuse hot temper. Very angry at first, but cools down & makes apology. Find men & carts about 3 miles on; two more axles have broken. Dine & La Ronde & Voudrie return to Fort for Milton & lodge, & to seek old Rouge, for whose loss La Ronde is very disconsolate. Spend afternoon in stitching up, repairing, writing log, &c. Milton & other two don't return.

Tuesday, September 9th.—Milton & La Ronde don't reappear; afraid the old horse cannot be found; idle about & expect their return. About 12 they turn up with the missing horse found this morning just at the back of the Fort, Milton having offered £2 reward. After dinner, about 2, we started. Messiter & I each sent a small present of cap-charges, & supple screw, &c., Milton his silver cup to Mackay for his kindness & hospitality, he refusing to accept anything for our 4 days' entertainment. Calculate we did 12 miles, going on until sundown, not coming before to water. I walked ahead of the carts with Messiter & spotted 3 brace of prairie chickens. Turned in rather tired, sleeping under the carts with lodge cover thrown over.

Wednesday, September 10th.—Up rather late; *very* cold on turning out about 6.30; water freezing, & little washing done. Away at 8.30. I walked ahead of the carts alone & got plenty of prairie hens to look at but very wild & only bagged a brace before dinner. Messiter ditto. La Ronde a lot of ducks, pot shots. About 10 miles before 12, then dinner. Teal & bain, very good. After dinner a brace of chickens & 6 ducks, 2 very beautiful green-winged teal. Day fine & hazy. Alternately scrub & prairie with copses of willow & poplar—occasional swamps. Came to very pretty glen with stream at bottom. Autumn tints very fine; half way between Fort Garry & Carlton. Set up Milton's new lodge for first time. Voted very comfortable. Bought of Indian at Fort Ellis for Calumet & cart-cover.

Thursday, September 11th.—Thro' similar country, fine sunny weather, cold frosty nights. Water in pails frozen 1/3 inch. Ducks abundant. Numerous swamps. Killed 10 ducks & 1 brace prairie chickens. Towards evening got amongst park-like scenery, copses & undulating prairie. Camped in evening near swamp. No incidents. Walked all day as since leaving Fort Ellis, Bucephalus' back being much galled with forced march; these men much astonished at any one walking who has a horse to ride. Remonstrate with me. "All right, monsieur. Indian horse always so — not hurt him." Larded prairie fowl to supper voted excellent. Think we did 20 miles.

Friday, September 12th.—Up very late. Milton not responding at all to the call to turn out. Nose bleeding in night destroyed his rest. Messiter angry & vows he will set forward alone with his carts & Voudrie. Won't come off. Away about 9. I walk on. Country as yesterday. Kill a couple of teal, & Messiter coming up, we come upon a great number of prairie fowl—some 20 brace—I bag 2½ brace, Messiter 1, we lost 2 brace which Rover would not find in the copse, having been licked for running in. Stop at creek for dinner about 1. Start again at 3. At 5 comes on very cloudy, & drops of rain begin to fall; camped therefore at first water, little pond amongst copses, & ran up the lodge. Rain however kept off. Wrote log & cut tobacco.

Saturday, September 13th.—Rain in early morning, & bad look-out for weather. Waited. Rain increased & clouds so threatening that we remained in camp. Lodge very useful now. All sat talking in lodge. Told them of the size of London, the Great Eastern, the pace of our railways, & the small time it takes to sail 2,000 miles to England, & excited intense astonishment. Milton writes up journal a month in arrears. Messiter & I play All Fours. Very long day.

Sunday, September 14th.—Started about 8. Fine misty morning, frosty. Boil coming on knee. Walk in morning & shoot ducks & prairie hens as usual. In afternoon ride in cart on account of leg. Very slow; get over about 20 miles in day. Country rolling prairie.

Monday, September 15th.—Rode in cart all day. Rolling prairie & copses; innumerable swamps, lakes & ducks. Ascending all day. No large wood; ducks—pemmican—galette & ring the changes. Mackenzie River speculation set on foot.

Tuesday, September 16th.—Leg 'bust' & nearly right; ride on horseback morning; walk afternoon. Usual shooting of some 5 or 6 brace of ducks & chickens. In fine health & rare appetites. Messiter after ducks finds skunk. Rover, bedewed, goes howling into the bushes. Messiter shoots him slightly & Rover goes in plucky & finishes him; skinned & eaten—smell pervades everything. About 23 miles.

Wednesday, September 17th.—Messiter & I give great yells to rouse camp about 6; off about 8. Shooting as usual. Messiter runs timber wolf & gets fall off grey amongst badger holes; not hurt. I pull up & observe the chase. Wolf disappears. Rover refuses to fetch any more ducks on account of cold; licked & won't do anything; see fox & won't hunt it. About 18 miles.

Thursday, September 18th.—Frosty night as usual. Day cold, windy, cloudy; a little hail. Rolling prairie, rounded hills, copses, innumerable lakes & ducks; can't get many, Rover having declined business. My horse requires discipline, having intense objection to leaving carts. At sundown come upon

Touchwood Hills.[15] Old Fort; pretty situation, rounded hills &c. Autumn tints at sunset very fine. Encamp just beyond Fort near pretty lake with round wooded island in centre very like a miniature Derwentwater. Strong resolutions made to rise earlier. Mackenzie River trip still talked of.

Friday, September 19th.—A most miserable gaunt Indian-looking dog made his appearance in the camp this morning; skin & bone; probably lost from train, or left behind on changing to New Fort; ate greedily of pemmican, & we induced him to come with us thinking he might be useful as train dog. The rest as usual.

Saturday, September 20th.—Country principally bare level prairie; ducks, &c., as usual. Encamped at night near lakes, &c. La Ronde kills another skunk with beautiful skin which commences Milton's hunt. Travelled very fast, horses at jog trot most of the time. At last my old horse very done & hardly able to get along till sundown (25 miles).

Sunday, September 21st.—Messiter & I afraid we have caught the itch from our boy. Pray for sulphur at Carlton. Then set good example by saying prayers. I shoot a beautiful small black & white duck with green crest. La Ronde says he has never seen one like it before. Milton therefore kindly skins it for me. About 20 miles.

Monday, September 22nd.—A most unlucky day. I commence by burning my boots & socks which were drying by the lodge fire. After starting with Messiter to walk ahead I find I have lost the top of the shot bag Milton lent me. I then miss 5 ducks in succession & fire 3 barrels at snipe without success. I give up shooting & rejoin the carts. See a badger running along the road in front of me. Milton & I give chase. I get within 30 yards & give him a charge of No. 3; it turns him over & he stops & grins at me; other barrel not loaded from losing shot bag. I run after him & turn him repeatedly, trying to cram in a charge of buck shot in gun. Voudrie comes up & hits him over nose with switch, but he succeeds in getting to earth to my chagrin, as I hoped to begin my hunt. Rain coming on, camp about 5.30 having made a short day.

Tuesday, September 23rd.—Over long tract of rolling prairie past several large salt lakes. Stopped to dine at one of them. Water very nasty. In the morning Messiter chivying two wolves on the grey got a tremendous pad on to his head, the horse falling on his nose from prairie dog holes; not hurt; at night La Ronde & I being ahead stop at swamp where we both thought we saw water, thinking to camp there. Carts come up, some horses taken out, enfarged. We go to shoot ducks for supper & find no water! The light-coloured mud, & some rushes having in the dusk the appearance of water & the shadows of bushes. Buckle to again & go on for about 2 miles in the dark. Milton gallops ahead to find water. His horse finds it in thick wood. Put up the lodge, &c., in the dark, the horses giving much trouble. Don't turn in until about 11. Saw hundreds of prairie hens. Milton spots 6 brace. I don't shoot at them. Up all afternoon.

Wednesday, September 24th.—Very slow in coming to time in the morning in consequence of late hours. Thro' woods, down into long level valley with large salt lakes, up again to camp by chain of swamps & camp there. Expect to reach Saskatchewan at noon tomorrow. Milton & Messiter squabbling all day. My gun shoots ducks well at last with 6 oz. shot No. 5, 2¾ dr. powder. Wet during afternoon & camp at 5 in consequence.

Thursday, September 25th.—Thro' wooded country with numerous lakes & arrive at South Saskatchewan at noon. Camp on bank, dine. After dinner men cut down trees, make raft, & cross for Company's barge; unload carts, & transfer all baggage & selves to other bank, leaving carts & horses behind to be fetched in morning. Saskatchewan about 80 yards wide here, muddy stream, wooded banks, muddy & stony at edges. Make Canada fire in road under trees & sleep in open air.

Friday, September 26th.—In early morning carts taken to pieces & brought across in barge. Then horses driven in & swam across, causing some trouble & enduring severe lodge-poling before they could be induced to enter the water. I contradict Messiter in the same manner he uses to others, & he becomes very irate. We don't speak for some time. I walk on 10 or 12 miles & the carts come up. I get my horse & stay behind to lunch on pemmican with Milton. I find that he & Messiter have had a violent quarrel about nothing & nearly come to blows. We agree that it will be better to separate, as his cross-grained temper will be monotonous during 6 months of winter. Milton does not like to mention it & pities him more than I do; left open. Milton's horse meantime breaks away

& I lend him mine to go for him; catches him at last, & brings back mine. We canter forward 5 or 6 miles & suddenly come into a broad track, & after about ½ mile of this, see the fort[16] in the valley below close to the river. Carts descending by another route. Find Mr. Lillie at Fort very civil & invites us to tea. Fresh buffalo meat for first time; steaks very good. Delighted with news that buffalo bulls are within half a day, the cows 2 days. Resolve to stay next day & Sunday & prepare, commence campaign on Monday. Lodge erected near river close to Fort. No Indians here except few old ones; rest after buffalo. Blackfeet not near except in spring. Snow comes on.

Saturday, September 27th.—Have famous sleep. The Company's jealousy of other traders: Mr. Lillie sends for La Ronde & pumps him about our rum & goods. Snow fallen some 4 inches during night & still continues (12 noon). Send to Fort for potatoes, milk & marrow fat, & have famous breakfast. Make what preparations we can but unable to get boxes on account of snow, not daring to uncover the carts. Very slow day. Fort better than Ellis; high pallisade with platform round & square towers at corners. North Saskatchewan very similar to South. Messiter very agreeable. Snow continued all day; in evening went to Fort & got some sulphur for our itch; bought 3 pairs moccasins (buffalo) 1s. per pair. Wretched old Cree with liver disease asks for rum; not got any.

Sunday, September 28th.—A very raw cold thaw; cleaned guns, patched bulb, & separated things for this hunt, sending the rest to the Fort until our return. In afternoon went to the Fort & prepared sulphur ointment. Invited to tea with Mr. Lillie who gave us stewed buffalo steaks; very good indeed. Milton made cartridges in the evening. Delighted with the news that 2 grisly bears were seen about 5 miles from the Fort. Mr. Lillie very kindly promised to keep the man (Peter the interpreter) who had seen them, to take us to the place at daybreak next morning. Peter had discovered the tracks whilst bringing in the horses to the Fort that evening; followed them & discovered two full grown enormous grislys tearing up roots; stated he dismounted, loaded his gun, & prepared to shoot at them when he suddenly remembered it was Sunday. La Ronde for some reason or other set himself against hunting the bears, thought he should not find them in

the morning, &c., &c. Went to bed rather late, giving in-
structions to be called at daybreak.

Monday, September 29th.—Not called until after sunrise.
Milton very dilatory in preparing for the bears. La Ronde
throwing cold water on it. Milton, Messiter & I get off about
8, find that Peter, tired of waiting for us, had started for the
hunter's camp whither he ought to have gone at dawn. Informed by Mr. Lillie that 2 half breeds had set out with the
horses & would pass the tracks & show us. Milton turns back
after a few hundred yards, thinking our chance of finding
small. Messiter & I canter forward. Rover won't follow us.
Cursing Peter and La Ronde for not accompanying us.
After 2 miles catch up the half breeds with the horses, go on
with them 4 miles & they show us the tracks in the snow.
We follow them, the tracks of yesterday, to the edge of some
pines, find some fresh sign & the place where they had evidently
breakfasted, the earth being torn up quite lately, grubbing for
roots; lost the tracks near the pines, & conclude they have gone
on to cover for the day; ride round the pines but see nothing
of the bears. Greatly disappointed. Excited while following
the fresh tracks, larger than a man's foot, & the impress of
their long claws very well marked in the snow. Canter back
to the Fort & find the carts started; get bread & cheese with
Mr. Lillie who sympathizes. He kindly gives me a pair of warm
gloves of which I stood much in need. I present him with
a fig of Chicago tobacco. He shows the road. We go on
some little distance, & it divides. Follow the one which has
cart-tracks; in about half a mile find the road end in a wood
near the River. Messiter proposes a cast round to find the
right one, I wish to return & examine where the cart-tracks
turn off. I agree to a cast, make a long circuit, & get back into
the road close to the Fort, before it branched; follow it & find
that the cart-tracks turned off from the road they followed at
first across into the other, which accounted for our being mis-
led. Confound the carts for leading us astray. Canter 5 miles
& find the fire burning where they had dined; about 10 more
bring us to Milton & La Ronde lying down smoking & waiting for us. Have a pipe with them & forward 7 or 8 miles or
more before we get to the camp. Milton baited at their going
so far; no water before. Camp on banks of river. Messiter
& I calculate we have ridden 45 miles. Peter & a Cree join
our train, latter a noted horse-stealer.

Tuesday, September 30th.—Milton felt seedy & stayed in bed until 11. I prepare for running, being now likely to see bulls any minute. La Ronde started already to look out for beef. Messiter goes off on Tom & we wait & dine expecting La Ronde to return. Voudrie informs me that the Cree, or rather half breed Cree with the Conies was out with the Cree war-party last winter who stole 130 horses from Blackfeet, & killed 35 men. Many horses I saw at Fort were, I found, Blackfoot horses, stolen from them by the Crees & sold to the Company. About 2 give up La Ronde's return & start; about 4 miles on, find buffalo bull lying in the road, recently killed & doubtless a victim of La Ronde's. The men stay to cut off some meat. Milton & I start to run some fine white timber wolves which were hanging about. Milton has a good start, & the one large white fellow. I some ½ mile behind. He gets close up to him on the Old Red & fires several balls at him without effect. I then come up on the little roan of Vital's which Milton lent me, my own horse having a galled back from the long journey of yesterday. I get close up & fire both barrels; miss. Little mare who had gone well, completely done, & I reluctantly give up the chase, the wolf being now able to run away from her. I strike out for the road & presently discern Milton in the distance. We canter along for 7 or 8 miles some time in the dark, at last see camp fire; arrive very cold & hungry & very cross. Milton blows up. Row with Messiter. Find he has killed 2 bulls & wounded another which he lost having expended all his bullets. Milton & Messiter very angry with one another about nothing as usual. Quieten down.

Wednesday, October 1st.—Set out at 8, somewhat excited, expecting to see bulls every moment. I ride the little roan mare again, my horse being still unfit. After some 3 miles the carts which were in advance pulled up as they saw 'les beufs' in the distance; we rode up & saw 8 or 9 feeding about a couple of miles off, & presently several more herds at small distances from each other; 30 or 40 in all; girths were forthwith tightened, arms prepared, Messiter & I taking loose powder & a charger, leaving our flasks behind. On went Milton a good deal excited, I feeling much as if I was in for something rather desperate, being however more afraid of not killing than of any danger. At a foot's pace in line, I on the right, Milton next, then La Ronde with Messiter on the left. When we got within ¼ mile of the largest herd, La Ronde began to low, the other groups then looked up from grazing & then trotted off to join the main body.

La Ronde then gave the word, & we broke into a canter, the large herd only looking round at us, & walking slowly forward, until joined by all the rest, when they began a slow lumbering canter: we quickened our pace a little & they kept on the same so that we soon got within 200 yards. Then La Ronde cried 'allez allez' & away we went, helter skelter, Milton leading on the Old Red by a couple of lengths, La Ronde next on the Grand Rouge, Messiter after on the Grey, I bringing up the rear on the little roan who did not go so freely as after the wolf the day before, being, I fancy, rather the worse for her severe course. Then, whip, whip, both heels hammering our horses ribs, arms flying, guns brandishing & yelling in true half-breed fashion.

As Milton nears them the band divides, the larger half bending to the right nearer me, giving me a chance to get pretty well in; $\frac{1}{2}$ mile & I am within 20 yards; another $\frac{1}{2}$ & I get within 7 or 8, my horse gaining very slowly; a comical appearance they presented, with head & shoulders covered with long hair, & bare quarters, like shaved French poodles, their long beards & fringed dewlaps wagging about, as they went along at a rolling gallop apparently very slow really a good pace. They looked venerable but dissipated & used up. When within 10 yards of the herd I fired both barrels at one & two separated. My horse made a vigorous effort to cut them off, & succeeded in separating one after whom I kept on, dropping into a canter to reload, soon came up to him again, fired one barrel of my gun & then 3 of revolver without any effect; knowing that I should lose ground if I reloaded & that he would probably stop before long, I kept on with my one barrel loaded, & in about 200 yards, up went his tail with the tuft at the end wagging about, & he turned round & faced me with head down, & looking very vicious indeed. Just as he turned his broadside & before he got under way to charge I fired, aiming behind the shoulder. He turned again away from me, walked two or three yards, then, stretched his legs & died. I felt highly elated at having succeeded in slaying my first buffalo, & had been highly excited during the run, screaming & shouting &c. like a madman. I went up to him, feeling afraid he might not be quite dead & get up & charge, dismounted however & looked for my shot. Found it exactly in the right place just behind the shoulder, nothing wonderful at 10 yards, but good for a quick shot. I took out the tongue & cut off his tail as a trophy. I hung them on to my saddle, marked the place & trotted off to rejoin the carts, after a mile & half descried the carts & Milton & La Ronde in the distance. La Ronde & Messiter each claimed to have killed two, Milton however found that one Messiter stated to be his was the one he had killed. A hot dispute. Evidence in favour of former, cartridge case being found by side of beast, La Ronde having killed one close to, & Milton describing the wounds correctly, Messiter reluctantly gives up. Milton had been unlucky, getting well in & a good chance of killing two or three, but cartridges kept missing fire. I took the boy Zear & we rode off together to bring the marrow bones of my buffalo. Very cold & raining slightly; strong north wind. Found him easily by the number of wolves around. They had already torn out his entrails. We set to work in the cold & rain cutting out the marrow-bones. Presently saw Messiter in the distance in full career after a herd of bulls, & then Zear cried out excitedly "Voila, Voila les beufs", & I saw 9 bulls galloping straight towards us over the hill 3 or 400 yards off. I dropped my knife, seized my gun & loaded, ran forward to get as near as possible when they passed, fired at the leader, heard the 'thud' of the ball; he dropped behind the rest & I gave him the other barrel; he staggered on a few yards & dropped dead. We ran up, I excited & delighted. Found one ball behind the ribs, the other just in the right place behind the shoulder. Measured the distance & found it 105 of the longest strides I could take. Not bad practice with a smooth bore on an animal at the run. Took half bones from each; we could not turn them over. The rain had come on fast & the wind very bitter & high before we started in search of the camp. I left the boy to choose the road & we made straight for the river. Saw a dead buffalo hamstrung & just killed, Messiter's victim doubtless. Saw wood before us & made for it; ½ mile off heard a shot & then another. Galloped ahead & found the lodge set up under trees. Wet through. Given me up & fired signals. Messiter not returned. All congratulated me & my good success in my first run. Rain & wind keep increasing. Messiter does not return; keep firing at intervals. La Ronde goes in search of him. Dark comes on. Put up lighted brand on top of pole. La Ronde goes out again & searches in other directions; can't see anything of him. Give him up till morning; fire shots occasionally. Probably out all night in cold & wet without matches! Turn in about 12, thanking our stars we are under shelter with good fire & food.

Thursday, October 2nd.—As soon as light La Ronde, Voudrie & Zear set out in search. 2 latter return about 7 with-

Our Night Camp on Eagle River.—Expecting the Crees.

out tidings. At 8 we saw 5 men on horseback coming towards camp, turned out to be Messiter & 4 Crees. After wandering about half numb with cold until an hour after dark he essayed to light a fire. Matches wet & could not succeed; on again for another hour or so; made for a wood & found there a camp of Crees; taken into Chief's lodge; given his place to sleep in. Things dried. Pipe sent round; large lodge of 15 skins. Meat & muskeg tea. Fat & water as cordial after, Squaws & men get up in night. Cook, smoke, spit, rise & whack dogs; dogs rush out & seized by others waiting at door; & grand fight; so on throughout night. Surcingle lost. Old chief rouses camp at midnight to find it. In morning makes them understand he wants to find camp. Go with him; presents them with knives &c. They come into our lodge & breakfast. Pipe went round. Ask for powder, salt, &c; given them, ask for more, guns, rum, &c., which La Ronde will not translate & gets out of; chief said we could not be great men if we hadn't rum. Stay until 1; dine. We make a move then. Chief Junior (rather fine looking fellow, Roman nose, spangled shirt, cap with ribands, medicine bag) gets up & makes oration. Translated by La Ronde; wishes to know what purport of visit to his country, for he had been frightened by the Company's men telling him numbers of white men would soon enter his country & he must beware of them. Told him to hunt, see the country & visit him. He would be glad to see us, & we might go where we wished & hunt as we liked. Thanked him, shook hands, & away they went. La Ronde frightened for our horses which they admired & asked many questions about; young chief told La Ronde 5 times that he had once been drunk which is considered a very great honour & glory. Move on two or 3 miles; & camp again. On the way Milton consults me about telling Messiter, as we had long talked of & well considered that we did not get on well & had better not pass the winter together which would be very foolish. I agree that it would be best to do so & give him time to make new plans. After tea tell him, much cut up. Can't see it is necessary. We are firm; men come in & left open. La Ronde & Voudrie watch all night; horses driven into camp; all guns loaded for Crees if they come. No alarm.

Friday, October 3rd.—Messiter renews attempt at acommodation. Don't agree. No more said. Cold & misty with hoar frost; start due south for the cows; pass several herds of bulls; but leave them alone not to disturb the cows. Day clears up.

Come to small river & camp; beaver dam. Salt water. La Ronde goes ahead to search for cows. We have washing & journal writing afternoon. La Ronde comes back at dusk having seen many herds of bulls but no cows. Resolve therefore to run the former tomorrow. In the open prairie on fighting ground of Crees & Blackfeet, Bruneau & Zear therefore keep watch.

A war party of Blackfeet said to be in the neighbourhood on the lookout for Crees.

Saturday, October 4th.—After breakfast went out in search of bulls; 2 carts for meat. Find 7 1½ mile forward lying down. Approach as before & get within 100 yards, then Hurrah, Hurrah from La Ronde, and a mad rush at the herd. Milton again leading on the Old Red, La Ronde next on the Grand Rouge, Messiter next on the Grey, I bringing up the rear as before on the right, but nearer much than in the former run. Bucephalus pricking his ears & setting into it might & main. 2 bulls separate to the right & I turn after them; Messiter brings up another & we charge them pretty well together; they separate again, 2 going with Messiter & follow the other, quickly overhaul him; put both barrels in, but too much behind, proceed to load again & find that every bullet had fallen out of my pouch (18) & I had only one which from some presentiment I had put in my shirt pocket. Rushed ahead with my forlorn hope, & as I came up he charged; Bucephalus merely stared stupidly at him, I only just got his head round, & gave him a cut of the whip, the bull's head being within a few inches of his quarters. The beast pulled up, & I pulled up some 6 or 7 yards from him when he charged again. I was ready this time, & got away easily, putting my only ball into him as he turned from me, but again in the wrong place, & away he went at top speed, faster than ever. I followed him for some 1½ miles, hoping he would drop; but he went ahead the same as ever, & I reluctantly turned back, my horse having had quite enough; cursing my ill luck. A very young bull & unusually fast. Then to the camp for more bullets, hoping for another run. I had lost my hat in the first rush. No stopping for that. Borrowed Voudrie's cap, got ammunition, & then after the rest; found them hard at work cutting up, Milton having spotted 3, Messiter 2, La Ronde 1, mine being therefore the only one of the herd which escaped. Confound it. Tried to stalk the wolves hanging round the carcases, but they were too wary. La Ronde thought me lost & had gone in search. All herds dispersed & no more running. Returned to camp about 1 hour before sundown, I greatly disgusted with my day's performance.

Watch set at night to guard against our friends the Crees.

Sunday, October 5th.—Wrote journal &c. Decided not to run, being Sunday, La Ronde having scruples. Messiter tries rifle-practice, & then all the men try their guns, making a regular fusillade. Milton expostulates, as it will disturb the country; about noon La Ronde cried out 'Les Sauvages' & presently saw two approaching on foot. Turned out to be two young Crees, sons of a Chief of 25 lodges camped near who were on their way to visit friends at another camp. Told us that a large herd of cows were making directly for us when the firing began which turned them away at once towards the N. E. Curse Messiter's powder-burning mania. Voudrie goes out to try & discover them but fails. The young Crees dine, & express their intention of honouring us with their company for the night. La Ronde in a great funk about the horses. The younger Indian, a boy of 16, told us, with great pride that he had already been 10 times on the warpath! & last spring stole 6 horses from the Blackfeet. Also that his father clothed him well (white blanket & trousers of do. with the stripes conspicuous round the bottom) whereas his brother was avaricious, & his father would do nothing for him. We all sat up late, & the Indians came into the lodge to sleep. The men being very sleepy from previous two nights watching, Milton took 2 or 3 hours at the commencement, & then awoke me, & I did 2 or 3 more; a beautiful moonlight night, very cold & frosty. Wrapped up in Milton's great cloak, & cooked a buffalo rib; very good; when tired, awoke Bruneau & Zear to take my place.

Monday, October 6th.—Came across the prairie by the road at a great pace, arriving about 4 o'clock at the place where we camped on the 2nd. night of our way out. A family of Crees before us. Squaw stretches lodge for us beautifully & presents with a mess which Milton & Messiter vote good, I detestable; a nauseous mixture of meat, berries, fat & water. Present man with a little powder & tobacco; old boy wouldn't smoke having a vow to his manitou; squaw, tobacco, needles & thread, Company's hunters & train of carts with meat for Carlton come in & camp at dark.

Tuesday, October 7th.—On with the carts. At noon caught up Company's train at dinner. Mr. Sinclair, bourgeois in charge very civil & gave us good cow beef & sugar to tea.

Ride on after carts, camp for night at swamp which we passed on first day; some 18 miles from Fort. Messiter had chivyed a wolf 3 or 4 miles, & then came upon 4 buffalo bulls; ran them 3 or 4 more & killed one. Poor Tom!

Wednesday, October 8th.—Rode on with Mr. Sinclair & arrived at the Fort just in time for dinner to which Mr. Lillie kindly invited us. Carts arrived about 4 o'clock. Lodge put up in the old place, got potatoes & milk from the Fort. Sinclair informed us that the two Cree chiefs had told him that they had followed our trail the day after they visited us but lost it where we turned off from the river at right angles to go on to the open prairie, the mist having effaced our tracks. They had fully resolved to have our horses, not being well pleased with our treatment of them. We had thought it very handsome. Goitre frequent amongst dwellers on banks of Saskatchewan; limestone & carbonate of lime plentiful.

Thursday, October 9th.—Messiter looking about for a man. Engages a villainous looking half breed Cree who cannot talk English & only a few words of French for £2 a month. His Father-in-law Atagakouph (Star of the Blanket) is a noted free hunter living at the Montagne du Bois. There Messiter intends to go, build a house near, & hunt with Atagakouph. Milton & I buy a few things, arrange accounts with Messiter & the men. Write letters home & to Dr. D——. The men desire a ball, & Mr. Lillie kindly lends a room. I feeling tired & not in the humour for gaiety turn into bed, sending the men. Voudrie came back in an hour & asked me if I would not like to go. On my telling him that I was too comfortable to move & he might go back, he bolted out of the lodge & returned at full speed, delighted to get back to the dancing. Sometime in the morning all returned, uncommonly merry & laughing. I feigned sleep.

Friday, October 10th.—Milton very seedy after the ball & stays in bed. I get everything ready & in the afternoon Voudrie & Zear start on their return to Fort Garry with letters & the horses. Things taken out of the Fort & crossed in the barge; Messiter crosses too. He & Milton quarrel about Snuffer. Milton lost toss for him & I sold my share for 3 lbs. of powder. Messiter's man wants to take out all his pay in advance. Messiter by Lillie's advice dismisses him at once & engages a young English half-breed instead. Milton & I go to Fort & say goodbye. In meantime barge has crossed; dark. Milton & I go over to N. bank in buffalo hide canoe & find men & Messiter there unloading. Sleep very comfortably in the open air. Fine bright night.

Saturday, October 11th.—Men engaged during the morning in bringing carts & horses across. 2 Yankees arrive from Edmonton on horseback & with a pack horse each. Emigrants to goldfields going back to families at Fort Garry to winter. Seem unwilling to be communicative as to the prospects of mines on the Saskatchewan. State that the majority have crossed the mountains, the rest out prospecting, intending to try their fortune on this side in the spring. Left buffalo bulls last night. Good hopes of having them near Lac Vert in the winter. Milton & Messiter quarrel again about Snuffer. All ready by dinner time. Dine, & Messiter says goodbye & sets out with his old guide & young man. The old fellow has crossed the Rocky mountains 16 times, & we have engaged him to take us over in the spring. All ready. Help to push the carts up the steep ascent. Rover missing. Bruneau goes back & finds him in the Fort. Set out about 3 & sleep under the carts. Country scrub copses & swamps. (Yesterday the old Cree whom we met on our return from the prairies told Milton we had been so kind to him & his squaw that he wished to present Milton with a horse. Milton very pleased but La Ronde said it only meant rum, & he declined the gift).

Sunday, October 12th.—Ordinary day through ordinary country; plenty of swamps, but the ducks all gone for winter. Idle; short journey.

Monday, October 13th.—Pretty well a copy of yesterday. Late in the morning & make poor travelling.

Tuesday, October 14th.—Arrive at Salt Lakes for dinner. By the side the track ends in nothing; keep on in right direction & come into track again after about ½ mile. Towards evening track again disappears; keep on. Milton going ahead to find water nearly bogged in trembling marsh. Camp by side. & La Ronde goes off to find a crossing. My Father's birthday. Melancholy reminiscences.

Wednesday, October 15th.—My Birthday. Hope they are having a jollification at Oxford & Hawksworth. Intend to celebrate it myself on being established in Winter hut. About a mile to place of crossing the bog; cut down branches for carts to cross; I get up behind Milton & the horse sticks fast; therefore try a cart; ½ mile beyond again find the track; along a valley with swamp at bottom; camp.

Thursday, October 16th.—At noon arrive at river Cocquille (Shell River); (or the day before?) help to haul the carts across. Shannan looks ill but gets over easily. Dine on north bank. Camp by swamp at night. 2 bullock-carts of Company's returning from fishery near Lac Vert. They give us two very good whitefish.

Friday, October 17th.—On a long journey & over the 'Jolie Prairie'[17] surrounded by woods & small hills & one or two lakes in the opening; a pretty promontory jutting into one lake, covered with pine & poplar. Strikes both Milton & myself as a very beautiful site for a house; dine at a swamp in scrub; ½ a mile further come to River Crochet (Crooked River). Very warm day & I strip & help the carts across; water like ice, but the bathe delightful. 2 plunges over head and out again. On catching up to the carts about 2 miles on, see smoke a little ahead; camp close to 2 houses; one, empty, belonging to the Company & set up in opposition to the other, built by Mr. Pruden, then a free-trader, & afterwards sold by him to an Indian. Bruneau put up the lodge in an open space, & Milton & I went on to the house where we found La Ronde already smoking his pipe. Old boy, squaw & several children; a comfortable house, two rooms in one of which lives old boy's son-in-law & family. Smoked away, & La Ronde discoursed. They had heard we had rum with us & asked us, as we were great swells, to give them a little; promised to send some in the morning. Old boy presented Lord Milton with 4 beaver skins; but said he must have the liquor at once. Milton & I went back to the lodge, drew off some into the little keg & watered it, & sent off 3 pints with one of water in a tin bottle. Just after we had got the barrel replaced & covered up in the cart we heard the Old boy[18] coming down, singing & shouting & he presently appeared, empty bottle in hand & accompanied by his son-in-law,[19] squaw & son. Both men very drunk, talkative & noisy. Produced some marten & other skins & required more rum. La Ronde explained that we had not come to trade, & had only a little for our own use during the winter. Very pertinacious, however, & after 2 hours discussion & nearly midnight we gave them a small quantity more. How they chuckled over it & hugged the pot! Squaws, children & all. They soon after went away singing & laughing & exclaiming "tarpoys," "tarpoys" i.e. "its true," "it is true"; I presume hardly being able to realize the delightful fact that they were actually drunk once more. Old boy rubbing his hands & chuckling tremendously, singing the praises of the ookee mow. Turned in very uncomfortable & forseeing the trouble the possession of the rum would cause us.

Saturday, October 18th.—Before we were up, both the men were back with skins to trade for rum. Explained that we did not want to trade & sent them away with the remainder of the little barrel. We then cached the big barrels. In about 2 hours they returned very drunk, accompanied by two others, relatives; & presently another, the Company's fisherman here, arrived on horseback accompanied by his squaw & kid. He informed us Mr. Christie was his father, & he hoped we would give him some rum. Directly after another employee of the Co. arrived, already screwed, having doubtless gone shares at the house with the rest. He informed us that his name was John Smith, a half breed, Mr. Lillie his master, & he wanted rum. Kept offering a beaver skin first to Milton & then to me & crying out 'rum my master', 'my master rum'; 'I want a dram', 'give me a dram.' The old man's son then came in very drunk & proceeded to take off his coat & then his shirt which he passed over to me. I shook my head, but he persisted in offering it, but presently lapsed into insensibility, fell into the arms of his squaw & spued. La Ronde then came in having been absent after the horses, & explained that we had not come to trade but hunt, & had only a small quantity left which we wanted for our own use during the winter. They persisted however in demanding & we in refusing, & we spent nearly the whole day sitting in the lodge amidst the most infernal clamour. We sat them out however & did not give them a drop more, Mr. Christie, being the most lasting, staying about an hour after the rest. We were not quit of them until nearly dark. We then held a grand counsel as to what must be done, & decided that the barrels must be safely cached at some distance that night, & next morning we would retrace our steps as far as the Jolie prairie, there build a hut on the promontory of the lake which we had noticed as such a nice site on our way here. About midnight we took a little out of our barrels into the little bottle & Bruneau & La Ronde shouldered them & departed to hide them across the river; towards morning they returned very cold & wet from crossing the river twice, had some tea & turned in. They had hid the barrels securely about 50 yards from the road some ½ mile beyond the river.

Our Winter Hut.—La Jolie or Belle Prairie.

Sunday, October 19th.—In the morning the son-in-law came (a friend of La Ronde's, a noted trapper & hunter), brought a dressed moose-skin for which he wanted 6 medicines: viz. a purge, an emetic, an astringent for haemoptysis, a medicine for headache, one for sore eyes, & pain killer. I gave him 3 Pil Col Co, 2 Acct. Lead & opium, 3 grains Sulph., Zinc, Do. Carb. Ammonia, some Moss's ointment & a bottle of painkiller. Skin worth 16 s. at Fort Garry. He wanted me to see a child of his which was ill. I went & found a case of Che. hydrocephalus, but not very severe; a strong child & improving, 4 years old; sutures partly open & fontanelles membranous. Gave them hopes of recovery & prescribed fish oil & gentle pressure to head by bandages. Then struck tent & departed. Son & son-in-law followed us to river & assist in crossing. Bucephalus & Saudris mired & stuck fast; had to be taken out & carts dragged up by the men. Gave the two Indians a little rum for their trouble; delighted. Pushed forward. One of Milton's carts broke down in the swamp & had to leave it & put the load on the others; therefore progressed very slowly & had to camp for the night about 1½ mile from the Jolie prairie. Took in our rum casks on the way.

Monday, October 20th.—Arrived at our promontory about 10. Found plenty of wood. Water a little brackish but not unpleasant. Find no clay for the chimney, but hope to meet with it at greater depth, & all things appearing favourable we commence to cut down trees for the house after dinner, fixing upon the centre of the clump of trees on the south side of a few pines as the site; very sheltered & completely hid from the prairie. Our two friends the Old boy & the hunter[20] come in just before dinner, bringing the mitlas we had left with them to be made, and also some parchment & sinew for racquettes. Beads asked for & given in payment for the millinery, rum asked for parchment & refused, La Ronde telling them they would never get any to drink here but perhaps in course of time we might give them a small quantity to take away with them, but we had but little for our own use. They seemed quite satisfied, but the hunter took his parchment away with him. It then struck us that we had better cache our barrels at once, & were engaged in drawing off a small supply when I heard the sound of horses' feet approaching. I rushed out past the carts to see, & La Ronde threw my bed over the barrel. It turned out to be Mr. Christie's hopeful to whom La Ronde had promised a mouthful of liquor on the day when they were all so troublesome, he having had none given him then. He brought the parchment again, & we therefore gave him a little rum for himself & some for the hunter in payment for the skin, sending him off at once. Away he went at full gallop, & in about ½ an hour we heard a great singing & hullabaloo in the distance. The others had been awaiting his return, & they were having a carouse about ½ mile off. Presently the singing came nearer, & the hunter, Mr. Christie, & another youth made their appearance singing & very screwed. The hunter very civil, the two others very clamorous for more. Mr. Christie in particular being very pertinacious, & when going away, saying he hoped we should play no more jokes of that kind. What the devil did we want in their country if we would not trade? &c., &c. The others sang our praises & shook hands most affectionately, saying we were first rate 'ookee mous'. Afterwards just laid the first logs of the house 15 feet by 13.

Tuesday, October 21st.—Built some 4 feet of the walls, the house to be made like a box, the windows & doors cut out afterwards. I went & surveyed the country, looking for stone for chimney; shot a young skunk which the men ate with delight; stunk us out for a week.

Wednesday, October 22nd.—Raised the walls to about 6 feet in front, 5 feet behind to allow slant for roof, logs being placed with thick end to the front. I worked away digging out the earth two feet to increase height inside; good sand for floor. Two windows & one door now commenced to be cut out; very sharp frost set in.

Thursday, October 23rd.—House at full height—Door & windows cut out. In afternoon fetched straight dry pine from other side prairie to make roof. I finish my digging. Dwelling begins to look promising. Wind very high & bitter; very severe frost, 2 inch snow fell in night. Hunter & friend call on way to Fort for ammunition. Promise to bring our letters; don't ask for rum.

Friday, October 24th.—Eliza's birthday; drink her health. High cold wind, as yesterday. I take a walk & shoot some perdreaux; putting on the roof & heaping earth against the sides. Bitterly cold. Can't find any good clay.

Saturday, October 25th.—Beautiful frosty morning without wind. Lake completely frozen over. La Ronde discovers clay in the prairie but not good. Must make shift with it. Bruneau gets cartload of swamp grass, & we finish the roof with that & earth over it. I go out shooting, for we want fresh meat, having had nothing but dry for some days; kill 2½ brace perdreaux & one pheasant; see several rabbits but the cover too dense, & the only two chances I had, the gun missed fire. I had set my heart on one for dinner.

Sunday, October 26th.—A thaw, clear, warm high wind; men disappear, perchance to pray in the woods. I write up journal, clean gun. Milton arranges boxes & guns. Men return about 4 o'clock having been to the cart we abandoned on the road to fetch planks for the house. Harry's birthday, remember it & drink his health.

Monday, October 27th.—Fetching clay & building the chimney. I provide fresh meat in the way of perdreaux & pheasants. Light a fire in the embryo chimney & part tumbles down; consternation; debate what is to be done. I engage to take a cart & fetch more stone in the morning, the chimney to be then built on larger scale & with broader foundation.

Tuesday, October 28th.—First thing I take a cart & fetch stone, Milton being engaged in fitting up wood-work for the support of the chimney, La Ronde & Bruneau in stopping the chinks between the logs of the house with a mixture of clay & chopped reeds. In the afternoon Milton & I make foundation larger & build up lower portion of the chimney. The hunter & other youth come in bringing Norwester from Mr. Lillie on which was written that the Post from Fort Garry had arrived at Carlton, but alas! brought no letters for any of us. In addition we find that Georgetown has been abandoned in consequence of the Sioux massacres at Redwood & the neighbourhood (vide Norwester for Sept. 24th. 1862) & therefore probably there will be no post to Fort Garry thro' the States for some time, & our chance of letters at an end for the winter. Good news however as to buffalo advancing, still advancing; bulls already only 2 days from us & still coming on. Almost certain therefore to be almost at the door during winter. Hurrah! no fear of want of food or sport now.

Wednesday, October 29th.—In the morning "John Smith" arrives with 2 large fish to exchange for pemmican but reports that the fishery is so unproductive that Mr. Christie & the 'Old boy' have both given up for the present & gone after buffalo. I provide the usual supply of prairie chickens. La Ronde & Bruneau finish the chimney which now promises well, & Milton superintends. In evening make all preparations for Bruneau & myself to go to Carlton tomorrow with cart & Bucephalus, to buy dry meat & grease to last us until we get buffalo, & also to try & purchase dogs to 'rôder' with in the snow. Milton & La Ronde to stay behind & complete the internal arrangements of the house.

(On arriving at Carlton I found that we were a day wrong in our reckoning at the Jolie Prairie, it being only Thursday when we arrived there. The mistake no doubt arose whilst we were busy building the house, my journal being neglected somewhat during that period.)

We actually therefore set out on *Wednesday, October 29th* & did not start very early on account of the time it took to find the horses which had wandered far away. About 9 got under way, & I went in advance at full stretch 4 miles an hour, Bruneau following with the cart at a trot. Along a valley over the hills to the right of the 'Joli Bent', and on to a considerable prairie where we discovered 3 persons ahead whom we soon caught up & found to be John Smith, wife & the 'sharp boy', asked for his wife to ride in the cart she being enceinte; rather pretty Cree half breed; took her on board & camped a little after noon by a small stream ¼ day's journey from the river Cocquille. Fed the party. After dinner forward to the river; partly frozen. Walked over on the ice & broke it up for the cart to pass. Camped for the night ¼ day from Lac Salit. Cold north wind very bitter, & a little snow falling. Made a large fire under cover of bushes, hung up cart-cover for screen from the wind, cut rushes for bed; fish & bain for supper. Very comfortable indeed. Lay 'tout ensemble' squaw & all.

Thursday, October 30th.—Up at daybreak & off at sunrise; kept walking ahead, Bucephalus, Bruneau & the other two at a trot. Passed Lac Salit in the middle of the morning. Camped for dinner after a very good march by a swamp & in some bushes. Day cold, bitter north wind, snowing throughout. After dinner a very long tramp, & very hard work, the snow falling under one's feet tremendously, I finding my boots in this respect a great disadvantage, the tendon Achilles of my right foot becoming very painful. I was therefore very thankful to see Carlton at dusk. Found the river partly frozen over, full of loose ice in the middle. At the bank two carts

& a lodge set up, descried Snuffer, & then knew Messiter's property & that he must be at the Fort. Fired several shots & shouted for them to come & fetch us. Some one essayed to bring over a canoe & failing shouted to us to wait until next morning when the barge was coming over. Bitterly cold standing about. Ran back to Messiter's deserted lodge & made fire & supper, turning in very comfortably, thanking our stars we had found it, as there was no large wood for an out-door fire.

Friday, October 31st.—Cold bright day. Idled about waiting for the barge which we saw loading on the other side. About 2 it was brought over with some difficulty, Messiter giving one of his loud 'whoops' on seeing me. I could not make him out, his appearance being so altered by white capote & fur cap. Mr. Lillie accompanied & the Columbian—the latter arrived a few days before & not knowing what to do during the winter had made arrangements to stay with Atagakouph. 2 carts also & men for Fort Pitt. Sat & smoked in the lodge until the barge was unloaded. Ate more of Messiter's provisions, which we had found so acceptable the night before & then set off across river, crossed to the ice on the other side but had not force enough to pass her along against stream to the landing place. Lillie & myself got out & walked over the ice to the bank & to the Fort, sending more men to help; two men fell thro' the ice overhead & nearly drowned; dragged out by ropes, half-frozen. Messiter's house nearly finished; double high-pitched roof. Atagakouph & friends would have all his rum; give him skins, get drunk; dirty Indian gets into Messiter's bed, turns him out; ditto do., ditto do. At last takes him by shoulders & turns him out of lodge; Indian walks off indignantly, & Messiter expects to have his throat cut in consequence; but nothing ensues. Atagakouph keeps digging him in the ribs during the night whenever he goes to sleep in order that he may listen to his singing! Messiter arrived on Tuesday & had all ready to start on Wednesday. Badger did not come back in lodge; therefore all right without fire, & nothing to eat & drink but dry meat & water! At noon on Thursday Lillie met Badger & found out. Too cold to cross. Lillie comes over for him in canoe & takes him back to Fort. Badger dismissed but taken on again. Alcohol & spree the cause of his neglect. Lillie gives me supper & bed in his house. Very civil indeed.

Saturday, November 1st.—River stopped a little above &

below the Fort, open & clear of ice in the middle opposite so that we pass over easily into the barge. Sinclair & 2 horses with another man for Fort Pitt to catch up the carts which started yesterday. Sinclair refuses to sell his train of dogs; no other first-rate train. Take 100 lbs. dried meat, 20 lbs. fresh, 2 bags pemmican (90 lbs. each), 40 lbs. soft grease, 20 hard. Brought cart across to sandy promontory where barge landed us. In going back ice gave way, Bucephalus down & struggling; with difficulty got out unhurt; take him across without cart which Bruneau unloads & pulls on to the ice & in about 20 yards loads it again, like a great fool; of course the ice breaks thro' again; on my return find what he has done & make him carry all heavy things to bank, when the cart passes easily. Quite 3 o'clock when all this is over & we get fairly under way. About 10 miles before dark & camp in wood. (Lillie told me of soldiers going to bed at Abercrombie where Sioux appeared & driven out to fight by officers with revolvers to their heads. Also Driver playing the devil with his alcohol. All men drunk & selling their blankets for liquor).

Sunday, November 2nd.—Start soon after sunrise; fast. Camp for dinner just beyond Lac Salit; a good journey. At night camp on South bank of river Cocquille.

Monday, November 3rd.—Find ice strong enough to bear horse & cart, the heavy things being carried over. A very long tramp to the far side of the Jolie. But to dinner, only 4 or 5 miles from home, my tendon Achilles very painful & I borrow Bruneau's moccasins to finish the journey. Home in about an hour; find the horses on the way & bring them in. Find them in the house, door & windows in & beds up; chimney stood all right. Very glad to see us back, hardly expecting us so soon, thinking the river would be impracticable; a long chat before bed.

Tuesday, November 4th.—I rest my tendon Achilles & open & arrange boxes & goods. Milton also rearranges everything. La Ronde & Bruneau planking floor. Old Indian (old boy) 2 days ago had brought daughter for sale. Married a few days ago for a horse. Husband stole horse back. Old boy therefore stole daughter back & vowed he would kill his son-in-law; wanted one of us to take the daughter; declined with thanks. Not bad looking though.

Wednesday, November 5th.—Writing up Journal, making a

candlestick, & preparing strychnine for wolves & wolverines. La Ronde making a table. Milton arranging. Bruneau making high platform outside for meat out of reach of dogs & wolves.

Thursday, November 6th.—I & Milton engaged in putting up shelves & arranging things thereon. Bruneau & La Ronde finish the planking. In the afternoon I commence cutting out a chair wherein to smoke withal. Milton ennuyeed.

Friday, November 7th.—La Ronde sets out for 3 days tour to find trapping ground. Milton & Bruneau go off to the "Old Boy's" to see how the tailoring goes on & flirt with La petite sauvagesse. I work all day at my chair forgetful of dinner, alone with Rover, & complete it by sundown. At dark, Bruneau returned alone milord being trop 'fatigué' to come back the same day. Bright frosty weather.

Saturday, November 8th.—In the morning I made another candlestick & prepared strychnine. Bruneau washing. At noon Milton returned, very cold, accompanied by the Old Boy, hunter & another Indian & small boy. In the afternoon I placed poisoned meat for the wolves; found plenty of tracks. On returning found that the Indians had ensconced themselves in the lodge, intending to stay the night. Milton had given them a pint of rum for 2 martens.

Sunday, November 9th.—Indians still here, very quiet. Milton & I set out to see the effect of the poison. One piece gone; follow the tracks about ½ a mile each way but cannot find the fox. Search again in afternoon without success. La Ronde returned at dusk, having only found tracks a good day's journey into the woods; nothing near. The Indians departed after a good chat with La Ronde, making only a feeble request for more rum which they did not get, our excuse being that it was Sunday.

Monday, November 10th.—Bright cold day, north wind very bitter; 6 inch snow fallen in the night. I go out to place poison again. Milton does nothing but smoke. La Ronde & Bruneau making sleds, or rather felling trees for them.

Tuesday, November 11th.—No success with the poison. Yesterday over again. No tracks.

Wednesday, November 12th.—Much colder; very severe on the lake; my ears chapped & numb from the cold. Have fur put round my cap to cover ears by Milton in the evening.

A Marten Trap.

Thursday, November 13th.—Wolf tracks close to my baits, but afraid to go near yet. La Ronde & Bruneau still at work on the sleds. Still cold, clear, with bitter north wind; my ear-caps very comfortable. Colder by far than the severest weather I have known in England. Wish we had a thermometer.

Friday, November 14th.—Doing nothing but smoke all morning except watching the completion of the sleds. At noon Milton & La Ronde set out for the Old boy's to fetch the shirts, &c., which they had been making for us. I went as usual after my baits, & again without finding any dead wolves. In the evening practised French with Bruneau. About midnight La Ronde came back accompanied by the Chasseur who, although he had only just returned from his trapping, & very tired, had come to get a pint of rum for a marten he had sold to Milton. He departed singing after about an hour's incessant talking with La Ronde, the latter enjoining him not to drink on the way.

Saturday, November 15th.—Up late. La Ronde sets out to look at his traps to return on Monday. I went with him to the end of the lake to look at 2 he had set there; on the way he showed me the difference between the tracks of a fox, little wolf & wild cat. In one trap we found a very large fisher—worth some 20 s.; got back at sundown & found Milton just returned very faint & hungry & having sat down several times on the road & once gone to sleep! In the evening set to work & altered my duffle shirt which had been most villainously made by the Indian women, Milton kindly helping me; kept us up late. Bruneau's culottes made so tight that he could not walk except by slewing his legs round as if half paralysed!

Sunday, November 16th.—Went off at daybreak, rifle in hand & poison in pocket to spend the day in making traps & placing poison round the lake. Took a very long time to build & set one trap & left it with great doubts as to whether it could possibly go off at all. On my way back at the point descried mine ancient enemy the great wolf, lying dead. A monster with a fine skin. Detached my belt & dragged him thereby to the hut; heavy work as the snow was rough. In the evening patched bullets & made other preparations for our buffalo hunt. On my return found the young son[21] of the Chasseur had arrived to go with us; gave him a fillet of rum, & the young dog kept us awake half the night by singing &

talking. Had to get up & Milton & I both sat & drank rum & water to enable us to sleep; found the remedy successful.

Monday, November 17th.—First thing after breakfast took Bruneau round my beat to shew him all my traps & poisons in order that he might attend to them during my absence. Found all the baits eaten except one, 3 wolves & 2 foxes having been having a corrobory of them; spent a long time in following the tracks without success. Very disappointing as 2 of them evidently very bad & walking with difficulty. The foxes also probably valuable cross ones, the footprint being very small. In the evening wrote up journal & completed preparations for our hunt, intending to start at daybreak tomorrow. Hurrah!

Tuesday, November 18th.—Started late, having some trouble to find the horses. Took the 2 roans, made one stage, very hot & the snow going fast. Camped at sundown under some pines on the bank of a small lake at the commencement of the hilly country. Water a strong smack of Harrogate.

Wednesday, November 19th.—Off at daybreak. Spent rather an unhappy night, being in momentary dread of a pine which was half burnt thro' by the fire, & seemed by the flickering light to bend tremendously to the strong north wind which blew, & about to fall directly upon us. I woke La Ronde but he was too sleepy to cut it down & with an 'all right' 'pas de danger' snored again. It didn't tumble after all. The day turned out very warm again & we took off our coats. Terribly hard work for the horses, the snow melting & binding to the sleds; & in many places no snow at all. At our dining place, La Ronde found track of a Fisher & straight-way made a trap for him. Our track disappeared in the course of the afternoon, & we steered across a large lake, the horses crossing with difficulty from deficiency of snow—obliged to make a push & get over as it would be impo' 'ble in the morning when the surface was refrozen. Nearly dark when we camped other side of lake.

Thursday, November 20th.—A long day thro' undulating country covered with scrub & the latter part of it burnt some two or three years ago; had been dense forest & the burnt & fallen trees gave us much trouble with the sleds which continually caught & occasionally broke against them. La Ronde went in advance & returned just as the small savage & I had prepared camp, bringing the welcome news that he had seen the plains which were close ahead; too dark to make out buffalo.

Friday, November 21st.—Reached the ridge of the hill in about an hour after breakfast & saw the plains below. La Ronde could see only 5 buffalo about $1\frac{1}{2}$ miles off. It took me some time to make them out amongst the scrub & willows. Made camp under some pines, ate, drank & smoked & then set out leisurely to slaughter our bulls, the weather being so warm that in an evil moment I cast off my duffle shirt & La Ronde his capote. After much dodging about round hillocks & through scrub, I not knowing exactly where the beasts were, we crawled some 200 yards on hands & knees, & then La Ronde whispered me & pointed through the bushes, & there sure enough were the 5 bulls lying asleep & only some 20 yards off! And now we made a mess of it, La Ronde whispering in a mixture of French & English, & I being highly excited, my heart thumping against my ribs very loudly, I could not make out whether he meant me to shoot then or not. He on the other hand could not make out what I was going to do, & so we waited: at last he put up his gun to shoot, & I afraid of being too late incautiously exposed my head & shoulders rather suddenly, when off they all were in a twinkling, exposing only their sterns for us to shoot at, bang, bang, bang, but no result. La Ronde cursed me & I abused him, but we were soon all right again tho' both much vexed at the unfortunate event. No more bulls to be seen, & what's to be done? Come for meat & must have it. Follow the 5 & see them about $1\frac{1}{2}$ miles off feeding. La Ronde & the young Indian[22] set off again, I lending the former my gun as it was a question of victuals & wishing to give him every chance of killing. I followed leisurely until I heard 3 shots & then set off at speed & at length caught up the young savage waiting for me, La Ronde having gone in chase of 2 wounded ones We followed at speed & presently heard three more shots, & soon La Ronde appeared for more ammunition, exhausted & out of breath. Had made 2 safe & another badly wounded which he set off again to try & get. We walked after & shortly saw one bull walking slowly along. I gave him one behind the shoulder which downed him at once. The youthful cree amusing himself by firing at him until he was very dead indeed. La Ronde came back unable to get the third & to search for the other dead one. Found him some 200 yards off. The sun had already gone down & we were now 5 or 6 miles from camp. Resolved to camp by buffalo. Oh how we regretted our coats!—A bitterly cold night, & nothing but our shirts & a reeking buffalo hide to cover us. Made a good fire; but of course it went out before morning, & the hide froze in an arch over us, letting the wind in dreadfully; like sleeping in a railway tunnel. Very little sleep either, & a wearisomely long night.

Saturday, November 22nd.—Very stiff & cramped from my futile endeavours to make myself small enough to hide completely under my covering. Gradually thawed before a good fire. Resolved that I go & look for the wounded bull, La Ronde & the young Cree to fetch the sleds for the meat. I followed the tracks for 3 or 4 miles but could find nothing; they had evidently gone far the night before, the dung being frozen & blood in the track. Gave it up & return to the camp where I sit waiting very cold & half asleep until La Ronde & the young Cree return in the course of the afternoon when we move our camp to a more sheltered place where there was a little more wood. In the evening I prepared poisoned baits, La Ronde being very keen to bag a black fox he had seen, & I expecting a good haul of furs as there were tracks of cross foxes everywhere, & of wolves, without end.

Sunday, November 23rd.—La Ronde & young Cree stay in camp to dry meat & place it on the trains. I go out to a high hill from whence I could view all quarters of the plains for 20 or 30 miles. Could not see a buffalo. In returning saw La Ronde going also to look out. (Found all baits gone in the morning but no dead foxes or wolves). Placed more poison treble strength. La Ronde had gone out to look for me thinking me long, for I had sat some time on the hill smoking & looking for buffalo. In the evening he returned having viewed 8 or 9 buffalo close at hand; resolve to go in chase in the morning.

Monday, November 24th.—Start directly after sunrise, not sans chemise this time, the boy following behind with the horses. After long detour La Ronde brings me within 50 yards of the 3 buffalo; peeping over the crest of a little mound, I see them all fast asleep. La Ronde & Cree go round to the opposite side of them, instructing me to shoot in case they should begin to move off, but otherwise to wait until I saw his head above the opposite mound on the other side of them. They started off & I waited & waited, every now & then cautiously raising my head to see if the bulls were still undisturbed. Can't see a sign of La Ronde, look again cautiously, & one of the bulls was on his legs looking round. I raise my gun & cover him well; but cannot see La Ronde yet, & as the beast seems tranquil, I drop my head under cover of the hill & wait once more. Now I presume I had one of my fits of absence of mind, my thoughts for some unaccountable reason being busy with home affairs & Bingley & its neighbourhood. How long this went on I don't know for the next thing I remember was that I heard a great shouting, & on popping up my head, saw the 3 bulls coming past at full speed some 30 yards off, La Ronde & the young Cree trotting after & adjuring me to shoot. I shot aiming very carefully at the last which presented a good broadside; he staggered & dropped behind, following the others very slowly. I was so certain that he was settled that I did not give him the second barrel but fired at another with what effect I could not see as they were by this time some distance. La Ronde fired several shots with great rapidity but without much chance of killing as they were only stern on to him. I reloaded as fast as I could & ran after them, La Ronde being already in chase in advance, his trade gun giving him great advantage in loading quickly. I found to my surprise that the wounded bull had again joined the rest who had pulled up a little to look round, & they were all again under way, quickly disappearing over a hill. On joining La Ronde, I found him in an awful temper sacréing[23] & d—ing dreadfully, swearing he had been cachéd on the other side the buffalo for a good half-hour waiting for me to shoot; then he whistled low & the bulls arose & looked round, & he saw me as he thought about to fire, but to his disgust saw me withdraw under cover again: then he called out in a loud whisper, Fire, Fire, then louder, Fire, & at last provoked beyond longer endurance he shouted as loud as he could Fi-er, when of course the bulls set off, & he shouted again to me to look out. The wind was strong against me, & I did not hear until the last sound. I could not see him for he was well hid from me & the buffalo too. He declared however that I could have seen him well, & he waved his hand & cap & did everything he could to induce me to shoot. He was so vexed that he would not go after the wounded one, saying I had missed, & that it was the young Cree who had hit one, for there was the blood in the track of mine & he could not get over that. As they had gone straight away from the camp & we were already a long distance from it, I did not choose to follow them alone. We then retired to a mound to smoke a pipe of peace, regain our good temper & our wind to look round & consider the next move. La Ronde at the first glance spied 10 buffalo about a mile off, having assembled on a hill like ourselves to see what the firing meant. This put us in better humour, & having finished our pipes, we set off again to stalk up to the 10. After a long round we got within 50 yards, & then resolving to give the young Cree a chance sent him round to some good cover close to them on the off side, expecting they would come straight to us when he fired. After waiting some little time, we heard the shot, but on cautiously looking out saw them going away some 100 yds. off. Bang, bang, bang, my 2 barrels, La Ronde's one, & thud, thud, thud—three hit but none stopped; plenty of blood in the tracks; load like smoke & after them at a run; follow for 2 or 3 miles; but they keep going; at last they stopped & began to feed a little, some mile ahead of us, moving on slowly after a time. Then commenced another stalk, crawling on our bellies over exposed places, rushing along at full speed when well hidden, to the place we expected to find them. Gone again! cautiously forward for another half mile, still going on! We pull up in despair & have a pipe, screened from view. Look around again when we have had our smoke & find they have stopped once more & begun to feed more steadily. Try it again, says La Ronde, & off we go again with the same alternation of crawling, stooping, & rushing along for another mile, an awful pace & I very nearly cried a go, but my old boating training stood me in good stead, although awfully done I was determined not to give in & stuck to it; at last we stopped, & La Ronde said they were feeding slowly on & would appear directly round the hill behind which we were ensconced. It was now La Ronde's chance of first shot, & as the first head came in sight he began to aim & shot deliberately as he showed his shoulder. I was determined that no more wounded ones should get away if I could help it, & seeing he did not turn over at once I gave him a barrel, which put him all of a heap, & my second to the others; then loading again frantically I broke my ramrod, but rushed along to cut off the rest who were making a circuit rather towards me; gave both barrels to a wounded one which lagged behind some 300 yards but all went away & we were both too tired to follow far. The one we both fired at first was lying dead having only gone a few yards, & we found the young one already arrived with the horses & at work cutting him up. He turned out a splendid young bull with a beautiful coat & quite fat. Very good meat. La Ronde was indignant at my shooting at his bull, but I told him we had lost too many & I was determined to bag something, & I triumphed when upon examination it turned out that my ball had gone through the heart & killed, his only through the shoulder blade & too high, not doing any material injury. We were both so done with our 5 or 6 miles chase that it was with the greatest difficulty that we placed the beast in the proper position for cutting up, not a hard task otherwise for 2 strong men. Having had nothing to eat all day, & it being now sundown, we made a fire & cooked steaks & made tea, working away at cutting up, I like any butcher up to the armpits in blood; dark before we had finished & loaded the horses, many miles from camp. A young moon of only 3 days. Cloudy also; steered for camp as well as we could, tramped on for several hours, unable to find camp although sure we were close to it; nearly midnight. Can't find any dry wood. At last meet with some, & in despair of finding our camp in the dark make a fire & supper & turn in, La Ronde under one of the young one's capotes, himself under another, I under a cartcover. Another cold night; waterproof damp. Breath condenses & drops on to my face. Can't sleep much. La Ronde & young one the same, always somebody up mending fire; "wish for the day".

Tuesday, November 25th.—Awoke very cold & stiff before daylight. Wonder where we are; heard wolves howling through the night not very far off. As soon as we could see, go to a little hill near to find our bearings. Find we are not half a mile off, adjourn tout de suite. Find wolves have eaten half the meat on the sled farthest from the fire; the other untouched. Having enough load, however, for the horses as there is still no snow, don't much care. Feed, load the sleds & start for home; reach our first camp in view of plains before sundown. Horses very done.

Wednesday, November 26th.—2 rather short stages through the burnt country & scrub, & camp a short distance before coming to the lake. Very monotonous work driving a sled. In the evening La Ronde tells me of some fights with the Sioux; 60 half-breeds attacked by some 2000 Sioux who brought women leading horses to carry away the spoil. Had intelligence of their coming & barricade of carts. Horses round inside & men next; women & children in the centre; two days; 30 horses killed; no half breeds; 10 Sioux. Priest with them exhorting them. Another time single combat with Sioux, on horseback. Pots the Sioux after much maneuvering to get first chance of fair shot.

Thursday, November 27th.—All morning crossing the lake. La Ronde drags the sleds over the ice; heavy work. Young Cree & I lead horses through woods; ice too slippery to cross them; much trouble with the beasts; cutting road for them to pass; I have two to lead. Always one on the wrong side of a tree; one will come along sometimes & the other won't. I thought they would have driven me wild. At last get round to opposite side. La Ronde already there with sleds & made fire; pemmican & tea & off again; camp in thick wood.

Friday, November 28th.—Up & down hill; horses done; La Ronde finds a Fisher in one of his traps. The Sandris refusing to proceed along the side of a hill rears & over goes he on to his side; the sled turns over & throws him on his back helpless, sled upside down, he supine kicking his legs in the air; I suggest unharnessing, but La Ronde 'Oh no, help me to roll him over,' & we give him a lift & turn him rolling downhill until he & the sled come right side up! Thats the way they do things in this country! Camp at night at our old place of the first night out. Snows 4 inches in the night. Sleds go like smoke.

Saturday, November 29th.—Take a straight line for the Jolie Prairie; have to cut road most of the way; little breakfast. One long stage with empty stomach. La Ronde makes a bee line & brings us to the house soon after noon. Order pancakes immediately, having an intense longing for some vegetable food after a fortnight with nothing but meat. Find Dalilah; disgusted. Say nothing till next day. La Ronde makes up his mind to get drunk, having had a dream to that effect. Gets very lively. Chasseur, John Smith & another arrive. He treats them. Encamp outside; I sleep there too. Singing & howling all night. I say never any more of this. Bruneau nearly mad with drink. Pulls Milton out of bed 4 times for liquor. At last Milton kicks him out; very indignant. Comes to our camp & howls, shouts & raves. Throws his arms about theatrically & cries continually, 'O le bon Dieu' &c. The Indians singing; wild scene. La Ronde & I force Bruneau to turn in under a blanket. Indians keep turning up all night, & I get devilish little rest even in sleep.

Sunday, November 30th.—Indians still drunk; La Ronde

all right; Bruneau muggy; expostulate with Milton about D. They depart for the Old Boys. I work all day mending culottes. &c. & preparing for trapping expedition. La Ronde & Milton return in evening without D. & with small sled & two dogs bought of Old Boy.

Monday, December 1st.—Writing journal morning & evening. In afternoon try snow-shoes for first time; get on very well; 4 or 5 falls in the wood; 9 or 10 miles; more tired than if 20 without. To start in morning with La Ronde for 4 or 5 days trapping in the woods. Sauteux comes in in evening on trapping expedition. Gives poor account of prospects of fur.

Tuesday, December 2nd.—Milton engaged in my absence the wife of an Indian near, "L'homme tranquille" as La Ronde & Bruneau call him from his silent equanimity, to wash. She came, & continuing to wash until midnight & the eternal scrub, scrub, splash, splash, poking the fire, & rattling of pails preventing any possibility of sleep, he ventured to remonstrate mildly; without effect; it becoming unbearable towards morning, he jumped up, emptied the water & put out the fire, greatly to her disgust. She rested quietly until she thought he must be asleep & then again lighted the fire and resumed her washing. He was beaten & resigned himself to his fate with many maledictions. Started after breakfast for the woods to commence trapping. I took up my bundle & placed it on my back with many misgivings; it felt *very* heavy; 2 blankets, 20 lbs pemmican, 5 or 6 grease, 2 pair extra moccasins. La Ronde, meat, tea, salt, tin pot & 2 cups, baits for traps. In addition I had my belt with axe, knife, bullet & tobacco pouch, tinder & flint & steel ditto; powder horn, shot belt, gun, mittaines, 3 pair socks on, leather breeches, mittas jersey, flannel shirt, tweed waistcoat, leather shirt, duffle shirt! O! by Jove! I could hardly move, trudged along with stern resolution. La Ronde going a great pace in spite of a load heavier than mine, but I was too proud to request him to be more moderate. 2 miles across the lake, & then plunged into the thick woods, & I soon found it very heavy work, my back aching before the first mile, the 4 inches of snow hiding the obstacles in the path which didn't exist & making footing very slippery & uncertain. After 4 miles of this work, when I had begun to curse my folly in making such a beast of burden of myself, La Ronde very considerately proposed a pipe to which I acceded without protest, & I seated myself on a fallen tree perspiring at every pore, for the day was extremely warm for the time of year. On again same distance & dine; devilish glad of it. After dinner on to large lake for night. See a few Marten tracks on the way; 3 traps with baits eaten by magpies & ermine, warm weather having thawed them. Thank my stars able to lighten my load by eating pemmican, & gorge myself with that view, utterly careless of food for future emergencies! Saw a fresh moose track; no wind.

Wednesday. December 3rd.—Same style of thing as yesterday. Beast of burden half repents. La Ronde goes, as he calls it, 'doucement' & I call at a severe pace struggling after. All traps the same; baits gone. Over a hill covered with fallen trees. Camp over the other side. Thank goodness.

Thursday, December 4th.—Get to the end of traps previously made by La Ronde, & commence lengthening the line by making some 6 more, La Ronde instructing me how to make them; know a marten's, fisher's & mink's tracks. Camp for night on the other side of first hill; steering N.N.W. Over our camp-fire La Ronde tells me of Company. No free trading allowed. 13 years ago, 5 men imprisoned for it; Canadian half breeds go armed to the Court which sits 2 days & a night in terrorem. Law against free trading repealed immediately in consequence.

Friday, December 5th.—Forward making traps (all marten) every 3 or 400 yards. I turn off to shoot brace of partridges. La Ronde thinking I had gone too much to the right, keeps more to the left. I had however kept bearing to the left, he not having noticed that I had come back after turning aside; going ahead of him to make another trap, come on my own track! Call out to him, & he comes up. Says some Indians; take out my compass & find we are going due South, instead of N. N. W. & following back track a little come upon a trap made, as we thought, 2 miles behind us! La Ronde very much chagrined. Never happened to him before. Dense pine forest, very cloudy day, not a glimpse of sun; awful work, stumbling over fallen trees; hurting one's feet on stumps, putting eyes out with branches. Camp early & La Ronde goes ahead to view country. Comes back no wiser; dense forest & no hills. Fine pines covered with snow, intense stillness; made 20 traps.

Saturday, December 6th.—Leave our bundles behind us & go on nearly all day making 15 traps, returning in evening to former camp. Dense fine pine forest. Covered with snow & duffle shirt found objectionable, the snow sticking to it & freezing on. Plenty of marten tracks; one moose track. Start for home at daybreak having made 45 traps which with 25 La Ronde had made before 70 in all.

Sunday, December 7th.—Plod home, the bundles feeling heavy in spite of the pemmican being reduced to very small compass. Weight increased by 5 martens we find in traps: 2 in those of my own construction; satisfactory. Camp for night at encampment of 2nd. night. Sleep little always towards morning when fire gets low & feet very cold; woke with them numb & obliged to rub vigorously.

Monday, December 8th.—Very sultry, & walk very slowly, a long stage, & into the house in afternoon; placed poisoned baits at all camps, for benefit of wolverines who follow track & smash all traps. Milton & Bruneau glad to see us back; bored; ordered pancakes & broiled fish 'tout de suite'. After dinner Bruneau came in & announced the arrival of some dog trains from the direction of Carlton. I went out to meet them & saw three trains coming across the lake. When they came up, recognized Badger (Messiter's man) as the driver of the first, Peter then comes with the 2nd., & another fort man with a third. Badger informed me that Messiter was a little behind, & I went forward & met him on the lake. The same as ever, talking like one o'clock. Full of trading for furs. Had made 70 marten, besides deer, bear & other skins of his 2 gals. rum, knives, flour, &c. Had been racing Peter all the way to get hold of the 'Chasseur's' furs first. Bought martens on the way in the face of Peter &c. In the evening he recounted his experience of the liquor traffic. One occasion Atagakouph wanted rum as a present. Messiter refused, wanting a marten. Atagakouph went out, fetched the marten (being already pretty well screwed), crumpled it up & threw it in Messiter's face. Messiter enraged, hit him in the face with his fist. Atagakouph drew his knife & stabbed at him, held back by Badger. 4 other Indians also present (in Messiter's house) & also drunk, immediately drew knives & rushed on Messiter & Badger. The Columbian coming at the time, got a cut across the face; knives chopping about in all directions. One Indian seized the candle, dashed it on the floor, & then collared the rum cask. Messiter in the corner farthest from the door & unarmed, made a rush, got a cut on the hand, one through the hair at the back of his neck, & another gash in the breast; none severe; met a man on the way; bright thought struck him; stooped down, seized him by the legs & chucked him over his head with a crash; gained the door, having seized the barrel, snatched up his gun which was close to the door & loaded, & seating himself on the barrel outside the house, kept guard over it with both barrels on full cock, vowing to shoot the first man who interfered with him. Sat some time in considerable doubt. Then up rose Tambout like a giant refreshed with wine; (Tambout a man of enormous strength, half-breed, 6 feet 3 & built in proportion, known as the strongest & bravest in these parts). Messiter had been kind to Tambout in giving him several little things. He was drunk & lying on the floor, but being at length aroused by the din, & understanding what was going on, he rose up, seized Atagakouph (6 feet 2 & built in proportion)& banged him against the wall most unmercifully, Atagakouph a trifle in his hands; declared he would kill the first man who touched Messiter (had killed one with a blow of his fist): Ataqakouph gave in, & all marched to their lodges under terror of Tambout's vengeance, Tambout assuring Messiter that not one would stir again. And Messiter accordingly slept that night in peace.

Tuesday, December 9th.—Peter & Badger racing to the Chasseur's before daybreak; Messiter awaiting their return. Spent the day talking & smoking. Milton bought Messiter's little rum keg for his best fisher. I sold Messiter 2 gals. of rum for 30 martens; subsequently he called off the 2nd gal. if the first did not pay. Played at whist in evening, Milton & Messiter for marten; ended quits; late to bed.

Wednesday, December 10th.—Peter & Badger returned soon after breakfast. The former very indignant with Messiter for trading. Wrote forthwith to Mr. Lillie to stop further supplies to him. Peter had gone to meet the Chasseur returning from his hunt & collared his furs first; Badger had however sold all his liquor to the Chasseur on tick. (In the middle of the night I had been aroused by the entrance of the Chasseur who aroused La Ronde & conversed; it turned out that he had come the 8 miles in the middle of the night in the hope of getting more groq; disappointed however.) Peter & Messiter with Badger started early, & soon after Milton & La Ronde for a few days trapping. Bruneau also to look at some traps, & I was left to spend the afternoon alone which I occupied by cleaning guns & writing.—[Messiter told me his experience with scabies. Still suffering, & not being able to manufacture ung. sulph. satisfactorily, he, by the advice of his Columbian, made a decoction of tobacco boiled down to thick paste, & rubbed this in hard for an hour, standing before the fire; soon ill; vomiting & raving delirium all night; Columbian dreadfully frightened & essays to send for me. Horses cannot be found. No help for it. Toward morning Messiter better, but unable to move for a day. Itch quite cured. Atagakouph still in bed to this day from Tambout's treatment].

Thursday, December 11th.—Out after breakfast for the day with Bruneau: left Chewshew the new dog bought of the Sauteux trapper in the house & fastened the door, taking Rover with us. Went S.S.W. Over a large lake into the woods; no tracks; lost our way several times, & only able to steer at all in the thick wood by the help of my compass. Dined & made 3 traps for fisher "sans design"; snowing a little, cloudy, foggy, raw east wind. Wonder how Milton likes it. Arrive at home an hour after dark. Find that Chewshew has taken a large piece of meat from a high shelf & eaten the whole for which he gets well licked by Bruneau. In evening write up Journal & then pipe & to bed.

Friday, December 12th.—Bruneau went off to see marten traps across the lake. I remained at home cleaning gun, mending my clothes &c. Just before dinner the dog trains for La Crosse arrived. A young Sinclair commis en charge. Very agreeable; 3 trains. Bells &c; jolly tinkling as they trotted along; the two men cooked dinner, delighted to have fresh meat & flour; only fish & barley in the grain at La Crosse. After dinner they started again. Bruneau came back. I went across the lake & set a fisher trap to rights, there being a fresh track. After that quietly to bed.

Saturday, December 13th.—Across the lake in the middle of the day en racquette to set marten trap on our walk, view my two traps at the far end of the lake & try poison again for the foxes. At the point saw La Ronde emerging from the wood. Met him half way across, carrying Milton's pack as well as his own, Milton not yet in sight; close to border of lake met Milton marching very, very slowly; said they must have come 16 miles since daybreak; 5 or 6 I think; forward, placed poison, rebaited traps; back after dark; snow-shoes blistered my feet. La Ronde had made thirty, Milton one.

Sunday, December 14th.—Did nothing particular all day; having severe cold; caught it with staying in the house, the first since leaving England! Decided not to start with La Ronde to see my traps until Tuesday. In evening, to our surprise Messiter appeared with the Columbian having walked over from the Montagne du Bois. The latter vowing he was nearly killed; about 30 miles walk. Messiter had come for the gallon of rum I had sold him for 15 martens. Sat up till midnight & then played whist. Milton & Messiter began squabbling as usual. Very slow whist. Messiter had heard of a camp of Indians as yet unvisited by traders & anxious to set out with rum to get the furs before John Company.

Monday, December 15th.—After breakfasting Messiter & the Columbian set out to return; the latter generously promised to send over the wherewithal to make a plum pudding for Christmas. In the evening had rather warm discussion with Milton about furs, he wanting to take all La Ronde killed, have the 30 which La Ronde made when they were out together to his own cheek, & not allow me to have any made for myself ! ! As I pay La Ronde half his wages, I didn't see that at all. Offered to put all the skins together & divide in 3 parts, 1 to La Ronde, 1 part to Milton, 1 to myself. After a long time he agreed. He had nominally bought La Ronde's hunt for tobacco. &c., but I had certainly a right to his services to make traps for me if he made for him & merely proposed the dividing into 3 parts for the sake of simplicity, & as being an arrangement sufficiently to the advantage of Milton, as I was able to make traps, Milton not. (I had made 20, Milton 1).

Tuesday, December 16th.—After breakfast, being ready to start, I said, "Oh, I'll go with you to see your traps when I come back if you like." "Oh no," said he "for you'll find out my walk & be poaching on my manor"! "Well but," said I, "it will make no difference, for the whole will be divided into 3 as we agreed last night." "Oh no," he replied "those are my private ones." I had 3 or 4 times explained with the utmost particularity that I meant the whole, both his traps, La Ronde's & what I made. I told him that wasn't the bargain at all. It was mere folly to suppose that I had offered to make an arrangement to give him a third of the traps which La Ronde & I had made on our walk, seeing that I had made more than a third with my own hands & those in the very best part of the walk! Another warm discussion. I persisting that I had a right, as I paid half, to have half labour. I told him either that or he must pay La Ronde entirely himself & left him to think it over until my return.

Set out late in consequence, very late & did very short stage before camping for night.

Wednesday, December 17th.—A good journey; cold better with the fresh journey, & I found my two blankets & 20 lbs of meat nothing. Fine bright day. Found 1 marten. Wolverine had broken most of our traps. Camped for night at old place on the hill. Saw 3 tracks of elk, 1 of moose.

Thursday, December 18th.—La Ronde set out in advance to arrange the traps at the furthest end of the walk, I following quickly after to arrange the nearest; so return at dark to same camp. I found all traps broken, & the remnant of 1 marten. The wolverine again. Eaten of the Yankee strychnine & made him hungry! Confound the Yankees! I set right all my traps with a bad heart, & got back to camp about an hour before sundown; made fire & prepared supper, when La Ronde came in; he had not arranged a single trap, the wolverine having broken all & eaten nine martens of which he had found the remains, perhaps more. In a great rage, vowing vengeance against the wolverines. Very unusual for a wolverine to touch a marten. La Ronde thinks him half devil.

Friday, December 19th.—A long march; only pemmican to eat; very heavy stuff to walk on: hard work in snow; last night cold very severe & in spite of a tremendous fire & two blankets awoke with cold feet, & neither able to sleep for many hours before daybreak. Arrive at the house before sundown, & find Bruneau solus. Milton being at the Old boy's. Eat fish & bain with greediness.

Saturday, December 20th.—Enjoy the 'dolce far niente' all day over a pipe & tea. In the evening Milton returned with the young sauvage to drive the dog train; brought in 30 fish from the Old boy out of the 200 he owes us for net.

Sunday, December 21st.—Milton, La Ronde & the young one go over to the Indians to make arrangements with the Chasseur to take us to the Wood Cree Camp on the border of the plains to hunt Buffalo whilst La Ronde & Bruneau go to Red River for supplies of flour, tea & sugar. Only sending 600 miles for necessaries! ! to be back in 2 months. No flour at Carlton, tea & sugar very dear, 5/.- & 2/.- the lb. Bruneau & I rest quietly at home mending moccasins, &c. Remember it is the shortest day.

TRIP ACROSS CANADA

Monday, December 22nd.—Awakened at daybreak by knocking at the door. Sinclair the commis from Carlton to Lac Vert with flour & pemmican for the fort there; 5 dog sleighs. Give them breakfast. Sinclair informs me that Lillie had seized the train of dogs which he had sold to Messiter & refused any further supplies, Badger having come to the fort for some things with the dog train. This done in consequence of his trading & racing Peter the commis all over the country for furs. He had written to Lillie to explain that he was only purchasing a few furs for his lady friends; but that wouldn't wash. In afternoon Milton & La Ronde came back, having made all arrangements with Chasseur & the two intending to set out for Carlton tomorrow, the latter to go forward with Bruneau to Red River, the former to return here with a few small supplies, & then we set out for the plains. In meantime I go with Chasseur's son to look at the traps & endeavour to poison the wolverine.

Tuesday, December 23rd.—La Ronde had violent cold from standing out of doors with wet feet, & I prohibited the journey to Carlton for some days. Nothing occurred.

Wednesday, December 24th.—Patient rather better, still feverish. Milton & Bruneau start for Carlton, La Ronde to follow as soon as well enough. Here's a Christmas eve! Here I am alone with La Ronde & the young Indian, writing up my journal, the former smoking, the latter looking with great delight at the plates in my Surgeon's Vademecum. No mince pies, no good things, no family meeting this year. Not after all so melancholy a Xmas as the last. But sad thoughts of home & its melancholy associations are getting hold of me. I will stop & essay to keep Xmas Eve as appropriately as I can with a tin can of rum punch & a pipe.

Thursday, December 25th.—Xmas day. As yesterday sit in house with my patient who is nearly convalescent. The Xmas dinner consisted of galette & hot pot! In the evening I made some rum punch which La Ronde & I discussed with gusto, & found it raised our spirits, & we passed the evening merrily, having been very melancholy all day. Prepared to start tomorrow.

Friday, December 26th.—My Mother's birthday. Wish her health & prosperity. La Ronde set out for his long voyage in good spirits, calling at Carlton for a dog train, provisions

& Bruneau. Immediately after I set out with Nashquapamayoo for the woods intent on the destruction of the wolverine. Weather still fine & warm in the middle of the day. Carried two blankets, a sack of fresh meat cut up small & mixed with pemmican, & a few onions; quite enough I found with a large axe also in my belt. The young 'un carried a gun, blanket, tea, flour—(a very little of the latter). Rover accompanied us. Camped half a journey from the hill. Saw 1 moose track, the wolverine broken all traps. Put poisoned baits in them.

Saturday, December 27th.—Dinner on the hill. At the lake this side found a great number of fox tracks, & the wolverines everywhere. The reason, an immense number of small fish shut into a small space of shallow water where a stream entered the lake & where it was not frozen, the animals & a number of crows fed constantly on them; put 3 poisons; camped for night at half day from last trap. All broken by wolverine; mended young one's moccasin he not being able to work needle & thread. He went into fits of laughter at the result, it being all on one side. Much amused also at my attempts at Cree with help of La Ronde's vocabulary.

Sunday, December 28th.—Visited traps as far as we had baits, & then returned camping for night at encampment of first day. Wolverine had taken all poisoned baits out of traps, tasted & dropped them, confound him! Set my 3 hook device without much hope of catching him. All traps broken again.

Monday, December 29th.—March home without a single skin. Arrive 2 hours before sundown. An hour after, Messiter & Badger arrive & report Milton on the road, & he arrives about an hour later still. I find that he got to the fort on Xmas day in time for dinner, 26 hours! Reports La Ronde & Bruneau have set out for Fort Garry. Milton & Messiter rush off straightway to Chasseur's, the former in an awful excitement about Messiter getting the furs there, & threatening strychnine & all kinds of devilry. I laugh at him, tell him that is all nonsense & rubbish & advise him not to make a fool of himself; a jolly good sleep after.

Tuesday, December 30th.—Messiter & Badger come in at noon, reporting Milton to follow after dinner. Milton comes in before dark in great excitement. They had come to knives drawn about martens the night before, both having skins owed,

Messiter's for Farquharson, but Milton having first debt,
Messiter had taken some in payment. Milton vowing to
poison again. I say I will try & settle it with Messiter & he
cools down a little. Atagakouph gets dram for trouble. Old
boy (alias Crooked nose in Cree) came & spent night. I write
up journal & listen to Milton's anathemas against Messiter;
very tired of it.

Wednesday, December 31st.—We think of starting for
the buffalo in 4 days, after I & the young one have been to find
out the result of our machinations against the wolverine.
Crooked nose & Nashquapamayoo very energetic in explaining
something & some reason why I should not set out for my
traps, & Milton for the other house tomorrow. The whole
thing was cleared up just before dark by the arrival of Kinamontayoo, wife, kid & D—h with all traps & two sleds, come
to spend New Year's day with us, & ready to start for the
plains as soon as we liked! Their custom to visit their friends
on New Year's day & eat & drink all the good things they
can qet. We come to the conclusion that it will be best not
to disappoint our friend & start at once tomorrow. Milton
& D. camp out much to the astonishment of the Indians.

Thursday, January 1st, 1863.—First thing Crooked Nose
& the young one go outside with their guns & fire a salute
of six shots in honour of the new year. After that a general
shaking of hands & qood wishes. We omit kissing the women
which was part of the ceremony properly. Complete preparations & load the sledges, after which qive the two men half
a pint of rum as new year's gift for which they are very grateful & sinq the praises of the two Okee Mows. Then start.
Milton ahead on snowshoes, going very well at first. Dogs
very unwilling to leave & requiring some licking. Left Chasseur's wife & Apitwaitimackiow in charge of Fort Milton during
our absence. I find sled-driving very tiresome, the abominable
things always turning over or pulling up against a tree. Went
on after dark to get to La Ronde's & my old camp. Milton
very disgusted & swearing he was killing himself, leading the
way on snowshoes at about a mile an hour the latter part.
Both very glad to camp. Not very cold.

Friday, January 2nd.—Started well & did a fair day's
journey. Milton soon after the start very unhappy & having
serious misqivings that the two Indians who were leading
would not think it necessary to stop for dinner, wearying me

with his complaints & curses that he had ever come & wanting to stop and make a fire with every rotten stick he saw. We stopped the Chasseur when we overtook him making a trap; he was evidently quite astonished that we wanted dinner & hurried us off again very hastily after a renewal of groaning & complaint from Milton whom I had great difficulty in inducing to go on & do a fair day's march. The Hunter apologized over our camp fire for not knowing we liked to dine; very cold feet; intense frost.

Saturday, January 3rd.—Long journeys; Milton grumbling; cold; sleds great bother; nothing else; Saturday, January 3rd was an unfortunate day. I lost my Coke knife & sheath, Milton his bullet pouch, Chasseur his pipe, & both axes broke.

Sunday, January 4th.—Milton in the same mood, & I had almost a quarrel with him to get him along. Bitterly cold north wind & scanty snowing; crossed a lake in afternoon and camped in clump of trees with plenty of dry wood. On arriving, Milton's nose frozen; first case I had seen; he had been riding in the sleigh; only silk handkerchief round his face; rubbed it gently under my direction & it was soon all right again. Made a very good camp, fed heartily & regained good temper; *cold very severe.* Found the camp we expected to reach was broken up & the Indians dispersed in different directions after buffalo. We had followed one of the tracks leading N. N. W.

Monday, January 5th.—Kinamontayoo arranged that we should all stay in present camp whilst he went out alone to look for buffalo. We were rather anxious all day about his success as our provisions were nearly exhausted; a few pounds of pemmican & a little flour. The dogs were condemned to fast completely until we got meat, & we had selected one as a victim to our appetites in case buffalo were not forthcoming. I and Nashquapamayoo spend the day in collecting wood & mending moccasins, &c., Milton in smoking pipes & congratulating himself upon his happy condition in not having to face the road that day. Wait—wait—wait. No Chasseur; dark; no Chasseur. Have supper; still he does not turn up. Speculate whether it is a good or bad omen of his success. Nashquapamayoo gets very anxious about his father & listens intently for sound of gun. Induces me to fire several shots at intervals; no reply. Fire again & young one fancies he hears one in return; two more shots & then give up. Wait—wait—

nearly asleep. Nashquapamayoo sitting listening most intently, motionless, absorbed; at last a little before midnight the sound of footsteps & Kinamontayoo appeared carrying something on his back. Fresh meat by Jove! He had been a long way without seeing a trace of buffalo, coming back, & just at dark he discovered a solitary bull & killed him. Nearly frozen & obliged to make a fire. Brought the heart & tongue which we cooked & ate forthwith thankfully. Colder than ever.

Tuesday, January 6th.—Struck camp & went off 6 or 7 miles to skin buffalo which was fortunately where there was plenty of dry wood although small & giving me & the young one much trouble to collect in sufficient quantity which we did whilst the Chasseur cut up the beast; all finished by dark; still intensely cold; Milton's face swelled a little with gumboil.

Wednesday, January 7th.—Milton's face a little more swelled & he resolves to stay in camp with Nashquapamayoo, whilst I went out with Kinamontayoo to look for buffalo. We set out, I having by this time nearly got accustomed to my snowshoes & marching bravely behind the Chasseur in the deep snow (2 feet in many places). After some 4 or 5 miles trudging, we came upon the fresh tracks of 2 bulls & followed them for about a mile on the undulating prairie, when suddenly the Chasseur pulled up, & at the same moment I saw the head of a bull peering at us; we quietly dropped out of sight all our length in the snow, & Kinamontayoo motioning to me to stay behind as there was no cover & the stalk difficult; crawled on alone to the edge of the hollow in which they were feeding. I did not object as the buffalo were so scarce & we wanted the meat. He got within 40 yards & then, stealthily withdrawing the cover of his gun, took a long aim & fired. I heard the thud & one of the beasts began moving; thought all right; again he fired, 5 shots in succession, without the bulls running off, then I saw them mounting the opposite side of the hill very slowly, & Chasseur darted off to the right under cover of the uneven ground, got near again & fired two more shots; 1st bull very lame, 2nd following very slowly behind. Again Kinamontayoo darted off & I at length saw him 3 or 4 miles off like a speck on the prairie, making a tremendous circuit to cut off the 2nd bull which had now gone off fast ahead of the lame one which kept stopping every few hundred yards, able to go fast, but evidently in pain. Having been above an hour lying in the snow with my blanket over me, & being almost frozen, I resolved to start after the hindmost bull, taking the hunter's blanket & snowshoes with me. I followed the tracks & discovered the wounded bull standing about ½ mile off—on the bare prairie. I determined to have a stalk on my own hook but looked a long time in vain for any cover by which to approach him. At last I observed a small bush which would hide me if I made a long detour so as to come up for some distance in a line with it. I set to work & approached within some 300 yards very cautiously & slowly, & so successfully eluded his observation that he lay down. Then just as I was congratulating myself on the almost certainty of success, who should appear but Kinamontayoo! Confound him. He thinking the beast was done walked straight up to him & of course off he went at full gallop, a great sell, & very stupid of him for he saw me carefully crawling up; if I had made such a faux pas with La Ronde, wouldn't he have "sacré maladroited" me. The buffalo quickly disappeared in a gully, & Kinamontayoo assuring me that we were sure to find him on the morrow, & it being nearly dark, we gave up the chase & laboured home again "en raquette"; the other buffalo he had chased a long way but he refused to stop although wounded in the body. Found Milton with supper ready in camp.

Thursday, January 8th.—Milton's face much swollen & painful. I therefore remain in camp with him, sending the other two to look after the wounded buffalo. At dark they came in with the two dog trains heavily laden with beautiful meat. They found the animal close to where we had seen him disappear, his leg had frozen & the wolves had pulled him down. Meat frozen, & they had to make a large fire round him before cutting up. In spite of which the Chasseur broke his knife, a good one, & he was very disconsolate until we promised to replace it. Milton rubs his face with pain-killer.

Friday, January 9th.—On waking up, Milton found one eye swelled up; he had got erysipelas! Here was a nice fix! 100 miles out in the wilds; only plan to start at once, wrapping the patient up in duffle, blankets & my buffalo robe & putting him on a sleigh; we managed to get off by noon, & camped a few miles beyond our old lake camp. Patient no worse; & I am inclined to blame the pain-killer. Very cold.

Saturday, January 10th.—Milton's face a little better. Weather warmer; tie him on the sleigh again, rolled in buffalo robe. He was of course quite helpless, & I found it an infernal bother lifting up the sled which was continually upsetting, or running amuck against trees. The dogs had as much as they could do to get along with a heavy load, the track being snowed up in most places. Comyun asthmatic, I push on, weak though willing. Kuskitaostaquarn lame from frost-bite. Milton pretty happy now he had to make no exertion. Camped for the night with lots of wood & had a roaring fire.

Sunday, January 11th.—Milton's face nearly right, & as I have a deal of trouble with him lying on the sled, like a sack of flour & making it so wide that it was continually catching trees & stumps, I suggested the advisability of his riding untied, & jumping off when there was any difficulty. After dinner we did this with great advantage, except that he grumbled frightfully at having to walk up a few steep hills & swore it would kill him. However we got in at last to our old camp of the lodge poles. Very exposed place & not much wood; burnt the lodge poles.

Monday, January 12th.—A long journey trying to reach home that night, but darkness overtook us & we encamped some 10 miles short. Bitterly cold again, not much wood. Chasseur proposes starting in morning without lighting fire or breakfasting. Vehemently negatived by Milton. Both very thankful to be so near home, as our ideas of travelling are so very different that we both lose our good tempers in the disagreement.

Tuesday, January 13th.—Dogs very done & road very bad; progress very slowly & Milton wearying me with fruitless questions every few minutes whether we are nearly there; wondering whether the Chasseur has lost his way. Groaning & moaning as he walks up every hill, & I almost quarrel with him, using very strong language occasionally. He declares he is killing himself, & shall be laid up for a week, &c., &c. I pooh-pooh it. At last we get home about 2 o'clock & find that the women have the house much neater than it had ever been before. They prepare a sumptuous feast of fish & bain which we both eat to repletion. Milton quite lively now his troubles are over. Have a drop of rum & give Kinamontavoo ½ pt. on which he gets glorious & shakes hands continually, assuring us that we have only to speak & he is ready to do anything for us we can wish. I feel very tired & turn in early. In a fix about D. now; never mind till tomorrow.

Wednesday, January 14th.—Discussion about D——; arrange that he & Milton go off to Crooked Nose's today, & they accordingly set out in the afternoon, with supplies. Flour nearly finished. Chasseur goes out & spears rats. I smoke & write up my journal. Chasseur watches with staring eyes.

Thursday, January 15th.—Mending things, cleaning gun, &c. Intensely cold outside. We feast on muskrats which I find very eatable. At noon young one arrives with note from Milton to say Crooked Nose & wife are off next day to buffalo, & wanting me to send over the Hunter, wife, & family immediately. He begs to stay till tomorrow on account of extreme cold. I agree. Expect letter express to Carlton every day now.

Friday, January 16th.—After breakfast the whole kit set out for the other house to my great delight. They had employed nearly their whole time in cooking & eating, & were a great nuisance, squatting about the floor, & surrounding the fire-place. Felt quite jolly all alone & cooked a fish & some meat; after which put on my snowshoes & went across the lake to look at my home traps. The wolverine had visited all & broken them. I therefore reset them & placed some poisoned baits near. Got back before dark; chopped wood & made some chips to light my fire with in the morning. Cooked fish for supper, smoked sundry pipes & retired to bed very contentedly.

Saturday, January 17th.—About midday Nashquapamayoo appeared with a dog train & informed me that Milton, the Hunter & Kekwapkosis were close behind, & they shortly appeared. They had brought a few fish, & the Hunter quietly informed me that the meat was finished & he must be off to the plains at once for more; the Old boy also. I was rather taken aback at this as I had thought we had enough for a fortnight or so. As it turned out on inquiry that the Hunter had 10 fish, the Old boy 12, Milton 13 at the other house, & I two here, & this was all our provisions except 2 pounds of flour, I decided at once that it would be absurd to start for the plains to starve ourselves & dogs & leave Milton to starve here, but the plan was to make a forced march to Carlton & get hold of some pemmican first. Milton agreed. The Old boy immediately signified his intention of going there for pemmican also.

Sunday, January 18th.—Turned out of bed at daybreak

by the Hunter. They had not breakfasted, but had cooked a little scrap of meat, about a pound, for Milton & myself. I gave half mine to the young one, the others doing without. We left 13 fish for Milton to live on during our absence, the Old boy took 5, the Hunter 5, I, 2; the rest left for the Indian's family. I took the little flour there was, Milton having his desiccated vegetables to fall back upon. We had also (literally) 1 handful of tea which I mixed with some ground coffee to eke it out. We had 9 dogs, 3 men & a boy, therefore to feed for at least two days on 12 fish & a morsel of flour! Allowance for each dog & man 2 fish per diem properly. We got under way about noon; rather cold; snow very deep & no track; heavy work. Camped at night at pines other side Cocquille river. Ravenously hungry when we stopped. Gave dogs a fish amongst 3. Ourselves a fish each. Cold north wind set in.

Monday, January 19th.—Nobody able to sleep for the cold; 2 blankets & great coat as nothing, the wind coming thro' as if they were gauze. Miserable work. At daylight they began to cook & kept on until nearly noon, the only answer to my remonstrances being 'Keeyarni kirni, warpuski marsgoot namoy kirin,' and I could not get them to face it. When we did start we really found it was 'kirin'. Stopped a few minutes to make tea, & shortly after for the night before dark; but the Hunter assured me it was the only place where we could get good shelter. Pines this side Salt lake; plenty of good dry wood.

Tuesday, January 20th.—I turned out before daybreak & got the others up, so that we were ready to start by the time it was sufficiently light. 2 small fish amongst the 4, nothing else; finished our tea. Dogs had nothing since the day before yesterday. I told my men I *must* & *would* be in the Fort that night 'Keeyarm'. Off we went; snow deep & snowshoes—no stopping in middle of the day. I felt very faint & suggested a stop; but the Hunter reminded me that we had nothing to cook, & that if we stopped we should not reach the Fort that night. I therefore gave up the point, set my teeth & went at it again, lighting up a pipe occasionally to ease the gnawing of my stomach. Oh that weary walk! How many vows I made never to be short of food again if I could help it! And I came to the conclusion that all those poor wretches who commit crime from force of hunger were deserving of the utmost pity. I'm sure I should have stolen then without scruple. No one who has not been in the same circumstances has the least idea of the suffering of hunger. Well, at last we came to a clump of firs which I recognized as only 8 or 9 miles from the fort. There the Hunter pulled up & sat down for a moment to light a pipe; before I could get my tobacco cut & my pipe lit he set off again; after 3 or 4 miles he said he was thirsty & broke open a rat house to drink. Getting done now, thought I. I improving fast. Some 5 miles from the Fort we came upon a hard cart track, & Kinamontayoo taking off his snowshoes, I did the same, the dogs set off at a gallop, & after them we ran at a tremendous pace, right into the Fort, I leading for the last mile, in magnificent wind & feeling as fresh as possible after getting rid of my snowshoes. Found Lillie & Ross hospitably bent & they ordered supper at once, i.e. in the course of ½ an hour; but I felt very comfortable & not at all ravenous until I began to eat; then I did wonders. Old bull went down like English beef. Bread, fresh butter & the potatoes went down deliciously; only not enough of them. Ordered the Indians & dogs as much as they could eat, & went to bed not the least tired.

Wednesday, January 21st.—The men & dogs required a day's rest. Got ready 2½ bags pemmican, 5 bladders grease, 4 lbs tea to send off tomorrow by the Indians to Milton at daybreak, promising the Hunter ¼ pint rum if he made all speed; he promised to be there on the third day. I resolved to stay for the mail packets, now expected every day, & to return with the La Crosse one. Enjoyed my rest at the Fort most tremendously, & idled the day away very pleasantly. Ross an old Peterhouse man, & an immense addition to Carlton society.

Thursday, January 23rd.—Monotonous day at the Fort.

Friday, January 24th.—In the evening the Edmonton Packet arrived, Mr. Hardisty in charge. He came in a cariole with a very fine train of dogs, harness set out with bells & plumes, very jolly; a yellow-haired Scotchman he, by descent, a Red River man born & bred, very pleasant fellow indeed & very obliging. No snow at Edmonton!

Saturday, January 25th.—An Indian came in from the woods half starved with a report that a terrible disease was raging at Fort La Corne. He gave such an accurate descrip-

tion of small-pox that I concluded it must be that, & finding
that Sinclair had some vaccine matter, I set to work & vaccin-
ated all the unprotected ones I could lay hold of. The matter
turned out worthless, & none of the cases came to anything.

Sunday, January 26th.—Nothing to record, except a treat
in the way of dinner, viz:—boiled rice with sugar & butter!

Monday, January 27th.—Nothing but smoke.

Tuesday, January 28th.—In the afternoon the packet from
Red River via Norway House & La Corne. Smallpox report
turned out a complete invention. Great excitement when the
letter boxes were opened. I felt intensely anxious, & my
disappointment was awful when there turned out to be none
for either Milton or myself! The rascally Sioux the cause,
I presume, for only 2 or 3 letters have reached here from Red
River. Had some slight consolation in reading the papers;
only home news death of Mr. Birkbeck.

Wednesday, January 29th.—Reading the papers.

Thursday, January 30th.—Begin to be very fidgetty about
returning to our home. Northern packet viâ La Crosse not
come in. Hardisty kindly offers me horses & cariole to return
with, but snow too deep. Find a freeman, Jemmy Isbister,
has good train of dogs & willing to take me back. Refuses
payment as I am a doctor & have prescribed for his child.
Wait one more day for express.

Friday, January 31st.—Express does not arrive. Prepare
to start tomorrow. Play Euchre at night.

Saturday, February 1st.—Set out after breakfast about 10
o'clock. Run after dogs first 5 miles; after that snowshoes;
pace awful, dogs leading fast; track very fair. Intensely cold;
strong bitter north wind. At first pines hear an axe at work,
turn in & find La Crosse train at dinner; delayed by late arrival
of train from Athabaska; no accidents, only slowness of green
hands in deep snow; dined with them & went on the same pace;
all I could do to keep up. Arms & legs swinging like fen
skaters. Camp at some pines just on the Carlton side of the
Salt Lake. Too cold to sleep much.

Sunday, February 2nd.—A very miserable night; not a
very good fire. Up long before daylight, & start before sunrise with the first dawn. Same frightful pace; bitterly cold;

neck frozen. Face ditto; thighs ditto; Johnson ditto, & sphincter vesicae partially paralysed so that I had great difficulty to retain. Nose bled from cold; neither able to get warm in spite of great coat & furious exercise. Dined on this side River Cocquille. Wind fearful. Off again about big hill, legs gave way & took off snowshoes & lagged behind; arrived at home thoroughly done; very stiff; a little after dark. No one there. Isbister made a fire, chopped wood for night & morning, fed his dogs, fitted up a cariole extempore & started back again in about 2 hours—arriving at Fort as I heard afterwards next day at 11 a.m. Very good travelling.

Monday, February 3rd.—Hardly able to sleep from stiffness; very painful turning out of bed; alone; anointed my frozen members, chopped wood, & cooked, smoking contentedly in the intervals. In evening a French half breed came in—said he was starving not having eaten for 2 days. Lodge near big hill. Came yesterday but finding no one only made a fire & drank some water, leaving food untouched! I fed him well on pemmican, & he was very grateful.

Tuesday, February 4th.—My dear Father's death a year ago. What changes since! A day of sorrow at home, I know. Gave the trapper some food & tea for his wife & set out myself for the Indians' dwelling; in the last mile one of my legs gave in, & I had great difficulty in reaching the place. Milton came out & was very pleased & surprised to see me, expecting I should return with La Crosse men. Warmly welcomed by the Indians. Talked till late, offered a partner in the shape of the Old boy's daughter; declined & she very much offended.

Wednesday, February 5th.—After breakfast Milton & I set out for our own house; my leg very bad, & road heavy. Lent Milton my snowshoes; we both found the journey very laborious. Found that the half breed[24] had brought his wife to stay a couple of days to wash & mend for us according to promise. He had however forgotten the fisher & cross fox he promised to bring me. Wife very English face & pleasant-looking; both very attentive & tried hard to make us comfortable.

Thursday, February 6th.—Wife washed & mended all day. Milton & I rested our legs & discussed news & plans for future. The Old boy's family had already made a great hole in the pemmican. The men & young one were away when we left the house, to bring in a moose the Hunter had killed. We left word for our two to come over the next day & bring plenty of fresh meat.

Friday, February 7th.—In afternoon the two arrived with the dog sleds & some meat. Feasted on tough moose. Hunter claimed his ¼ pint of rum which I had promised if he made all haste with the supplies from the Fort. That necessitated giving the halfbreed, his wife, & Nashquapamayoo a little. Then the halfbreed wished to stand treat to his friend. We agreed to give them another ½ pint between them on condition they did not ask for more. They promised & presently began to get very drunk (Milton having foolishly given them a pint instead of half one) & sing uproariously. Telling us how they loved us & would do anything for us. The halfbreed with every drop he took stood up & said 'Milor, aussi Docteur, je vous remercie deux fois.'—'Je vous salue,' 'Good luck,' About 9 o'clock the Hunter asked for a *little* drop more, *only* a little. He was very drunk but talked pretty well. The Canadian tried to interpret but could not get the words out. We reminded them both of their promise, & the halfbreed said he could not say another word for it was true. But Kinamontayoo was oblivious; nothing could make him understand; we continued firmly to refuse & he to ask. He explained that we were very fine fellows in some respects but our hearts were very hard; he sat down beside me, drew his knife, seized me by the arm & placed the point at my breast. I sat quite unmoved, but prepared for the emergency. However he explained that if he had been a plain Indian he should have stabbed me if I said no; but that he did not behave in that way. In spite of this theatrical display we still said no, the Hunter again begged, & at last said that if we would not give it he would return at once, & forthwith ordered the young one to get the sled ready. He remonstrated strongly but without avail & after tumbling about for some time, the Hunter set out singing & leaving us to our fate. The night bitterly cold & snowing. The halfbreed lay on the floor cursing, & in the interval stammering out, "Excusez, excusez, Milor, aussi Docteur, pour l'amour de dieu."

Saturday, February 8th.—The halfbreed's wife returned with a present of needles, &c., the man went off to the Hunter's to see how his friend fared. We sent a message to the effect that we were astonished at his behaviour & that he had not acted like another La Ronde as he considered himself. As it seemed probable that he might not return to duty, we made up our minds to make the best of it until La Ronde's return, I cutting wood & fetching water, Milton cook.

Sunday, February 9th.—I up first, made fire & fetched water. Milton then cooked breakfast after which I chopped a good pile of wood & then went out to shoot something if possible (for the Hunter had taken back the fresh meat) & also set snares for rabbits to eke out our provisions. Came back in about 3 hours with 1 partridge, found the Hunter & son again there with sleighs & meat; very penitent; said he was very drunk & understood nothing. It appeared he had only got to the other side of the lake when he missed the road & fell down almost insensible; but for his son he would have been frozen. Nashquapamayoo made a fire & they camped for the night within a mile of our house, arriving at home next day towards evening when they went to bed. There found by the halfbreed, & informed what he had done; very much shocked & resolved to come back & apologize next day. We fixed to start for plains day after tomorrow.

Monday, February 9th.—Sauteux trapper came in to consult me about a big-bellied little child of his with worms, & to sell a cross fox which Milton bought for a spade & adze & 2 skins; prepared to start tomorrow. Gave them a little fillet of rum & told them not to ask for more; no trouble this time. In the evening excited great wonder & respect by tricks at cards, they all trying to do them without success. Young one especially delighted.

Tuesday, February 10th.—Got under way a little before noon. Hunter, son & myself & two dog sleighs. Fine bright day quite warm. Left Milton paying for his fox skin & intending to go up to the Indian's house[25] till our return. Snow deep but arrived at pines where road divides by dusk, & there camped for the night. Pemmican & a little flour. Left Milton 1/3 bag pemmican & about 20 lbs flour. Hunter's wife to supply him with fresh moose meat.

Wednesday, February 11th.—Found snow too deep for dogs, & I therefore had to go ahead in addition to the hunter to tread out the track; very heavy work; shot rabbit & partridge for dinner; camped far beyond the old lodge. Cold, & my cheek

& nose frozen slightly; size of a pea. Young one's too. No incidents of consequence.

Thursday, February 12th.—Sara's birthday; wish her many happy returns. Heavy snow-shoe work again; making one's back ache; very near the end of our journey. Many misgivings as to finding our cache safe, for we find wolverine's track following ours for last 2 days. If meat gone, & no buffalo to be found, in a fix; pemmican nearly done; resolve in the worst case to give pemmican to the dogs & push to the Fort for supplies which we could reach in 2 days very hard travelling.

Friday, February 13th.—Wolverine's track still visible following our old one; give up all hope of finding the meat; in about 2 hours arrive at old camp by the lake where we stayed a day on our former expedition; there to our delight see the yesterday's track of a solitary buffalo; going at speed & probably frightened; fear they have been driven off by Indians; halt dogs at lake & Kinamontayoo goes ahead to reconnoitre; comes running back with report that 5 bulls are some ¼ mile off. I & the young one remain to make camp tho' not allowed to light a fire yet. I did not go after the buffalo because meat was the thing to be considered, not sport. After making a long circuit which the young one & I watched from an ambush in some bushes at the top of the hill we heard the report of one shot, & presently after saw only 4 buffalo going away in the distance. I had lent the hunter my gun; another more distant shot & the young one exclaiming "quatuck aceniow" (another Indian) got quite excited & started off to see what was going on. I went back to finish the camp, & in about an hour the young one came back with some fresh meat which we cooked & ate forthwith with great relish. He informed me that his father had killed one the first shot; very good meat; but that another Indian had then fired on them & spoilt his chance of more. We then moved our camp to a little dell with plenty of good wood & nearer the buffalo. Having prepared camp there & cut wood, young one & I took the sleds & dogs for the meat; only a few hundred yards off. Found Hunter nearly frozen for the day was intensely cold; on way met other Indian Gatchi Mohka-marn[26] returning from pursuit; had wounded one & followed it a long way without success. Sent him to camp to light fire & shortly followed with all the meat the dogs could draw. Covered up the rest & the skin with snow till next day. Dogs like wolves seizing the meat in the most savage manner; had

had devilish little for a long time before. At camp found Gatchi Mohkamarn with roaring fire; quickly put up some meat & marrow bones & had a tremendous feast. Gatchi Mohkamarn had fasted for two days & therefore did wonders. He had only arrived at the plains the day before via Atagakouph's, & the only buffalo he had seen were these 5. We were therefore very lucky. He told me that Messiter & Farquharson were almost starving, having only a little flour. Atagakouph been out 2 months on the plains for meat & not heard of since he started. Messiter sent Badger to Fort for pemmican. Lillie refused: & Messiter had now himself gone to try & get provisions, intending if successful to start for Red River in 5 days! Why? had enough?

Saturday, February 14th.—After another enormous feed Kinamontayoo & Gatchi Mohkamarn start again, the former to see after our cache as well as look for more bulls, the latter to pursue again the 4 of yesterday. Mishoo & I remained quietly in camp, I & he to have our shoot tomorrow if any could be seen to-day. At dusk Kinamontayoo returned with pleasing news that the cache was untouched, although wolverine had followed the track very near to it, & the wolves had gnawed the timber ferociously; he brought away the powder & shot &c, making the cache additionally secure again with more logs. Long after dark Gatchi came in covered with blood; he had killed the whole 4 bulls! seen no others. Hunter none. Valentines day.!

Sunday, February 15th.—Bought 2 buffalo of Gatchi 5 skins each as meat is scarce. Hunter & young one went off to cut up meat & protect it from wolves. Gatchi to take a little meat to his wife who had now had nothing for 3 days. I stopped in camp & cut wood &c. About noon "Mr. Christie" & son made their appearance; astonished to see me & very curious. Reported no buffalo at all & Indians starving. They had seen none for 2 months & had only a little dry meat left; they announced intention of staying night with us; very talkative & when Kinamontayoo & son returned at dusk, there was an incessant chatter till we turned in.

Monday, February 16th.—After breakfast Mr. Christie soon set out after buffalo; we all remained in camp. Before long Gatchi Mohkamarn returned with wife & effects, removing close to his meat; reported 5 lodges of Indians following, all starving. They soon came in with their dog-sleds &c. (dogs literally skin & bone); men very wan; woman looked in best case; we gave them some meat & a little tea as they passed for which they were very thankful; we were nearly all day cooking for them & hardly tasted ouselves; 2 young Indians who stayed after most of the rest, (one very smart with scarlet binding to his leggings & coat & vermillioned under the eyes) began gambling with the Hunter. They staked & valued all their shot, hairrings, knives, pipe, mittaines &c. And having done that put a blanket over their knees, (all the rest getting a frying pan or pot & drumming on it with a stick) & began to sing & move their bodies & arms about like a baby in a baby-jumper. They were greatly excited & delighted. The game appeared to be to guess in which hand a ramrod wire, a hair do., or nothing was: or rather to choose a hand & guess what was in it; the holder changing behind his back & under the blanket continually; they marked their success with sticks stuck in the ground & each guessed in turn, they were a long time before able to make up their minds which hand to choose & pointed several times & often held the pointing hand stretched out a long time before daring to risk the decisive word. This went on for about 2 hours & then ended by the Hunter winning all. The two others went away very contented, still singing & having now neither knife, shot, mittaines &c. The Hunter was greatly delighted at his good fortune, & told me that if he had lost he should have gone on until he had nothing, not even coat or gun! I told him I thought that very reprehensible, but he only said it was good & told me to observe how much it had done for him. The only persons left now were one man, his squaw with a child at the breast. This fellow was one of the most repulsive objects I ever saw, very tall, over 6 feet, very thin, a patch over the left eye, toothless gums & a very large nose perfectly flat on his face, this disfigurement I found was from a fight with a grisly bear. He was horribly dirty, & possessed neither gun, knife, pipe, or cooking utensil. It appeared that he had been at the Fort, & there gambled away everything, until he was reduced, as the Hunter expressed it, simply to his wife, child & dog! These unfortunates seemed resolved to put themselves upon us, & ate! oh! enough for weeks; they had starved for days; that fellow's toothless jaws never seemed to stop. The squaw (rather good looking) was nearly his match. As "Mr. Christie" had promised to send over a sled & dogs to assist in transporting the meat if we would wait until the day after tomorrow, we agreed to do so.

Tuesday, February 17th.—All day in camp doing nothing but eat & smoke. The ugly fellow & wife still with us, making snow-shoes. Former took sled & skeleton dog & fetched in the buffalo's head & part of skin spared by the wolves. Only food for them after we are gone except Gatchi Mohkamarn's meat.

Wednesday, February 18th.—Get sleds packed & ready to start, expecting Mr. Christie's son with other sled by noon. Waited all day but he did not appear. Cursed him & smoked; ugly fellow still hard at work on our meat. Resolve to start tomorrow with our two sleds & wait no more for the other. I am very tired of camp, & wood is getting very scarce. Weather very cold still. Hunter disgusted with Mr. Christie's son; "namouya quiusk, namouya quiusk" he kept saying. More starving Indians expected to pass.

Thursday, February 19th.—When ready to set out Mr. Christie's son appeared with a tiny sleigh drawn by one dog. It seems he had killed a buffalo the day before & sent out the other sled & dogs to fetch in the meat; this was his excuse for not coming yesterday himself, & not bringing a larger sled & more dogs today. We now arranged the meat on 3 sleds, borrowed the skeleton dog from the frightful party, & set out at last, about noon, promising to return for the other meat & bring a small quantity of rum as part payment, the rest to be tobacco, & ammunition. I gave the Ogre a pipe & some tobacco, to start him in life again & left him & squaw to live on their buffalo's head. We went on till dark making a good journey; no dinner; dismissed the skeleton dog as worse than useless & put in a pup instead who pulled like mad.

Friday, February 20th.—A long day's march, camping 2 miles beyond old lodge; much swearing; dogs obstinate; harness wrong; sleigh continually upsetting & getting off the track, which is like a line of a single rail, &, the snow being deep, requires no small exertion to get it on again; when you have effected that with immense labour, perhaps the leading dog won't start, you scramble past to lick him, & then the others lie down & howl & you can't get them to move forward until you have turned round & got behind them again, in doing which you catch your snow-shoes in the bushes & come on your nose in a yard of soft snow, & so on. Verily I believe driving a heavily laden dog-sled in a hilly country would spoil the temper of a saint.

TRIP ACROSS CANADA

Saturday, February 21st.—Very hilly country & much upsetting of sleds; down two steep hills dogs & sled went rolling down to the bottom, the sled overriding the dogs in spite of me. Kuskelas staquam the shaft dog being under the sled, & tied up in the harness in the most intricate manner. It took me with Mishquapamayoo a good ¼ hour to set them right; dined at the pines where we slept first night on way out; passed last camp on return former trip before dark; about 10 miles from home, dark; no wood near; Schushow keeps the track & the rest follow, a weary long way, but no use camping now if Schushow only can find the way which he did, never losing the track, only getting off it once although we could not see it, & could only find it by feeling for it with a pole, it being open country & all drifted level. Thanks to Schushow however we reached the house about 2 hours after dark & we were delighted to see a light in the window, hope La Ronde may have returned. A delighted "Hello Cheadle devilish glad to see you back, all alone here for 4 days & getting very 'down in the mouth'". Had brought over D——— for some things, but he refused to carry back Milton's bag & he therefore sent him off & remained alone. A jolly good feast & drop of grog; delightful being in a house once more.

Sunday, February 22nd.—Hunter & son start for their house with a sled of meat & promising to return in 5 days. Very pleasant time of it, I hewer of wood & drawer of water, Milton cook which he was with great success.

Monday, February 23rd.—Have a grand cleaning, for the house had become horribly dirty; took out 3 waterproof loads of dust, ashes, & chips. Milton made a besom & swept, I shoveling it into the waterproof with a plate! I nearly died with laughter at Milton on hands & knees, grubbing out the dirt from under the bedsteads with his hands. We then had a general tidying & were much gratified by the result, the hut really looking very neat & comfortable. This with cooking & cutting wood took us all day, but we went to rest with quiet consciences.

Tuesday, February 24th.—I went out to cut some Kinnikinick,[27] Milton staying at home to cook, & attempt a plum pudding with our little remnant of flour, & the currants & raisins sent us by Messiter; we had not before dared to attempt the manufacture; but Milton, inspired with a just confidence from his success in the savoury branch of the culinary art, resolved at my earnest request to attempt the sweets also. And on my

115

return I found him surveying the pudding; half boiled only already. On seeing me he suggested that it looked so tempting that we had better eat the outside, & boil the undone centre part after; but I would not consent although sorely tempted, & the pudding was again put back; a period of anxious suspense ensued which we mitigated by eating an apoulard, & a partridge I had shot. At length we thought it must be done & forthwith turned him out; hurrah! quite ready; we resolved to finish him; as big as my head; most delicious; not had such a treat since leaving Fort Garry! it really was good; would have held its head up in any company. Could not quite get through it; but pleased to think we should have thereby another treat next morning for breakfast. Childish very; but true; & anyone who has lived on meat only will easily understand the gratification. (Caps & buck-shot found in the pudding.)

Wednesday, February 25th.—Just finished the pudding when Hunter & Old boy turned up. Come to see if La Ronde had returned and ready to go off to plains for rest of meat. Mishquapamayoo laid up with stiff back from lifting at sleds. Hunter to go after moose tomorrow, give him & Crooked Nose a little rum, the very last drop. Former thereon performed sundry medicines, viz, took teaspoonful of rum, stretched out his arm at full length, held it so some little time & then threw the rum into the fire. Then a long prayer with great energy. Then [took] Milton's calumet which he filled & lit, then turned round several times; all this that he might be successful in his hunt of the morrow.

Thursday, February 26th.—Hunter set out at sunrise. I remained writing journal, Milton cooking & making Kinnikinick; Old boy cutting wood & fetching snow.

Friday, February 27th.—Old boy cut wood & then went out after rabbits; we remained at home doing various small necessities. In the afternoon we heard the crows, a pretty sure sign someone was coming, & Milton looking out cried out, D——it, here is Badger again. It turned out however to be Philip Tait,[28] with dog, cariole & attendant come to collect furs. He stayed the night, & we had a treat in the form of potatoes, sugar & seed cakes; we being only able to supply fresh meat. Informed us that Messiter intended to set out for Fort Garry in 3 or 4 days in company with the painter. Had tried to dissuade him as it was already so late that he could hardly hope to reach there with snow, and Messiter had only 1 train of dogs, the painter

2 half starved wretches. But they resolved to try it. Tait brought us also our bills from the Fort. Mine £17 odd with £6 off for the horse I sold; Milton's £32. We resolved to object to many of the items, such as £2.5.6. for a bag of pemmican, 10/- a buffalo skin, &c. horribly extortionate. Hunter returned at dusk, got close to a moose when dogs disturbed him.

Saturday, February 28th.—Philip Tait & Milton went off after breakfast to the other houses to return in the evening. I went to look if wolverine had taken poisoned baits; could find no fresh tracks; but too much snow had fallen in meantime & I could make nothing out. In evening Tait came back. Milton staying till next day. I resolved to go over with Tait next day to Messiter's to see his place, & get the 15 martens he owed me for the gallon of rum I sold him. Tait told me many accounts of starving this winter. At Fort Egg Lake they had to boil down a buffalo hide; two men arrived quite exhausted at Touchwood hills for supplies, but there they were at the last extremity, & could only give the men returning to Carlton with train that had brought express a very little pounded meat to return with; the last they had; at Fort La Corne they were reported to be starving sometime ago. The Carlton hunters were driven to eating a dog on their way out to find buffalo, & were about to kill a colt when they fortunately met with a solitary old bull buffalo far out, nearly as far west as Fort Pitt, & further south.

Sunday, March 1st.—Started with Philip Tait for Touch-wood Hills. Rode in cariole across plain beyond big hill, report 3 times whilst attempting to light my pipe, the track being high & the snow deep; dined just beyond the river & arrived at Atagakouph's 2 hours before sunset. Very warm day indeed, Snow-shoes very disagreeable from the snow thawing & freezing again on the bar under the sole of the foot. Found Messiter & the Painter just about to dine on what they called very poor food but which I enjoyed amazingly, viz—dry meat stew, with macaroni & bread! Messiter laid up with frozen great toe, a small piece sloughing off & nail also; very cold when going to Fort on snow-shoes, & he did not find out on his arrival that he was frost bitten & stood by the fire. Picked out my furs at night & had sardines & coffee for supper. Turner (the man who wishes to go across the mountains with us) seems to cook very well & is very obliging. They intend to start in a day or two. I represent the difficulties in rain. Philip Tait the same. I recommend them to try & get Isbister & his dogs to go with them; Messiter jumps at the idea.

Monday, March 2nd.—After breakfast bid goodbye to Messiter & Farquharson, the latter presenting me with 2 pair of white trousers; the former, a bottle of quinine & two cakes of brown Windsor [soap]. Very warm day again; did not get under way until nearly noon; snow-shoes great lumps of frozen snow; a weary walk tho' only 20 miles. Found Milton at the house, very tired of being alone. Found he had a row with the Old boy & family who were very discontented as they had not much to eat, & we refused to give them any of our small stock as they would devour it at once & be no better. He had also discarded D———— to my delight.

Tuesday, March 3rd.—A quiet day, I cutting wood & fetching water. Itch broken out on both Milton & myself; I have a warm bath & sulphur ointment. Curse Zear['s] Jane; only dry tough meat for food. Earnestly desire La Ronde's arrival with flour & news.

Wednesday, March 4th.—Feel seedy & get up late; Milton being actually up first & lighting the fire! I go out & try to shoot something for change of diet, the lean meat becoming very monotonous; abundance of fresh tracks but nothing else. Hot & bright.

Thursday, March 5th.—About noon Hunter arrives. Had killed two moose; beautiful meat. Mishquapamayoo sent us the nose as a present, which we boil forthwith, Milton squatting before the fire & eyeing the pot with greedy eyes, & eventually beginning to eat it long before cooked. I more prudently await its more finished state. Very good indeed; improved calf's head. Kinamontayoo stays night & promises to bring a sled load of meat day after tomorrow. Informs us that Old boy & family have gone off with lodge to a lake about 8 miles off. Very indignant we refused to give them meat; took off the dog Kuskituostaquam which we had hired for the season. Kinamontayoo very disgusted with their conduct.

Friday, March 6th.—Kinamontayoo goes off with dogs promising to return on the morrow with our meat & Mishoo. We are very much pleased with his conduct, and their supply of meat very acceptable as we have only 3 pieces of buffalo left, all tough & dry old bull. And this morning making arrangements to start for Fort as soon as we drew near the conclusion of it. What can have happened to La Ronde? 9 days behind the time he fixed for his return.

Saturday, March 7th.—Wood, water, cooking. Anxious expectation of Kinamontayoo & meat; and La Ronde; neither arrive; ennuyéed. What is La Ronde doing? I am tied by the leg, not liking to leave Milton alone, or I would be off in the woods trapping. Milton very full of plans for establishing himself near here when he comes out again, drawing ground-plan of prospective house, giving prospective wages & provisions to prospective men. I moralise on the uncertainty of all things & strain hard to catch philosophy; very high wind & bitterly cold out of doors.

Sunday, March 8th.—Indoors smoking. Afternoon brings Kinamontayoo & son with a sled-load of moose meat; too cold to come yesterday; cook some meat & marrow bones which we found delicious; the marrow not like or equal to buffalo do., the meat extremely tender, a cross between venison, mutton & beef. They would not allow us to give the scraps to the dogs, the moose being a very sacred animal to them.

Monday, March 9th.—Bitterly cold, high north wind again, which raised the snow in clouds like dust; we all stayed in therefore. I soled a pair of moccasins & mended my leather shirt ready for any excursion. Hunter collected a good supply of wood. We had a good feast of moose meat & listened to Kinamontayoo's account of being 10 days without food last winter but one, & many moose & elk hunts which he described most graphically, & I understood perfectly. Innumerable pipes.

Tuesday, March 10th.—Hunter returned; fetch his wife together with the meat from the place where he had killed the moose to their house, leaving the young one with us. Same weather as yesterday, & I lent him my Inverness cape to his great delight. We did nothing, both getting rather cross-grained & snappish; dreadfully ennuyéed with staying so long in the house; read King John in the evening.

Wednesday, March 11th.—Same as yesterday. Read Henry VIII aloud in the evening; Milton very attentive & pleased.

Thursday, March 12th.—Fine warm morning & bright. I went out to see if I could find La Ronde's old track to trap in case I should have to go out alone. I followed it with some difficulty as it was very indistinct, & as it were by instinct, & was immensely pleased with my improvement in the art of tracking. I should not have seen the trace of a road 6 months ago. Set 3 marten traps. Not a single marten track visible. This morning at breakfast used our sprinkling of tea, & driven to coffee for dinner; as it is of our own roasting & no sugar, we find it hard lines; *sole diet* meat & coffee! In evening young one informed us he should be off home again at daybreak tomorrow as they were going to have a great medicine feast at their house. 8 marrow bones, the ribs & head of moose, all to be eaten. He asked me to go too. I was not much inclined, but Milton very anxious to see the feast & taste the good things. I said I would go if he would, & he asked if he might come too. The young one said no, only me. Milton was rather offended but there was no help for it. I therefore told the young one my feet were too sore (the fact) & I would lend him my snow shoes & stay here, he to return next day.

Friday, March 13th.—Mishquapamayoo set out after breakfast. Shortly after Mr. Christie's son & another young Indian came in. Informed us that Gatchi Mohkamarn had almost given up expecting us to come for the meat, & had already been driven to consume most of it. Gave them tobacco for the use of dog & sled we hired.

Saturday, March 14th.—La Ronde arrived (as he stated it, this turned out to be Wednesday March 11th. so that it seems that I had managed to manufacture 2 days since I was last at the Fort on February 1st.). We heard some one outside, but never dreamt of La Ronde, having quite given up expecting his return. He looked very thin & worn, was very husky, & had a dreadful cough. He told us they had got out in 23 days, being only 7 days to Fort Pelley,[29] quickest on record at Fort Garry; had tremendous trouble to get Milton's cheque cashed, McTavish refusing for a long time but at last consenting; objecting on ground that the cheque was incorrectly drawn. La Ronde laid up with mal de Johnson from the cold. Snow much deeper than here. Set out on return last day of January; 2 days from Fort Pelley obliged to give up one train from weakness of dogs. Short of provisions & have to feed dogs on flour. At Fort Pelley found them short of provisions & took all the pemmican they had, only ½ bag, leaving a bag of flour there, the snow being too deep & the sled over-laden;

La Ronde frequently having to go twice over the track before the dogs could move. Had had his bronchitis 20 days & was very weak. Messiter was at the Fort, having given up the notion of going to Fort Garry in the snow, & waiting the thaw. Bruneau appeared shortly after with the sled; 20 lbs. tea, 5 gallons grog, half sack flour (having left one at Carlton to give place to pemmican); above all the letters at last! ! What a treat! All come together, with the exception of those written to Montreal & Toronto; 8 letters & 2 newspapers for me! Milton had also a large receipt; all news good for both of us, excepting we neither of us received news from our men of business. Delighted to find that they get on so well at Oxford & that Sara is so well cared for at Hawksworth'. The news of ma chère amie very perplexing. What am I to think of it? Jem seems to have had more reason for his escapade than I had expected. He will make his way I daresay. Heard from Dr. D. & Uncle; letters dated July 18. Home up to November 28th; Mrs. Horsfall the same date.

La Ronde brings very evil news from Red River; 2,000 Sioux camped two miles off the fort, come for ammunition to fight the Yankees with in the spring. Company have stopped the sale. Terror in the settlement. Troops sent for. Governor about raising troops of halfbreeds. A guard of do. at Fort at a guinea a day. Some one burnt all La Ronde's hay; suspects young Vital. Voudrie & Zear lost all horses but Old Red & Zear's horse. Left them to die close to Portage! Said they were all too ill & move on. But it appears that he rode them hard & at night tied them up to avoid the trouble of fetching them; they could therefore get but little to eat & at last could not go on. The men having no provisions left them, & after arriving at Red River, did not take the trouble to send after them, or they would probably have been saved, for they were seen alive some time after. There is no excuse for the fools, for it was a fine autumn & they could not have lost them but by the greatest stupidity. A great loss to Messiter. Tom cost £58, the grey £30, the Grand Rouge which Milton had given La Ronde cost £35 — ! Dreadful. La Ronde much enraged; Messiter & Milton also; thank goodness I kept mine here. (The next 3 days were really the dates 12th, 13th, 14th, & to rectify this veracious record, I will merely mention what occurred, & then proceed regularly according to date). On the night of La Ronde's arrival Milton & I were too excited with receiving our letters to go to bed until very late. Having

had a feast of pancakes & strong tea—Ah! what a treat!—
after the others had gone to bed, Milton set to work
& made galette which we ate, then retired after a pipe, when
quite midnight; when we were just comfortably asleep, we
were awakened by the dogs barking & heard a noise outside
& presently some one entered. Milton jumped up & struck
a match the light of which shewed us as I expected the Chasseur, & in addition the Old boy, his wife, & D. & the young
one. I was too sulky to turn out; but Milton smoked a pipe
& then intimated it was time to sleep. Most of them encamped outside amongst the coprolites. *Next morning* we
settled accounts with the Chasseur, son & Old man, giving
the former a skin a day, the young one ½ skin. It turned out
that the Chasseur had drunk all but 2 skins, the young one
22 skins entire. The Old boy owed 40 skins; 2 first satisfied;
the latter went off disgusted at owing so much. The old
woman abusing us & saying we had come into the country to
starve them, & so on. All at last went off. Soon after Mr.
Christie appeared, accompanied by the demon whom I had
seen starving on the plains; looked uglier than ever. Very
civil; begged for some rum, but we refused for the night.
Shortly after, they returned with the Old boy to whom I had
lent a steel trap; he reported that Gatchi Mohkamarn had
already given up the notion we should come for the meat & had
been driven to begin upon our cache. Bruneau therefore not to
go there but to Atagakouph's to try & buy meat there; if none,
on to the Fort for £2. 5s. 6d. pemmicans. The Old boy stayed
the night. *Day after,* Bruneau set out. Mr. Christie & one-eyed
man came; sold them a little liquor for fur. We sent them
off to drink it, & they did not return. I gave the Old man, who
still favoured us with his company a little medicine for a lynx
skin. He wished to trade a silver fox & Milton was anxious
to buy it, but next morning La Ronde discovered it was a red
one, very ingeniously dyed. He recognized it by the smell &
feel of the fur. Dodge often tried by the scoundrels. We
said nothing but declined the purchase. La Ronde somewhat
better but very down in the month. Attack of bronchitis, &
jaded with long journey.

Following day. Chasseur came in to borrow snow-shoes
to go after moose; stayed the night; La Ronde much the same.
Old Indian still here. Ennuyant. I have to cut wood, &c.,
La Ronde being too ill; Milton very idle about cooking.

TRIP ACROSS CANADA

Sunday, March 15th.—Chasseur & old Indian depart before night. Very glad to be rid of the dirty old beggar. Chasseur dilates on the delight he experiences in our company & assures us he will visit us again before long & bring us some moose-meat.

Monday, March 16th.—La Ronde somewhat better. Long after dark Bruneau arrives with pemmicans, &c.; had been able to buy none from Indians & went forward to the Fort. Re-read my letters.

Tuesday, March 17th.—Went out & set snares for rabbits & tried to shoot partridges for my patient but could find none. Resolve to visit my traps day after tomorrow if my patient is well enough to be left.

Wednesday, March 18th.—Nothing but prepare to start tomorrow for my traps.

Thursday, March 19th.—Set out with 3 dogs & train; a pemmican, a few potatoes & a little flour; day dull & cloudy. Found the track nearly as far as the first lake, then lost it & steered N. N. E., debouched on to the lake too much to the left. Not at all sure where the track re-entered the woods. The line I thought of taking appeared nearly W. by the compass. Sun not visible, therefore steered N. N. E. again thro' villainous country, little poplars & marshes; dreadful work cutting road, & getting the sled over fallen trees, &c. Afraid we are going wrong & camp early to wait for sun tomorrow, not having confidence in the compass. Soon after, the day cleared up & I mounted a pine to see where the hill was. Saw it not very far but in a somewhat different direction to what I expected. Saw several moose tracks during the day.

Friday, March 20th.—Worked hard all day cutting the road & dog-train driving; found one lake I recognized; but could not make out where to turn off; went at a guess & laboured all day through awful debris of fallen trees & little poplars; got pretty close to the hill before camping for the night; 1 marten track. Rather disappointed; more moose tracks. Slept delightfully in open air again.

Saturday, March 21st.—Found ourselves on the great lake at once. Did not know it again entering from another point, & therefore bore to the right fancying the required lake lay there; found ourselves in difficulties after passing through some pines into small poplars; therefore left dogs & ascended the hill to look; found it was the hill we sought but it being past noon resolved to cache our pemmican in the firs; camped there, dined, & then made 2 fisher & a marten traps having seen the tracks.

Sunday, March 22nd.—Started home again and arrived 2 hours before sundown; hot bright day & heavy walking the latter half, the snow thawing considerably & clogging the snowshoes. 1 fresh moose track, 2 lynx, numerous minks. Found La Ronde much better. Milton nervous about him, & they had been very dismal. Old Indian come back; we had taken his cooking kettle & he had to await our return; had sold his dyed fox to Crooked Nose who did not find out the deception until some days after. Heard this thro' Mr. Christie who called. Major died poisoned, having picked up a bait somewhere.

Monday, March 23rd.—Idle except favourite employment of clothes mending.

Tuesday, March 24th.—Start for trapping ground again with Bruneau. Tiger drawing our sled.

Wednesday, March 25th.—Arrived at old camp previous night & found cache untouched, the wolverine not having come yet. This morning we took half pemmican forward with us, Bruneau starting first, I staying after to arrange a gun for the wolverine. Arrived in the thick pine forest for dinner steering N. N. W. Went only 3 or 4 miles, having fallen into a region of swamps & burnt ground, with fallen timber, little poplars, stumps, &c., the very devil to travel amongst with snowshoes & a dog-train; & made a good camp.

Thursday, March 26th.—I set out N. N. E. Bruneau N. N. W.; continual succession of burnt ground, patches of pines, & swamps. Could not find the grand forest. Worked hard & made 13 traps; but few tracks. Made the last trap in the dark close to camp having seen a track there on going out. Found Bruneau already returned, having made 17. Nearly sundown.

Friday, March 27th.—Lenghtened the walk & made 6 traps more. Very warm & thawing in the middle of the day which quite used up my racquettes.

Saturday, March 28th.—Sent Bruneau to the house to see

how they were getting on; I remained in camp all day mending my snowshoes, having only Tiger for company.

Sunday, March 29th.—Started early to find the grand forest for better trapping ground, returned a little on our track out & then steered E.; found 3 fresh marten tracks in the first mile; soon came upon the great lake, following it nearly to the end; found the great forest continued along the south side & resolved to made traps in that quarter tomorrow. Came back the latter part by the walk & saw 2 traps, a marten in the one I had made in the dark close to the camp; a very little beast. Dined, then harnessed Tiger; loaded my sled & departed to form new camp on the road where I had branched from the main track, had finished cutting wood for 2 days when Bruneau appeared. News that La Ronde had gone off to hunt rats, leaving Milton alone in the house; provisions very short & must start for Fort, bidding good bye to our house immediately. I therefore resolve to visit traps tomorrow, give up all idea of making more, & start on return to house the following night.

Monday, March 30th.—Visit traps—find 1 marten; tremendous thaw; break my snowshoes; awful work walking without. Had dismantled all my traps on going out in order not to kill things uselessly, disgusted to find that a marten had passed one in the meantime; my consideration cost me dear. Arrive in camp before sundown rather tired. Bruneau arrived with "une belle marte". Resolve to start about midnight but oversleep ourselves.

Tuesday, March 31st.—Start at daybreak; arrive at cache; all right; take pemmican & proceed to next camp; sleep there all day; very hot, thawing rapidly; start when moon at height; awful work amongst little poplars & fallen trees. Not frozen much; break snowshoes hopelessly; killing work grinding along 4 or 5 miles without; in the marshes up to the knees in melting snow & water. Camp at moondown in wood close to our lake.

Wednesday, April 1st.—On again after sunrise, Milton & 2 young Indians. Very weary & sleepy; thawing rapidly. Never much more jaded than when finishing the last 2 miles over the lake. Bruneau & I breakfast & then turned in; aroused towards evening by Milton crying out the Schushew was poisoned; jumped up & found him in a state of tetanus;

paroxysm passed off & gave him gunpowder & alcohol at intervals, which appeared to prolong his life for 5 or 6 hours; suppose he picked up a bait at the point; La Ronde came in before dusk with a lot of rats, balls of fat, almost too rich; resolve to start day after tomorrow; one of young Indians saw 3 ducks pass over.

Thursday, April 2nd.—Bruneau to Old boy's at daybreak to fetch some things left there. La Ronde & young Indian to fetch up horses; Milton & myself packing up all day. Strong frost in the night.

Friday, April 3rd.—Set out about noon, leaving the house without a tear, but feeling some regret at parting from our winter quarters, where we had certainly endured much hardship, but however had some enjoyment & at least learnt much of Indian life. Horses very fat, & restive at starting. Milton on little roan mare, I on foot, Bucephalus in my cart. Rover refused to leave the house & Milton obliged to bring him in a string. Camped the house side of the big hill & ate musk rats for dinner; supply of pemmican very small & not sufficient to last to the Fort. La Ronde killed 6 more rats. We have nothing else. Feel quite independent again with all property in one's cart. Regret not seeing Hunter & young one to say good-bye. Camped for night before reaching River Cocquille.

Saturday, April 4th.—Reached Salt Lake & camped for night. La Ronde & I shot some prairie grouse to eke out supplies; very very wild.

Sunday, April 5th.—Easter day. Camped at Pines (the last before the Fort). Shot at first goose long way off. Eke out pemmican with Milton's vegetables & just have enough for supper & breakfast tomorrow.

Monday, April 6th.—Arrive at the Fort.[30] Find Messiter & the Painter there. Send over a man to look after our things on other side River; ice still strong & carts cross without difficulty. We stay at Fort. La Ronde & Bruneau camp on hill. Ask Lillie to give us dinner having nothing but small breakfast long time ago. Milton leaves all heavy things at Fort.

Tuesday, April 7th.—Settle accounts with men. Feed up. Talk to Messiter. Engage Baptiste Supernat at £12 per month to cross Rocky Mountains as guide.

TRIP ACROSS CANADA

Wednesday, April 8th.—Say good-bye to La Ronde who departs about noon. After that settle accounts with Lillie. Dine on roast goose. After dinner cross river to start, but Milton has so much packing & arranging that we give up the idea & return to the Fort after that is completed.

Thursday, April 9th.—After breakfast we again cross the river & set out for Fort Pitt with only our new man Baptiste. He proves very civil & handy & gives favourable account of shooting in the mountains. Make a short & easy day. Milton rides in cart, & I walk.

Friday, April 10th.—Just about to start when Philip Tait comes in with horses from Fort Pitt,[31] 5th day from there. Wait a little & smoke pipes & then say good-bye. Sherman indisposed & hardly able to get along; therefore soon camp for dinner & rest a long time which seems to do him good. See ducks & geese; all too wild.

Saturday, April 11th.—Undulating Prairie with copses. Baptiste kills a goose & duck which we find very good. Short day on account of Sherman who seems no better.

Sunday, April 12th.—Long day; level country; bleak hills in distance; little wood; enter a gorge & camp at the Spring (La Source); a river rising in a spring at the foot of a semi-circular range of hills; wood almost used up by constant camp-ings in this place. Baptiste wipes my eye at a goose, tells us stories at night of gold found by Indians near foot of Rocky Mountains, a lump size of end of finger, sent by Mr. Rowand to England & found to be pure gold. Indians instructed by Company to keep the matter secret for fear something terrible should happen to them. Copper found by an Indian near Montagne du Bois beyond Fort Ellice. Piece of iron found by Indian near Edmonton & placed many years ago on top of a hill, size of fist when placed there, now so large no one can raise it! place where originally found stream of red water! He himself found gold in creek near Fort Ellice. When in Rocky Mountains, found high up a little prairie in the woods: in that a lake round which were round things like clear stones, on shaking them something rattled inside — did not know then what gold or such things were, fancying all *made* in England; but believes now that there were diamonds inside!

Monday, April 13th.—Crossed the stream without difficulty

& several more in course of day; dreary country, bleak hills, with flat levels between the ranges, very monotonous & no wood; find a little scrub & dry poplars for dinner. Camp at night in better country. Lots of ducks & geese but very wild, & none for supper.

Tuesday, April 14th.—I went ahead & killed 4 ducks at the river, but we were unable to get any of them on account of depth & rapidity of stream. We turned to the left in order to avoid crossing this, but were obliged after making a long detour to camp early & make a raft to traverse it, for it *would* come in our way.

Wednesday, April 15th.—Completed raft & crossed the river. Cold raw morning & very cold dreary work slopping about in the water, for the banks of the stream were marshy. I crossed first, then hauled Milton over who set to work & made a fire whilst I & Baptiste crossed the baggage. After that hauled the horses & carts across; as much as Milton & I could do to pull the latter through. Made only a short journey before we came to another river similar to the first. Here Baptiste found a place where the ice was still unbroken but very thin in the middle of the stream; this we crossed by taking the wheels off the cart & pushing it before us, by which we made a bridge over the weak part, by this we carried over all the baggage, swam the horses across where the river was free, & hauled over the other cart without taking off the wheels; these broke thro' the thin ice, & we with difficulty pulled it through. Baptiste then crossed where the ice was already giving way, & by the time we had put the wheels on to the dismantled cart again, the river was open, ice broken up—only just in time. Camped for night at Jack Fish Lake. Milton set the prairie on fire.

Thursday, April 16th.—Spent the day in camp for some snow fell, & the wind in the east, high & cold; we did not like facing the water again, & Jack Fish River was only a mile ahead. Baptiste went out & killed a good supply of ducks; reported ice on lake not very safe for crossing with carts, & no wood near the river. Milton & I slept, cooked & smoked.

Friday, April 17th.—Crossed the river. Baptiste remained to cut wood for raft. Milton & I took carts on to river, unloaded. Milton then made fire & I returned with empty carts for wood for raft. Came back with wood, & Baptiste & I crossed first, then Milton & cooking apparatus. He made fire & began to cook whilst Baptiste & I crossed baggage; very wet banks, nearly a yard of melting snow. Whilst busy, saw 4 Indians galloping up to us. Crossed grog immediately & covered barrel up with blankets. They came up to other side, talked with B—. & then went round by the lake to come to us; turned out to be Gatchi Mohkamarn & 3 Wood Crees. Very civil & glad to see us. I bartered a burning glass for a Mountaineer stone pipe. Had dinner. Gave Indians a drop of grog to their great delight; accompanied us having heard of 4 bulls; 2 turned off shortly; Gatchi & another went forward & camped with us for the night. At the far end of the lake.

Saturday, April 18th.—Before starting The Wolf & John Smith came up at the head of a party from Carlton on their way to Fort Pitt to help to bring down barges; went along with us. Camped for dinner at wood; long stretch of prairie after. Crossed Turtle River before night; strong rapid. Men pushed & steadied carts. Prairie covered with pretty blue anemones.

Sunday, April 19th.—A good long day; crossed English River after dinner. Pretty steep banks & pines; like English trout stream—crossed baggage by fallen pine. Carts & horses taken round & hauled over. Short of provisions, Carlton men only 6 days pemmican given & a few charges of powder & shot. Nothing for the dogs who dragged the travailles; Lillie's stinginess. Gave them our pemmican.

Monday, April 20th.—Worked hard all morning for our dinners, & got forward some 16 or 17 miles. I killed 4 pheasants & a goose & with the rest made up 2 geese, 2 ducks & eight pheasants. Not much for 10 men; all ate greedily. After dinner another 12 or 14 miles; horses give in; continually expecting to see the Fort. Milton walks a long way & then tires out: leave carts 3 miles from Fort with Baptiste to come on in the morning, & Milton & I go on to the Fort arriving long after dark. Fresh meat & potatoes, milk; latter upset me & I couldn't eat; rather tired. Slept like a top.

Tuesday, April 21st.—Chantelaine gave us a man to go with Baptiste to barter for horses from the Indians. Make arrangements. Informs us that we shall have to pay 10 s. a day for living in the Fort. (We did not however pay 10 s. each but only 10 s. for the 3.)

Wednesday, April 22nd.—Indians keep coming in. Have heard that we have rum with us. Want to trade for some, but recommend us not to go to their camp with it as there are too many there & we might probably be pillaged, &c. Big Squirrel & friend offer to accompany Baptiste to visit the Blackfeet. But we do not coincide. Baptiste to visit the Assiniboine half-breed[32] engaged to go with him, put off their excursion until the departure of the Indians.

Thursday, April 23rd.—The Indians still keep coming in & departing. Big Squirrel taken rather ill & delays a little. Assiniboine's child very ill, & he cannot start tomorrow. Chantelaine very civil. Milton & Baptiste mixed liquor all day yesterday, & much too publicly. Continually bothered. Ennuyeed. Bright sunny hot weather.

Friday, April 24th.—Assiniboine's child worse. Plenty of other patients also. Fort Hunter comes in; buys up almost all the store to go on a state visit to the Blackfeet. Ribbons in hat, &c. Baptiste & Assiniboine to start tomorrow. More Indians.

Saturday, April 25th.—Assiniboine's child died in the night. Baptiste cannot therefore start. Decide to get one horse & go on to Edmonton & trade from there, following the track on the Fort side of the river for some days & then cross over, in order to avoid the Crees.

Milton buys a good strong horse from Chantelaine for his Reilly No. 12 gun & fittings. I think a satisfactory bargain for both parties.

Sunday, April 26th.—2 Blackfeet came in, the advanced guard of 6 coming to trade at the Fort; have heard that we have some liquor. Tell them a little for our own use, &c. Better looking & better dressed than the Crees. The men in handsome robes, & dress of blanket, better shaped heads & finer features than the Crees. The women attired in different manner from Cree women, or Chippewas, with long gowns of beautifully dressed buffalo hide, very soft, & dyed brown, with belts round the waist, of leather almost covered with round plates of brass, the size of half a crown. Faces of both sexes highly painted with vermilion. Men's features highly marked; good high foreheads, cheek bones not so prominent as Crees, nose large, well formed, straight, or a little Roman, mouth large but less blubber-lipped than Crees; beautiful teeth like all other Indians. The two chiefs very dignified, & submitting with great composure to the gaze of Fort men & Crees who looked with interest on a race seldom seen except when in battle with them. They expressed their intention of trading all their horses (11). We inspected them but found them all so lean, & having such dreadful sore backs that we were not very anxious about it; but came to the conclusion to trade for the 4 best on the morrow when we had moved out from the Fort some few miles in order not to offend Mr. Chantelaine. Mr. Chantelaine took their horses into the Fort yard as some of the young Crees had dropped hints that they would help themselves. The Crees had already stolen some 30 from the Blackfeet since the peace, & the Blackfeet rather more in return; so that hostilities will probably recommence before very long. Our horses were also placed in the stable yard with the Company's. Intend to set out in the morning.

Monday, April 27th.—The Blackfoot Chief will only sell one horse, a cream & good runner, he says. We therefore refuse to trade at all. I resolve to wait till the morrow, in order that they may be before us. They spend the morning in trading their buffalo skins & robes with Chantelaine for powder, ball & tobacco. A Cree came in last night with the intelligence that a Cree woman had been killed in the Black-foot camp. It appeared she went to be married to a Black-foot, but others in the camp took a fancy to her, a quarrel arose, & one of them, to prevent the others from obtaining her put an end to the dispute by stabbing the woman. He had also heard that some Blackfeet who were on a visit to the Assiniboine in their camp had suddenly disappeared in the night, leaving their tents standing & everything in them, having doubtless received intelligence of impending danger or trouble, & the Stoneys set fire to their tents; everything seemed to betoken war again very shortly, & Chantelaine went to the Blackfoot chief, related the news & advised him to cross the river & be off at once, which he thought would be wise too & set off in a few minutes. A few Crees came in some few hours after the others went, & reported that just as they en-countered the Blackfeet on their road from the Fort, another Blackfoot arrived from the big camp, breathless & with only his breech cloth, coming in haste to recall those who had come in to the Fort here; he told the Crees that all was right at the Camp; but they inferred that was merely a blind, & that hostilities had already begun there; lucky we did not send our liquor there, or take that road ourselves. Off tomorrow at any rate, if 10,000 Blackfeet arrive, for we are all tired of slow life here.

Tuesday, April 28th.—A beautiful hot summer's day. Packed our carts, & set out once more. Baptiste had arranged to stop a short distance from the Fort to buy 3 horses from some Wood Crees & Sauteux; horses stolen from the Blackfeet. We stayed accordingly about a mile from the Fort, & about 20 Indians soon appeared, one big fellow riding a tiny yearling. The Assiniboine came & assisted at the barter. The first horse, a little white stallion, one gallon of mixture, 40 trade balls, 2 pints powder, 2 yards tobacco, & a yard of red cloth. A little dun mare the same; a weedy chestnut gelding & a roarer, the same plus ½ gallon. We did not take very long bargaining & then set out in earnest; Assiniboine accompanied us to dining place. He then intimated that he would have been glad to have engaged with us to cross the mountains. We said we should have been glad to have had him, for we liked the man, & offered £3 1st month, £5 after if he would come now. He promised to join us next day if he decided to accept the offer. After dinner, horses & carts stuck in a bog. I stripped legs & went in to help; after, just as I had remounted the chestnut, one of our new purchases, he suddenly whipped round, the saddle which was quite loose, turned (surcingle much too long), & I fell on my back; it took my breath, the saddle got about the horses heels & he galloped off, kicking furiously, just missing me as I rolled over. Eventually brought up against a cart & captured. I remounted & took more care. Baptiste watched horses all night. I had had headache from my fall & could not watch my share. Milton & I slept little from anxiety about horses; no alarm. Revolvers ready.

Wednesday, April 29th.—I got up & lit fire, & Baptiste went to bed. Milton would not get up. Assiniboine's son[33] arrived with the sun, he was going with us & had sold his lodge & stock of provisions & would join us about noon, the boy taking back some horses to bring him along more quickly. I went out for 2 or 3 hours & shot some ducks; found both Milton & Baptiste still fast asleep on my return. Assiniboine arrived about noon with family. I went on foot. Just about to camp when we saw some people in front, some on horses & others on foot; one set off at a run. We thought they took us for Blackfeet. Assiniboine galloped after to ascertain

Swamp formed by Beaver. With Ancient Beaver House and Dam.

who they were. Came back with news that they were Wood Crees; one who ran was after a wounded goose. Expressed their desire to drink a couple of horses.

(The halfbreeds & people at Fort slightly smitten with gold fever, shewn specimens of micaceon, granite & schist; they were much disappointed it was not gold.)

Thursday, April 30th.—Sent Assiniboine ahead to Indian camp to bring up men with horses for sale on to the road. Found them soon after dinner. The two horses they had brought were an old blind beast & a 3 year old the size of a dog; declined to buy them; said they could not go back without some liquor, & one offered to sell a little roan stallion he had borrowed from his Father to ride here upon. We gave him 1½ gallon, a calumet & ammunition; dearest horse we have bought; crossed a little river & camped on high ground above. I rode all day having run a great piece of wood into my heel. Assiniboine's mare foaled; no delay; tied foal on to the travaille[34] first half of day; after that he walked.

Friday, May 1st.—A long tedious day. I still too lame to walk. In afternoon come to river, rather deep; broken down bridge across it of cut pines. Men set to work to make it passable & traverse carts, whilst Milton, I, & boy took horses across by a ford lower down; took most of afternoon. Camped early for night under some cypresses, or stone pines.

Saturday, May 2nd.—Louis Battenotte (the Assiniboine half-breed) went off with his son to his house, to see if his father-in-law was there, in order that he might leave some of his family & effects; to join us again in camp tomorrow. We went forward & camped at noon to await him. On our way heard 5 or 6 shots in succession, & saw train of carts passing along side of hill to right, about a mile off. Presently English half-breed rode up; turned out to be Company's train from Moose Lake. Wanted to know if we were free men or Company's! In afternoon went out with Baptiste to look for beaver in Dog River close to camp; found trees cut down, & following stream upwards, discovered the dam & lodge; plenty of beaver tracks; they must have been there for generations, for we found old rotten stumps cut off by the animals years & years before. It turned very cold & cloudy, & we went back to camp fearing rain.

Sunday, May 3rd.—Up very late; waiting for Assiniboine.

In afternoon he arrived with "Mr. Jem" Simpson, a young fellow the image of D. H. Cooper, & the former wife of Assiniboine, at present mistress to "Mr. Jem". The latter brought us a present of fish & turnips very acceptable indeed. After dinner tried for pike in the river, & at sunset watched the beaver-dam but saw nothing more; too much disturbed by the Indians.

Monday, May 4th.—Eliza (little 10 year old sister of Assiniboine's present wife) returned with Mr. Jem. Wife & son to cross the mountains with us, he taking 2 horses for them. Could not find his beau-père yesterday. Mr. Jem left us a little before noon, having been very civil & invited us if we came out to share his house! Eliza left with regret having been regularly made screwed by Milton whenever we took our rum. We set out soon after & made a long stage to a large lake where we were to rest & hunt elk on the morrow.

Tuesday, May 5th.—Cleaned guns & went out after red deer. We rode to the wooded ground the far side of the lake & there left our horses. I then went with Baptiste, Milton with Louis. Beautifully appropriate country, but no fresh tracks, hills, wood, lakes, open spaces. Found 2 tracks of chevreuil yesterday. Bears' digging of few days ago. Very hot out of wind which was high. Saw, too, places where the river had been turned into a series of small lakes by old beaver dams, now grown over with grass, & the old lodge a green mound. Tapped a birch tree & drank the sap which was like sugared water. Get back to where we left the horses some 2 hours before sundown & found Milton & Louis just arrived, having been equally unsuccessful, the former disgusted with his experience of stalking; shot ducks & geese on way back to camp; & arrived very hungry indeed; ate bainette.

Wednesday, May 6th.—Last night very sultry, & the musquitoes very tiresome. I had a restless night, & Milton strong symptoms of a fit; smelling rum & taking carb. ann. arrested it; 2 more symptoms before stopping for dinner but not so strong as one in night. Intensely hot; 2 fires still raging across the river. After dinner wind suddenly rose into a tremendous gale, the sun clouded over & it became intensely cold. We hurried on to a large lake where we expected to find a large camp of Wood Crees, but they had left. Camped there.

Thursday, May 7th.—Wind still continues; arrived at Saskatchewan for dinner having forded one stream by the way. Very cold still. In afternoon men go up river in search of wood for raft. Milton & I go fishing but find rivers too shallow. Men come back unsuccessful, but bringing specimens of auriferous quartz, as they think, but which I am afraid is only mica.

Friday, May 8th.—Men at work early, making hide canoe. Milton sleeps till midday. I write journal & try again for fish. Steered a good fish like a trout of 4 or 5 lbs 3 times but he would not take; stream too clear. Milton joined me & fished, wading across river, looking for gold also. Dined quite late when the canoe was finished, 6 feet long 2 feet wide 1½ feet deep; frame of green willows, & covered with buffalo skin. Baptiste ferried over the luggage; very crank boat; at dusk all baggage over & I went across with B——,[35] log tied to side of canoe to steady it; the canoe only just floating with the two heavy men, B—— & myself. Gave the men some rum for it was cold work, the wind being high. Milton came across, leaving Louis & family on the other side with horses & carts. Baptiste went back to them to carouse; very sharp frost.

Friday, May 8th.—Bright warm morning; ½ inch of ice in bucket; horses swam across. Carts crossed by tying to tail of my horse & the Minister. There was a very steep ascent up the bank & an extra horse was harnessed by tying a rope from the cart shaft to his tail which brought them up triumphantly, Milton & young one as postilions. The road only a horse track for the freemen from White-fish lake, & very hilly & uneven for the carts. We therefore did not make a very long journey & camped on a hill. Cold & windy.

Saturday, May 9th.—Nothing occurred; awkward road. Not yet in cart track. Snowy covering to the ground; very cold, raw wind; reached main track in afternoon & camped in burnt country near a swamp; one of the fires we had seen in the distance put out by the snow of last night. Duck shooting in plenty.

Sunday, May 10th.—In the morning in shooting ducks ahead of the carts put up a herd of caribou. I did not see them or might have got a good stalk. Ran within 200 yards of carts. Disappointed. In afternoon came on wet & rain, heavy for some time; cold high wind. Camped early in consequence. Shot a couple of white geese for dinner which were really

balls of fat, & pronounced "wuckassin mitorni" by the men;
we found them too greasy without salt; this had run out, &
the potatoes also; nothing but dried meat, grease, & ducks, of
all which we are very tired.

Monday, May 11th.—I and boy shoot ducks; cross very
deep little river, & have to unload the carts & carry baggage
across; swim horses & drag carts without wheels across old
gold seeker's bridge of 3 trees. Fair day's journey.

Tuesday, May 12th.—Meet a Wood Cree who gave us
eggs for tobacco. Had killed two bears; are to arrive at Fort
tomorrow.

Wednesday, May 13th.—Nothing of consequence. Found
we could not reach the Fort,[36] the horses soon tiring with the
heat & heavy road.

Thursday, May 14th.—The men took an awful time washing & dressing themselves in their best in order to make a
swell appearance at the Fort. Crossed 4 small streams during
the day; water low now & easily forded. After dinner passed
freemen on way to Red River, wanted to exchange a mare
& foal or lame gelding for Sharman; no go. Arrived in sight
of Fort & ahead of the carts, 3 or 4 hours before sundown.
Fort very prettily situated on high cliff above the river, banks
well wooded. Both of us much taken with the appearance of
the place. Descend the hill to the beach, & soon 2 men come
across with canoe full of holes & take us over in the barge,
which goes back for carts arriving in meantime. Hospitably
received by Hardisty. Go down to see luggage landed & find
men very screwed; been at my rum. Hardisty informs us that
there is to be a grand bear hunt at the Lake St. Albans settlement[36a] of freemen & Romish Mission, 9 miles from here; that
is from Edmonton I believe; 5 bears attacked a band of horses;
2 men narrowly escaped on horseback, one only by throwing
his coat to Old Grisly. Resolve to start at day break & join
the hunt & get out revolvers & clean guns accordingly.

Friday, May 15th.—Baptiste overslept & did not call us.
I up before he came; could not get Milton out for a long time,
& we squabbled tremendously; would wait for breakfast. Then
started; pretty ride; copsed country. Settlement on hill ½
mile from lake; 20 houses; most civilised place since Fort
Garry. Saw a priest[37] & rode up to inquire about the bear

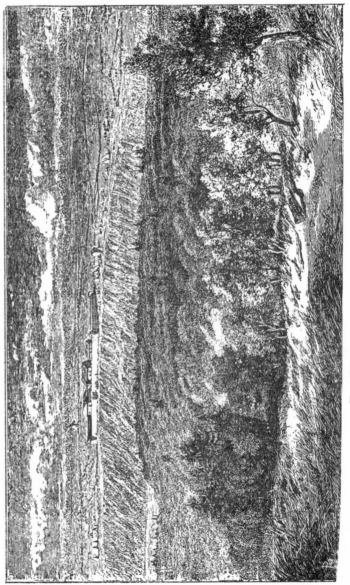

Fort Edmonton, on the North Saskatchewan.

hunt. Told us that no day had yet been fixed for it. Invited us into his house, a neat looking building, with nunnery adjoining it, & half of it used as school for girls who were taught in French, Boys having school in Fort & taught in English! French Canadian & therefore could speak a little English. Milk & pipes. Gave me pipe of birch-root, invited us to dinner; soup, dry meat, potatoes & turnips; pancakes & sugar. Mill near; horse power. Promised to tell his people on Sunday to arrange hunt on Monday or Tuesday; we agreed to come & camp there the night before. Left Priest busy having horses cut; very fine & fat; about 20; given as payment for absolution, &c.; best horse a fine black, taken from a poor widow whose husband died unconfessed & therefore priest would not read burial service; he therefore required hard work to get him out of purgatory, for which labour the priest received the black horse! Priest's room small, table & few chairs, pictures of Pope, Bishop of Marseilles, & Bishop of Red River, & a print of angels hauling saints out of flames of purgatory. On arriving at Fort again in afternoon found Mr. Pemberton of Lac La Biche going with boats to Norway House; 7 days from Fort Pitt.

Saturday, May 16th.—Idled about the Fort in the society of Mr. Pemberon, Macaulay & Hardisty. All hands busy getting the boats ready to start for Norway House. Mr. Pemberton had crossed the Mountains by Jasper's as far as Fort Colville; Hardisty only to the Boat Encampment. Mr. Pemberton amused us by telling us that you could only distinguish old *winter* camps by gazing up into the air & looking for old stumps cut off some 20 or 30 feet from the ground. The usual depth of the snow in many places. It is of course much too deep to remove when forming camp, & the plan is to cut green wood & make a firm platform for the fire & sleeping place on the top of the snow. He related that when he first crossed in winter he began to shovel away at the snow with a snowshoe in the usual manner, but having got down to his own depth without, to his surprise, finding any sign of ground, he sounded with a long pole, but was unable to reach the ground; he therefore desisted from his labour & cut greenwood in manner above.

Sunday, May 17th.—A day of rest indeed, for nearly all slept most of the day. Mr. Love, a Kentuckian & one of the batch of miners at work higher up the river, at White Mud

Creek, 50 miles West of Edmonton, came in today in a boat. He had been in California, thence to Columbia & from there on account of health, as he stated, had ascended the Fraser River in canoe with 4 others, & crossed here by Jasper's House. He described the navigation of Fraser River as extremely dangerous, & stated that he would not go down it for any consideration. It abounds in dangerous rapids, & frightful whirlpools amongst huge rocks; pine trees coming down stream disappear in them for a time, & come out with branches stripped off & completely shattered. A large boat belonging to the Company was sucked down & all hands lost; several other lives had been lost there. Love had brought down a small bag of pieces of fine dust, gold conglomerated by use of mercury, each about an inch square, being the work of 2 men & weighing about 2 oz. I was surprised at the lightness of the masses, but he said the gold was of the finest quality, & in very small grains & very loosely packed; 17 dollars the oz. They had made according to his account about £90 a piece, some having only worked 4 days, others 14. Found no nuggets or coarse gold, all the finest dust. Prefers the pursuit of the latter as the yield is always regular, & if there are no great finds, there are also no great disappointments. Told us we should find the roads pretty bad in the mountains, & worse the other side. He had come over to see some hunters about provisions & intended to work for the next week opposite the Fort to await their arrival. Said he was much delighted with the mining prospects here. Another party had started in spring for the north source of the north branch of the River where they expected to find it in greater abundance, but nothing had been heard of them since. Told us of Perry, a downright down-east Yankee. Pemberton who had seen him sometime at Jasper's House said he was the most determined fellow he ever knew. He crossed the prairies to the Rocky Mountains & over them into California with no means of transport but a wheelbarrow which he trundled before him! It contained all provisions, tools & effects; after that he returned to the States & set out from some place in Minnesota, I think Breckenridge, without a penny, & nothing except a gun & some ammunition, & the clothes he had on. He borrowed an axe at Breckenridge, cut down a large tree, made a canoe & paddled down Red River alone 6 or 700 miles to Fort Garry. From thence he made his way on foot, & supported by his gun, to Carlton where he obtained employment as driver of a cart to Edmonton; thence crossed Mountains with a party of Cariboo; was working a pretty good claim there, but finding another man working near was making about 5 times as much he, kicked his rocker & pick into the river & left in disgust. Love not knowing now where he is. Lots of gold found in Peace River. Pemberton found plenty near Jasper's House in small stream running into Athabaska river. Hardisty told us of contest between Priest & Methodist minister, Mr. Wolsey. Priest catches a convert & baptises him. Wolsey hears of it & baptises him over again, & so on ad infinitum, it being with great difficulty that convert knows whether he was made Papist or Protestant last. Quarrelled very fiercely at table about saying grace at dinner when both staying at the Fort. Mr. Brazeau who was in charge at the time told them if they did not behave better they should neither of them be allowed to say it at all. Whereupon they compromised & agreed to say it alternately. The Priest did not understand English, & Wolsey not French. Priest tried Latin; Wolsey at fault. They were therefore driven to Cree of which they neither knew much. Their "Keya Margastun, niya mirvarsin," "keya a rascal," "keya crapeau" intensely amused Brazeau & Macaulay who were the spectators. Wolsey trying to make a settlement near here in the woods. Failed & left his house, building another at lake near main river. Spent £1,000 mission money last year, & no settler but himself yet. Macaulay who is stationed at Jasper's now informed us that no man had yet escaped being obliged to eat horses there. He had to live on squirrels & kill an old stallion last winter. The plan pursued there is to camp about all summer in woods hunting moose for winter provision, the Fort being closed during that season, the Shushwaps coming in to trade only in winter. Last autumn on arriving at Fort, Macaulay found all parchment windows gone. Afraid the Fort had been robbed. Entered & heard something trotting about in loft overhead; went up & found wolverine who had evidently made his home there considerable time, but strange to say had not touched any goods, but lived on parchment, only eatable in Fort; chivied him out & killed him with sticks. Priest from Lake arrived in evening.

Monday, May 18th.—Engaged all day in writing letter to Harry. Milton in doing do. to Lady F. to be forwarded that evening by Mr. Pemberton who was to start for Norway House with boats. Mr. Macaulay to leave also next day for

Jasper's with pack horses. We left at sunset for the Lake to be ready for the bears on the morrow according to promise. Arrived at dark, & Baptiste took us to his uncle's who had begun a farm there. Hospitably received in one-roomed house, seemed well off; plenty of milk, potatoes & dry meat.

Tuesday, May 19th.—Set out rather late & called on the priest who found 4 half-breeds to go with us to look for the grislies. Out all day looking but found no fresh tracks; in low willow ground; ground dug up in 100 places in autumn & spring but nothing very new. Returning home much disappointed, met 2 men who informed us a man had seen a bear not very far off that day. Resolved to search again on the morrow with dogs, & reached priest's by dark. Supped with priest, & then hurried home in rain which became very heavy after we got in.

Wednesday, May 20th.—Cold rainy morning; but before noon it cleared up, & we started with 5 men & 6 dogs for the place where the bear had been reported to be seen yesterday. But not a trace could we find, and we came to conclusion that our informant had lied, especially as we found he had described a totally different spot to other people. We found numerous old diggings; spent the rest of the day in searching without success, & returned at sundown much disheartened; took up our old quarters at Alex Sioux's & found a woman just arrived who had seen a bear also that day; but we decided not to be done any more, at any rate for a few days, & our horses needed rest.

Thursday, May 21st.—Cantered back to Fort in time for dinner, having promised to send a present to our entertainers. Called at the priest's; gone to river gold seeking. Good looking nun flirting with Norwegian miner who had turned Romanist last winter to obtain a young girl of the settlement. I had caught a very bad cold & stayed in, reading "Alfred Leslie". Milton went across river to see the gold washing, but came back disgusted with smallness of result.

Friday, May 22nd.—Mr. O'Byrne returned from the Lake to worry us about taking him across with us. As I have omitted to mention him in the proper place when we first made his acquaintance, I will give his history & our acquaintance with him here. He introduced himself to Milton on Sunday evening & talked at him furiously & shortly after to me. From his own account it appeared he was a graduate of Cambridge, having been at Clare; knew Reverend T. Dixon of Bingley & Atkinson of Clare; most of the Bishops &c, & he crammed birth & aristocracy down my throat in nauseating doses, thinking doubtless it suited my palate. After leaving Cambridge, he studied law, apparently without success, & became connected with the press. After that private tutor to different swells' sons. Been in India without bettering himself (I could not discover in what capacity). Returned to England. Invited by prosperous friend to come out to Louisiana. Did well there till prosperous friend failed. After that engaged by planter at salary of $2000. as something or other & lived very comfortably & happily there until the war broke out. One day confounded by planter coming up & congratulating him upon being elected Captain of the home guard! As he is tremendous coward he was horror struck & decided that the only thing to be done was to escape at once which he effected by the assistance of a friend, but had to leave all money & valuables behind him; got recommendations to Bishop of New York, & appointed Classical Professor at Jackson College. But funds fell short on account of war, & Professors dismissed, he being owed £45; down Mississippi to Red River to seek appointment as teacher in school there. School broken up. Forwarded to Archdeacon Cochrane at the Portage. He sent him in with a half-breed also professed to be going across the mountains. But half-breed ate all provisions & left him at Carlton. Brought up in boats by Hardisty for which Governor Dallas[38] made Hardisty pay £16. 10 !! arrived here with nothing. Wolsey the Methodist Minister took pity on him & kept him during winter, & in spring he came back here & lived in miner's shanty, Mr. Christie kindly giving him some provisions to save him from starvation. He does not seem very grateful for the assistance he has received, & sneers at Wolsey's vulgarity. He is a great talker & I fancy a great humbug & "ne'er do well" who has been a dead weight on his friends throughout. Seems a well-informed fellow, however, & nearly knocked my head off with Latin quotations. Horribly afraid of bears & even wolves, & the men amuse themselves by exciting false alarms of bears being seen in his neighbourhood! He has left his shanty because he hears that bears are fond of willows which grow in plenty around the place, & taken to a lodge borrowed from some one in the Fort. The men put this up for him so that a storm of wind blew it down on to the top of him, & he has now merely thrown it over our cart under which he resides, a man of 60, clothed in long coat, & walking with a stick. He wishes to go with us, & intimates it will be our interest to take him, which we can't see as he is the most helpless fellow in the world. Intends to walk with us, carrying 30 lbs of pemmican on his back! poor provision for 36 days! Poor fellow, I wish we were not so short of carts, or we would willingly give him a lift, although he is an ungrateful dog.

Saturday, May 23rd.—Mr. Christie's little girl who had an attack of remittent fever when I arrived is now quite well; a pretty little child of 3 years old. Mrs. Christie raised in the country, but visited England with her husband last year. Nothing of note occurred.

Sunday, May 24th.—Rice pudding with very good rhubarb jam to it; a sleepy day.

Monday, May 25th.—3 women & 6 children suffering from secondary syphilis! The Fort will be in a nice state eventually, I expect. Bought a horse from an Indian, for $1\frac{1}{2}$ gal. of mixture, a blanket, & some tobacco. At night late bothered by another who came into our bedroom screwed, & wanted to sell his horse. But we were obdurate, & I very sulky so that he perceived it & asked if I wanted to fight with him. He was very good-humoured & jocose although pertinacious; we told him it was too late that night, but we would give him some in the morning. He said "you are very foolish for now I am drunk I don't care for my horse, but in the morning I shall be sober & shall be very fond of it." We said Keyarki; & he, finding it no go, left us.

Tuesday, May 26th.—In morning Indian brought his horse & we bought him for same price as the last; another came, but we could not trade, the liquor being finished. The last we bought a very good strong one. In afternoon we went across river to wash gold. Hardisty and Baptiste accompanied us; worked away at our tin pans, obtaining a perceptible quantity each time. They called us to supper, but forgot to send barge, & we had to wait an hour before we could make any one hear. After, tried to collect our gold dust with mercury, but owing to stupidity in using tin dishes, & bad manipulation we lost it all.

Wednesday, May 27th.—Looked at some tents & our horses; latter fattening fast but not yet fit to start. Arguing with Milton all day about taking a tent or a lodge, I voting strongly in favour of the former on account of lightness & small size, he for the latter because most comfortable.

TRIP ACROSS CANADA

Thursday, May 28th.—In quandary about Baptiste. Hardisty gets in André Cardinal who shows us map & explains the road; it appears that there can be no doubt of Baptiste's finding the road easily as the party which went last summer left a very visible trail. Decide therefore to go on as arranged with Assiniboine & Baptiste.

Friday, May 29th.—Very showery; nothing occurred.

Saturday, May 30th.—   do.   do.

Sunday, May 31st.—Decide to start on Wednesday or Thursday. Numerous patients with syphilis improving; 9 children & 4 women with syphilis ulcers & eruption.

Monday, June 1st.—Arranging our packages; looking at tents &c.

Tuesday, June 2nd.—Assiniboine has bought a lodge which of course finishes our argument as to whether it is most advisable to buy a tent or lodge; we employ him to change it for a larger which will be sufficient for all. Yesterday we made Mr. O'Byrne happy by consenting to take him with us; he made a most pathetic appeal to me as a Cambridge man, & although we knew it was foolish to burden ourselves with an extra mouth, yet we could not find the heart to refuse him. Resolve to set out tomorrow.

Wednesday, June 3rd.—Assiniboine neglected to change the lodge on account of his wish to have a private one, thinking, I suppose, that we should buy a tent if the thing were left till the last moment; but we sent him off, & he effected a change, we giving a shirt & some beads & tobacco to boot. This & trading with Indians for pieces of buffalo robe to put under the pack-saddles delayed us until dinner time. After dinner we sent the men off & followed ourselves after, saying goodbye to Hardisty & the rest over a drop of grog. During the morning the men of the Fort headed by the saddler, a Scotchman, commenced a subscription to present Mr. O'Byrne with a horse, & they soon collected £12, Milton & self giving one each. John Sinclair £2. Company sold the horse which was still at the big lake. Bridle given also. Arrived at the lake a little before sundown & found O'Byrne looking out for us; sent a man off for it, & at dusk he came in with a little black horse very lame; not worth £5. O'Byrne in a great way; did not seem very grateful. Wanted me to send a man over to the guard &

take another Company's horse on my own responsibility which I of course refused, & felt rather disgusted at his suggesting it.

Thursday, June 4th.—Sent off Baptiste with the horse for Hardisty to examine & a note from me explaining the matter. I went to see two patients. In afternoon Baptiste came back with a very good white horse, but rather thin & a note from Hardisty to say that he had never seen the horse before, & the man who sold it for his debt to the Company had done him. We were to have our choice of the horse sent, or another fatter one at the guard. When we paid our bill at the Fort (£23. 3. 4.) we found that we possessed only £23, & therefore had to deduct 3. 4. from what we had put down for the servants, not a six-pence left now! Starvation in Caribou! !

Friday, June 5th.—Got off late, Changed Sherman for a fine-looking cob yesterday, but he would not let Baptiste mount & a boy who took him into a bog to mount had his thumb put out & much cut by the cord which held him and the horse turned out a little lame also; it further appeared that he had not been ridden for 3 years; we therefore changed him again for a small black horse, very fat, but a bad goer & stumbling, but the best we could get. O'Byrne's horse very satisfactory now. A great trouble arranging all packs &c. for the first time, but fortunately all horses prove quiet except O'Byrne's, which is the fastest runner we have. Weather fine & hot. No incident occurred after departure; reached fine wooded & copsed country, pines & aspens, & camped near a prettily wooded river. O'Byrne's assistance is nil; most helpless fellow I ever saw: frightened of a horse, & shews very little disposition to help in anything without I ask it. Asks the men, rather tells them, to do little things for him, as if they were his servants & he an emperor. Does not even attempt to pack his own horse. I fear trouble with the men on his account. He is the greatest coward I ever saw, & I can hardly help laughing at his continual questions as to the chance of meeting grisly bears. The Assiniboine today stopped in the bush to light his pipe. O'Byrne who was behind passed him without seeing him & when he had just gone by, the Assiniboine set up a most fearful growling. O'Byrne took to his heels & ran for it immediately.

Saturday, June 6th.—Very wet morning & unable to set out until nearly noon. After 7 or 8 miles it clouded over & began to thunder, & before we could get the tent up, we were nearly wet through by a tremendous shower which continued till nearly dark; this day's journey at an end.

Sunday, June 7th.—Fine bright morning with nice breeze; reached Lake St. Ann's about noon, & dined there, getting fresh fish. After dinner went 7 or 8 miles round to the other side of the Lake where the Romish Church & Company's house & most of the settlers are. About 50 houses. The lake is very pretty, thickly wooded all round but a bad place I fancy for farming. The abundance of whitefish taken there seems the great advantage of the place. Called on Mr. Colin Fraser[39] who was very kind & promised us some fresh & smoked fish in the morning. Told us all about the fine old hunting times some 25 years ago when they supplied provisions from Wood Buffalo along the Peace River! And at Jasper's House one year, although their hunter died, & they had only a man & boy to hunt who understood nothing about it, yet game was so plentiful they never missed a meal off moose & bighorns. Said the Blackfeet were much belied. In his experience of 38 years in this country never knew an Englishman injured by them. Several Americans killed. Had spent a summer hunting with the Piegans & was treated like a prince. Once when out with Mr. Rowand, as they were resting in the middle of the day, a body of 200 Blackfeet, naked & in war-paint, moved on to them with fearful yells. Mr. Rowand jumped up & cried out 'stop you villains'; one of the chiefs fortunately recognized him & stopped the rest. They were profuse in their apologies & regrets for having frightened them; *many of them actually cried with vexation;* they had taken them for Yankees, & would certainly have scalped them if they had not recognized Mr. Rowand; asked permission to spend the night with them, & told them not to be afraid of their horses; & they made no attempt to steal.

Monday, June 8th.—Mr. Fraser kindly sent us new milk & fish this morning. Horses strayed & searching for them most of the morning. Found them just before dinner. Wood thick & separated from one another. Decided to wait till after dinner. In meantime Milton went to bathe, & I walked up to Colin Fraser's, & gave him some hints about his medicine chest for which he was very grateful. On going back, Baptiste preferred a request to stop for the rest of the day to see his relations whom he had not seen for 20 years. This we could not well refuse although we did not like the delay. In the afternoon Milton & I went over to Mr. Fraser's to drink milk & have a lesson in fly-making. We made several large flies on gimp hooks with worsted & coloured silk for bodies & speckled duck's feathers for wings; resembling no live fly I had seen, but Mr. Fraser assured us Rocky Mountain trout would take them greedily. Here Milton had a very severe sympton, followed by two more not quite so strong after our return to camp. He happily got through them all. Mr. Fraser told us he had been 38 years in the service, 27 in charge of a post, but through want of interest had never been promoted, & it was only for the last 2 years that his salary had been raised to £100 a year! If he had married a chief-trader's daughter instead of a poor woman it would have been very different. He had not seen Fort Garry for 30 years, & for 15 had never been further into civilisation than Edmonton!

Tuesday, June 9th.— Milton woke up very seedy & with bad headache, therefore did not start. Invited to Mr. Fraser's to dine & he gave us whitefish, potatoes & galette of barley flour which we enjoyed amazingly. Spoke very highly of Dr. Hector,[40] & indeed of the whole party, & found great fault with the Company for refusing to advance provisions &c. to the party when they had exhausted their order on the Company. Lord Southesk[41] fortunately came up & very kindly advanced money which got them out of the difficulty. Lord Southesk[41] very indignant. It appears it was Sir G. Simpson's express orders. Formerly, no stranger who passed was charged a farthing for board & lodging in the Fort! In afternoon we weighed camp & set out, Milton being now all right again. We stayed behind the rest & had a parting pipe & drink of milk with Mr. Fraser whom we presented with a little Deane & Adams pistol; he was quite overwhelmed, & almost offended at first, thinking we supposed he wanted pay for what he had done for us. He offered to get anything done for us before we returned to this country, & we asked him to find some moose & jumping deer skins for trousers & shirt. We parted from him with regret; a very fine old fellow indeed, & of Highland hospitality as well as birth. Along an awful road, in thick wood, bogs up to the horses' middles & fallen trees; path like a woodland path in England, & I expected to see the stiles every moment. Found our men already camped in an open space with good feeding for horses, about 7 miles on; Mr. O'Byrne much impressed with the difficulties he had encountered, & said he had never seen travelling before, although he had been in nearly every country.

Wednesday, June 10th.—I got up at sunrise & got them to prepare breakfast earlier than heretofore. Milton very sulky at having to get up in decent time. Reached a fine lake for dinner, & were nearly all the rest of the day in passing along its banks. Saw Emigrant's old camp about ½ way in afternoon. Camped by a swampy lake but very good feeding for horses. All very sleepy at night. Have made a very fair journey. Men grumble at O'Byrne's helplessness; road rather better.

Thursday, June 11th.—Up directly after sunrise, & Milton soon after; awfully sleepy; the musquitoes were very bad & I had to smoke out the tent at daybreak & then fell asleep again for a short time. Last night made O'Byrne help us to unpack the horses instead of disappearing with a pipe as is his usual custom. Pretty copsed hilly country.

I started in good time on foot, having first assisted to pack the horses. Shot some ducks during which the others passed me; I caught them up in about 3 miles & found they had already crossed Pembina river. Sent my horse back for me. River not more than 4 feet in the deepest place. Found 2 freemen on the other side returning from trapping beaver; they had only killed 24 between them. Steel traps; had one immense beaver whole; the first I had seen. Also greater part of 2 year old black bear killed yesterday. As Milton was anxious to try for gold here, we unharnessed & proceeded to dine at once, although only about 10 o'clock, the freemen of course as usual kindly giving us their assistance in consuming our provisions. We thought we found a trace of gold in river bed but nothing conclusive. The river shallow & stony, flows down a deep narrow valley with precipitous cliffs in many places, in which are to be seen seams of coal, in one place apparently some 12 feet thick; the sandbanks & shores were strewed with blocks of coal, & it cropped out along the shore; did not seem of the finest quality, rather soft & dirty, like engine coal. Went on rather late owing to delay from rain, & camped in smart shower, close to a river we had followed for a long time.

Friday, June 12th.—All through the day bad swampy ground, often covered with fallen timber, & very heavy work for the horses; in the morning heard a rustling in the bushes, probably a wolf, which horrified O'Byrne who was sure it was a grisly bear. Weather sunny & breezy.

Saturday, June 13th.—Heavy rain at daybreak, & we don't

149

get up as early as usual. I led on foot, & took them a good spell as the road was nearly all sound, although thickly wooded. One part of the road was very pretty, lying along the edge of a beautifully wooded little valley with a stream at the bottom. Fresh track of black bear. Other parts through what resembled pine & larch plantations in England. After dinner did not get more than 3 or 4 miles, the path the whole way lying thro' swamp, up to the bellies of the horses not unfrequently. O'Byrne came & joined us at some bread & butter in the evening & proved rather amusing with his account of American life & manners; boys at school revolver the 'Professors' &c. His own experience. Musquitoes dreadful. Woods on fire, looking at first like approaching storm.

Sunday, June 14th.—Up directly after sunrise; a sharp frost last night; O'Byrne's boots frozen. All morning passing thro' a bog, very monotonous, these places are generally wooded with small firs & covered with very thick soft moss; this makes it very heavy to travel over. I led them a good long stage before dinner, much to Milton's disgust, & stayed for dinner at an old beaver dam, where a river had been converted into a lake, a tiny stream & a patch of grass. After that through pretty wooded country with firm path to a little river where we camped. After arranging the things, the Assiniboine took his gun to look for beaver, Baptiste having seen 'sign' when looking for fire-wood, I was on the point of accompanying him, but it struck me that there might be trout in the stream as it was very like a Yorkshire moor stream, & I therefore walked down it. Saw a small fish rising & went back for tackle. I had unfortunately lost the flies which Mr. Fraser helped me to make at St. Ann's; they were contained in a little brass box which had belonged to my grandfather, (the one with burning glass as a top), and I regretted the loss much on that account; the box fell out of my pocket somewhere. I therefore set to work & whipped a very rough fly & tried the fish with that; but although they came at it twice they would not take. Water very clear & brown; had recourse to a small spinner, & soon captured a small trout of some 2 oz. but could not get another run; the fish was very like an English burn trout, but instead of the red spots, it had a red line along each side about $\frac{1}{8}$ inch broad; the black spots similar to English variety; it ate like our own fish. Just at dark the Assiniboine returned in great excitement; he had followed the stream upwards, wounded a beaver & could not get him; after that wandered up stream 2 or 3 miles. On his return when about ¼ of mile from camp heard a cracking in the bushes, & thinking the horses had wandered that far went up; to his astonishment he found himself within 10 yards of an enormous grisly bear, who rose from his employment of tearing open rotten wood for the insects therein; the man stood still & the bear ran up to him growling horribly until within 3 or 4 yards; he pulled the trigger but the gun missed fire. He had Baptiste's double barrel, but one barrel was loaded with small shot. At the bear's growling, two other great big fellows came running up, & they in turn walked up to him, growling & shewing their teeth horribly. They retired again, & he cautiously withdrew, & made a tour, coming upon them from another quarter & up wind, having recapped the gun. One of them, the largest, immediately came up growling again, the other two going off at speed. Again the gun missed fire. After some time the biggest bear which had remained, still perambulating backwards & forwards & showing great disposition to fight, the Assiniboine stole off, crossed the little stream & succeeded in regaining the camp in safety. I had already returned from fishing when he returned very pale & excited, & related rather incoherently at first what an escape he had had. I immediately called out to Mr. O'Byrne who put his head in at the door of the tent & his naturally long visage rapidly lengthened, & his face expressed the greatest terror as I related what had happened. He begged to sleep in the tent & borrow my revolver, but I told him very maliciously that it was liable to go off unprovoked, which made him in as great a fright of that as a bear, & he eventually arranged his bed alongside the lodge, & took the big axe as a bedfellow. We were all too excited to go to sleep until very late, & resolved to go in quest of the Grislies in the morning, it being dark already when the Assiniboine returned, Milton agreeing to get up at daybreak. Hoped at any rate to find the big one the man left growling & walking about.

Monday, June 15th.—We started at sunrise & found the bear tracks, & the Assiniboine explained how they had run up to him, &c. &c. We followed the tracks across the river. & there found that they were all 3 together again having only traversed it that morning, their foot-steps being quite wet. After a good deal of careful tracking, & crossing numerous other bear-tracks we found fresh dung, soon after a bees-nest quite freshly pulled open, & expected to come upon them very shortly. We sat down to rest a little & have a pipe, as we knew they would not now move far, it being already nearly noon; the place was very thickly clothed with underwood & cypress, & we should probably not view them until very close indeed. We were however disappointed. The men lost the track on some bare ground & could not regain it just as we were hoping for success. Query? did the men lose it purposely, & did the Assiniboine pull a trigger at all at them yesterday? As we were returning home disconsolate, we came upon a moose-track of yesterday, & I decided to follow it up with the Assiniboine whilst Milton with Baptiste went back & raised camp, we to rejoin them further on; away went the Assiniboine at a great pace, & it certainly astonished me to see the ease with which he followed what I could only discern by carefully stopping to investigate. After an hour or so the moose still going straight & at speed occasionally, & the weather looking very threatening, we gave up, & were already on our way back, when we crossed a fresh moose-track of this morning & set to work to follow that; in the middle of this it began to rain heavily & we sat down & got a jolly good wetting over our pipes; we then recommenced our hunt, & soon got to where the moose had begun to circle, preparatory to stopping to eat & lie down; we now had to be very careful, & the rain having soaked the fallen leaves & dead grass helped us much; but there was a great quantity of dead wood & it was very difficult to avoid breaking the dry twigs; we found three places where he had been lying & fresh dung some of which was still warm, but the moose had walked off; we followed the track down to the river where we lost it, & as the beast was evidently bent on a long walk, we gave up & set out for camp. About ½ way met our party, & joined in with very empty bellies, & altogether very uncomfortable, cold & wet. Had to recross our little river & a long stretch of boggy ground before we found a camping ground, & a very poor one too. I immediately made a big fire, & walked into some cold pemmican very handsomely, having had nothing to eat all day.

Tuesday, June 16th.—I going ahead as usual on foot, after about 4 miles took the wrong track which led me through a most dismal pine swamp up to the knees in mud & water. I had some misgivings & sat down to smoke a pipe, & see if the rest came up. But as they did not appear, I retraced my steps & gained the right path; found they had passed already. Fired my gun at intervals to intimate that I was in the rear, in order that they might not go on too long, thinking to find me at some fit camping place ahead. But they did not hear until they had already camped in despair, & I had a good two hours hard walk after them. Milton had thought me ahead & that I was making them march so far on purpose & much disgusted in consequence. In the evening we reached McLeod s river & camped in a pretty open spot on the banks. A fresh bear track we found there renewed Mr. O'Byrne's fears, & we had a good laugh. Found some oak fern which brought thoughts of home.

Wednesday, June 17th.—Up at sunrise. In consequence of expostulations with Milton from myself & the men, we got him out in good time. We crossed McLeod's river about $\frac{1}{2}$ a mile above where we first struck it; here it was very shallow; water very low & clear. It is a pretty river, apparently as broad as the Saskatchewan, & the high banks handsomely clothed with fine pines & poplar. I had hoped to find trout in it but could [find] only some small fish like dace which were taking the fly. After crossing Milton & I stayed behind to wash for gold, & only found a doubtful trace of it; when we had finished we found our horses had broken loose & followed the rest & Milton was very unhappy at the prospect of a long walk to catch up the party. We found his horse, however, brought up by the bridle catching a fallen tree about $\frac{1}{2}$ a mile on; & presently we crossed a small river. I had some little difficulty in finding the track, Milton staying behind to wash for gold at the mouth of the stream. I found the men camped about 4 miles on, & discovered that my horse had arrived before me, having lost his bridle; and also that the big axe had tumbled out of one of the saddle bags. We therefore sent the Assiniboine back to look for these, & waited a long time for his return; therefore setting out late, meantime Milton came back having found no gold, but having seen a moose, which he took for the horse of some one sent in search of him, & called out & whistled to him thinking he was hiding in the wood to frighten him! He as usual had given some one else his rifle to carry. What bad luck mine not to have had such a chance! In the afternoon we had a tremendously long stage, finding no camping place, & stopping at last in the thick wood where we saw others had camped before. Found a note on a tree in pencil from

Macaulay[42] of Jasper's House stating this was the only fit place for some distance. He got there on the 29th May, leaving Edmonton on the 19th, so that we were only 2 days longer from St. Ann's. Milton very unhappy at not being able to camp before dark.

Thursday, June 18th.—Nothing of consequence; made short journeys to rest horses, & stopping early; in pretty good feeding ground to make up for yesterday. Along banks of river all day in the thick pines. At noon Milton found very "good colours" of gold in this river. After camping for the night, Baptiste went ahead & found moose & bear tracks & 2 small rivers in one of which were trout, & in the other beaver. We fix to move on to the little river, fish & hunt for one day.

Friday, June 19th.—Assiniboine & I off at sunrise after moose, the others to move camp to fishing place. After a hard day's work we cannot find fresh moose tracks; innumerable old ones; plenty fresh bear; but we saw nothing; very hot. O'Byrne set fire to the country & spoilt chance of beaver. Baptiste & Milton quarrel about the site of the lodge. Former packs up his "petit train" to start but repents. We kill several fish, some resembling dace, others small trout, & the boy kills a very fine large trout of 2 lbs with a partridge bait, & loses 2 or 3 more.

Saturday, June 20th.—The road now turns off at right angles from the elbow of the river & leaving the thick pines on the bank, passes thro' a more open & copsy country, with hills & vales, doubtless the first hint of the Rocky Mountains. The first part is burnt & affords tolerable pasturage. Today we saw the last of our guide Baptiste Supernat. I thought the storm had blown over, but after helping to pack the horses, & seeing the others start, he remained to light his pipe, he said, & we never saw him after. I had as usual started first to do the shooting, & did not observe his absence for some 2 or 3 miles; then however, seeing he was not there, & remembering his sulkiness & conduct the day before, I enquired of the Assiniboine who declared that he knew nothing except that when they started he said he must stop to light his pipe, & he had not seen him since. He was riding the grey, one of our best horses, & had on him the saddle-bags of O'Byrne, who was in great consternation thinking his pemmican & tea were gone. But on investigation it turned out that Baptiste had packed his things in the old man's bags,

& taken nothing but those, the horse & some pemmican & tea. We soon pulled up & held a council of war. Assiniboine said he could find the track, & we made him guide at once with Baptiste's wages. The prospect before was now one of hard work, our only man being a one-handed one. As we owed Baptiste £10 wages the loss of the horse was not much. Camped at night by little stream, close to where the hunting track joins this one, making good wide road forwards.

Sunday, June 21st.—Make a fair start; rather a grind having so much work to do, & no joke lifting 180 lbs over the back of a tall horse. We are all in good spirits, the only one much out of sorts being Milton who sorely longs for revenge on Baptiste & cannot forgive the loss of his horse. This morning we again reached the McLeod River & continued to follow it all day, camping for the night on its banks. The scenery begins to be very pretty, the country ahead being hilly & full of streams. The McLeod rolling down a fine, deep, narrow valley well wooded. In fact, the whole country is covered with pine & poplar. We passed one or two beautiful little spots, tiny prairies, with clumps of pine, cypress & poplar most beautifully arranged, with rounded knolls & hills around, very park-like. The young one fished for trout in one of the little streams with a gad-fly. But they were too lazy to eat, & I had to stand on one side of the stream to stir them up with a long pole, whilst he put the bait before their noses. In this way we caught two, but we both fell into the water with a great splash which however did not frighten away the fish. Bathed in McLeod River. Day of misfortunes. Assiniboine, Milton, self, & Old boy lost our pipes, O'Byrne the only one who found again. A great misfortune as I have only 2 left now; started with 6 from Edmonton.

Monday, June 22nd.—Can't get up as early as I wish; men don't back up well, & Milton's laziness a great drawback. About noon we begin to suspect that we have taken the wrong track as our road begins to appear less beaten, & still keeps the bed of the river. The Assiniboine had observed another path turning to the right, but had preferred this on account of seeing bullock-tracks. But it struck him that these might be those of the Yankees who went up the McLeod to look for gold this spring, & the path we were following merely a hunting road. It led us through a bog &

The Forest on Fire.

to the top of a high bank over the side where it appeared to cross. The matter was now becoming serious, & we therefore unpacked horses, although there was nothing for them to eat, & Assiniboine went out to see the road. In meantime we had dinner, & very nearly set the forest on fire, the horses trampling some of the embers of their fire into a fallen pine tree which quickly set fire to some neighbouring standing trees, & I thought we could not save it. I seized an axe & cut down the nearest trees. But then the little black horse getting burnt a little, got frightened & rolled in the fire & I had to seize a great pole & beat him about the head before he would get out again. I thought he was done for, but he turned out little injured. Whilst this was going on, the fire had again got head, & I set to work with the axe, & shouted to the rest to bring water, & Milton's activity & presence of mind in helping me to some at once saved us, & we got the fire under by sundry pansful. Whilst I was energetically cutting trees & crying for water, I observed O'Byrne sitting down, tugging away at a boot. I shouted to him very angrily, "Mr. O'Byrne, what on earth are you doing! why the devil don't you bring some water?" "I can't, I've got only one boot on", he said. "Are you a fool staying to put on a boot, when the forest will be on fire in a minute & you burnt to a cinder?", this frightened him, & he jumped up & limped up with a pan of water very assiduously. In an hour or so the Assiniboine came back, having found the road some few (6) miles back; & we packed off & got there by sundown, going at a great pace, keeping O'Byrne at a run, for he dare not be left behind for fear of bears & losing the road. Quite exhausted when he came in. Camped for night in pretty open space where road forks.

Tuesday, June 23rd.—A good stage thro' the usual routine of bogs, pine woods & poplar; passed close to a large lake in the morning. Camped for dinner in some spruce firs near a marsh, the Yankees had camped there before. Soon after we started in the afternoon, it began to thunder & rain heavily, but as we were wet thro' almost immediately, I did not stop until we found a good feeding place for the horses. The storm was a very heavy one, reminding us of the one on Red River, but not nearly so severe as that. We were completely drenched, & very glad to get the lodge up, light a fire & change our things. Here we found written on a tree the name of Hutchison the miner & stating that his party had come this far, & *finding they were on the banks of the Athabaska,* had turned again to follow the McLeod. Are we on the right road to Jasper's House? at any rate we must go on & see the road.

Wednesday, June 24th.—Started late, having to dry all our baggage, & hope to find the Athabaska before night, making only one long stage. Just as we were ready to start it began to thunder heavily, & we were very glad to get the lodge put up and goods covered before the heavy rain came down. We had to give up the idea of going on & dozed away in the lodge, whilst Assiniboine went ahead to view the road. He came back before dark with the news that *we were within ½ a mile of the Athabaska* which was tremendously swelled by the rain, & probably inpassable! Oh dear! Too late again; two days earlier would have saved us this. Will Milton never learn the value of time?

Thursday, June 25th.—Fine morning, & we set off for the place where the crossing of the river is usually made, intending if the river is still too high to wait there & hunt until it lowers sufficiently. All morning along the banks of the Athabaska now more swollen than before. It is a fine river very like the McLeod but not so winding, here nearly ⅛ mile broad & full to the banks. On a little bare knoll in the thick wood of the high bank I stopped & awaited the others behind, & had my first view of the Rocky Mountains. A beautiful prospect, & a bluish haze softened off the picture very completely. In the foreground below us rolled the rapid Athabaska between its high banks, clothed with pine, spruce & poplar. Beyond, ranges of hills clothed with pines, & running nearly north & south. Farther still & parallel dimly in the haze stood out the first chain of the mountains 'de facto', backed by still higher ones behind; the sun shone on the snow still lying in the hollows & on the peaks. A cleft in the range, cut clean as if with a knife, shewed us what we supposed to be the position of Jasper's House & the opening of the gorge through which we were to pass across. It looked not more than 12 or 15 miles off, & we hoped to reach it by sundown; but, alas, the day clouded over after dinner, & when we had gone about 2 miles, it began to rain heavily, & we stopped & unpacked the horses; when we had finished, it cleared up & we packed again, but before we could start, it began to thunder & rain tremendously, & we gave it up,

& raised our lodge. Very heavy rain all night. We shall have a nice piece of work to cross the river.

Friday, June 26th.—Very wet morning, & we don't hurry to set out as we shall probably have to wait for the river to go down before we are able to cross it; showery all day; we have several views of the mountains which remind one forcibly of some pictures of scenes in the Alps, the snow-clad tops, abrupt cliffs, covered with soft blue haze, & amid lower hills clothed with pine. We crossed several little rivers already swollen into torrents, & some beautiful glades, park-like spots ornamented with pine, spruce & poplar very effectively. Camped for the night by a small stream, where there was some splendid feeding for the horses. Mountains now look quite close, & we hope to dine there tomorrow; during the night frost; ⅛ inch of ice in O'Byrne's tea cup in the morning.

Saturday, June 27th.—Beautiful bright morning, & I turn Milton out in fair time, (perhaps 5 o'clock); at which proceeding he became very crabbed & vicious, and we had one of our usual squabbles as to the advisability of starting early & doing fairly long journeys; to reach here we have already doubled the time usually taken. We made a good long morning & stayed to dine at a beautiful little lake where there was a splendid view of which I give a sort of plan.
Before sundown we again reached the Athabaska, here expanding into a lake with several islands, and passing close under the cliff to the right; on the way the grey stallion stuck fast in a quagmire, & Assiniboine & I had to unload him, no one else came to help, & I was very wrath with O'Byrne. On the road I saw the Gallardia picta in full bloom, roses, tiger-lilies, a pretty red orchis, & abundance of red & white vetches; the blue borage, & in the moist places, the marsh violet which Sarah & I found on the road to the Beacon near Bolton Abbey. In the evening there were numerous branches of the road, the one we followed finished in the river, & we went on by a small track which led us to a log cabin, doubtless a cache for provisions when out hunting from the Fort, but now empty. We were compelled to camp here in order to search out the road tomorrow, it being already late; we were now between the two most distant hills marked in the plan—fairly in the mountains.

Sunday, June 28th.—Resting whilst Milton makes Kinni-kinick, I fish, & Assiniboine investigates the road, & handles the big axe, ready to work at the raft, & looks out for a place to cross.

Assiniboine discovers the grand path still leading along this side the river, & probably we are still a day's journey from the Fort. Caught no fish, water being too heavy. Very wearisome long day. Fearful amount of gad-flies. Horses half mad.

Monday, June 29th.—Horses rampaging about all day yesterday, & during the night. Up at sunrise having had a very poor night's rest. During the course of the night O'Byrne crept into the lodge, being in terrible fear of being trampled on by the horses of which indeed there was some danger for they did nothing but rush about the lodge & all over, tormented to death by flies; & they kicked against the tent poles & disturbed us dreadfully. About daybreak Milton jumped up in his sleep with one of his usual shouts of "Holloa, Holloa! what's the matter?" O'Byrne started up in horrible terror exclaiming, "What is it, my lord, what is it?" I smothered my laughter under the bed-clothes, Milton subsided again under his, & O'Byrne unable to make it all out & quite disgusted at the continual disturbances, got up & breakfasted. During the morning's journey we found our road obstructed by fallen timber caused by a fire which was still alight, slumbering amongst the turf. We therefore had to waste a long time in cutting a way thro' with the axe. When emerging from these difficulties, I found myself without gun, & camped for dinner in order to go back & search for it at once, and Assiniboine to my delight soon returned with it, having found it where I dismounted to fetch some horses out of the wood into the path again.

We are now in the mountains in earnest, passing up the vale of the Athabaska, passing the foot of the straight cut cliff I have mentioned before. The river spreads out here into numerous channels, & winds round some fine islands very prettily. The valley some half mile broad. After dinner the Assiniboine who was ahead found some very fresh sheep tracks, & went after them, & I dismounted & followed; we followed a sheep track half way up the face of the cliff, & there I caught sight of a "mouton blanc" & lamb not very far ahead; we could not find any bighorns, although plenty of tracks. We therefore made a stalk up to these, a long round up

Over the Mountain, Near Jasper House.

narrow path loose stones & slippery rocks; could not see them; cursed the others who had been shouting & making a great noise; coming back we found we had mistaken the point where we thought they were, & carefully advanced to the edge of the cliff where we had marked them really; & some 15 yards below I descried the head of the goat looking up. This was all I could see, & I aimed between the eyes & bowled him over; he got up again & presented his broadside; my second barrel missed fire; the Assiniboine therefore gave it her behind the shoulder; she staggered down the cliff, & we reloaded & followed. We had now only small shot, & I got very close & fired into the goat which was still able to scramble down the cliff. The Assiniboine shot the lamb in the head & he fell a tremendous crasher down to the foot of the cliff below. Assiniboine now cautiously approached the old one who was still alive, & heaved over the edge, & crash she went, & lay quite dead at the bottom; we then descended. And when I looked up at the face of the rock, I could not believe it possible that I had come down there; but in the excitement of the moment I thought nothing of it. We now cut up the old one, took two legs & the head & brisket, & hanging these & the lamb on to a pole, Assiniboine & I set off to catch up the rest; saw Jasper House in the distance, 3 miles off; in the valley; road now went nearly straight up the mountain side; and I never had such an awful grind in my life as carrying our heavy load up this mountain side. We rested 3 or 4 times, fairly done up before we reached the top, & coming down was nearly as hard work. At the top we saw the camp fire in the Valley below, & fired shots in the hope that they would send horses to meet us; but we had nearly arrived before we met Milton & the young one coming to look for us; & soon after we arrived in camp thoroughly tired. The mutton we enjoyed very much; rather strong-flavoured but we had not tasted fresh meat for 2 months.

Tuesday, June 30th.—Up very late, being so dreadfully tired. Lamb cutlets fried in paste for the grease, delicious; afterwards moved camp up to the crossing place. Fine weather but cloudy. Stream running tremendously. Our camp on the sandy shore of the river. All rest of morning, cutting dry trees to make the raft. Very heavy work as the axes are both very small, & we require large timber for our raft, on account of the great stream & number of persons &

baggage. I was regularly chawed up by dinner time, not having quite got over my hard work of yesterday, and the wood-cutting devolving on myself & Assiniboine. After our noon's rest we detailed into 3 parties to carry the cut timber to the river side, the place selected for our start being about 300 yards above the Fort, where there was a little inlet of still water. Assiniboine & I one party, to carry the heavy logs, Milton & O'Byrne, & wife & boy, 2 other detachments for the lighter ones. It was all Assiniboine & I could do to stagger on under our heavy loads, & we required the assistance of all the rest to get them on our shoulders. Walking over the pebbles & shingle of the shore with heavy loads soon cut our moccasins thro' & hurt my feet tremendously. Milton very much disgusted with his helpmate O'Byrne who gave much advice, & exerted himself not at all. He would not put one end of the log they were carrying (very light ones) on his shoulder, but held it with one hand, and after going a few yards would let it down with a run saying he was exhausted & thereby hurting Milton considerably by the jar, not being too exhausted to give a great many orders all the time. I and Assiniboine met them coming with their last, when O'Byrne pulled up; Milton working well & dragging along the log alone. Assiniboine very indignant, gave vent to some very strong language in French, & seizing the wood put it on his shoulder & ran off with it. Milton came up to me very vexed with O'Byrne, & he, overhearing, I suppose, what we were saying, came up & said it was all very well for me with shoulders like the Durham Ox, but he was not so strong. I told him that I had had to lift more than double the weight, & that I had strained under it until the perspiration poured off me, whilst he seemed very comfortable. And I said Milton had shown great contrast to himself. "Oh!" he said, "he is fired with the emulation of youth." I said I wish he had a little more of such spirit. He said his hand was sore & showed me a little scratch on his thumb. But I exhibited to him my hands perfectly raw with blisters, & that finally shamed him, or rather shut him up. When all the wood was collected, the sun being now only about an hour from setting, we decided that it was too late to attempt to traverse that night, & retired to supper & bed. Heard a distant shot in afternoon.

Wednesday, July 1st.—When I awoke found a stranger in the camp, one of Macaulay's party, which had divided at McLeod's River; he was head of the moose division, Macaulay with 3 others going after sheep, & agreeing to meet here today. This man told us it was very lucky we had not crossed, as by following the river for a day's journey on this side, we should find a better crossing place, & also avoid a very bad river which was probably now impassable. He expected Macaulay today. We therefore decided to go on two or 3 miles to a good feeding place for the horses, by a lake where there were plenty of whitefish, & a Company's fishery, & stay there for the day hoping for Macaulay's arrival. On our way there was a rapid stream, rather deep for 2 or 3 yards. We were all on horseback except O'Byrne, who was behind, & he getting into the deeper part was nearly carried off his legs by the stream, having to hold on to his stick very firmly. He was in a tremendous fright, & cried out, "Oh dear! Oh dear! I shall be carried off!" I had delayed a little to see how he got on, & was really rather pleased to see him in difficulties as he is so very fond of advising and ordering other people; but thinking he would lose his presence of mind & be in some danger, I shouted to him to get back which he did, & the man with us trotted up & gave him a hand across; he clung to his stirrup in great fear — but came easily enough thus. We camped by the fish lake, and went pike-fishing in a little river which flows out of it, in the afternoon. Water very thick, & killed nothing. Intensely hot; saw bighorns on the cliff opposite but too hot to go after them. Had a bathe in the lake which brought on one of Milton's symptoms, & he did not stay in long although the water was very warm & beautifully clear. An old half-breed who wanted to go with us as far as Tête Jaune Cache, but told him we had no means of paying him unless he went all the way to Kamloops,[43] or we would take him for 2 or 3 days for the first part of the road to help us across the Athabaska & Myette rivers, & pay him in ammunition, &c. He took till next day to consider. 2 Shushwaps dressed only in small marmot robes & shirts, sans culottes & moccasins, came in & we bought some dried fish for powder & shot. In the evening the Company's men put out a net & caught a whitefish immediately, which they gave us. After dark the 2 Shuswaps went out in the canoe & speared fish by torchlight, a very pretty sight.

This valley of the Athabaska is very fine, surrounded by lofty mountains on every side, clothed 2/3 of the way with pines, the upper part bare rocks covered with snow & capped

View from the Hill opposite Jasper House.—The Upper Lake of the Athabasca River and Priest's Rock.

with clouds, the river winding in the valley below with numerous lakes & smaller streams. Some parts of the valley were like a garden with wild flowers, the most showy being the Gallardia picta, white & purple vetches, & a brilliant red flower something like the scarlet lychnis in effect. The Fort is merely a little house, surrounded with low paling, very clean looking & pretty, on the west side the river, the ground around covered with wild flowers. We only of course saw it at the distance of some 4 or 5 hundred yards.

Thursday, July 2nd.—I had intended starting at daybreak with Assiniboine to hunt bighorns, but during the night Milton had two symptoms, & I could not go; and rain coming on at early dawn, Assiniboine remained in camp also. After getting up, Milton had another symptom but got through. The 2 Shuswaps brought us 11 fresh fish speared the preceding evening, for which we gave them a small piece of soap & a pint of flour. The old half-breed agreed to see us across the river for ammunition & medicine. Very hot sun & high wind in afternoon. Intend to start again tomorrow.

Friday, July 3rd.—Milton awaking with the bad headache which had troubled him all yesterday & during the night, was not fit to go on, & we were obliged to stop another day, although very hard on our provisions, every one around of course honouring us with their company at meals. Poor devils, they were starving. I bought a moose skin dressed with the grain, & a cariboo skin for a little medicine. Before dinner I again tried fishing, but the water was too thick if there were any fish, which I doubt. After that read all my letters over again & wished for later news. Just finishing dinner when Macaulay arrived. Camped close to us. Had killed 10 sheep, & at a lake nearly a day from here had killed 42 large trout in about 2 hours. Invited us to his tent & feasted us on trout & fresh mutton which we appreciated highly. And he kindly sent over a quarter of bighorn to our camp. O'Byrne came also to Macaulay's camp & ate enormously. The poor fellow had begged some tea of Macaulay before. We invited Macaulay to breakfast before starting, & O'Byrne.

Short commons at Jasper House in winter. The wolverine. The Shushwaps.

Saturday, July 4th.—After a roughish journey of some 8 or 9 miles along sides of mountains, thro' several lakes & small rivers, many of them taking the horses above the belly, & which

O'Byrne considered highly perilous, we camped for dinner Macaulay accompanied us. On the way we had to go out of the road on account of the high water. O'Byrne, as usual being fearful of urging his horse beyond a slow walk, lagged behind, & when he arrived here was quite nonplussed. We heard him bawling away in the rear, & Macaulay, Milton & I went back to look for him. We found him leading his horse & in a great fright; lost the road. Telling him that he would be left or lost if he did not take care not to lag behind again, or perhaps devoured by a grisly, we helped him on his horse again. I never saw such an old woman in my life, or such a nuisance. He had changed his sore-backed horse for a very fat little chestnut stallion, who was uncommonly lazy, & coming up one of the hills lay down with O'Byrne. "Poor fellow," said he, "quite fatigued with my weight!" He only wanted a thick stick, but O'Byrne was much too frightned to lick him. Went on after dinner to a nice still place in the river. To make a raft tomorrow. Yankees crossed here leaving names on a tree. Macaulay stayed the night with us. About 15 miles from Fort, 300 perhaps from Edmonton. Calculated by Yankee party, 360 miles from Edmonton to Tête Jaune Cache.[44] I believe at least 400.

Sunday, July 5th.—Men cut wood & made raft during the morning; there were some very large pines, & we had all to help to carry them & work very hard too. As usual O'Byrne waited until he thought everything was done, & then came up with his, "Oh Doctor, can I be of any use?" I said, "You are a *great deal* too late, Mr. O'Byrne," very sternly, & he slunk away. As we were putting the raft together Assiniboine became greatly enraged at O'Byrne's idleness & swore he should not cross unless he either worked or paid. I said I had excused him, but he took no notice, & I had to speak very shortly to him, at which he was much offended. Always a quarrel with men about this old fellow. Before we set out, we got Macaulay to give O'Byrne a good talking to about his idleness & interference in the management of affairs; and it produced good effect, for he was very diligent in loading the raft. (It should have been mentioned in the account of the day before yesterday that I had on my own responsibility & greatly against Milton's inclination engaged an old interpreter[45] here as guide to Tête Jaune Cache, giving a horse, for his trouble, only one of the little pack animals we bought of the Indians for rum. But Milton thought the man was exorbitant

Crossing the Athabasca River. In the Rocky Mountains.

& very angry with me for my obstinacy. But I had no confidence in Assiniboine & was glad to get hold of a man who bore a good character like this fellow. I should not have cared had I had one able-bodied man with me but to be left alone with Milton & O'Byrne to haul to Cariboo,[46] would be too great an undertaking). We finished the rum here at which treat the men were much pleased, Milton giving the barrel to Macaulay, I gave him my telescopic cap & he was gratified. We crossed famously on our raft, landing exactly where the Yankees did, on the 16th June. Horses driven across first. Loaded & off at once for a few miles before sundown. Assiniboine's horse (roan) very lame; afraid in the shoulder.

Monday, July 6th.—Quite a change come over O'Byrne's conduct in consequence of Macaulay's talking; very active in giving every help he could & not interfering or ordering at all; so far so good. He finished all his provisions yesterday & was obliged to ask me for something to breakfast on in the morning. Poor devil! I gave him a good lump of pemmican & hope he will use it carefully, or we shall be short. I told him before we left Edmonton that this would be the case but "30 lbs were enough for him, he was quite sure he could not eat more than ½ lb per day." He has actually eaten 40 lbs before we are half way, besides contributions of bread, fresh meat, &c., from every meal of ours. We reached the "Petite Maison" or old fort for dinner. *I presume it is the site of the former Jasper's House.* Much more prettily situated, on a little prairie, backed by fine hills, which in this case are green nearly to the top, & covered by scattered spruce. We are still in the Athabaska valley & going South, but turn west before night & follow the River Myette, a small but deep stream. And an awful journey we had on account of fallen timber & rocks; the worst road I ever saw; like walking amongst game of spillikins. We had to have the two men ahead with the axe & often jump our horses over the fallen trees. This was too much for O'Byrne who dismounted & led his horse. Camped amongst fallen timber on banks of Myette. O'Byrne told me story of missionary preaching about crucifixion. Indians delighted & wished him to give diagram showing how it was done. Missionary fled in terror.

Tuesday, July 7th.—Showery weather; tried the Myette for trout last night but no success. After a short piece of awful road crossed the Amiette (or Myette) by a raft & dined whilst the men were constructing it. The road we had come was the worst we had yet had, awful fallen timber; the two men with axes ahead of us all the time; frequently had to leap the horses over fallen timber, lots of rocky ground; up a narrow defile between high hills resembling Yorkshire, but sometimes covered with pine. Crossed the Myette & its branches 6 times in the course of the afternoon; the last very difficult, tremendous fall, immense rocks, something like the wharf just below the Strid. O'Byrne was pretty much frightened, & his face grew very long. I could hardly help laughing, as he followed me closely as I told him; no accident whatever; then on until just dark, when we found a camping place, all the rest of the road being through sand & stones. To cross the river finally by raft to-morrow. Whole country seems to be burnt, & we shall probably have same difficulties with fallen timber for some time. Very irritating work driving horses, will fork out of the path. Can't ride after them on account of timber, dismount, whack them & chivy them back, they rushing & leaping & crashing about, I expecting they must break their legs; the lame horse still follows us of his own accord.

Wednesday, July 8th.—Fine bright morning, but a heavy shower came on before we had got under way & delayed us a little; continued showery until afternoon when it finally cleared up & was a beautiful evening. Yesterday my horse fell 3 times, & Milton's twice, & he rolled off once. I had no fall. Coming again through marsh & willows along the banks to the rafting place, we found the Yankees ahead had left their raft attached to the other side. Young one stripped to his shirt & wanted Milton to accompany him which he declined. And he mounted his yellow horse & whipped him into the stream; the horse crossed well, but the landing place being steep he could not get up & fairly turned round & swam back, in spite of the efforts of the young one who now began to get in a funk, especially when the horse reared in the water, & they came back without having effected their object of taking a rope across to the raft. We then drove all the horses across except the O'Byrne's, & the Assiniboine attaching a rope to his tail, & holding on to the mane easily succeeded in gaining the raft; but the horse going ahead, pulled his tail loose from the rope, & the Assiniboine just missed gripping it as it went back into the river. This caused him to forget to remove the O'Byrne's bridle whereby it was lost by the horse. Now how was the rope to be crossed? I proposed to throw it, but they pitched it round Papillon who quickly swam across with it to his master. During the afternoon we crossed rough ground along the side of hills, & frequently obstructed with timber. Fine hills around covered with pine nearly to the top, with high hills beyond covered with snow. One resembling top of Norman Church tower. Nearer ones in valley of Myette strongly reminding us of the Vale of Todmorden. I had a nasty fall, chivying one of the pack-horses amongst the fallen timber. I put my horse at a fallen tree, & giving a tremendous buck-jump on one side, the saddle turned & I fell on my back against a fallen tree, bruising myself no little; gun strange to say unhurt. Camped for night in beautiful feeding ground close to Pipestone River, a source of Myette. Found many wild flowers in this open ground.

Thursday, July 9th.—Made a long morning, camping for dinner at the head of Buffalo Dung Lake. Road pretty good all the way. I drove one horse & followed after the guide, & we lost sight of all the rest. My horse had a fall, but picked himself up again. Found the buckle holes of girth broke yesterday, which accounts for my fall. After we had arrived about ½ an hour, Milton was heard shouting in the distance & presently came up in an awful passion with me & the guide for getting so far ahead. I told him I had one horse & that the worst, & he had continually led me after him into the wood to bring him back into the road, & I thought that the others might manage one apiece as well as myself. It turned out that the little grey had been left behind at one of the little rivers & the young one & father had both gone back to find him, leaving all the horses to Milton & the woman. Our guide told us this lake was a great fishing place for the Shushwaps, & there were plenty of trout. We therefore stopped early & camped for the night at an open place near burnt ground. (We had in the morning passed the height of land & the little streams now flowed to the westward, but we had ascended so gradually from Jasper's House that it was not perceptible). Here 2 constructed a raft, & put out a long line into the lakes with many hooks, whilst Milton & I tried the spinner & fly from the raft, & the others fished from the bank; but it was no use; no trout to be had; great disappointment. Assiniboine & wife in great rage with O'Byrne who had a horse in front of him in the morning & quietly let him hide himself in the bushes, without attempting to fetch him out, or telling any one; & the wife had to go back & seek him. Beautiful weather.

Friday, July 10th.—A glorious morning. Milton chose a fine hill to the left as his mountain, & I a still higher to the right.[46a] His cone-like & terraced, mine a long range of very rugged rocks, very high & snow-clad with green slopes, & bright pines half way up. Very fine indeed; seen better after leaving Buffalo Lake & striking the Fraser which we did this morning. During our matutinal march we went ahead, the road being pretty good, except here & there a bog, or obstructed by fallen trees. Whilst we were going on, O'Byrne as usual quite behind, I heard a great bawling & went back; found O'Byrne leading his horse very disconsolate, & with an awful long face; his horse had shied at a Shushwap tent of bark, & he had fallen over his head; he was very frightened, but not hurt. I adjured him very strongly to keep up to the party; but he would not whip up & come along. I told him he would be lost or eaten by bears if he lagged behind so. We stayed to dine in thick wood. After dinner we had an awful experience of muskegs, overflowing streams, marshes, &c., & did not reach Moose lake as we had hoped, being compelled to camp for night in a muskeg. The worst road & hardest work, as well as longest day we ever had, track frequently under water, & the little rivers we had to cross up to the horses bellies. O'Byrne almost distracted with his horse. He still lagged behind, & I again heard an awful shouting in the rear. I again went back, & found him leading his horse which had the saddle under his belly, & in his shirt sleeves & with a more lugubrious face than ever. It appeared that his horse had fallen in a bog & rolled on to him, & he thought he was killed; therefore holloa'd for me. In pulling himself from under tore his coat into two pieces. He seemed shaken & horribly frightened, & said he had the narrowest possible escape of being killed; it was a most awful journey; I gave him another lecture about lagging behind, & we followed the rest at a better pace. We caught them up where they had diverged from the track, & were waiting in the wood whilst the two men sought out a better road, the track being in too deep water. Having found it, O'Byrne took on himself to lead the way; next the guide, & in a few minutes of course neglected to keep him in sight; horses all got wrong, & a pretty bother we had to get them right in thick wood & no path. I was very angry with O'Byrne, blew him up & sent him to the rear. Again muskeg, water, mire, marsh, in the low ground next the Fraser, & we had some two hours more of it before we camped. O'Byrne keeping now close behind but on foot, driving his horse before him thro' everything, because he was too frightened to keep him at a jog trot! Everybody was tired & glad to camp, & we had a feast of bread & vegetable soup, this being the hardest day we have had, & during the afternoon the worst road. Memorable 10th. of July! O'Byrne says he shall never forget the horrors of it as long as he lives & I believe him. Milton & I could not help laughing at him as he dilated on the fearful perils we had gone through. Mountains high with rugged tops on each side, Fraser valley, half way down, thickly clothed with pine, & the valley a muskeg with thick pines. Only accidents to Milton & self, were Milton fairly dragged on to the tail of his horse passing thro' thick bushes, but he held on & scrambled on again like a monkey without stopping; my horse taking a tremendous buck-jump over small fallen tree, rammed my head into a great dry pine branch & scratched my face handsomely, & the Savage kicked me tremendously over the shins whilst flogging him up; not hurt.

Saturday, July 11th.—A glorious morning again. Detained a long time searching for Bucephalus, who was eventually found on the other side the Fraser, the Assiniboine having to swim over to fetch him. Our experience was as bad or worse than yesterday. Water overflowing everywhere, & one marsh the horses only just helped swimming; all the bags got well soaked, but we found no place to stop. We crossed Moose river by fording; stream strong & deep in some places, but our man found a good passage, the water however streaming over our horses' shoulders as we faced the stream; O'Byrne as usual being in a horrible fright, nearly got into difficulties; not guiding his horse carefully in the line shown by the guide, he was very nearly carried off his legs, but O'Byrne fortunately stuck on, with most desperate resolution, & the horse got into shallower water again. His face as usual was never to be forgotten. "Hair breadth escape, doctor," &c., &c. After this we emerged on to the shores of Moose Lake, apparently some 14 or 15 miles long, & very handsome, a sort of cross between Wast water & Ulleswater, the hills enclosing it on each side being very lofty & rising as it were directly out of the lake, covered with dense pine nearly to the summit, with here & there brilliant green patches of willows or grass, & streaked with numerous rivulets & waterfalls one of which on the opposite

side seemed to be very fine indeed. The road now lay along
the edge of the lake; as it was strewed with collections of drift-
wood, we were frequently obliged to go out into the water &
some times ascend the steep cliff above us to pass; we were
obliged each to lead a pack horse, they having a great liking
for going out & having a swim in the lake, to the great det-
riment of supplies. In trying to get up the mountain side
beset with loose stones & fallen timber, the Savage missed footing & rolled a complete somersault; I thought he must be killed,
but he brought up somehow & right side up & tried it again.
Another tumble & at it again which succeeded; neither he nor
his pack were at all injured tho' he rolled down an awful place.
And yesterday the little grey tumbled thro' a Yankee bridge
into a deep stream, came up & out all right although he hung
some time with his hind-legs in the bridge & his head down in
the water. Gisquakarn fell down the hillside 3 times, & they
were obliged to unpack him & carry his load to the top. This
delayed us some time, & we re-assembled on a little open knoll,
wishful to stop for dinner; but there was nothing for the horses,
& our guide told us we must press on to the other end of the
lake, the only place where there was any pasturage; we therefore got under way again, & in the water & out again, up sides
of hills, over drift wood as before until sundown, when the
guide pulled up; we could not reach the end of the lake that
night, & the horses were compelled to fast or eat branches &
pickings amongst the rocks. Milton rode thro' most of the
difficult ascents & descents —but at last confessed this beat
hunting in Ireland, & dismounted, his saddle always slipping
loose. All the rest on foot; when we got in we looked at our
provisions & found ½ the pemmican soaked, but fortunately
only a small quantity of flour. But all my "petit train" was
wet through, & we had to have a general drying. Fortunately
only ½ lb of powder wet. Hardisty when he crossed had all
pemmican putrid, threw it away & starved utterly for 5 days.

Sunday, July 12th.—Drying things. Beautiful bright morning, sunlight & mist on the snow-topped mountains very lovely.
Start to find pasturage for horses, which we did soon after
noon in a fine open place close to the banks of the river below
the lake. The poor things fell to furiously for they had had
next to nothing for two days & presented a very nipped-up,
hollow-flanked appearance. We resolved to rest here for the
remainder of the day to finish drying our things, & on account
of horses. On careful investigation we discovered that more

than half the pemmican was soaked, all my shirts & property of every kind wet through; Milton's in his big leather bag escaped. The flour was very slightly injured. Everything was spread out in the grass & bushes in the sun which was tremendously hot, & completely melted one side of a roll of gutta-percha which I carried for splints; the pemmican we partly dried by heating in the pots & frying pans. But I am afraid it will not keep. O'Byrne very much distressed with his horse; saddle would come round, &c. Holloa'd tremendously when left a little behind but, no one now regarding, he found the road without assistance, appearing at the end bearing his saddle, cloth, & blanket, & he said he had come to the conclusion that he was much happier walking, & he would lend us his horse to pack if we would only give him a lift crossing the rivers. Part of our road today was awful, thro' thick wood (out of the regular track which was in the water) & pushing thro' bushes past & over fallen trees, very rotten boggy ground. Gisquakarn fell twice with me, & my horse carrying the flour twice also; Milton & the rest no misfortune.

Monday, July 13th.—Another bright hot morning, turning out one of the most sultry days we have had, & very hard work we had to do. Milton, I & O'Byrne get left behind with 2 horses, & the timber was very large & frequently 2 or 3 great trees lying on one another across the road; this fatigued the horses dreadfully, their mode of progression being merely a succession of jumps, their loads heavy, & the weather oppressive. At last the horses would not go ahead at all, & did nothing but fork out of the road & try & hide in the thick wood. And as the road was so obstructed, frequently impassable, we had to make long circuits to avoid the obstacles & great difficulty in bringing the horses back to the path again. Some of them under the pressure of repeated blows of the stick took some extraordinary leaps, & placed themselves in most awkward situations, sometimes with fore-legs over a tree over which they could not get their hind ones; now jammed fast between two trees too close together to allow the packs to pass; or trying to pass under a tree arched over the path too low for the pack-saddle. Milton got quite wild & savage, O'Byrne very confused. All 3 perspiring at every pore & quarrelling dreadfully. At last I caught the horses, led the worst myself, & gave other to O'Byrne, & thus we arrived at the camping place for dinner very much out of temper, Milton being very aggravating by abusing the guide for not stopping sooner, whereas he had pulled up at the only place where there was any feeding for the horses. After dinner I went on foot & took a horse. The others would lag behind & I heard Milton storming & raging at his horse & continually crying out for us to stop. We got tired of this (I & the guides) & went on, presently Milton came up in a furious passion, having left his horse because we would not wait. I sent the guide back for another for me to drive & took 2 for the rest of the day; Milton too sulky to do anything. Just before sunset we came to a precipice with a narrow path along the side, & a sheer descent into the Fraser 100 feet below. We all pulled up & the guide led his horse across.

We waited intelligence of the state of the path, & he returned to say that a large rock had slipped down, probably since the Yankee party passed, & overhung the road in such a manner as to render it impossible for a pack-horse to pass without the almost certainty that the pack would catch & probably hurl the horse from the narrow footing into the river below. The American party last year had lost a horse & all contained in the pack, viz. guns, ammunition & flour, by an accident of the kind at this very place. Assiniboine, the guide, & I therefore set to work with pine poles for levers, & after some ¼ hour's work loosened the rock & hurled it down with mighty bounds & crashes into the stream below. We then led the horses across singly, & without mishap; the path was about a foot broad, of hard rock covered in most places with loose slate. This so delayed us that it was quite dark & we had not found any place to camp where there was feeding ground for the horses & were compelled to pull up amongst big pines & willows; ground covered with moss & nothing on earth for the horses. It turned out that we had stopped not more than ¼ mile short of a beautiful little open place with nice grass. We had come to no other place with any food whatever the whole of the afternoon, the country being entirely hilly & nothing but rocks & moss. But Milton chose to kick up a bobbery about not stopping sooner, & blamed the guide &c. Some angry words passed between us about it. We had been descending rapidly all day. The Fraser is here a rapid stream boiling over rocks at a great pace. The scene where we passed the precipice was very fine. I try to give a faint idea of it.

Tuesday, July 14th.—We started early, & in an hour arrived at the Grand Fork of the Fraser; here we unpacked the horses to feed a little, whilst the guide & Assiniboine went to explore the passage of the numerous streams, or perhaps mouths of the same, which spread out over a large open space covered with a little grass & a few willows. In about ½ an hour we again started & crossed some 5 or 6 streams, very rapid & swollen. but not more than up to the horses' bellies. O'Byrne in a great funk. One of the horses took it into his head to swim down the main Fraser & soak our pemmican again. I thought he would be drowned, but he came safely under the bank, & we hauled him out with a rope. Another carrying the flour walked into a deep place out of the road & soaked that also. We had an awful bother with them & were very glad to be past all the water. This Grand Fork is the original 'Tête Jaune Cache' & is certainly the finest scene I have ever viewed. To the right Robson Peak, a magnificent mountain, high, rugged, covered with deep snow, the top now clearly seen, although generally covered with clouds. Ranges of other mountains & pine-clad hills run along the Fraser on each side, & in the blue haze were quite fairy-like. The road followed the Fraser pretty closely. We were again delayed by numerous streams to be crossed & which seemed rather deep; they were a long time discovering the path. but at last we got over without accident. The last channel being a tremendously strong stream, & though not more than a yard deep, our horses had all they could do to breast it. O'Byrne horribly afraid, let go the horse he was leading, & Assiniboine nearly carried off going after him on foot. After this we got into higher ground & continued thro' thick wood, bogs & fallen timber, until suddenly arrested by Milton in a great passion, & we camped where there was only a little equisetum for the horses & wanting 4 or 5 hours to sundown. He began abusing me, & the guide for going on & we had a grand quarrel. It had been brewing for several days, & its first origin was that Milton had neither the patience, activity or constant attention necessary to drive horses in the woods. I got on famously & had mine always close at the heels of the guide, whilst he was always in difficulties & calling out for the rest to stop. I bullied him tremendously about this & recommended him not to drive any more, taking two myself, he having left his to his fate in a great temper. This day before yesterday, & similarly again yesterday morning. I certainly was greatly to blame in pushing the matter so far, & saying the severe things I did; but if driving horses was aggravating to him, so it was to me. Whenever I was near I ran and helped him out of all his difficulties, but I got tired of pulling up every 5 minutes when he shouted for me. Being thoroughly out of temper at all this, he took occasion to find all possible fault with the guide, who, poor man, had done his best throughout, & had not so far made a mistake, having been driven to camp in bad places twice only because we did not travel fast enough to reach good ones. Before this he had not attempted to even ascertain what we were going to do for the day, leaving it to me to make all inquiries & not even asking me, I gratuitously imparting the information. For 2 days I succeeded in persuading him not to interfere with the guide, who by the usage of this country is always captain of camps, & startings &c, & escaped pulling up in a wretched marsh when there was a beautiful camp not ¼ mile ahead. Yesterday however, although leaving the place where we rested in the morning with the full understanding that we should try & reach the Cache that night, which the guide said he thought we could easily, he, getting in a rage driving his horse, left him, & pulled us up in this miserable place, without anything for the horses to eat, & nothing having arisen in the meantime to cause any alteration, except that he got out of temper because he could not keep his horse up to the guide & myself; & I had two horses to drive. He abused the guide & me for passing places fit to camp in when there were not any such, &c. &c. We had both so completely lost temper that I would not stop to quarrel & walked off. And after a couple of hours, both having cooled down, we talked the matter over pretty calmly. I apologised for my hard words about the horses, but told him he was quite wrong about the guide & from being in a passion with me had unjustly used the man; but he would not allow this altho' perfectly true & declared he would do just the same again. I therefore said at once that I would have nothing more to do with the management of affairs under those circumstances, & he could not expect that I would if after everything being always left to me to look after & everything prospering, he only interfered to set all wrong. And we went to bed with the matter unadjusted, Milton giving orders that we should not start early because he wished to write his journal, & dry some 'bois gris'! And this with horses starving & good feed near! Yet he declared that the reason he pulled up was because he wished to save them!

Wednesday, July 15th.—A day to be remembered during the rest of my life, as eventful & crowded with misfortune. In the morning both Milton & I were very sulky & would hardly speak to one another, & the Assiniboine said he & family would leave us at the Cache if Milton was so discontented, &

he then said it was very hard I would not help him with the men. I said I would do all I could to keep matters straight, but *would not* have anything more to do with the management if he did not agree to not interfere with the guide again in that way he had done the day before. But he would not, & so we started, I leading the grey, who carried the flour. *The boy following close behind with my horse & Gisquakarn who carried all the personal property we possessed.* Milton of course lagged behind & got into difficulties with his horse. And to make matters worse the saddle turned with him & shot him head first into a pool of muddy water rather deep, out of which he was hauled by O'Byrne; & he came up where we had stopped, close to the river in a worse temper than ever. The reason of our stoppage was this. I had been leading my horse (the little grey), but the river having overflowed so much I pulled up to get on. The saddle which was not girthed up turned, & I tumbled over on the other side on to my head; this stopped the young one & the two horses he was driving, and Gisquakarn, rightly so named (the fool), wandered off into the water, & the more the boy tried to arrest him, the more determined was he to go on, & at last plunged into the stream & was carried down at a great pace. Bucephalus followed his companion, & in spite of all the boy's efforts he too plunged in & was carried off. I could not ride to help for my saddle was turned, & before I could put it to rights, it was too late. The boy & guide started off in pursuit, & I waited for the rest of the party to come up, & then Milton pitched into me again & we had another set-to. I had the best of the game this time, for the boy had followed me close with 2 horses. We followed on again with Assiniboine as guide, & Milton, self & woman driving. I told Milton the horses had gone into the river & were probably both lost, the men discontented, & the best thing & wisest for us to do was to give up quarrelling & wipe out all that had passed, and do our best to work together or we should be left in a most unpleasant fix. He seemed to see this & we had no more words about it. Boy & guide presently came back with the intelligence *that the 2 horses had gone a long way down stream, & we went a good mile before we saw them* on a tiny bare sand bank in the middle of the stream. We passed in a small open space close to the edge of the river & the horses seeing us began to neigh & presently Bucephalus started off & made for this bank, Gisquakarn who followed however keeping straight down stream, & my horse seeing him, when nearly at our bank turned & followed after;

The Assiniboine Rescues Bucephalus.

& away they went down stream at 10 miles an hour; both men & the boy hurried off, & Milton & I followed; but viewing one of the horses going down still in the middle of the current, a good mile ahead, we gave up & went back to the horses & taking them on a few hundred yards camped in beautiful ground, like a garden with white & purple vetch, red Lychnis, &c; & waited the return of the men.

The guide appeared first & said he had seen no more than we had, & then set out again, and about 3 o'clock all returned bringing the brown with them. It appeared that both horses had again landed on the other side and again started; hearing the boy's horse neigh, the brown again attempting to reach this side, but the other continuing straight down stream he followed & they got into a tremendous rapid, my horse pulling up in the stream 8 or 10 yards from the side, the other passing straight on. The Assiniboine rushed into the frightful current, just reached the horse; carried off his legs & under the belly of the horse, but clung to him desperately & succeeded in bringing him to shallow water by the side; but the horse was too exhausted to come out until the Assiniboine had pitched off the bags into the water; they were of course a tremendous weight now. He spread the things on the bank & left them, & when he reached the top of the river bank, he saw Gisquakarn close to the opposite bank, standing up to the girth in water with his head in the bushes. After the man had refreshed, Milton & I went down with him to see our things, & arrange them, & viewed Gisquakarn still there. The Iroquois hastening on to the Cache to send up the Indians there with canoe to rescue the horse. It was nearly dark when we reached camp again, some 2 miles, the horse still there when we left, unable to mount the steep bank. We were much astonished with the bravery of the Assiniboine in facing such a current & rocks as he did, & we promised him £5 on the spot. Went to bed, I in better spirits at recovering my horse & some of my effects, Milton rather down at the probable loss of his. Even of the things we had got back most were spoilt, & medicine chests soaked. Milton's completely spoilt & mine not much better, but medicines little injured. Trousers, shirts, socks, pistols (Milton's revolver & box), ½ lb of powder spoilt, wads &c; & it seemed likely to set in wet again.

Thursday, July 16th.—Very heavy showers all morning & rivière visibly rising. We wait anxiously for return of guide & Indians & he arrived with two. They had been unable to ascend the rapids with the canoe, had come on foot, & observed that the horse was not there. They told us the news that the last party of miners, 5 who went down Fraser from here in 2 canoes, had been all drowned. They had found the bodies & canoes not very far down last spring. Poor fellows! They further told us that Hutchinson's party which we had followed so closely after they gave up the McLeod & resolved to cross to Cariboo, had only left the Cache the day before yesterday! having rested here 9 days. They had bought 2 canoes with their horses & taken two Shushwaps with them as far as below the Grand Rapid. When they arrived here they had only a tiny piece of pemmican, no trousers, only their shirt, no shoes; they killed their two oxen here & dried the meat. We induced one of the Indians to cross the river on a small raft & search for the horse; he returned at dusk, said that he had seen the place where the horse was, that he had tried to get up the bank & failed, & after that he had turned in to the stream once more, and as there were nothing but high banks, rock & rapid below there could not be much doubt that he had perished. A great loss to all, even O'Byrne; for he carried Milton's great leather bag with best suit, great coat, all moccasins, silk handkerchiefs, shirts & socks, besides, worst of all, his letters & papers, including cheque book & passport. May make serious difficulties for us, the loss of these papers. I have lost sextant, all powder & caps, revolver, cash box containing all matches, watch, ring, breast-pin, all keepsakes, papers & letters, some tea & all my tobacco. Hardest lines of all, my botanical collection utterly rotten & spoilt, Milton also lost his smoke, Aimen mitorni! this O'Byrne remarked very characteristically that that was a great misfortune, for he was out, & meant to have begged some that day! just as he remarked when thro' his carelessness my boot was lost (one which I had lent him to wear). Oh dear! I would not have taken £5 for that boot. No allusion to my loss! —O'Byrne lost his letters of introduction to the Governor and the Bishop, and his tea-kettle, but as the tea is nearly finished that don't matter. Very hard lines, no tea or tobacco. Wet all day; heavy showers.

Friday, July 17th.— Milton & I have pretty nearly ascertained our respective losses. He is reduced to 6 plugs tobacco, one pair of very dirty & holey canvas trousers, 1 pair moccasins worn out, no boots, no coat, only leather shirt. Loss including horse estimated at £45. Mine estimated at £30. Watch, ring, sextant &c. mounting up. Yet Milton & I had a good laugh over it, & I think it has at least restored good feeling amongst us all. During morning we moved on to real Cache de Tête Jaune, a half day's journey. Assiniboine & son looking along river for the horse in vain. I had a great row with O'Byrne; he was behind with the woman who was driving the little black horse. We had just crossed a bad swamp when he came running up to me & said, "Doctor, Doctor, you had better go back. I hear the woman calling out." I said: "What's the matter?" "Oh," he said, "I expect the horse has stuck in the bog." I said, "Why on earth did you not stop & help her?" "Oh," said he, "I ran away as fast as I could, afraid of losing you." I said, "You miserable old woman, to leave another in such a fix," & running back I found the black down & fast enough in the quagmire, the woman having taken off the packs & trying to whack him into sufficient exertion to get out again. I set to work & helped her but, had not Assiniboine fortunately just come up in the nick of time, & it was all the 3 could do to haul him out. I walked back & found others already camped at the present Tête Jaune Cache. I blew up O'Byrne handsomely for leaving the woman in the lurch, & told him he would have to cry out a long time before any one came to help him now. He denied that the horse was fast when he passed, but the woman assured me it was so, & I believe her. He is the fellow who always cries out for help & needs it most from others, yet he is never ready to offer assistance & escapes giving it if possible. We have hardly spoken since. I think he richly deserved the lecture I gave him. The Fraser here is very rapid & rocky for the whole day's journey; now very swollen; the Cache is just above the Grand fork of the Fraser & a small open space of a few acres of burnt ground on each side the river. We saw the smoke of the Shushwaps back slant on the other side & hope to cross there to-morrow. Dried things during the evening. We are supposed now to be on the other side the mountains, but we see nothing but their snowy tops on every side still.

Saturday, July 18th.—The two Shushwaps transported all our baggage to the other side & ourselves also in a small dug-out which would barely carry 3 people, and it was rather exciting work rushing down the rapid & over the waves; I was afraid O'Byrne would upset, but he came across very well, loosening his cravat in case he upset! — We bought a great lot of wild pears, about the size of bilberrys, but rather lighter colour, growing on a small bush 1, 2 or 3 feet high; very good, & growing in enormous quantities here. They would have brought any amount for needles & thread, but we were obliged to stop the sale. An old woman made us a map of our road to Kamloops. No guide to be got, the two old men having gone with Yankees. Young ones know nothing. Total here 2 old men & wives, & 2 young men & do., several children. Women clothed in marmot-robes. Men in capotes & moose-skin breeches. Kids nearly naked. Live on the wild goats & marmots. Milton bought two marmot-robes, and I gave Harry's old brown blanket and an old flannel shirt for another. Milton also purchased some roots of a kind of lily which they eat; quite spoilt our rubaboo; very bitter; Milton of course swore it was delicious.

To remember to write to Dr. Hector for Louis Caropontier, Iroquois half-breed at Fort Jasper House, that he has given in charge to Mr. Christie, Edmonton, but received no acknowledgment, viz. 2 marmots (pair), 1 pair large mountain squirrel, 1 pair of "gros suisse", 1 pair small mountain rabbit, 1 pair white mountain partridge, 1 pair of pied mountain ducks, ready stuffed.

Sunday, July 19th.—Prepared for an early start, but heavy rain set in, & we went to bed again. The rain continued with slight intermissions all day & we were unable to move away, much to my disappointment. We went in the evening & ate wild pears. One of Shushwaps will come with us for a day if we give him a shirt. I promise him one of my 3 remaining white shirts. The Shushwap language very odd. Like speaking of idiot who cannot get his words out. Some words same as Cree. All anxious to start again. I sent letter by guide to Macaulay of Jasper's House, detailing our loss in case anything should turn up there by the Indians.

Monday, July 20th.—Up & writing this before the sun; very suspicious looking clouds about; hope rain will keep off. Our road follows pretty wide valley running nearly N. & S. & nearly at right angles to the gorge thro' which we have come. This valley runs on to Kamloops they tell us. The Iroquois prepares to return to Jasper House & crones over the little grey which he is to have in payment. When we are packing up, O'Byrne's horse is not there with the rest. Iroquois states he brought him up most of the way with one of his horses & could not bring him quite here. And Assiniboine states that he saw him then, & that he is probably close to somewhere, but he will not look for the property of such an idle old fellow as O'Byrne. We thought it was merely a little ill-will on his part towards O'Byrne, & that the horse was really close at hand & did not therefore interfere as it would do O'Byrne good to be frightened, & perhaps make him look after his things a little. Just before we started, the guide went off & shouted adieu from the other side of the river. The boy was then sent off by his father to look again for the horse. And the rest started leaving O'Byrne & his things to await the arrival of the boy with the horse. About ½ mile on we met the young one; no horse. I now began to get very uneasy about the matter, & went back with the youth to assist in the search. And we searched well, asked the Shushwaps; they knew nothing, & what was conclusive of foul play somewhere, had found their band of horses with which the chocolate[47] had associated since we arrived here. I therefore gave up the search, & taking O'Byrne's saddle & blanket he walked on & I followed. Presently descried Milton in the distance, returning from an unsuccessful tour, & further on our Shushwap guide & the young one do. do. We were evidently done somewhere, & Milton & I of course suspected that Mister Assiniboine had cached him intending to pick him up if he returned this way, and were considerably puzzled how to act, for we could not afford to have a complete rupture with Assiniboine & be left to our own resources. But when we catch up to our party the matter begins to leak out. Assiniboine says he has little doubt that the old Iroquois has bagged him, for he had told the boy that as O'Byrne was not content with his bargain, he would take the horse. And if we did not pay him satisfactorily he would bag all ours! And had tried to induce him to persuade his father to leave us here, as we had lost all our property & would not be able to pay him, &c. &c. We therefore concluded that the old fellow had got him, but no doubt with Assiniboine's privity. O'Byrne, as he says, almost heartbroken as he has now lost everything of any value, viz. papers & horse. We make a very good journey; fallen timber small, fine road; level barren sand, with small cypress; dine near a lake; & camp for a night near where the road divides for last time. Americans with A. Cardinal very little further in two days; no rain but dull.

Tuesday, July 21st.—Dull morning. We paid the Shushwap in the red coat who had come thus far as guide, one of my 2 remaining white shirts, & 4 fish-hooks; very good pay for an easy day's work. He returned, & we went forward about a mile to a river in front of us which we had been told we should have

Our Misadventure with the Raft in Crossing Canoe River.

to raft. (Is this the Canoe R?) From the high plain of the valley above we had a steep descent to the valley of the river, which we cut nearly at right angles. The river was high & the stream very strong; we followed it up some little distance before we found a place at all suitable for crossing. We then drove the horses across, & set to work to cut wood for the raft. We had now only the Assiniboine's axe, & I relieved him by an occasional spell at chopping. Then came the carrying to the bank. I took O'Byrne as partner & was hardly able to get along for laughing at him. We took some of the biggest logs, I taking the larger end, & although the weight was really not at all crushing, he literally hardly moved along, giving vent to the most awful groans at every step, & crying out, "steady Doctor" 'steady' &c. I seduced him into carrying another quite as heavy under the pretext it was quite a light one. When he arrived at the bank, he declared that another such effort would kill him. I being tired of my partner took the young one instead, & he tripped along with a load as heavy very easily, O'Byrne dragging slowly & painfully along the ground some little poles to put across the raft. Then another ½ hour to tie the raft which Assiniboine did firmly & strongly, a most fortunate circumstance as it turned out. We saw that we should have to run a long way down as the bank on the other side was beset with drift, & trees overhanging the stream, which was running at a great pace. We had some trouble in all getting on the raft on account of the current, & as soon as the last man got on we were rapidly drifting down, & I commenced pushing out as hard as I could, for which Assiniboine swore at me dreadfully. Away we went down stream at a fearful pace, it appearing certain that we must run foul of a tree overhanging the bank on the side we started from. Very vigorous poling, urged on by the frantic shouts of the Assiniboine, we just succeeded in escaping it; but the current setting in strong for the other side from this point, before we knew it, or could make any real effort to resist it, we were on the far side of the river, straight for a little rapid which we passed over like an arrow, & then to what seemed certain destruction, a large pine closely overhanging the water & through the branches of which the water was rushing & boiling like a mill stream at the wheel. Assiniboine shouted "land with the rope", jumping himself with one up to the shoulders in the stream, & catching a small tree round which he whipped the rope like lightning; but it snapped like a thread, and the other, which I had leaped ashore with as the raft neared the land for an instant before rushing under the pine, was dragged out of my hand in a moment. The raft rushed under the tree, I saw only O'Byrne struggling in the branches, everything & everybody seeming to be swept off like flies, & when I caught a glimpse of the raft on the other side, I saw O'Byrne sailing down-stream as if steering, sitting in the stern quite motionless. All the rest I thought were in the stream drowned or drowning, when I heard a gurgling shout from the tree & saw Milton & the woman clinging to it. I jumped straight from where I was at the tree, caught one of the branches, pulled myself up, & proceeded to give a hand to Milton, having shouted all the time to encourage them. Milton said very nobly "Never mind me, help the woman," & I was going to her first, but observing that she was in a much better position for holding on, viz, lying on her back past the tree with her arms stretched above her head holding to the branches, whilst he was on the upper side of the tree; his body being sucked under the tree, & his hold much more difficult, I gave him a hand, & he soon climbed up beside me; he was very cool & collected. We then got hold of the woman, but here was difficulty. She was further up the tree, where it overhung so high, that we could not haul her up & how to pass her along to shore clear of the branches we did not see. The young one came up & was in a great state of mind, but suggested a rope. Where was the Assiniboine? The boy ran off crying out for his father & a rope, & I then espied Mr. O'Byrne walking on the bank, with a face which betokened perfect imbecility. I shouted to him, "For God's sake try & bring us a rope or the woman will be drowned;" but he only held up his hands in dismay. I shouted at him again, & he sent his neckkerchief by the boy who now came running up. I now saw the Assiniboine on the raft which had brought up lower down, evidently working with all his might to untie a rope. I called to him to be quick with the cord. Milton held up the woman's head with O'Byrne's handkerchief, & I held her firmly by her girdle & arm; & we had her firmly enough. After what seemed an age, though really very quickly I suppose, Assiniboine came up with the cord, & with his assistance we soon landed the woman all safe, though fearfully numb & cold, the water being like ice. It seemed that when Assiniboine & I jumped to land with the ropes, young one followed his father, Milton & woman brushed off by tree, O'Byrne though submerged when under tree stuck to the raft & eventually brought up against a tree, with the assistance of Assiniboine who seized the rope & held her. He was in a great rage with O'Byrne. He said that he followed the raft not knowing what had become of the rest, & called O'Byrne to throw him the rope (which he actually held in his hand at the time) as he neared the land. But he only shook his head & cried, "No, no, no," & when at last the ship brought to, he jumped ashore, & ran away as fast as he could, Assiniboine wanting his assistance to secure the raft. O'Byrne told me afterwards that he had no recollection of what passed after the raft went under the tree. We all went down to where the raft brought up & found our provisions safe & dry. Everything safe except Assiniboine's bags & saddle which had floated away, & with them our remnant of tea? Assiniboine & wife absolutely destitute. I lent her & Milton dry things, & gave them a drop of rum. We had very great difficulty in making a fire as rain came on, & we had no matches; very little dry tinder. We had then to dry some of our things, & moved on about 2 miles to camp for the night, O'Byrne being quite miserable until out of hearing of the sound of the river.

Wednesday, July 22nd.—Started late on account of the horses having strayed back to the good feeding by the river; but made a long morning, over very rocky ground along the side of the valley. We had made a long detour to the right to get round the hill we had observed, apparently blocking up the valley down which we had come.

We were obliged to camp for dinner on the bare rocky side of a hill, in consequence of having lost our frying-pan which Assiniboine & I went back 2 or 3 miles to seek but without success. The day before, I lost my whip, & Milton his tinder bag; & in the river his fire-bag & cap. Now therefore the only flint & steel in the party is Assiniboine's; no matches. Milton has to have the cap he gave me, & I go bareheaded; bread baked in the soup-kettle & on plates, & sichan made in former also!—After dinner lost our road for a short time, & soon after we recovered it, we found such a splendid fording place for the horses by the banks of the little river we had been following, that we resolved to camp there although early. A splendid glacier mountain ahead.

Thursday, July 23rd.—A good start & a long day. A magnificent mountain covered with glaciers appears to shut in the valley before us; we made very great progress towards it to-day & succeeded in reaching a very nice place to camp for the night; during the day we had passed the height of land, &

A View on the North Thompson, Looking Eastward.

come into the watershed of the Thompson, the country being mostly rocky & burnt. Tracks of bears very numerous. Afternoon thick pines of enormous size, oasis in word, little stream & marshy ground. Here Milton & I made Kinnikinick, our tobacco being nearly finished. O'Byrne of course too idle to do the same, but begging some of ours when he found it good. The American party had camped here last year, & left a notice about a black stallion lost. I presume one which André Cardinal had cached. Horses getting very slow & sluggish. Little red nearly finished.

Friday, July 24th.—A long morning thro' dense pine forest, camping in thick wood for dinner; fallen timber & muskegs made it dreadfully severe work for horses. In afternoon we crossed the river. Stream very strong & rather deep, rushing over one's knees as we sat in the saddle. Put the packs high on the top of the saddle & crossed them thus; 2 more small rivers after gaining this side before camping for night in place with only a little grass & equisetum, & intersected with numerous tiny streams, & timber not very close. Saw some enormous timber, some pine, but the largest Tamasquatty Cedar, 2 close together being one $6\frac{1}{2}$ embraces, or about 39 feet round, the other 5 or about 30 feet, & of tremendous height. Ate plentifully of a large kind of bilberry as big as sloes. Bear & beaver tracks everywhere. Country opens out a little ahead.

Saturday, July 25th.—A gloriously bright clear morning. We had many difficulties this morning. First all horses squandered in a muskeg beset with heavy timber & underwood & a dreadful bother to bring them all into the track again. Then stopped by an *arm of river very deep* & we had to unpack the horses & lead them carefully over a half broken-through old beaver dam, carrying their packs across ourselves. After that the grey fell in a little gully full of water & could not get up again; had to cut the ropes which tied the packs & haul him out. Flour a good deal wet. This all wasted so much time that we had only done 2 or 3 miles when we camped at noon. After dinner 2 hours brought us to banks of main Thompson where we were obliged to pull up & camp in order to ascertain where the road now went.

Assiniboine crossed the branch we had been following, but found only old Indian foot track there. The map given us by the old woman does not agree with road followed by the Yankees. For according to her map we ought not to have crossed the branch we had followed until long after its junction with main branch. What is to be done? Resolve to cross main branch, & follow the main river & American road as long as in right direction. At this Camp the Yankees had evidently stayed some time, & we found a notice on a tree to the effect [that] A. Cardinal had returned from here.

Sunday, July 26th.—Sand flies & musquitoes terribly annoying. O'Byrne in great funk at having to raft again & full of advice. No rest today as provisions are running short; Assiniboine goes off to see for place to cross. Find a place on main branch for horses, & at Junction for the raft. Assiniboine has a prejudice against crossing on Sunday, but says he will cut the wood today, & we can cross tomorrow morning. Great approval from O'Byrne who is delighted to have another day's respite from the perils before him. Much discussion during the day as to what course we ought to pursue. Assiniboine has completely investigated the other side of the river below junction & no road there. There must therefore be either a road following main river down to Kamloops on right bank, or the Yankee road there turns N. W. & follows up the main branch to Cariboo. Milton for going to Cariboo direct. I advise under present shortness of provisions that it will be wiser to follow the river to Kamloops if we find a practicable road; if not, follow Yankees wherever they go. We observed what is I believe common in these mountain rivers, that the water rises at least a foot at evening, going down rapidly during night & next morning. Effect of sun & frost on mountain tops alternately. I assist Assiniboine to cut logs for raft, very hot work, & in evening we carry some to the river bank; a nice sandy inlet to start from. O'Byrne gave vent to the usual groans & sighs whilst staggering under a small tree. Resolve to husband our provisions, but Milton will make no definite plan.

Monday, July 27th.—Milton's birthday, but a day of work, putting raft together & crossing. Musquitoes & sand flies fearful at night. Glorious weather. Very anxious to get to the other side to see where Yankees have steered; found bullock's bones in their camp here. We drove the horses across without much trouble & then packed our raft & set out on our voyage. We were much favoured by the conditions of the place, for a large tree which had drifted down had stuck in the middle of the river & caused a large eddy there, which we gained easily,

& then poled like mad across the stream beyond into the shallow bank on the far side, landing easily & safely. The moment we neared the shore O'Byrne made a rush for land, but I collared him & made him wait. He said Assiniboine had told him to jump ashore, but I doubt it; & he certainly never showed such activity before. After we had put everything in order & *untied the raft,* & fetched up the horses & dined, it being now about 4 o'clock, Assiniboine proceeded to investigate, & presently came back in great disgust to say that we were on an island! & where the Yankees had gone he could not well make out. We immediately secured 6 logs of the raft which had not yet floated away, & then Assiniboine went off again to investigate, to try & shoot a beaver, of which tracks were very numerous. He came back at dusk quite nonplussed with the Yankees who had evidently landed on this island, gone forward about ¼ mile & then camped; & he could not make out their course afterwards.

In the place we are it is very difficult to find a road; rivers on all sides & sand banks frequently flooded leave no trace. We must have a thorough investigation tomorrow & find out where the Americans went & if there is an Indian trail forward to Kamloops. O'Byrne thunderstruck at being taken in in this way. He fancied all rafting was over; before starting he said he had a strange presentiment of evil. I showed him it was only his own foolish fears & rallied him about it when we were safely over. Thus it is presentiments still hold their own.

Tuesday, July 28th.—Assiniboine off early to search the road & comes back before Milton is up to say that he has found it. The Yankees appear to have been rather at fault. They had recrossed the main branch making the road nearly due west—(towards Cariboo probably). After a short distance of this they had camped evidently for a day, roads leaving & coming in in various directions; but the marked road again crossed the *main branch!* & then followed the main river on the right bank, making now I suppose for the Fort. We had awful work to cut into this road. First, to carry all our baggage over the drift timber collected against an old beaver dam across the fork of the main branch which made the island, thus forming a natural bridge. It was very difficult work in some places, having only a small pine to walk along over the rushing stream, & carrying as I did a heavy weight, viz. the horse-packs containing the flour. O'Byrne was rushing off to get over without carrying anything but I stopped him, and when he got safe over, he would not go back for anything more, until Assiniboine threatened to strike him over the head, when he set off in great haste, & carried 4 lots more! ! After this a good half hour to make the horses cross, who got half way & then stood in a shallow & would not move in spite of sticks, stones & yells till we were quite mad with vexation. Next to carry all the things up a steep precipice along the side of which the road lay, & pack the horses in this narrow path. And when we set out, the road was much beset with fallen timber, & sometimes passing in the river, then low, but now so full that we were obliged to cut a new one alongside of hill. Assiniboine completely done when we camped at night & all tired. Miserable place for horses.

Wednesday, July 29th.—Milton will delay to have moccasins made, although I offered to lend him a pair to enable us to go forward to some feeding for the horses. Much squabbling between us during last few days, & I have now completely resigned all share in management or rather such mismanagement. Assiniboine very much put out, & I myself thoroughly sick of such childish work. Assiniboine sets out first to investigate the road, & comes back after 2 or 3 hours, having been obliged to cut a road up the hill, the Yankee road going into the river. We got off a little before noon & had very heavy work up the hill & over fallen timber. Very severe work for horses. A succession of hills or ranges of hills come down to the river at intervals of a few miles, with very steep descent towards the stream; here also the timber is heavier, & the ground more obstructed by debris. We worked away a long time before finding any place for our cattle; about 2 hours before sundown came to a little swamp with equisetum; return. Here we pulled up to camp for the night; a ¼ mile before, we came upon a great number of trees cut down, a number of pack saddles & harness, &c. It now became quite plain that many of the American party at any rate had become weary of the difficulties of the road, & had made canoes & rafts to go down the river. They had also killed up their oxen & dried the meat, for there was a large "chapeau" for that purpose: (On a tree written Slaughter Camp, Sept. 22nd, 1862 & 4 names) and they had spent some days here, by the beaten ground & tracks about. What had they done with their horses? We were tremendously non-plussed at this event, as the road appeared at an end. But in going forward to find a suitable

The Trail at an End.

Mr. O'B. Triumphantly Crosses the River.

place to "mettre à terre" we came upon a continuation of the road, & were once more at ease. After feeding (it deserves no better name for we have now only pemmican & flour, & neither tea, salt, or grease) O'Byrne, Milton & I walked forward to look at the road; numerous fresh tracks of Cariboo deer. The other two turned back, but I continued on, the road led me through a muskeg to the banks of a small division of the river here making an island with the main stream. Here again were trees cut down, 5 or 6 pack saddles, &c. A hundred yards further, more trees & chips & no road to be found! I came to the disagreeable conclusion that all the party must have embarked, & that we should now have to cut our own road to Kamloops! Pleasant prospect this with such great obstructions & only one little axe. After searching in vain for the road for a considerable time I returned with my evil tidings to camp. O'Byrne awfully knocked over, having calculated on 30 miles tomorrow. Milton indifferent. The rest not much cast down, Assiniboine bravely exhorting us not to be down, for we would get out of the mess. We had many jokes about eating horse, &c. We have provisions for 10 days yet, & in that time ought to be near the Fort & perhaps in open country. All went to sleep in good spirits except O'Byrne; Assiniboine engaging to start at daybreak & view the country, perhaps kill a cariboo.

Thursday, July 30th.—We had very uncomfortable night of it. Sand flies & musquitoes almost prevented sleep, & at dawn heavy rain came on which continued until 10 or 11 o'clock, preventing Assiniboine from starting. After eating he set out, it having cleared up a little, but showers afterwards all day. Soon after we heard a shot, & Papillon[48] in full cry. Hope for bear or Cariboo; but the sound died away in the distance, & no other shot; therefore not much expectation. I writing journal & smoking Kinnikinick. Loss of tobacco felt more than ever now. After 3 or 4 hours hear sound of axe in distance & anxiously awaiting Assiniboine's return; to our delight he appears bearing a black bear over his shoulders, a yearling cub. All set to work to skin & cut him up, & a great feast we had making bread & apoulards. First fresh meat since leaving Jasper's House, but the want of salt an immense drawback. This gives us 2 more days provisions at least & with 1-3 of a pemmican & ¼ bag flour ought to take us into Kamloops which cannot be more than *100 miles off*, and Assiniboine reports that the country appears to be favourable for some distance ahead. Timber very large but standing widely apart & not much fallen. Hills getting lower & lower to the right. Perhaps cut our road without much difficulty.

Friday, July 31st.—Very heavy rain set in at daybreak, & continued till noon when it cleared up & we hope to start shortly; 2 or 3 very loud thunder claps. We got off, but it continued showery all the way, & set in very heavily just before we camped for the night by the river with plenty of "prelle"![49] We had very harassing work keeping horses straight as there is now no track except that made by leading horse, & that not very perceptible, the road being so beset by red-willow, & the great-leaved prickly plant which trails along the ground, pierces one's moccasins & trousers & trips up the horses. The road also bad from fallen timber part of the way at first; after that pretty open.

Saturday, August 1st.—A very hard day of it & very slow progress. Although not stopping for dinner, yet I doubt whether our day's work is more than 6 or 7 miles, & as harassing to the horses as 30 decent road. Fallen timber up & down mountain sides, ground all as rotten as the timber & abounding in bogs, quagmires, & concealed springs. The whole so thickly covered with that infernally prickly trailer (the stems sometimes 2 yards long & an inch diameter, leaves as large as rhubarb leaf & shaped like raspberry, bears spike of dirty reddish green flowers, stems & leaves thickly covered with thorns like the briar) & the red willow that it is impossible to see what is before you when you make your path. Horses very slow & hesitating in consequence not knowing where to put their feet. Sometimes up to the hocks in soft ground, about the roots of trees, which thus makes a little hole to let the hoof in, & they have to struggle tremendously to get loose again, &c., &c. We seem to be passing the last mountain with snow on it to the right; to the left the hills have for some time rapidly lessened in size & become pine clad over the summit. Perhaps this first-named mountain to the right may be one which the old woman (wretched old impostor!) said was not very far from the Fort.[50] I don't expect to reach the Fort for above a week yet. The rest more sanguine. Economise victuals by having only two meals a day. No stoppage in middle of day for dinner. Horses to be beaten all day long. Jump, crash, stumble, rush; tumble; refuse to go on, &c. During day the river opened out into several streams forming three islands. Assiniboine found marks where Yankees had put 3 horses ashore, & probably some one with them, but could not stop to investigate. Frightfully hungry all of us at night, but had only half a bellyful of rubbaboo.[51] Assiniboine almost disabled by thorns in hands & legs; showery day.

Sunday, August 2nd.—Fine bright morning. Assiniboine, getting tired of making road through thorns & underwood, essayed to mount the hill in order to find clearer ground above. But the horses could not do it, it being so steep & embarrassed with fallen timber; one rolled back against a tree & broke his pack-saddle; & here was ½ an hour's delay to get him right. And Assiniboine mounting the hill & finding that although there was less underwood, there were more fallen trees, we turned tail like the King of France & came down again. During the morning I don't think we made more than 3 miles, & stopped for dinner as the horses were very done by their rough work & usage. After this we made another mile, all horses got along with difficulty. I tumbled on to track which Assiniboine supposes to be made by Yankees with horses unshipped from raft. Follows this & camps by marsh. Milton, I, & O'Byrne behind with 4 horses. Grey, after being 3 times prevented, obstinately rushes into a very bad place, a sort of triangle of fallen trees, rolls on his side & is helpless. Remove load & lick him; no use; haul with tail & rope to neck, but no go, & have to get axe & cut wood away before we can release him; another hour's job. Comes on very heavy rain. Milton & I seriously discuss the course to be pursued if horses stuck up. I am for leaving them & walking, but he won't listen to that. Provisions getting very small ⅛ pemmican & ¼ bag flour!

Monday, August 3rd.—Heavy rain in night, bright morning, clouding over after. We have fairly passed big hill. Valley widening rapidly, & hills still lower to the right. Did perhaps three miles before dinner, & 4 or 5 after, camping at night at a long marsh where there was some splendid feeding for the horses. And this being the first time we had been in any open space since crossing the river a week ago, the effect upon me was like coming out of a darkened room into broad sunlight. The gloom of the forest being so great Milton & I, upon my strong representation agreed not to discuss disagreeable subjects, or squabble any more & got on very well during the day. Innumerable bilberries of the two large sizes of which all ate freely. Several patches of raspberries as large as English garden fruit. Large bracken, taller & slenderer than English variety. Fern growing like English male fern but not so good as ours. Beech fern & oak. Big red got foot into hole between two huge trees, & Milton & I had to cut it out. Wearisome work driving 3 horses which won't go in spite of any amount of blows; thorns in our legs & hands; one's feet stabbed; bellies empty; Keyarm. Assiniboine begins to get down-hearted, & I have exhorted Milton to shew more readiness in getting up & off in morning to which he agrees; will he perform? Shot 4 partridges which make a supper for us. On the whole the country has opened out more than usual, & road somewhat better than we have had since commencing cutting our way. Crossed very rapid little stream; O'Byrne traversed as usual[52] Showers during day. All wet through to middle in long underwood.

Tuesday, August 4th.—Dull morning. Milton gets up well. Our procession goes thus: Assiniboine leads with axe; wife follows leading horse with cord; then young one driving 2 horses; then Milton on horseback to give rest lead; then I with 3 horses & on foot; last O'Byrne with little black. First mile through the marsh which we got over very quickly. After that bad road, muskeg, & rocky hill sides; several horses fell badly, & their legs are barked all over, & swelled as if they had the gout, & they are so frightened at every nasty place that it requires tremendous thrashing to get them over. During the morning we came upon an immense quantity of wild raspberries which we stayed half an hour to eat, as large but not as sweet or well-flavoured as English garden ones. We all ate enormously. Bear tracks very numerous. Beaver also. Country changed wonderfully for the better, large valley, last snowy mountain to the right; to the left only one small hill to be seen; a range a long distance away & running East & West across the valley suggests that the fork of the river & Fort may be there. Tremendous rain came on & gave us no choice but to camp & lie snug all afternoon. Very hard to do under our circumstances.

Wednesday, August 5th.—Late start owing to necessary repair of moccasins. Came at once upon mossy ground with very little obstruction, & made 2 or 3 miles at a good pace, a little of old sort before dinner, killed 2 partridges, therefore stopped at midday. After, Assiniboine's hand too painful to

allow him to use the axe! I had to go in front with him for
that purpose. Papillon killed a skunk for supper. During the
afternoon we came upon the hill we had seen yesterday, a small
pine-clad, rounded eminence commanding the valley, but *no
prairie.* Vast woods still before us. Immediately after this
crossed two mouths of a river coming down western valley.
After that pretty unencumbered ground till sunset. Rivers
very rocky & strong current, rather full. Should have thought
it dangerous at one time. Pemmican size of ½ man's head!
Very economical on the whole, but Milton will have bread
which is extravagant. No rain all day. Musquitoes murderous.

Thursday, August 6th.—Dull morning. Early start for us.
I had again to go ahead with the axe; the first part was good,
& we found a path along which horses had passed, perhaps
some of the Yankees; but after some three miles the obstructions
became greater & greater, & the underwood thick. It was
terribly hard work forcing one's way first thro' all this, &
about 2 o'clock I felt rather weak & doubled up, but recovered
rapidly & finished up bravely at night. We had no rest all
day & no refreshment, starting at soon after sunrise & stopping
only after sunset. We camped on a low swampy point, very
densely covered with underwood & had to cut it away to camp.
All this on a little watery rubbaboo. The valley ahead seems
to expand widely a short distance on, & we have some hope
of better country. We should now be very glad to see some
one; pemmican size of fist; flour very little in bottom of sack!
killed 2 partridges which we enjoyed for supper. Discussion
about killing horses very frequent, I wishing to starve a little
first, Milton not intending to hesitate.

Friday, August 7th.—Rather weary on turning out, & Milton
sleeps heavily; hope to do a good day as horses have fed well;
dull & showery morning. Yesterday wet through from head
to foot in bushes. After some little bad road we got into a
large marsh, which quickly opened out, bringing us into a large
valley, the confluence of 5. Here was a grand expanse of
marsh, bog & burnt ground. In the morning Assiniboine saw
a bear but could not get near enough for a shot as he took to
the river. And Papillon chased another which *would* not *tree*
& therefore we never saw him. We found immense quantities
of beautiful bilberries & stopped a short time to dine on them
& gather a few for rubbaboo; only killed one partridge, saw
3 ducks but they went away wild; 5 geese passed at night too

high, very disappointing this when there is only one day's provision in camp & not half rations. Much discussion at our council fire in our camp in the marsh. What are we to do? Milton & O'Byrne vote for stopping here tomorrow to let Assiniboine hunt; & as the bear tracks are exceedingly numerous, perhaps he might succeed. Assiniboine objects on ground that we have already passed thro' & disturbed all the open country, & there was apparently nothing but thick wood before us, where it is almost impossible to see game. Bears are the most uncertain of any game, wandering far in a day. And we are probably now not above 3 or 4 days from the Fort & might get in by husbanding provisions, & shooting partridges, &c. I agree for my part, but explain to Assiniboine that Milton will not be able to get along like the rest on *very* short commons, & he decides to try hunting tomorrow. Milton vowing to kill a horse if he does not succeed in finding game.

Saturday, August 8th.—Assiniboine off early. Young one & I after geese & ducks to a little lake ahead; Milton a good sleep & rest. We see some ducks but cannot get near to have a shot. On returning to camp found Assiniboine already there having been quite unsuccessful in his hunt. Found Milton & O'Byrne gone to look at the dead body of an Indian discovered by Assiniboine in his rambles; it was close to where the young one & I had passed in the morning, not 10 yards off. But the grass was so long that we could not easily see the body. Milton & O'Byrne returned without being able to find the body. In afternoon young one & I & Rover went again to search, & also try & shoot a supper (for we had eaten our last morsel of pemmican to breakfast, a piece the size of the fist in a thin rubbaboo which served 6 persons, & for dinner only a marten in do. which was very disgusting, & made O'Byrne vomit). We easily found it now & investigated. The head was entirely wanting, the rest of the body in a sitting posture, crouching with hands over knees over old fire; the interior of body full of chrysales of maggots; skin dried into parchment over back & shoulders; rest of bones nearly bare; clothes entire, American shirt, knitted drawers, a tiny marmot robe & a bit of old buffalo ditto. Close by lay his axe, his knife & fire bag, a birch basket containing a net, Indian fish-hooks & cedar bark, & another with a few onions which had grown in the basket. Just behind were a number of bones broken into very small pieces evidently to get all nutriment possible out of them, what appeared to be part of the head

The Headless Indian.

(judging from teeth) & ribs of a horse. He had evidently changed camp once, for there was another camp-fire about 10 yards off, at which he had left one of the birch-baskets. The fires were made only with small sticks. The bones & body were extremely small, more like a woman's than a man's. But the dress & 'agreement' (charge of shot, axe, &c) were that of a man. The onions told us that it was spring when he died, as well as the state of decomposition of the body. The broken bones told of probable starvation & want, & the fire of small sticks, of illness & weakness. He had probably killed his horse long ago, & chipped up the bones of his last remnant, or been seized with sudden illness & unable to hunt. There was no gun to be found, but a large 2 gallon American cooking kettle! *And the body had no head.* In vain we searched the grass & bushes around. What could have become of it? We could find no explanation. For any animal that would have eaten the head would have meddled with the rest. Assiniboine suggested he had met with foul play; probably from some Americans, who of course having such a bad name are accused at once if any crime is suspected. But this seems improbable from the quiet crouching posture of the body, & the natural position of the axe, bag, &c. He had probably died naturally from illness & starvation. Soon after we got back Assiniboine & wife returned, the former having again been quite unsuccessful in his hunt. The woman brought a large quantity of bilberries, which we ate for supper, made into a paste with a handful of flour. It was very good but not satisfying. Milton then urged the necessity of killing a horse tomorrow as he was determined not to go on any longer without a good feed, being quite done up with his short commons. Assiniboine voted, & I also, for going on a couple of days to see what might turn up, & the flour would last that time with what we could pick up in the way of partridges, &c. But knowing Milton would never get along in this way, we agreed to sentence the little black horse to die tomorrow morning. Then no one could be found willing to perform the bloody deed. Assiniboine & I said we were not far enough gone in hunger to do the thing, & it being Milton's proposition he ought to execute it. But he would not, & we went to bed with the point unsettled. And in rather poor spirits from what we had to do next morning as well as from the effect of the sight of the dead Indian who had been in a very similar but worse position than ourselves in this very place.

TRIP ACROSS CANADA

Sunday, August 9th.—Moved camp in the morning first thing to a place where there was plenty of dry wood, made a rack for drying meat & then executed "Blackie" with a ball behind the ear, & a gash across the throat afterwards. Soon had some meat in the kettle, & tasted it with anxiety. All found it very sweet & good although lean & a little hard, except Milton who swore it tasted strongly of stable, & he could hardly swallow it. I & the rest ate ravenously, & Milton during the day managed to pick a good deal. They were engaged all day in cutting & drying meat. I wrote my journal, ate, went & got raspberries with O'Byrne on a hill near & Kinnickinick. Today O'Byrne declared he was at last tired of Paley, & had begun to doubt some of his propositions, & think with me that he was a special-pleader. He had not missed a day reading hard at him since we left Edmonton. Hope to start again at noon tomorrow. Very hot day, & Milton & I very weak & languid, & feel as if we could not walk ¼ mile, or hardly lift a hand; effect of 10 days' hard work on a little to eat. (Assiniboine shot Blackie after long contention with Milton).

Monday, August 10th.—Assiniboine makes up fire all night & meat all nearly dry at breakfast time. We get off after dinner, having during the morning overhauled harness & bags, &c., & packed our dry meat which looks wonderfully small quantity now & weighs light enough, not more than 30 or 40 lbs, perhaps enough for a week, but shall we get there by that time? We got over 4 or 5 miles, & by dint of keeping away from the river a little, took advantage of several small swamps. Assiniboine's hand being better he & I both went ahead with axes, having thought it no crime to take the dead Indians little axe in our present need. Shot at a duck & two partridges but only got a partridge, the powder having become so weak from damp, it is little use. Camped on bank of river, having apparently a very bad piece before us tomorrow, side of hill coming on very perpendicularly into river. Horses much improved from rest & good food.

Tuesday, August 11th.—Assiniboine away at daybreak to mount the hill ahead & view the road. We were off late in consequence & after 2 miles hard cutting through some of the greatest obstructions we had yet met with, Assiniboine was quite chawed up, & we had to camp for dinner. I presume it took us quite 3½ hours to do this short bit. Very hot indeed.

Last night I set some lines & caught 2 large white trout, 1 some 2 lbs., the other 1 lb. & a small one; very good eating; gave them to Milton who cannot get on with horse. In afternoon did perhaps 3 miles; road nearly as bad as in morning. The river here runs thro' narrowish valley, but hills low & none to be seen a little distance ahead; but plenty of bad road ahead. I'm afraid. Assiniboine very 'démonté' yesterday. Could not understand why we came this pass in preference to the other. Found it strange that we did not bring a proper number of men & horses & do the thing in style if we were "bourgeois" as we said we were, &c., &c. I explained as well as I could.

Wednesday, August 12th.—I got up early & draw my lines; 2 fish, one 2 pounder before sunrise; others turn out then & I hope we shall be off earlier. Assiniboine went forward & cut a piece of the road, whilst the rest of us packed the horses. We were much disappointed in the country as we went along. Instead of opening out as we expected, the hills came nearer & nearer together, ground rocky, covered only with moss & timber & almost destitute of other growths. The current of the river increased, & at last flows through the narrow pass in a rocky bed, between high pine-clad hills as a grand rapid; great rocks in the boiling stream; no raft could live there. To our surprise we observed a road cut on the other side. The Yankees had I presume, given up the raft here & taken to land again, but the ground appears much more difficult than on this side. During the day Papillon treed a great porcupine which Assiniboine shot with a ball. We were able to find nothing for the horses & therefore were unable to stop for dinner, & at night were compelled to camp in bare mossy ground. Poor beasts! they have hardly eaten since leaving the marsh 3 days ago. There being no great obstructions we came on better than usual, & flatter ourselves we may have done 10 miles. Heavy work for horses, so much up & down hill work, having to ascend frequently to avoid the cliffs with sheer descent into river. Feasted on the porcupine at night, & found it delicious, like sucking pig but strongish-flavoured; skin $1/4$ inch thick, & loaded with rich fat. The rapid apparently continues several miles further. I think we have had 3 of it already.

Thursday, August 13th.—Everybody anxious to see what is at the end of the rapid. I prophesy the grand finale & descent on to alluvial plains. All keep spirits up well, though it is disheartening work cutting through thick wood for nearly a month, and I could not help contrasting my luncheon of a scrap of dried horse flesh & water therewith to the many good feeds I have had on the moors on bygone twelfths of August. Again hard work nearly all day up & down acclivities, cutting through timber. The ground is now merely large rocks covered with moss & trees. The difficulties may be imagined by the fact that 3 horses fell amongst rocks & timber in such places & positions that they had to be unpacked, timber cut away, & then hauled out; pack cords cut, &c. We see now nothing before us but the continuation of this rapid thro' its narrow gorge — no other hills or indication of opening out. We went on until dusk, & then coming to a place apparently impassable, viz. an abrupt descent into the river, beset with rocks & timber, we were again obliged to camp without pasturage for the horses, poor things. I hope this will not last long for our sakes as well as theirs.

We have now only provision for 3 days more, & 7 or 8 charges of powder. Dried lean horse-meat goes fast, & is very poor stuff to work on we find — Assiniboine fairly knocked over with the increasing difficulties & discouraging prospects, but works like a man, & the wife too who took my place ahead yesterday & cut away much better than I can. Milton beginning to be rather dismayed, & our only consolation is in talking of what good things we shall get at the Fort when we do arrive there. His health keeps up well, although he says he is weak, as in truth am I & all the rest.

Did not unpack for dinner, eating a little dry meat as we stood, perhaps 6 or 8 miles.

Friday, August 14th.—Assiniboine off early to find a road. Shall we get past this confounded valley today? O'Byrne has now neither pipe nor spectacles, & very fidgety & disconsolate. Assiniboine returns with very evil intelligence of our path. Get off late as he was long away to find out how we could pass. We had to gradually ascend for some distance, leading the horses with cords, the exceedingly steep side of the river bank (or rather mountain) & then pass along a few hundred yards & again descend. When I had got my horse over the worst position, I looked back for O'Byrne, the only one behind me, but he was not in sight, & after waiting some little time I went back to look after him, & he presently hove in sight panting up the hill. "Where is the horse?" said I. "Oh he's dead gone, tumbled down the precipice; he fell headlong &

must be smashed to pieces." "Good heavens," said I "let us go at any rate & look for him," & turned him back with me. The place where he had slipped & fallen over was at the heighth of the ascent & when I saw what a cropper he must have gone I gave him up as killed. The ground is merely loose small rocks, covered with moss, & very treacherous indeed. I descended to the edge of the river & there found Bucephalus on his legs astride of a large tree which lay across a hollow; he had fallen fully a hundred feet, nearly perpendicularly, over huge trees, & finally with a grand plump over a rock some 20 feet high on to the tree. It was the most extraordinary escape possible. O'Byrne & I unpacked him, & rolled him off the tree, & I found a place to lead him round up the ascent again. Then I had to carry the bags up the steep, very killing work, for I felt weak enough; pack him again & off. Leading the grey, I stopped an instant to watch O'Byrne behind, the horse when standing still moved a foot, slipped and away he went rolling down but fortunately was brought up on his back about 10 yards down by two trees. Cords to cut, head & tail to haul at, baggage to carry up, &c., a second time. After this we had no more accidents & soon caught up our party who waited for us. The road after this was pretty good. The river continued to narrow until making a sudden turn between two huge rocks about 60 feet high thro' a narrow opening about 15 yards wide, boiling along thro' this narrow passage some 50 yards. Very like the Strid at Bolton Abbey, a little larger, but then much larger river also. Certain destruction for raft or even canoe I should think. Named by Assiniboine 'La Porte d'Enfer'. We continued on the top of the bank until, coming to a little marsh, we stopped rather early. Rapids still as far as we can see & hills. I fished & caught only one white trout of some 2 lbs. Finding every one downhearted, I discoursed, showing how at the pace we were compelled to travel we could not have come the distance, & by the map the river ran through a valley with mountains on each bank up to the very Fort. This put everybody in better spirits, & it was high time, Milton getting down about it. O'Byrne bears up like a brick & I find he improves on being tried hard. We consumed our last morsel of flour in a rubbaboo of 2 partridges, dried meat, & berries which was a great luxury, & everybody went to bed comparatively happy. Come 4 or 5 miles only. Assiniboine cut his foot badly & can hardly walk.

Saturday, August 15th.—I up at daylight to look at my

fishing lines; no more fish; a long hard day keeping along the top of the range of hills running parallel to the river, finding the timber smaller & obstructions less difficult. Stopped for a few minutes in the middle of the day without unpacking the horses, ate a morsel of uncooked dry meat, smoked a pipe of Kinnikinick, & on again. We kept on until nearly dusk & by that time left the rapid behind us & descended the hill-side on to a flat point covered with willows & fern & a little "prelle". It had been raining slightly all afternoon, & set in hard just as we camped, all getting thoroughly soaked before the lodge was up. The country has now changed its aspect, the hills still large as ever, but valley again wider & river flowing in several channels round numerous islands quietly enough. At night we boiled our last bit dry meat; one fish only provision in camp. Set my lines in the rain. Papillon came in with nose, jaws, & tongue stuck full of porcupine quills; he had killed one somewhere. Milton & I worked away with forceps a long time, but finding it useless to attempt pulling those in his mouth, we gave it up. I suppose he will die, poor devil.

Sunday, August 16th.—Rose late in consequence of wet weather, & no expectation of breakfast. I went disconsolately to look at my lines & found a small trout. To my surprise found the woman cutting up dry meat. She had hid some from us all & we now found the value of it. This with the shakings of the flour bag which had been wet, & which the woman scraped diligently, we made a handsome rubbaboo; but this is really the last except 2 fish; and it must be another horse to-morrow. Yesterday we were cheered by numerous old trees cut down by Indians, & at night some branches cut this spring. Hurrah! — Found one of the fish wouldn't keep, therefore made a second breakfast of the two, & very delicious they were. Just as it began to rain again we started, and an awful time of it we had, in fern as high as our heads, close willows, fallen timber & muskeg. Assiniboine turned very sulky; it certainly was very harassing work, & bitterly cold, all wet to the skin & rain falling heavily. Crossing a little river, a horse fell & was nearly drowned before we could disentangle his feet from matted willows. Poor O'Byrne's things sopping again, & part of Milton's bed; whole place full of water from beaver dam in little river. After about a mile which took us above 1½ hour, being almost numb with cold & wet, & the rain continuing to fall heavily, we pulled up on a little dry spot where there was plenty of prelle & camped, resolving to kill another horse at once in order to save time. The lot fell on Assiniboine's red, he having a very bad back but otherwise in good condition, we to recompense him in some way. Turned out capital meat, much better than the little black. It is astonishing how we all enjoyed a feast on fresh horse after the dry meat. Milton ate it now with avidity. Tried to get to river to set my lines but stopped by water everywhere.

Monday, August 17th.—Rainy morning; refitting in every way & drying meat; trousers all torn & in rags, moccasins, &c., a sorry turn out. We shall go into the Fort nearly naked. A wearisome long day, nothing but eat & smoke, mend things & keep up the fire for drying meat; all this on a wet day, camped on a tiny dry spot in the middle of a muskeg, water all around, dank high fern & red willow; huge pines & cedars overhead. And then one cannot help speculating about the Fort, how far it is, when we shall get there if ever; if there is a road on the other side the river. Whether the Yankees cut the road we saw on the other side the river forward to the Fort, or made fresh rafts after the rapids. Assiniboine resolves to investigate on arriving at a suitable place. This horse-killing is most unprofitable work, delays us two days, & after that we have dry meat for only 5 or 6 more; dreadful. I expect this is not the last business of the kind. Again discuss the question of rafting or walking in the last emergency. I decidedly advocate the latter, having all my love of rafting destroyed by the sight of the fearful rapids we have just passed. Only Milton advocates the raft. He is very irritable & provoking & tries my temper continually. I am dreadfully bored by being compelled to be at a standstill thus for 2 days. I think of home & its comforts, & the eatables & drinkables till we are quite wild with appetite for them. And then we have no tobacco! What would I give for 1 lb shag? & a yard of clay, a quart of beer! But I cannot stand this, I must change my thoughts, & resort to gnawing the shoulder blade of a horse. And horse is really very good meat if one had only something to it, and could get out of this cursed forest; 2½ months now without daylight.

Tuesday, August 18th.—Heard a crow this morning, an almost sure sign of open country near. Hurrah! fresh hope. Meat to be dry by noon, & then forward again. It was some time after dinner before we got under way & then had to renew our labour of cutting thro' willows, pushing thro' bracken, & wading water. After ½ mile of this we came to signs of a road being cut, & presently to a little river of which the bottom was such soft mud we were compelled to unpack the horses & carry over the packs ourselves by a temporary bridge of trees & boughs. It being late, & a thunderstorm coming on, we left the horses there to feed, & camped on the farther side. At the other camp we had lost the only knife belonging to our cuisine now, the others having been all lost, & this reducing us to O'Byrne's clasp knife, mine, & Milton's razor. The Assiniboine & boy went back & searched again, to our great delight finding it buried in the ashes of the fire. I tried fishing without success. O'Byrne went to look at the new road ahead which he pronounces tolerable. This has raised our spirits wonderfully, and Assiniboine who had become very sour & disagreeable, is quite amiable again.

A large boil coming on my knee almost prevents my walking except in great pain, but "Keyana"! March! Hope this is the Yankee road.

Wednesday, August 19th.—To bring horses across little river, & investigate; our road followed the road we had come upon along the edge of the river. It was apparently an Indian trapping-road, improved probably by the Yankees; horses had passed, by the frequent horse dung; but still it was no grand track, & when we came to a large marsh & sort of prairie in the afternoon, we could find it no longer. Here we rested a short time & ate & gathered a quantity of berries. Some large raspberries were delicious, & most delighted us, beautiful flavour tho' watery. Large haws, like those of English thorn, but large & black; very nice; Pembina berries, & several other kinds which I did not appreciate. Milton & O'Byrne squabbled over them like 2 small kids. I had the greatest possible difficulty in walking along on account of an immense boil on my knee which swelled to size of two fists; no help for it.

Camped at night near river with swamp for horses. Shushwap cutting all day. Weather fine & apparently settled.

Thursday, August 20th.—Fine morning. I forgot to mention yesterday in my notes that the young one & Milton had a great row. Milton, I & O'Byrne being behind, the young one appeared coming back on foot. Milton asked him something about the road, which he answered, but Milton not understanding spoke very sharply in English, which the young one did not reply to. Then Milton began to swear at him very loudly, at which young one lost his temper & took out his gun to shoot Milton. I doubt however if it was loaded, but I ran up & stopped the fun immediately, blew the boy up soundly & Milton too, showing the latter the folly of bullying & quarrelling with the child now in our present circumstances, & so the matter ended. During the day the valley continued to widen, the river flowed round several islands with good stretches of gravel, & we had a sort of track along which horses had passed by the edge of the river. The obstructions were fewer, & we had stretches of marsh & muskeg; in the latter we found a great number of beautiful bilberries, & had a feast; dusk came on before we had time to get out of the bog, & we had to hasten to river-side to camp in dark. Many bear tracks. Lots of sign now, some pretty fresh, in shape of camps, wood cut, &c. Altogether in better spirits, the look of country improving so much, & opening out. Did perhaps 6 miles. Weather fine, slight thunderstorms. I have suffered horribly from anxiety the last few weeks on Milton's account. Apathetic, holding back, utterly reckless of the value of time, not appreciating the awkwardness of our position, I having no fear for myself but for him on account of his being unable to walk or endure prolonged fatigue in case of emergency, & in addition always finding fault & quarrelling about small things of no consequence, & causing Assiniboine to threaten to desert us, & I knowing that it would not require much provocation to make him do this if things became much worse. Altogether a weary time. General peacemaker. Oh! for the Fort. Have finished our fresh meat.

Friday, August 21st.—Fine morning again, & set out with brighter hopes. Road better, more signs of civilised life, several camps; burnt ground & swamps; immense number of bilberries, raspberries, ground mulberries, big raspberries, gooseberries, Pembina berries, pears, eat our fill. Stop in middle of day, it being tremendously hot, having come fast tho' not very long. At night camp near good feeding ground, where Yankees apparently coming up river from direction of Kamloops had made a canoe & left a notice on a tree which we could not quite make out, but somewhat like this "This trale goos to thy steame land". Assiniboine finds we have now a good horse road forward, the trees marked. Expect a good long march tomorrow to try & get in without sacrificing another horse. Musquitoes murderous.

TRIP ACROSS CANADA

Saturday, August 22nd.—To my astonishment Lord Milton calls me at daybreak, & we get up & make fire before rest arise, who are delighted at this change as I also. Bravo! — We made a splendid journey, doing some 18 miles, camped for dinner at a real little prairie. Shot 8 partridges & a marten which ekes out our provisions a little. Road improved fast after starting, & except a little cutting at starting, a very good path indeed; better than most between Jasper House & Edmonton. Cypress, sand & rocks. River again a rapid, not so fierce as other. Valley ahead now blocked up by great hill ahead. Expect a river there, & to sleep near Fort day after tomorrow, perhaps starving a bit, but no more horses to kill. Lots of bilberries at night, delicious like best Ribstone pippins.

Sunday, August 23rd.—Up before light & off early in high spirits. Tremendous quantity of magnificent bilberries, pluck fistful at a grasp, like grapes. Meet old Shushwap, wife & kids; from signs infer we may reach Fort tonight. Peg along. Beautiful country. Partially wooded hills, cliffs, little park-like prairies. Road very good indeed. Do 25 miles at least. I find myself very weak. Shoot 6 partridges for dinner. At night only morsel of dried horse. Camp after sundown; no sign of Fort near; glorious bright hot day.

Monday, August 24th.—Beautiful morning. Up & off early at sunrise. Eat our last scrap of horse & push for the Fort. Find some wild cherries on the way which help to stop a gap. After a few miles a road turns off to cross river, & we saw 2 women & kids on the other side, & canoe in water. Called out to them, but they would not come across, & finding a good road which went forward we kept on & followed that; over small prairie & little river; when we had crossed this, O'Byrne who was behind holloa'd out "Doctor, Doctor, come here," & presently appeared leading a Shushwap by the hand, who was ugly as Caliban, & presently another younger & better-looking fellow appeared; we explained that we wanted to go to Kamloops & had nothing to eat, & they intimated that if we would come a few yards & have some berries, they would afterwards go our way, but they had no fish, & it was a long way yet to Kamloops; we should have to sleep 4 times on the road yet, but when we got there we should find plenty of bacon, flour, sugar, treacle, tobacco & all good things; trade articles he named in English, & also whiskey. We turned aside & went with them, & there found two women & several half naked kids;

they had some berries cooking in a pot, which they gave us
to eat, & most delicious they proved, as sweet as any jam in
the world, the red berries of a kind of lily which we had observed frequently in large quantities on the road but feared to
eat. After this they brought a rabbit, & wanted a shirt for it,
Milton giving an old one he had on. Then O'Byrne came out
& bought two more for one of his shirts. Presently the man
we had met yesterday appeared quite done up; he had followed
us in all haste, having some potatoes to sell! We gave him
a bag & he went off & shortly returned with a few in the bottom, just dug up; these we bought with another old shirt of
Assiniboine's, & with a partridge we had shot made a very
good dinner, understanding we might get some fish tonight.
After eating we went on, the younger fellow accompanying
us till we came to a large clear river, which they told us flowed
from Lake Cariboo. Here the others who had come down to
this point in canoe landed & then brought our baggage &
selves across the new branch; for this we gave them an old
buffalo robe each. Dirty ugly fellow discontented, other
pleased. The former had the cheek to ask a shirt for a piece
of rope tobacco ½ an inch! After this we found the younger
fellow & wife camped close to & wishing us to do the same.
Others gone on. This we did & made a rubbaboo of our
potatoes, berries & a partridge. We were disappointed in our
hopes of fish, but made out from his signs & word "fish" we
should get plenty tomorrow. Also that his wife had lots of
potatoes at some place further on. We must do as we can;
I gave him my trousers & told him he must give me fish &
potatoes for them.

Tuesday, August 25th.—Up before sun. Shushwap & wife
off in canoe, giving us to understand he would meet us somewhere where there was fish, & recommending us to be quick.
After 5 or 6 miles part of which was very bad road (beset with
underwood), we found the Indians waiting for us, told us they
would   transfer   our   things   &   selves   to   opposite   bank   a
little further down, there being a better road on the other side.
On our way we passed two dead Indians laid out, covered with
blanket, all goods & chattels around, not yet completely rotten.
Probably man & wife. Could not make out whether from starvation or small-pox; think the former. They give fearful
accounts of ravages of the latter lately. Young fellow's squaw
much pitted in face. More pushing thro' underwood, musquitoes

being killing! & then we emerged on to the stony beach of the river where were the rest awaiting us. Fire made & cooking berries. They gave us a mess of cooked berries of which I ate greedily; Milton sparingly. After this the woman made a present of two fish, some lily-roots & a basket of berries to Assiniboine's wife. We cooked the berries & I again ate freely. The Indians then transported us & our baggage across. Whilst loading the horses here I began to feel decidedly unwell, & by the time all was ready had such dreadful griping & feeling of sickness that I could not walk, & Assiniboine kindly offered his chestnut horse which I was glad enough to accept. The young fellow here led the way for us on foot & I followed in considerable agony for several miles, when we pulled up by the bank of the river & found the canoes awaiting us. They took the younger Indian, Milton, Assiniboine's wife, & some baggage on board, leaving the rest to bring on the horses, giving us to understand that the road was very bad. But here I felt so ill that I was quite unable to proceed at present, & lay down with bridle in hand until I might be better. In the morning, as I had walked along, I had plucked the lily berries rather largely, being awfully empty, & also eaten freely of them & roots at dinner time. I stayed here some ½ hour, with a most violent attack of vomiting & purging, and then, feeling slightly better, got on my horse & followed the rest, and with difficulty & great pain. The road was dangerously bad, beset with fallen timber, along ledges of slippery & sharp rock on the sides of precipices. But I was too ill to walk, & really at the time cared little whether I & the horse fell over or not. Some miles passed in this way when I met Assiniboine returning on foot. A horse had fallen over into the river & he was going in search with help of one of the Shushwaps in canoe, asking me to hurry the others on as we had a long way to go yet; a little further on, I found them at the ascent of a rocky mountain. High in the air we had to go, on a slippery sharp path, with descent of many hundred feet into river, the canoes waiting in the river below, anxiously watching our passage. Here we drove the horses along one by one, & before we finished, Assiniboine came up with missing animal. All got safe over; and as I followed last with my horse some 200 yards behind, I heard a shouting & angry words evidently between Assiniboine & O'Byrne but thought nothing more of it. When I got down & caught up the others I inquired of Assiniboine where O'Byrne was, & he told me that he had gone off, that he had told him to take two horses but he refused to do so, upon which he being very hot & out of temper at the time from contending with the horses, in his anger struck him a blow of his fist, & that he had gone off at a run, although they had called to him to stop. It now became rapidly dark, & Assiniboine took the lead, finding the road at a great pace in the most wonderful manner. But at last it became quite dark & I feeling so ill called to camp by a little stream, losing our hopes of supper, & meeting Milton. But I was too bad to care for that. It was thick wood with cutting for the horses. We made a small fire, & I got out my small supply of rum & some medicine; we all turned in with empty bellies. What has become of O'Byrne? Knowing his propensity for losing the way I was unhappy about him.

Wednesday, August 26th.—Off very early to meet the rest & get something to eat; 4 or 5 miles brought us to where they were camped on the sandy bank of the river. I felt nearly all right again; before we arrived the two Indians came to meet us, bringing two or three potatoes in their pockets which we ate greedily. To our surprise found O'Byrne already here & very glum, indeed he was. Lots of potatoes cooked ready, & we ate at once, but not much. Milton had paid his saddle for our big kettle full & for his passage in canoe down river. Many of our things being wet, we resolved to spend a couple of hours drying them in the sun which was intensely hot. From what Milton told me, it appeared that O'Byrne had arrived at the camp sometime during the night, & woke him up in a most fearful state of mind. Relating that Assiniboine had struck a most fearful blow with the back of the axe & that he had fled for his life; dark coming on soon after, he had wandered out of the road & lost his tin pot, eventually stumbling on the camp. Talked very largely of murderous assault, conspiracy against his life between Assiniboine & Shushwaps, "escaped only by his presence of mind in running away," "giving Assiniboine up to justice on arrival at Kamloops," "Irons & imprisonment;" and would have started with the light to make his way to the Fort alone on foot if Milton had not expostulated with him on the folly of his conduct. I examined him on the point, & he declared that the axe was used, & murder intended, & that it was only out of deference to Milton & myself that he stayed & did not give him up to justice. I looked at his head and found only a slight swelling on the occiput (right side) near protuberance & not even discoloured! I then went & examined Assiniboine on the subject, & he declared solemnly he struck him only with his fist, not with all his might, & threatened him afterwards with the axe if he did not take on the horses as he was told. This I was convinced was true from appearance of blow, & fact that he ran off talking, &c.; more frightened than hurt. I blew up Assiniboine, sympathised with O'Byrne, but laughed at his notion of murderous assault &c; & succeeded in putting things nearly square again. Milton persuaded the younger Indian to take him on in canoe to the place where we were to arrive with the horses tomorrow, & where he expected we might get salmon from other Indians there. For this he gave him the waterproof cart-cover, & expected to get in that night, & feast on salmon. We wished them good speed, & they paddled off, & the other returned up river to where we left his family the day before. We then packed up & set out. Sun intensely hot. I felt still very seedy & had been hardly able to eat anything; [(we had only a few potatoes, O'Byrne having purchased a small bagful with his beaverteen trousers, & Milton with his saddle); the place where we met Milton's party being small prairie with a good many potato gardens]; and was compelled to mount Bucephalus. When we had crossed the prairie, where we found another corpse laid as the rest, we had a tremendous rocky ascent along the side of a hill, & by the time I got up, the poor horse was completely done, & I had to dismount & make my way on foot as well as I could. The scenery was fine all way, indeed as it has been ever since we struck the good road. Rounded hills covered with large stone pines at almost regular intervals with grass between, or craggy & rough, rising out of flat prairie valley very suddenly, or crossing up close to the river edge. Road on the whole very good. We camped for night close to the edge on a beautiful rich prairie, where we saw our first prairie bird! Couldn't get him for supper, and tried fishing for supper, with hooks on bits of lines attached to pack ropes. No go & obliged to be content with a few potatoes, none able to eat many dry. Musquitoes awful, & unable to sleep until nearly midnight. 15 miles.

Thursday, August 27th.—Started off in good time hoping to reach Milton & salmon at camp tonight. Road good & well beaten now. Found brood of prairie hens but could not make anything of them, as Papillon was too exhausted to assist me. Going for about 3 hours, when I heard the jingling of bells, & presently two men rode up on horses with foals at their heels, one very Spanish-looking, with old brass-mounted horse pistol in belt, Mexican saddle, bells on bridle, wide-awake & loose trousers. The other in corduroy bags & similar equipment of steed. Thought they were miners, but turned out to be Shushwaps; they pulled up & dismounted, filled pipes & gave us a smoke round, which we enjoyed amazingly, the strong rope tobacco making O'Byrne & self quite drunk for a minute or two. After that Spanish-looking fellow made me get up behind him, & I had a painful ride (being very lean myself & horse bony) for 4 or 5 miles. When we turned down to the river & found Milton's baggage tied to a pole & stuck in a tree. This we packed on the horses & went forward another mile where we found 2 other Indians, squaws, & children. Milton lying under shelter of reed mat laid across slant.

— Men & women better dressed than we had yet seen. Had had a grand washing day that morning & all in clean clothes. Women in red paint, hair combed out. One, very smart in green bodice & white canvas petticoat, prepared a good mess of potatoes, & some dishes of weak coffee well sugared; which I found the greatest treat I had yet had.

I gave her a silk handkerchief which she put on her head at once, greatly delighted. Bought two ducks for waistcoat & shot, & pan of potatoes for pair stockings of an old woman. Gave several presents of shot, handkerchiefs, &c., & then started again. Young Indian came with us — hurried us along over rocky road most of way, evidently making for some camping place, saying "salmon couchen" & just at dusk we arrived at a flat open space by the river where we found a camp of 2 or 3 families; bought a dish of flour for bit of buffalo-skin, & fish for two hooks, which with 2 ducks, 2 partridges I had shot, & potatoes, made most glorious feast for months past. To our surprise a man came up who talked to us in French & English! turned out to be halfbreed from other side who came over when a boy; knew Colin Fraser, &c. Told us only 17 miles from Fort & good road. All kinds of good things there; newspapers; Yankee war yet unfinished, South the best of it. Hurrah, Hurrah! Went to bed happy.

Friday, August 28th.—Horses wandered far, & off late. Bought two more fish for a piece of buffalo skin. Hurrah for Mr. Mackay & Kamloops; no more hardship after today. Fearfully hot & dusty, & a wearisome tramp I found it, being very footsore & rather weak, & the great heat making one languid in the extreme, added to this dyspepsia from potato diet. After

7 or 8 miles all glad to pull up at a stream & rest in the shade;
cook a few more potatoes. Assiniboine & wife wash & put on
clean things. Milton makes Kinnikinick in expectation of
tobacco tonight. I & O'Byrne take time by the forelock &
start immediately after feeding, in order to stroll slowly forward in advance of the rest, although in the heat of midday,
leaving the rest to pack up & follow. The road was generally
level thro' flats sparsely covered with large spruce or "cyprèe",
the reddish bark of which, & the brown grassed ground making
the scene very eastern. The rounded hills occasionally coming
close down to the river, & the path here being rather steep &
rocky, but nowhere dangerous for the horses; the halfbreed
we had met at the camp of the previous night had told us
the Fort was only reckoned 17 miles distant but he only considered it 15, & that we should arrive easily before sundown.
But we must have done more than that before Milton caught
up O'Byrne & myself, & we agreed to stop a few minutes &
have a smoke with some tobacco which he had bought of
some Indians we had just passed coming from the Fort, & who
assured us it was quite close. I had some distrust of the state-
ment from former experience of reported proximity of forts
(as Fort Pitt for instance), & walked on quickly pipe in mouth,
enjoying much my first smoke of pure tobacco for some 6 weeks
I presume; after a mile or so the rest overtook me; the sun was
already set, no signs of the Fort. Assiniboine proposed that I
should take his chestnut horse, & ride ahead with Milton, trying at any rate to get ourselves in, & get canoes ready to cross
the rest. I gladly agreed, being very done with over 20 miles
in the hot sun, & my feet very sore, & we cantered away as
well as our tired horses could go; and a deal of whacking they
took. To our amusement O'Byrne appeared tearing after us,
being I suppose afraid to be left in the rear with Assiniboine!
Getting dark fast when we emerged on to a wide plain, stretch-
ing long before us, backed by a range of hills running East
& West, & in front of which the "South branch" *must* flow.
Darker still, but at last in the twilight we discern a long ram-
bling shanty, & riding round to the front found several people
seated round a tarpaulin stretched on the ground eating —
pots & kettles on the fire near. An old man jumped up & in
a curious mixture of French, English & Indian invited us to
eat, saying "Une piastre chaque, Monsieur," "Une piastre chaque, monsieur", "Campez, campez ici," I said, All right we must
eat if it costs £50 a piece, & straight let loose our horses & sat

down to the remains of the repast which consisted of a greasy soup of bacon, cabbage & pease in a tin dish, beautiful white galette, & tea & sugar. Milton & I did wonders! Fat bacon, cabbage & pease & the greasy liquid went down fast, & galette after galette called for; we meant to do all we could to have our dollar's worth. O'Byrne shortly appeared & joined us heartily & coolly, altho' I informed him it was a dollar a head! After eating all we could get hold of with perfect ferocity we desisted, telling them to prepare for 3 more to arrive shortly. The old man informed us he was Captain St. Paul "un Canadien" of whom we must have heard; showed us into a kind of out-house with 2 broken-down bedsteads in it & fowls roosting on the beams. The old boy told us there was to be a dance given that night, & that all the world would be here very soon. After it was quite dark Assiniboine turned up with the pack horses very tired out, having been on the point of camping when he arrived in view of the house & came forward. They had to wait for more cooking, before feeding, & meantime we got a fire in our 'bedroom', & baggage taken in, beds prepared, &c. The arrivals for the dance now commenced. A Canadian in charge of Company's horses here, who civilly supplied me with tobacco, & halfbreed cook for Company, 2 Lanes who gave the dance, sons of late Chief Trader here, Indians, both sexes all gaudily dressed, & with some Spanish or Mexican air about them, in bright petticoats & shirts, men gay caps, or hats like muliero or bright-coloured silk handkerchiefs round their heads. Men smaller than Indians of other side, more civilised & better dressed. All anxious to know who we were, where from, whether intending to mine or seek employment, & seemed rather incredulous when informed that we were a mere party of *pleasure*. Our ragged appearance & gaunt looks greatly against us. Milton's trousers literally rags, mine little better; shirts the same, moccasins in holes; our persons dirty, unwashed & unshaven. Assiniboine & wife in same condition. Horses & dog skeletons.

These people informed us that McKay who is chief Trader in charge here[53] was away at Lillooet, but expected daily & the person in charge in the meantime was Mr. Martin, who had been a midshipman in the navy. O'Byrne as usual then began about the Martins of this place & the other. Shortly after the Canadian brought up Mr. Martin, who was very civil, nephew of Admiral Martin; family in the navy for a century. Handsome, boyish-looking fellow of some 25, full of chaff & oaths, a complete sailor in manner; told us he had left the navy after serving in Crimea & Baltic; went into East India Company's service; invalided from there in debt & with liver complaint; came out here after row at home; worked in mines in Cariboo; broken twice; could not get work; begged down to Victoria; lived out there in tent with a lot of others in same fix; boat along coast; rows with Indians; shot several, became too dangerous living by gun; at last gave letters of introduction to H. B. Company in Victoria who gave him clerk's place at once, & he was sent here some 10 months ago. Asked us to come over to the Fort which we agreed to do tomorrow. I went into the dance for about an hour, & had a drop of rum, after which escaped on plea of fatigue, being really unable to keep my eyes open. Milton stayed a little longer; continually disturbed by noise & thumping on floor of dancers in next room. At last towards morning peace & rest.

Saturday, August 29th.—Up early from old habits, internally hungry & longing for more galette & bacon; but the inmates, wearied by late hours of preceding night, slept long, & we did not get our breakfast of bacon, bread & potatoes until 10 or 11 o'clock; again eat everything before us. Horses when brought up looked so bad, that we thought it not safe to cross them, & decided to leave them with old St. Paul until they recovered a little; ourselves & baggage going forward to Fort across the South branch in canoe, for which transport we paid 2 old stinking buffalo-robe-saddlecloths! Old St. Paul impressed upon us his importance. How the magistrate always stayed with him on making his rounds; always "Monsieur St. Paul" from him & Governor; great extent of land which he owned on that side of river; no one allowed to graze a horse, or cut wood without his permission. Called our attention to two notices fixed up to trees, "Indian Reserve Lands", "Not to be trespassed upon." Cox Chief Magistrate. We were landed close to the Fort which consisted of two or three detached wooden buildings, not yet completed, the Old Fort which had been abandoned only this summer being on the opposite side of the main river. Here we found a Mr. Burgess one of the clerks, a civil gentlemanly youth who took our baggage into the store, & promised to arrange quarters for us in the house. We then purchased trousers & shirts in the store, towels & soap, & Burgess showing us a good bathing place, we went down to the river & had a regular scrub-down, & swim after-

wards; put on our new apparel & felt really comfortable once
more. After this Martin arrived, & a Mr. Bingham, a shrewd
middle-aged man who had been in India, China, California &
Cariboo & now in Company's service, having come to grief I
suppose on his own hook. Then — Ah! then — dinner!

*Mutton chops, potatoes, fresh butter, delicious galette,
rice pudding!* Never shall I forget that delightful meal. *Strong
tea & plenty of sugar.* Talk of intellectual enjoyment! pooh!
pooh! Your stomach is the door of true delight. No use in
describing how we ate & drank. O'Byrne of course coolly
entered & sat down without explaining his case to anyone,
& did more justice to grub than even we. We heard a good
deal of what was news to us. Taking of Vicksburg by the
North, Mexico by the French; marriage of Prince of Wales,
&c. But although we had heard nothing for 8 months, very
little seemed to have happened in meantime. 300 Indians carried off by small-pox last winter. Order famously kept in
Cariboo; Governor Douglas very efficient; only 2 murders this
year. Disappointed to learn we are too late to get on to
Cariboo, it being 12 days' journey from here by horse, & everybody except winter miners leaving before end of next month,
the snow preventing horse communication after that time. Milton declares he will spend another year out here in order to visit
the place. No surface gold in Cariboo; deep workings requiring capital; plenty of gold; therefore so many disappointed.
In California lots of surface gold at first which is now exhausted. Provisions very cheap in Cariboo comparatively this
year. Flour 20 cents lb. & so on; last year 2 dollars. Here
everything dear also on account of transport. Tobacco $3 1 lb;
butter $1 a lb.; flour 12 dollars per 50 lb. sack; bacon 1 dollar
per lb.; flannel shirts, 5 dollars, &c. Description of Cariboo
gold region; one large mountain covered with timber & almost
impassable from fallen wood & rocks; in the creeks coming
from this as a centre the gold is found.

Great nutritiousness of pasturage about Kamloops. Bunch
grass. Cattle brought from all around to winter. Get fat in
very short time. Would not have believed this of a country
which looks the colour of a lithograph. Wheat grows well
where fairly tried; potatoes & peas flourish as we have seen.

Sunday, August 30th.—Rest, eat, smoke & talk; still as
ravenous as ever. I was astonished at my gaunt appearance
& meagre, hatchet face. Milton quite fat. In afternoon 2

Yankees came in. They were tall, stout fellows on good horses with Mexican trappings, one armed with knife & revolver, the other double gun & do. on the look out for the two murderers (an Englishman & a Yankee) of the clerk of a Mr. Dodge who was shot returning with money from Cariboo, in open daylight & within a few hundred yards from House. Money was in saddle of other clerk whose horse took fright & ran off with him. There is a reward of $6.000 for them; supposed to be hiding in hills & not yet to have passed Kamloops; seen & shot at about 30 miles from here by Mr. Lane & me a week ago; 8 shots & all missed. Older Yankee, a tall pock-marked man, with nasal twang, & 'I guess', & 'calculate' complete; told us great stories of experience in California, &c.; want of water; catching "mustus nipee" in caps; saved life of lot of boys in salt prairies by roastinq stems of soap plants & catching drippings of sap. Told Martin & rest about O'Byrne, & they resolve to be rid of him like us; he has not yet said a word about his case, & comes in to meals; bought several dollars worth without a word! too cool; expects to go on with us, I suppose, but no go. Our sympathy much destroyed by his cool assurance; sickens everybody by his talking of this great person & another in one country or another, trying to fix himself on to someone on strength of mutual acquaintanceship with 3rd party.

Monday, August 31st.—Poor Jem's birthday; where is he? Martin reminds me much of him. Yankees depart on way back. Gave us astounding information that America & France were at war, and also Russia, Prussia, & England, but further than the bare fact he knew nothing. I write journal & clean gun. Martin to explain with O'Byrne today. Bingham very intelligent fellow. In afternoon Martin asked O'Byrne what he intended to do. He said that he thought of waiting here until we went forward. Martin hinted that he fancied we did not expect his company any further, & that there was now a good road forward, & houses at which he might sleep all along. He then said he thought he would set out tomorrow, & Martin told him he was quite welcome to stay & rest himself until then. In the evening he called me aside & asked me if I could supply him with a pair of socks, a silk necktie, some tea & sugar, a little bread & money enough for the steamer from Yale to Victoria. I said I would talk with Milton on the matter, & also about a letter to certify that the letter of introduction from Archdeacon Collian to the Governor was lost in the Fraser.

Tuesday, September 1st.—Milton kindly wrote O'Byrne's letter & supplied him with tea, tobacco & matches for his journey; Martin, with cakes & bacon; he was in a horrible fright of having to go alone, but we assured him there was no danger except for persons known to have a sum of money with them. He then called me aside & said, "Look here, I've got no money for the road," in the coolest manner, as if it was my duty to supply anything he liked to order. This rather put my back up, & I entered into a full explanation of the reasons which made Milton & myself rather backward in exerting ourselves to help him as much as we might do; showing him how badly he had played his cards with us, in exhibiting so little inclination to do what he could to assist us in little things during the journey, & in presuming actually to order us & the men what to do; complaining of the mismanagement & ill equipment of our party, &c; & lastly that neither Martin nor ourselves were pleased at his purchasing things in the store, coming to table, & assuming he was one of our party without a word of explanation with anyone. He wanted to laugh this off, but I made him hear me out, & he then said he had tried to do all he could, & behave as politely as he was able to us. I said we had not found it so. He then actually had the impudence to begin about Assiniboine, *our man,* knowing that his horse was about to be stolen & hinting that we were thus somewhat responsible! I told him that seeing both Milton & myself had subscribed for the horse, & had brought him over here without a farthing of cost to himself, I thought it was a most disgusting & ungrateful speech for him to make, & that perhaps the conversation had better end, walking away indignant. He bid us good-bye coolly & set out, pack on back, saying we should probably never meet again, & he bore us no ill-will! I suppose we may drop on him again in Victoria. I have no doubt he will abuse us heartily behind our backs. In the evening tried fishing without any success. Enormous appetite still continues, & as we have only 2 meals a day, tho' good ones, we are compelled to get odd bits with Assiniboine in the lodge. Play whist at night.

Horses brought over & put with Company's band; Bucephalus nearly drowned; so weak.

TRIP ACROSS CANADA

The country is what one might imagine the Cape: brown yellow except trees which are nearly all the large "Cyprèe".

Wednesday, September 2nd.—A most disgraceful scene at breakfast. Martin used some oaths & very strong language about McKay[54] & his delay in arriving here. Bingham who is McKay's uncle took it up rather warmly as well he might. Martin lost his temper & shied a cup of tea in Bingham's face, calling him a liar, & McKay a d — d halfbreed; at which Bingham retaliated by shying his cup, tea & all, at Martin who responded with his cup. Martin then rushed at the other & there was a regular scuffle for a short time, plates being smashed, victuals upset, & an awful mess. Bingham walked off in disgust; Milton & I thought Martin sorely to blame, but it was no affair of ours, & we quietly finished our breakfast after it was all over. Afterwards Bingham apologized to us. Martin had not the grace to do the same. In the afternoon a Mr. Jerome Harper arrived on horseback; he was bringing in a drove of 500 cattle from Oregon; a Virginian & staunch supporter of the South. He treated us to a tremendous tirade against the North, whom he called by all the vile names he could think of, hoped every Yankee would leave his bones on Southern soil; South would never be conquered; if they were, North would then set upon England whom they hated as heartily as they did the South, & we should find our mistake in not having acknowledged the Southern Confederacy at once. Said he was bitter because his mother & family had been driven out of their homes in Virginia where they had nice estates & left penniless. In the evening when we had all turned in he began again a long tirade, in penny-a-lining strain about art of ruling men, intellectual greatness of Southerners; General Lee equal to Napoleon & Wellington; and again about weakness of English Government in delaying recognition of Jeff Davis' Government, asserting that they were "truckling to Lincoln" from fear. We showed that they had no fear in the Trent question, that they were acting as they did contrary to their own interests (cotton) & their own personal sympathies, &; therefore it might be inferred from motives of political justice only. He could not answer this but still went on rhodomontading until midnight, wearying everyone.

Thursday, September 3rd.—Mr Harper set out again to meet his cattle. Wish McKay would arrive with news, & enable us to make another start as we are now rested, & anxious to get to Victoria for letters. What may not have happened in the 9 months since we have heard? Visit old boy with bad leg across river. Do nothing else but idle about, & finish reading all old newspapers. As we were at dinner, McKay arrived. Undersized man in cowhide coat and breeches, jack-boots & large-peaked cap; like an overgrown jockey; dark complexioned, but features remarkably like Fanny Essex. He made himself particularly agreeable, sympathized with our hardships, & told us all the news in which he was very well up indeed. We heard of Conquest of Mexico by French, taking of Vicksburg by Yankees &c. He is very well informed on most subjects & amused us with budget of intelligence until late. Informed us that so far from mining being a failure, the gold escort had this last trip brought down 97,000 ounces of gold which, at 3.10 per ounce (under its average value), gives an equivalent of £339,500! at one go; the fact being that the late murder had caused many who usually conveyed their gold by private hand to send it now under more efficient protection; thus the amounts coming down became more clearly known.— Land near Victoria which McKay had bought for £1 per [acre] sold for £24 shortly after.

Friday, September 4th.—Explained the fix we were in to McKay who kindly said he would take us on with him as he was going back to Yale on Tuesday & would provide us with horses which would save the expense of buying them & selling at a disadvantage at Lytton or Yale. Also that he would arrange our money matters & we could remit a cheque from Westminster or Victoria. Very kind indeed & getting us nicely out of what might have been an unpleasant fix if he had not turned out a good fellow.

Saturday, September 5th.—Spent the day in looking at horses the other side the river. Some shockingly injured by bad packing & brutality; ribs broken, &c. They put one yearling filly's neck out today with the lasso when they threw it.

Sunday, September 6th.—Went out pheasant shooting with Martin whose only open day it is. Turned out very showery, & we only found 3 brace of birds, where they had killed 22 brace a fortnight before. We returned home early, much disappointed. Mr. Bingham rather screwed but very quiet. Pity such a shrewd fellow should be so lost. In evening McKay showed us specimens of Opal found on Kamloops lake, & gave us each one. Vein of pure Copper found 20 miles below this place. The rhombic crystals given by Tête Jaune Cache Indians to Milton & used by them as flints, stated by McKay to be iron pyrites.

Monday, September 7th.—Arranging. Agree to camp out on way down as being less expensive & pleasanter also. To take only one pair of saddle-bags. We to take 3 horses on to Cook's ferry for Assiniboine, wife, & boy, McKay providing 3 more for Milton, self, & baggage. Indian arrives with Intelligence that little English murderer is taken about 3 miles below McLean's place. Other stole Indian's canoe & crossed river to this side, supposed to be lurking not far from here.

Tuesday, September 8th.—Set out rather late, McKay having so many last orders & preparations. The horse he gave us to pack kicked off everything twice before he became manageable. Bid a hearty goodbye to Martin & Burgess, & jogged along; had milk at MacIvor's 'ranch' but did not stop for dinner; camped at little stream about 3 miles short of the end of Kamloops lake, having got over some 18 miles. All day along lake which is nowhere more than a mile broad; fine hills running close up to the lake; of the same character, rounded, rugged in places, sparsely timbered, yellow with bunch grass. McKay full of talk on all kinds of subjects. Enormous appetite still continues altho' I am quite fat. Road tolerably good; up & down hill.

Wednesday, September 9th.—A long weary day, over 20 miles without stopping & at a foot's pace. Crossed the Thompson at the foot of the lake, followed the other side for 15 miles, & then kept to the right to cut into Bonaparte Valley. Milton's saddle & mine also were very uncomfortable, & we were uncommonly glad to camp on little stream where we cut into the waggon road from Clinton to Lytton. The trail had been thro' the same rugged country as before, one rather dangerous precipice to pass along, & we were obliged to dismount. McKay intended to have pushed on to McLean's, 6 miles up the Bonaparte Valley that night, but meeting his son received news he would not return from Lillooet where he had gone with the murderer until tomorrow.

Thursday, September 10th.—McKay started for McLean's immediately after breakfast, leaving us to go forward quietly until he caught us up, or await him at Cook's Ferry where the road crosses the Thompson. He recommended us to camp near the company of Engineers engaged in constructing the road some 16 miles on, & kindly gave us a note to Lieut. Palmer who is in command. Passed the "ranches" of the two Cornwalls; said to be Old Cantabs & men of some property who have taken to stock farming out here; plain wooden houses, but much more finished than any we have seen. Towards evening came to a portion of unfinished road; trail very rugged & precipitous; in a little ravine came upon a camp of some dozen tents & presuming it must be that of the Engineers which had been described as close, we arranged our own camp & proceeded to inquire for Lieut. Palmer; much disappointed to find, that this was only a camp of contractor's gang, the other being some 2 miles further. No end of cooking was going on in enormous tin kettles, & presently about 25 men came trooping in to supper. We fed & a man came up & smoked his pipe with us, not one of the contractor's men; could not make him out, English or Canadian; spoke well, had been up the North Thompson prospecting, following the east side however above the rapid; no gold. Said he had seen a letter from Colonial Secretary to the Governor, inquiring if anything had been heard of us on this side; but more particulars he would not give, being I presume afraid we might be impostors & make use of his information. I am afraid there is much anxiety about us in the two homes in England; perhaps not received our last letters from Carlton. Said he had come up to try to get information about the other murderer. Very rough bed amongst the rocks.

Friday, September 11th.—3 more miles of rugged trail amongst rocks & precipices; then made road again to Cook's Ferry where we arrived about noon. Did not call on the Engineers' camp near the Ferry house; very dusty place. Saw Chinamen at work, to great amazement of Assiniboine & family. Anxiously await McKay's arrival until dark; he does not come; then being short of provisions get beef & flour on tick. Invited by Chinaman who regulates cuisine to dine at Ferry house, but having no cash we were compelled to decline; bothered by Indians to sell horses; they often pick up good bargains from "broken" men coming down from mines. Number of men on foot passed during afternoon, blanket on back, seeming halting & footsore, unsuccessful miners on way back I presume.

Saturday, September 12th.—Still no McKay up to noon during which time I occupy myself with this veracious record. Very tantalizing now we have heard there are inquiries for us.

Prospect of nothing to do but idle about this wretched place. Road must be expensive; frequently cut out of nearly perpendicular precipice overhanging river; rocky & rugged; many places of the kind where I should be sorry to drive on a dark night; no fence whatever, & certain death if fall over precipices into river. On the way here saw several gardens tolerably flourishing: potatoes, cabbages, beans & cucumbers doing well, but oats, the only kind of corn I observed, very poor crops, short in the straw & small yield; all irrigated. Waited about wearily all afternoon for McKay. At dusk, 3 gentlemen & horses arrived & put up at the house. I asked the eldest of the party, a well-dressed middle-aged man of gentlemanly manners, if he had seen anything of McKay, & he informed me that they had left him encamping with Lieut. Palmer at the Engineers' Camp & that he would come forward in the morning. He took me for one of the Company's men, & when I informed him I had no connection with them, he said he presumed I was one of Lord Milton's party & made many inquiries about our journey, &c. Told me that this valley was one of the most barren parts of B. C. Better land in neighbourhood of William's Lake & on towards Cariboo. But the country had been grossly misrepresented, & B. C. would never be a great farming country. Quite my own impression from what I had seen so far.

Sunday, September 13th.—Just before daybreak very heavy rain came on which we endured for some time under our waterproofs, but at length it became too severe, & we, i.e. Milton, myself, & the boy bolted into the hay store where we lay very comfortably. Two of our horses had broken loose during the night but were found 2 or 3 miles on road back. The heavy showers still continuing, we breakfasted in the house; very good feed of beef-steaks, potatoes & hot rolls & butter &c; one dollar. Mr. Fraser at parting was very obliging & offered us the loan of his own saddle-horse down to Yale. But we declined as McKay had provided us. Observing our inferior style of dress, he insisted on lending Milton a coat & trousers, telling him his name was Fraser & he was always to be found at the Hotel de France, Victoria. From the Victoria paper we discovered the Hon. Donald Fraser had just been in Cariboo; & concluded this was our man; our host told us the other two were Mr. Smith, a large packer to Cariboo, & a Mr. Nuttall, in business there. We got all ready to start immediately after breakfast but McKay did not arrive until we were just sitting down to dinner. We had to get him to pay our bill which amounted to $42; he rather stared. Not bad for two days! Horse barley 25 per lb, bacon 50 per lb; flour, sugar, tea. We had a drink of really beautiful French brandy & then crossed the Ferry; sending our men to camp some ¼ mile on, we went into the house & made the acquaintance of Mr. Cook, an Ohio man; usual Yankee but quieter. Had delicious supper there, very clean & well cooked, best we have had since St. Pauls.

McKay has to wait here tomorrow to meet his pack trains coming in. We all go on Tuesday. Lieut. Palmer will accompany us. Assiniboine & family in waggons when they arrive. Hear that gold escort did not bring 97000oz as I stated previously, but $150.000! — And that Cameron had not made $300.000 but probably not more than $10.000. This from Mr. Fraser who, McKay tells us, is *Times* Correspondent & wealthy man in Victoria. He has been all over the world. He says this country greatly resembles South America in aspect. Views in Cariboo exceed anything he saw in Andes or Himalayas. Milton & I both went to bed with headaches in consequence of three 'drinks' of brandy during the day.

Monday, September 14th.—Breakfast at Mr. Cook's; excellent white salmon, fish rather resembling the bass. Milton engaged in bargaining with old Indian & wife for sale of our two remaining horses which they want for winter provisions; $30 a piece. McKay told us when talking of wolverines that woodrat of this country is very similar in mischief. In pulling down old Fort at Kamloops this summer found knives & forks, bullets & every variety of articles they had in the store secreted by them between the walls.

Tuesday, September 15th.—Indians came in to tell of body found in river close by; went to see it with Cook & McKay. Beginning to decompose. From moccasin, & tattooing on arm concluded it was other murderer of Clegg, drowned in attempting to swim Thompson. Leaving our baggage to come on with Assiniboine & family by the waggons, Milton, McKay & myself rode on to Lytton, 23 miles, at the junction of Thompson with the Fraser. We had a very pleasant ride, the road following the river very closely, hilly, but good sound road, following the gulches which come in to the river, & thus being very winding.

At Lytton we found Captain Ball the magistrate, a very jolly fellow indeed; flies in his hat; told us good fishing in streams about Yale & Hope; none to be killed in Fraser or Thompson. Stayed at Houtin's Hotel. Lytton one of the towns which was

The Terraces on the Fraser River.

raised by Fraser River excitement, numerous bars being worked; near "Canaka Bar", "Boston Bar", "Chapman's Bar" which were celebrated. It has now 'gone in' very much. On a point between the two rivers which has been cleared of timbers. The timber is beginning to change along the rivers as we go down, the spruce, firs, other pines & some few birch (small) lying & mingle with the eternal yellow-backed "pinus sylvestris" or "cyprèe"; & instead of the absence of underwood & bunch grass clothing the "benches" of the Thompson & Fraser we are getting thick growth of deciduous shrubs & a moister soil.

Wednesday, September 16th.—Rode on to Boston Bar about 27 miles, & there stayed the night; this place is another little assemblage of wooden houses "caved in" since the river mines have been abandoned. Some very fruitful little patches have been cleared here; but the mountains which from the river banks are so steep & often rocky that there is but the little space contained in the few small flats which can be cultivated, sufficient for gardens. A different climate after leaving Thompson River, rainy & mild; very different also to Fraser above also, which has flats & dry soil & climate like Thompson. The river banks & bars have been extensively worked all along, & we still saw Chinamen at work in a few places with a rocker, making from $1 to even $10 per day each.

Thursday, September 17th.—From Boston Bar to Yale 24 miles; a beautiful ride past the Jackass Mountain & Zigzag Nicaragua Slide over the suspension bridge which is just completed.

The road was unfinished round Nicaragua Slide, which is a great bluff of granite overhanging the river; the road is blasted thro' this & passes along the edge at the height of 7 or 800 feet above the Fraser; sheer descent. Sent our horses along the trail which went up the mountain by a zigzag, up to the very top, a very roundabout & dangerous trail, & the death of many a pack animal; whilst we walked along the unfinished waggon road *passing round the face of the bluff.* The granite here is a most beautiful grey variety, frequently with veins of quartz intermingled something like a plaid pattern very often, & in the water-worn portions, the granite has been worn away & the seams of quartz left projecting, less affected by the action of the water. The Canyons (as they are called) above Yale are worth [seeing]; occur at intervals for many miles. The river forcing

Yale, on the Fraser River.

its way thro' the granite passes. Large rocks standing out in several places in the middle of the narrowed stream thro' which the water rushes at a great pace. One of them very narrow called La Porte d'Enfer! not so fine however as the one we named like it on the North Branch of Thompson.

May not this have been the barrier which dammed up the rivers, & caused the chain of lakes so evidently shown to have existed by the benches of the Fraser & Thompson? Burst thro' at length by some convulsion of nature or wear & tear of water! What a curious country this must have been in those days! Chains of lakes & hills between, mountain tops now, no level land except perhaps the high level of "green timber" as it is called. Arrived in Yale about 4 & went to Colonial where we invited McKay to dine with us, & a capital dinner they gave, so it seemed to us at least. McKay reappeared in dress of English Gentleman of the period, & informed us that Finlaison, Chief Factor at Victoria, was there & had received letter of credit from Lord F———— for £400 which was at Milton's disposal. This eased our financial difficulties at once. Finlaison[55] very obliging. Found Donald Fraser & party at Hotel having been too late for steamer of Tuesday. Spent evening with Mr. & Mrs. McKay. Latter nice-looking woman of 23 or 24 but delicate. Maiden name Helen Holmes, at Miss Chalmer's with Elise.

Friday, September 18th.—Bade good bye to McKay & sailed on Reliance, Captain Irving, for New Westminster. The river widens rapidly below Yale into a fine broad stream ¼ mile wide with low banks covered with large timber; the hills receding rapidly. We passed Hope, a town of 30 or 40 houses, size of Yale, but now 'gone in'. It is most beautifully situated in a large flat with a magnificent amphitheatre of mountains behind. Prettiest site I have seen in the Colony. Further down Fort Langley, an old Hudson's Bay Station, with little but the Company's buildings; a fine site & selected as capital of British Columbia until Colonel Moody[56] changed to New Westminster for military reasons. By dark we arrived at New Westminster & went to Colonial. New Westminster stands on rising ground above the river, amidst the densest forest, which has cost fortunes to clear away, averaging $3 a stump, Captain Spalding, the Justice of Peace there, told me. It is finely placed & will be a pretty place in time. A deep bay of river forms a suitable harbour, & the town is extremely well laid out by Col. Moody.

Engineers' camp about ½ mile along river. Substantial buildings, Church & barrack rooms &c. Col. Moody's house very prettily situated. All the low land along the lower Fraser is said to be rich soil, but overflowed in summer (to a great extent) & covered with enormous timber, a great drawback to cultivation here where labour is so dear. An exception to this is the Plains of Sumas where some farming is carried on, & many cattle are wintered. But the musquitoes there are said to be terrible. And indeed men from all countries agree that the musquitoes of B.C. are unmatched for number & ferocity. In the evening Milton had one of his attacks, & I sat up with him greater part of the night; he had had several symptoms during the day.

Saturday, September 19th.—On board Enterprise steamer to Victoria. Belonging to Hudson's Bay Company. Formerly one of Sacramento river boats. Very nicely fitted up & stewards very attentive. Milton of course very seedy & had one or two more symptoms which passed off. We had a severe time of it going down, every one pressing us to drink. Amongst others the noted Billy Ballou, a regular Yankee, formerly had the Express & I hear showed wonderful energy & perseverance in carrying on the communications in the old time of no roads & hard trails almost impassable in the snow. At first sight a loud-talking rowdy, nasal twang excessive. A fine steam down to Victoria. River expands into Gulf. Mount Baker shows magnificent with its snowy upper half. Boundary line visible, a long vista cut in the forest. The low shores of much disputed Island of San Juan or 'San Wawn' as the Yankees call it. Sail right round Victoria before you get there. Night when we arrived. Donald Fraser recommends Hotel de France & delivers us to an obliging youngster to guide there. Proprietor observing our disreputable appearance in leather shirts &c. "has no room". We walk off, but he, hearing from our conductor who we are, runs after to entreat us to stay as he has found it was a mistake. Our guide had introduced us to two young fellows sitting in the Coffee room, viz. Judson Young, Governor Douglas's private secretary & Elwyn, 2nd. in command of Gold escort & Justice of Peace. They kindly took us to the St. George where Elwyn himself resides & we were provided with nice rooms there. Milton being so seedy went to bed at once & I had some supper & then went with Elwyn & Young to buy a suit of clothes. On return waiter introduced me to Col. Moody, a gentlemanly old bird who treated me to a full & complete history of the Colony, resources &c, lasting about $1\frac{1}{2}$ hours.

Sunday, September 20th.—Young called, & we went out & caught the tailor coming home from Church who let us into his shop, & we there both fitted out satisfactorily.

Monday, September 21st.—Called on the Governor who kept us to dinner with him, a fine old fellow with magnificent presence, but rather affected drawling air. Met Donald Fraser there.

From this date to the 29th. we spent our time in looking after Assiniboine & family who were delighted with Victoria & dining with the Governor[58] &c. We took Assiniboine & Co on board the Sutlej, which was just on her way out of the harbour for San Francisco. As they were only going out under sail & the breeze had completely fallen we easily caught them up about 2 miles out & got on board. Admiral Keigcome was very kind & gave us lunch in his cabin, but a breeze springing up in the midst of it, he turned us out very unceremoniously in the pouring rain. Our boatman had refused to hold on to the rope & be towed, & consequently the Admiral had to heave to & take in sail to enable him to come alongside & take us off; the rain soon ceased after we took boat, & we rowed back comfortably to Esquimault. We had driven a buggy & pair of dashing horses down in the morning, I driving with Milton on the box, & Assiniboine & family behind inside, to their immense satisfaction, & they compared this style of travelling to our wearisome march thro' the woods a short time ago. In the evening we took them to the theatre, a great surprise for them. Everyone knew "Our Indians," & they had numerous visitors in the old cabin they lived in by permission of the Hudson's Bay Company. At the theatre the "Marsh troupe" were performing. Young girls of 17 or 18, many of them dressed as small girls of 12 which did not at all agree with their womanly development. They acted very well. About 30,000 people in Victoria during Fraser River excitement[59] of '58, living in tents. Harris the Mayor began life by getting a sheep from Hudson's Bay Co. on credit, & selling it retail from a tent.

Tuesday, September 29th.—After much trouble to get our clothes from photographer who was out, we at last got on board the other steamer which took the place of the Enterprise broken down. Fine sail through the islands, mostly rocky & all thickly wooded. Good, the Under Colonial Secretary & old Oxonian, came up with us. Ran away with Governor's daughter to American side, & there married. Governor would not see them. Good, by advice of his friends went to call on him & propitiate. Governor knocked him down! afterwards all made up. Magnificent view of Mount Baker; large conical mountain covered with snow apparently $\frac{3}{4}$ way down, in American territory. San Juan.[60] Boundary line & obelisk. Heard of narrow escape of the Enterprise going up with Governor & party on board. Very rough sea, shaft gave way, & within a few yards of being dashed on the rocks.

Arrived in Westminster about 7, & after making arrangements for Assiniboine & Co to remain on board to sleep & feed, we adjourned to the Colonial & had supper. Young came to invite us to breakfast with Governor at 8.30.

Wednesday, September 30th.—Before breakfast transferred Assiniboine & Co to Reliance & gave them in charge of Captain Tovine who was so kind to them before. I had given them a note to Mr. Alard, Hudson's Bay officer in charge at Yale, to look after them. Also sent packet of books to McKay. At breakfast were Good, Young, & Bushby (in some Gov't post). Nice little wooden house on road to the camp. Governor smoked his pipe with us after breakfast & related with great gusto how the Yankee officer with some 20 men in possession of St. Juan had actually kept off the British men-of-war by his effrontery & swagger; & how when General Scott was sent to settle affairs the Governor had informed him that the only arrangement he was able to agree to was that the Yankee troops should be immediately withdrawn, to which Scott at once consented!

Finding that the Douglas steamer 'Hope' had not yet come in & therefore probably would not return until afternoon or tomorrow, we walked over to the Engineers' camp to call on Colonel Moody whom we found in his office, & just about to walk over to New Westminster to look after the sale of some Town lands by auction which was to take place today. He gave a most tempting description of the prospects of New Westminster, & the desirability of the investment that we were induced to walk back with him & promise to look in at the sale. Called at Governor's as we passed & received a circular letter addressed officially to the Gold Commissioners requesting them to assist us in all ways, likely to be very useful, especially as we shall probably

be short of cash. Went to the sale at the Court House, &
Milton, carried away by the excitement bought 7 lots ranging
from 3 to 9 acres at from £20 to 32£ each. I bid for one lot,
but Milton bid against me by mistake, & I of course stopped
bidding, therefore did not buy at all; ¼ to be paid at once,
rest by Xmas.

During sale Reliance sailed for Yale, carrying Governor &
suite, & Assiniboine & family. I therefore did not say good bye.
After went with Good & Captain Spalding the Magistrate &
Postmaster General to view the newly acquired property about
½ mile at the back of the town, but the forest was so thick &
the marks so indistinct that we could not make them out. On
return found Hope had come in but would not start back till
tomorrow. Archdeacon Wright & Attorney General Creese
had left cards.

Thursday, October 1st.—Good came to breakfast with us
& afterwards took us to Assay Office to see the gold dust melted
into ingots, & assaying process explained. After which were
introduced to Creese, a good looking bearded fellow like some
one I know; got on board about 2 o'clock. All night, nearly,
wooding & but little sleep in our narrow berths, for which they
charged us $2 each.

Friday, October 2nd.—Going before daybreak, having anch-
ored most of the night; a great flat boat full of hay lashed alongside & delaying our progress, so that we did not reach Douglas
until 6 o'clock. 45 miles from New Westminster. Douglas
Lake 45 miles long; immense numbers of salmon splashing about
in shallows of rapid in Harrison River. Indian boys in canoes
spearing them now in bad season. Bill on boat $10 each for 3
meals, passage & bed. Douglas a vile hole in hollow formed by
continuation of lake basin up to hill beyond lake; put up at
Macdonald's; wretched supper of pork & liver. Miners gambling
& drinking. Yankees preponderating; scarcity of women. Silver
mine on Harrison lake; talk of working it.

Saturday, October 3rd.—Find stage will not go till Monday.
Walk up to inquire of Mr. Gaggin the Judge if there are any
other means of getting forward. Regular jolly Irishman from
Cork; kindly promises to lend Milton a horse if I can find an-
other. Agree to start on horseback tomorrow. Introduced to a
Captain Nunn, very stout & barefaced, small featured; & Dr.
Sylvester a handsome young fellow with slightly grey hair &
shaky hand. Gaggin told us of miners & Chinamen coming

down in canoes without their heads. Barrett Lennard never came further than Harrison Lake into British Columbia, & Macdonald (another author) never beyond Langley. Delayed us with beer. About 5, stage came in with 10 miners. Prisoner brought in. Going up to see Gaggin, met a Sywash prisoner who had escaped, just recaptured, shot in the neck by constable altho' he did not resist; trotted along with string to the ring of his gyves.

Sunday, October 4th.—After sundry beers & procrastinations we set out. Gaggin having found a mule for me for which I had to pay $10 for the 29 miles. The Judge accompanied us on a grey horse which had been left behind by a Mr. Flinn gone down to Victoria. "The Judge" turned out a "whale for drink," & we pulled up at every wayside house to refresh; as we started late our chance of getting thro' looked small; dined at the 10-mile house where we were so strongly advised by the Governor to have a feed; & a very nice clean dinner we had. Kept by a German named Perrin. From there we trotted on to the 16-mile house kept by an old Scotch ship's-carpenter named Waite, & finding it late, we resolved to stay the night & ride forward in time for the steamer in the morning. Gaggin & I had two jugs of mulled claret which made us sleep like tops.

Monday, October 5th.—Off at 7 to catch the steamer at 12. At the 20-mile house there is a hot spring & baths; rude wooden affairs. Water a slight smell of sulphuretted hydrogen, & said by bath proprietor to contain common salt & nitrate of soda; reputation for cure of rheumatism; the water runs out of the solid rock at the foot of the hill in a small stream the size of one's finger; hot enough to boil an egg; similar spring at the foot of Harrison Lake. My mule 'Yank' falling lame, I rode on, leaving Milton & Gaggin at the 24-mile house refreshing. Arrived at foot of the little lake (29-mile house) an hour before the steamer started, dined & waited in vain for Milton & Gaggin; the steamer at last starting & leaving us in the lurch; much annoyed at thus losing a day. Presently stage came in from Douglas, bringing only one passenger, Mr. Flinn whose horse Gaggin had impressed to ride along with us. Also "Hard Cussie" & another fellow of the well-known "Hard Cussie" claim. About 4 o'clock Milton & "The Judge" arrived, the latter having met some friends at the last house & gone through ½ doz. of stout!—

Introduced to Mr. Flinn who has a farm & the ferry at Lillooet & kindly offered me his horse to ride over the portages.

Gaggin & the landlady (an Irishwoman) had chaff all the evening; very nice clean beds. Country between Douglas & Little Lillooet Lake thickly wooded; very little farming country; flat patches of small extent; usual gorges & hills; mostly rocky ground.

Passed Summit Lake, water flowing in opposite directions supplying 2 rivers.

Tuesday, October 6th.—Steamer brought in 2 prostitutes, white woman & negress, having spent the season in Cariboo (made fortunes). Over Little Lillooet Lake in tiny steamer, then portage past rapids (some $\frac{1}{4}$ mile) which are not passable at lower water; & then in fine steamer "Prince of Wales" over Great Lillooet Lake to Pemberton, a miserable rocky place. Gaggin accompanied us. Continual liquorings up, which Milton & I shirked as well as we could. Lakes surrounded with lofty rocky mountains sparsely wooded with pine & poplar. Arrived at dark.

Wednesday, October 7th.—Bid a kind adieu to Gaggin, & then forward 24 miles to Anderson Lake; pretty good road & usual scenery; a little farming land called The Meadows 2 or 3 miles from Pemberton. Milton rode Gaggin's mare, & I Flinn's grey, both capital hackneys, & we went thro' at a great pace. Flinn borrowed a horse, & "Charley Chapman" the owner of the steamer, accompanied us. For dinner we stayed at the house half-way owned by a Virginian of the name of Ketterel. He had only been there a year. There is a fine open flat of I suppose 100 acres partly under cultivation, such good open land is rare. He bought at 2,000 dollars, & the first year's crops paid the purchase. The seller who was led away by the Bentinck Arm route excitement went there, then thro' Cariboo, & eventually set up an opposition house within a mile of his old quarters, but no good land! Ketterel was an ardent Southerner & the most gentlemanly American we have met, very quiet & does not "blow". He & Flinn praised the Governor highly, & assured us that, were there to be an election for the office, he would have 99% of the votes. Ketterel had two pretty little daughters whom he evidently idolized & the youngest who could hardly talk informed us lispingly that she was "for Jeff Davis", & when she went home she should "fight the Yankees". Rode on rapidly to Anderson where we slept; Nice clean house kept by Frenchman; meals $1 each. Beds $1. Horses $1 per bed.

Thursday, October 8th.—Away at 6.30 over Anderson

Lake; in slow old steamer which took 3 hours to do some 16 miles; then portage of a mile to Seaton Lake where we had a fast boat which brought us across the lake in 1½ hours. The scenery on this lake is finer than the others, the mountains being higher, steeper & more rugged, descending nearly perpendicularly into the water. The brilliant yellow & red autumn tints contrasting with the dark green & black of the pines, & the bright green of the poplars, together with the varied shades of the rocks were more beautiful than I ever saw before. From Seaton, Milton & Flinn rode in. We loaded a "Lywarle" with our small baggage, & I walked in the 4 miles to Lillooet, a town of one street on one of the terraces of the Fraser. Very fair accommodation at the Stage Hotel.

Introduced us to "Judge Elliot", a pleasant little man who had crossed the Atlantic with Milton when he came out to New York before. He invited us to his house & introduced us to Mrs. Elliot, a very ladylike woman, with whom I was rather smitten, having a most remarkable likeness to Mrs. Tylor in both face & manner. In evening met Dr. Walker just arrived from Cariboo, out with McClintock in the Fox, now on some investigations for one of the societies. Very jolly fellow indeed; in Cariboo 5 months; gave us very unpromising news; snow, slush, mire already; not likely to get in with horses if at all. Miners phrases, "You bet," "You bet your gumboots!" "Your bottom dollar," "putting on frills," "piling the agonies," "getting into the mines," &c. "Caved in," "Played out."

Friday, October 9th.—Resolve to go by stage tomorrow. Rather a disturbed night. A half tipsy miner burst into our bedroom & swore it was his, & that it had 3 beds in beforetime. I assured him that it had now only two, & was not his & he made tracks; then at daybreak they rowed us out to ask if we were going on to Seaton by the stage; later on, the bottom of my bed which consisted of nothing but laths nailed on to the frame gave way & I came bump on to the floor, & was compelled to move the mattress on to the floor at the side & try again. Two men passing my door & seeing my boots outside where I had put them in vain hope of their being cleaned a little called out "Who's that d—d d—l, putting on the frills he is?" After breakfast wrote up my notes, & talked with Walker. A poor fellow nearly dying of Cardiac dropsy came in yesterday evening & was very thankful to get me to prescribe for him; better today. Dined with Elliot & met Reverend Brown the parson here, &

The "Rattlesnake Grade."
Pavillion Mountain, British Columbia; Altitude, 4,000 feet.

author of the essay. After leaving there visited Subsheriff Hudson, newly married man; Walker & Flinn there; nice music, "Glorious Apollo" & other glees. "O wert thou in the cauld blast," reminding me of home; not in bed till 12.

Saturday, October 10th.—Up at 7, hoping to start at eight & make the 47-mile house (Clinton). But did not leave until 10.30, owing to packing of freight ¾ ton, & only 3 passengers viz. ourselves & Mr. Hall, the Canadian whose horse had foundered over Flinn's ferry and along hilly road, mostly cut out of side of mountains & narrow. Our Jehu, a Yankee, drove well & rattled us down the hills; cranky stage, & overweighted, (nearly a ton), & if anything should give way, why, over the precipice. Fraser river scenery. Stayed for night at 15-mile house; wretched place, no fire, no beds. Milton slept under the counter, I alongside it, Hall on the top; 4 or 5 miners along the floor.

Sunday, October 11th.—Under way about 7. Passed Judge Begbie[61] on horseback. Everybody praises his just severity as the salvation of Cariboo & terror of rowdies. After about 10 miles come to Captain Marltey's roadside house; has a ranch near & flourishing. Then up the Pavilion mountain with a tremendous ascent, stage road winding along side of hill, but we walked straight up the mountain side, awfully steep & killing; I think 5000 feet above level. Extraordinary appearance of mountain slope on east of creek at bottom, as if waves of land beginning half way down in small waves, & gradually increasing to larger billows towards the bottom. Volcanic eruption or water? 3 miles along level top brought us to 29-mile house where we got fair dinner; passed numerous returning miners & pack trains. Then after ascending still higher, commence descent of Pavilion by "rattlesnake grade", the most dangerous carriage road I ever saw; the road turns 6 times, is very narrow except at the turns, the mountain side terrifically steep. We rattled down at a fearful pace, a wheel coming off, the brake giving way, or a restive horse being almost certain death. At the bottom a lake; at the further end a farm; better land; level road all the way along a valley up to 47-mile house, junction of Lytton & Lillooet roads; several large ranches; only hay, oats, & vegetables grown. Passed a magnificent camel grazing alongside of road; one of the two brought out, first tried in California & then here; failures in both countries. Met Mr. Smith the packer at Clinton; horse given in.

Monday, October 12th.—Thro' level country of "cyprèe" & lakes to 70-mile house for dinner, & forward to 84 to sleep. Miserable teams, horses wretchedly thin & one lame. Passed this morning a curious chasm in the earth 300 or 400 yards wide height 200 or 300 feet perpendicular. Valley sides as if cut with knife, commencing in a gradual depression & ending abruptly in a valley to the south. Passed the stage going down, full; learnt that the horses for next relay at 84 were still lost; therefore no going on beyond there tonight! & the same horses to go on 17 miles tomorrow! Cameron said to be coming down with 540 lbs weight of gold! real weight 630 lbs, 40 or 50 miners on foot; several mule pack trains. Last porter at 70-mile house 1¼ dollar per pint bottle!

Tuesday, October 13th.—Started late as we had only 16 miles to do. Came on heavy rain, giving us a good soaking before arrival, cleared up after. Afternoon to spend here at 100-mile house for want of horses. Met express waggon here. Express left mouth of Quesnel yesterday morning at 6; since then 60 miles by steamer & 78 by waggon! — On the road passed a covered waggon which they told us conveyed a sick miner; found out on our arrival at 100-mile house that it was the man who cut his throat a week ago & had been lying there ever since; now sent down to Lillooet for Doctor. The man is mad. All day thro' high table land thickly wooded with small 'cyprèe,' sandy, rocky & barren. To 100-mile house descended for nearly 3 miles to low ground; apparently better soil; a little open land & scattered poplars, rather reminding one of the Saskatchewan. Three of the 4 Indians condemned to death for murder of 7 whites (which they confessed) are said to have escaped, their jailor taking them out into the woods with him unfettered, & left them there to wait for his return whilst he went to change his boots! — Frequently sent to store for bacon, &c! (This is report of Express party.)

Wednesday, October 14th.—Now out of high land with a series of valleys continued from that of last night, strongly resembling 'park-like' country of Saskatchewan; numerous streams & lakes; hills thickly timbered with pines. Along here many "ranches" where oats, barley & vegetables seem to grow pretty well but very short in the straw. Only these "bottoms" that seem at all likely to repay a farmer. At night passed the spot where Clegg was murdered, not ¼ mile from the next house. Thro' roughish road & down hill to Davidson's (150-mile post), a large square unfinished house; billiard room; lots of geese, ducks & chickens. All kinds of vegetables. Mr. Davidson was exceedingly kind & hospitable, as also Mr. Hudson, brother of the man we met at Lillooet. Gave us some very good Hudson's Bay port to supper. Davidson has an extensive farm here & makes money fast, although he says farming land is not first rate & scarce.

Thursday, October 15th.—My Birthday, but I forgot to keep it. A long ride with tired horses; dined at Frank Way's 114-mile, he has farm of valley 4 miles long & $\frac{1}{4}$ wide; over 200 acres; a considerable part of this growing oats & barley which is cut principally for hay. Then, leaving the valleys, we crossed timbered hills, descending by a sinuous & very steep road into the valley of the Fraser once more at Soda Creek to wait here, where there were a few houses, for the steamer at noon tomorrow. House kept by a Yankee. All 'Docs' & 'Caps'.

Friday October 16th.—Steamer came in about 2 o'clock bringing a host of miners 2 of whom were very drunk & continued to imbibe every 5 minutes; during the time we stayed in the house they must have had 20 drinks. The swearing was something fearful. After we had been on board a short time the Captain, finding out who we were, gave us the use of his cabin, a comfortable little room, & supplied us with cigars & a decanter of cocktail, also books & papers. We were fetched out every few minutes to have a drink with some one, the Captain taking the lead by standing champagne all round. We had some dozen to do before supper; no one the least affected, Milton & I shirking in quantity. The 'Cap' told us the boat was built on the river, all the timber sawn by hand, the shaft in 5 pieces packed up on mules, cylinders in two, boiler plates brought in same manner. Boat cost $75.000!

Saturday, October 17th.—As we did not leave Soda Creek until 4 & the boat makes very slow progress against the powerful current, we had to anchor for night after doing only some 10 miles. At daybreak went on 4 or 5 miles, & then delayed by the dense fogs which prevail on the river in the early morning at this season. Passed Fort Alexander about 10. No great trade there now; depot of furs from the north; 20 miles from Soda Creek. Country more level & under usual Fraser benches, & low wooded hills; river banks sandy; few rocks; River about

A Way Side House.—Arrival of Miners.

A Way Side House at Midnight.

size of Saskatchewan at Edmonton; Coal found on banks. Continually called out to have a drink.

Sunday, October 18th.—Arrived about 9, at Quesnel mouth, a little collection of about 20 houses on the wooded banks of the Fraser. Quesnel at the north side of the Fort. Large new stores & cards all lying about the street. A drizzling rain all day. We made up our pack & set out. Captain Done met us in street half seas over & insisted to treat us to champagne, &c., at every bar in the place. At last escaped & walked to 4-mile house where we found Hall & another man who had started before us waiting for us. We stayed there all night. Packers playing cards. Proprietor one of the Canadians who had come overland & down the Fraser last year. Gave fearful account of hardships especially on the raft.

Monday, October 19th.—On foot to Smith's, 2 miles beyond the Cottonwood. Awful trail, nothing but stumps, roots & mud up to the ankles. Saw 6 horses lying dead in the road, hundreds probably a little way off in bush. Thro' nothing but small pines & poplars. Tall 'Maine' man killed 2 martens which crossed the road & we treed, and 2 partridges with his revolver. Very tired and footsore tho' only 20 miles. Milton got thro' famously, walking in moccasins!

Tuesday, October 20th.—Sharp frost. Mudholes frozen. Big boots excruciating. Milton & I, each picked up a pair of cast away gumboots on the road & left our own at houses till return; 14 miles to dinner & 6 more after to Beaver Pass where we found the Gold Escort & 40 miners; 12 dead horses & mules on the road. I had an awful cold, sore heels & pack of 30 lbs which I found too heavy before dinner. Awful night last night; wind blowing thro' cracks in walls & floor; only one blanket a-piece; 20 men in room; one afflicted with cramp in his leg which brought him on his feet swearing every ½ hour. Milton & another talking in their sleep; rest snoring; my nose running; little sleep.

Wednesday, October 21st.—In the morning passed along Lightning Creek to Van Winkle; past Welsh Company's claim which is stopped as wheel is broken. Milton walked very well; my heels very sore; snow getting deeper up to 3 inches. Called at Irishwoman's named Edwards, 3 miles short of Van Winkle, & had a cup of coffee for which she charged us ½ dollar each. Passed Welsh Company's claim which had stopped working

Miners Washing for Gold

on account of ice having broken wheel. At Van Winkle about a dozen houses (Lightning Creek). Passed on 2 miles further to a house where we got a capital dinner, beefsteak pie & beefsteak & onions & pancakes! a long weary walk winding along hill sides past the Bald mountain into William's Creek. Milton held out well walking like a man, carrying his hat slung like a pack although there was frost. At dusk we arrived at Richfield, the first part where gold was struck on this creek, & it was quite dark before we reached Cameron Town below, passing thro' Barkerville or Middle town. The whole 3 towns extending almost continuously down the creek for a mile, & containing about 60 or 70 houses apiece. This spring were only 3 or 4 houses at Cameron Town! Our path was a difficult one over endless sluices, flumes & ditches, across icy planks & logs, all getting tumbles, gumboots being very treacherous. Putnam the "Maine man", took us to his home & treated us, recommending Mr. Cusheon's as a good place to stay at. They gave us a good supper & plenty of blankets.

Thursday October 22nd.—Got up very late, being very stiff & sore. In afternoon, Cusheon took us to Cameron Co's hut & introduced us to Steele & the other 3 partners of the Cameron Co, except Cameron & Stevenson who had gone down; they treated us to brandy & water & then took us down to view the operations below. The shaft about 30 feet down thro' gravel & clay to bedrock of slate. Numerous shafts all supported by timber & very closely roofed in with flat crosspieces. Wet, damp, dark & gloomy; the shafts being in many parts very low, the "pay dirt" not being extensive perpendicularly. At the bottom shaft the pay dirt was best high up; at the upper end, down close to the bedrock; they kindly helped us to wash out two pans which yielded some beautiful gold to the value of $21, nearly 1 1/3 oz; we could see the nuggets lying in the gravel before loosened out by the pick! The claim was bought for a mere nothing, & the thing quite a fluke. Steele showed me about $1000 of gold in a bag, & the Company's books, showing weekly expenses averaging 7000 dollars, the yield being generally from 40 to 112 oz. per shaft (of which there were 3) per day or $29. on to $29.000 per week! over 100 feet of claim yet quite untouched. Steele very kind & intelligent.

Friday, October 23rd.—Got up very late, & towards noon walked up the mile to Richfield to see Mr. Cox, a capital fellow. Fat, tall, thick set fellow with very short coat, large features, retiring forehead, no whiskers & large moustache very German; but not in manner. Delicately polite, gentlemanly & jolly. Captain FitzStubbs came in. What a name! had been in army, came out with Barrett Lennard, now speculating in claims. Stayed there until ½ past 4 & on getting back to Cusheon's we found they had eaten our dinner. We had however a very nice one in adjacent house of mother-in-law & daughter who treated us hospitably. Steele invited us to Miner's cabin to have a pipe & we got much information from him.

Saturday, October 24th.—FitzStubbs took us to visit the Caledonian claim: did not go down himself for fear of dirtying his coat! Two or three proprietors took us round & helped Milton to wash a pan of dirt which produced nearly an ounce of very coarse gold. The shafts in this mine were very low & wet, the pay dirt being not of great depth. Then had lunch in miners' hut & smoked pipes with them. A large portion of this mine yet unworked. On return were introduced to Mr. Raby, a Cornishman & proprietor of the Raby claim. Also Mr Courtney, a lawyer from Dublin; wonderful number of Irishmen. Raby took us down the "Raby claim" & showed us some rich pockets of gold. The dirt visibly full of it & we could see the 'plums', the bits of gold in the face of the cutting. The place where we found this "pocket" was under a large boulder & this is where they are usually met with. And it is easy to understand how, when the boulder was lying in what was then the bed of the creek, & the water rippling past it, the gold would lodge in the crevices *under* the stone. Mr. Raby picked out a few lumps of the rich dirt, as much as would fill a quart pot perhaps, & Milton washed it. There was about an ounce. The Raby claim is very extensive, 1,000 feet, the pay dirt very extensive, being found high above the bed rock as well as on it, the claim being already worked on drifts 12 feet high in some places; gold has also been found plentifully in the gravel above the drifts & Mr. Raby expects to work this from the surface after the drifts are worked out. Enough to last & pay highly for 3 years. The gold seems evidently to have been washed down the old bed of the stream. The difficulty is to find out where the bed of the creek originally was, & the only way seems to be by following the lead. Claims are sometimes taken up & worked on the present bed, & it is found that the "lead" is not there; it passes right into the hill perhaps on one

The Cameron "Claim," William's Creek, Cariboo.

side or the other of the narrow valley; some slide, or volcanic eruption having changed the course of the stream.

We heard of the Dillon & Currie claim where 102 lbs. of gold were taken out as result of 8 hours work! The Wattie shaft where out of 100 feet of which it consisted $120.000 were taken, leaving over $70.000 clear profit.

Talking to one of the miners, he remarked "Well, Doctor, I've the greatest repect for both the professions of law & medicine; but its a curious fact that in this creek last year we had neither lawyers nor doctors, & we lived without litigation & free from illness. This year there has been a large influx of both lawyers & doctors, & there has been nothing but lawsuits & deaths in the place!" The appearance of William's Creek (so named from William Dietz, a Prussian the discoverer) is merely a narrow valley shut in by pine clad hills, the edges & bottom partially cleared & covered with wooden huts, flumes, waterwheels, windlasses, shafts, ditches & tunnels. In the evening went with Stuart, the Cameron Co's. foreman, to see a Scotchwoman who possessed the most beautiful specimen of native gold I have yet seen. Not more than 2 or 3 oz, but like the most perfectly frosted jeweler's gold & of fantastic shape.

Sunday, October 25th.—Did but little till afternoon, when Mr. Greer called & took us up to Richfield to call at his cabin to view some 'specimens'. I am already beginning to hate the name. But these were very fine, one nearly 6 oz. the other 7 oz. Both from Loughea; frosted looking bright gold with quartz. He kindly gave us several nice nuggets from the Greer claim on this creek. Introduced to Dr. Black practising here & who promised to go over to Loughea tomorrow with us, 3 miles from this. Dined with "Judge" Cox who was exceedingly pleasant. Present Courtney, a young Canadian, & an Englishman whose names I did not catch. A jolly evening, & home by bright moonlight in the snow.

Monday, October 26th.—Went over with Black to Loughea. He was very pleasant, having seen a great deal of mining in Australia. Loughea very like William's Creek, only smaller scale; 4 claims working, "Sage Miller", Vaughan, Crane's & another. Pays well, & beautifully fine gold; all done by tunnelling. Milton bought $37 worth of gold from Miller, I contented myself with $10. Miller had been all over the world, California, Australia & up the Amazon which he describes as a magnificent country; found gold (flower) in pan. Had pleasant walk over the hill back to William's Creek 3 miles. The great wants here are capital & steam power. Waterwheels freeze up early. Currie & another are now bringing up engines by the first sleighs. "Mr. Dixie", a nigger barber from Tennessee, was introduced to Milton, & as he said he should die happy if he could only shave a real live lord, he is to operate on Milton tomorrow.

Tuesday, October 27th.—Went to Bowling Alley with Cusheon, & he & I each licked Milton. Thence to see Mr. Raby of whom Milton bought 2 oz gold & I $10 of specimens. Witnessed washing up of one shaft Raby claim, shift & a half, (15 hours) over $4,000! A preserved meat tin case full.

At 6 went up to the Hospital the other side of the creek on the top of the hill. Found there Courtney, Mr. Blenkinsopp, an old H. B. Chief Trader now mining, Mr. Cocker, manager of Macdonald's bank here, Dr. Bell, a G. P. Brown, a young Irishman assisting Dr. Black, & Billy Farren, a successful miner in the Caledonia Claim, a rough boisterous Irishman who had been a sailor. Also Janet Morris a Scotchwoman, fair, fat & forty, the wife of a man who keeps a store, & who came to make the plum-pudding &c, & of course sat down & dined with us. Champagne ad-lib, & Dr. Bell rapidly became maudlin. He was a little smooth-faced man in dress coat, with large mouth & white teeth always smiling, under some obligation to the Fitz-William family under whom his father is tenant in Northamptonshire. He rose after the first glass before we had got to pudding & proposed in the most fulsome & absurd manner Milton's health & the Aristocracy of England. "Gentlemen, Dr. Black invited me here to meet a noble scion of the noblest house in England. I don't exaggerate when I say so. I can't exaggerate. I feel grateful to Dr. Black, deeply grateful for asking me here to meet the "noble scion" of one of the noblest houses England ever produced. It is a proud day for all of us & for this creek; it is the commencement of a new era," &c &c, quite nauseous, & he continued to propose toasts. Interlude, "He's a jolly good fellow" & sentiments, all full of the "Noble Scion". Then Dr Black overflowing with loyalty, laying his hand upon his heart & willing to die at once for his Queen & country; proposing the health of Her Majesty. Interlude "God save the Queen". My health. Interlude "He's a jolly good fellow" &c. We then adjourned to the kitchen & had more healths; songs. And then Janet presented Milton very prettily with a handsome nugget (25 dollars) for him to give his mother from her. After which in a "gushing" speech Black presented Milton with a large gold ring made on the Creek out of "never sweat" gold worth some $50. Billy Farren then gave me a nice gold & quartz specimen, & Janet another. After all which Dr. Bell essayed several speeches but was sung down by the company in Auld Lang Syne, & after sitting half asleep for some time made a bolt for the door which he thought was next the chimney, & was led off to bed by Mr. Brown. He rolled off with a crash twice during the evening, cutting his head against the stove. The dinner was held in the Hospital ward, the only patient a poor devil with anasarca being covered up with a piece of baize hanging from the wall. We had whist & 7 up pitch, after which supper & hot grog with numerous arguments about the mining laws until two o'clock when I persuaded Milton to come home. Both quite sober.

Wednesday, October 28th.—Milton went down another shaft of the Caledonia, & I, sick of going down in buckets, & crouching along drifts, walked on to Richfield & had pipe with the Judge where Milton joined me shortly; we entered into negotiations to borrow $500 from Cox, who was very kind & lent it us gladly; we were already out of cash, having spent $2000 since leaving Victoria, & Cox said that was very moderate indeed! ($200 of this went towards Milton's purchase of land at New Westminster.) To call next day for the money.

Thursday, October 29th.—Went with Black to call on 'Janet' & bade her an affectionate goodbye. Introduced to Mr Stenhouse, who had been a man of property in England, ruined by a 'Derby', afterwards made a large fortune as stage coach proprietor in Australia which he again lost, & is now living on speculations & his wits here; a very coarse vulgar but amusing man withal. Face purple-red like Bardolph's. Volunteers to go down with us tomorrow. Called at the Judge's for cash. Snowstorm; now nearly a foot of snow here, but not cold except at night when it is down to 5°. In evening Black called & took us into Jem O'B's of the Caledonia to drink whiskey punch.

Friday, October 30th.—Bade goodbye to Cusheon & Cameron Town, called & bid adieu to Cox. Our bill for 8 days was 78 dollars each, & very moderate for the place. An Irishman caught us up & walked in company as far as the Edwards 4 miles from Van Winkle. He amused me keeping a constant talk all the way. He was a cattle driver & said he knew the whole country well. Had hunted cattle nearly up to the head of the Fraser & round to Fort George, starting from Antler Creek! a few nights ago in danger from a pack of wolves at Cottonwood. Out on horseback. Climbed into a tree & set fire to the gum &c, & they eventually cleared off. At Edwards we found Stuart (Cameron foreman) & Mathieson (partner in Victoria firm & in claims here); they were on their way to look at two men prospecting the 'Ayrshire Lass' claim on Lightning above on the hill; & we accompanied them down the creek, leaving the trail to the left. Our path lay along the top of the bank above the creek, & in a hollow of what appeared to be the old bed of a stream; at the further end was the 'Ayrshire Lass'; here we found 2 men working at a tunnel into the side of the mountain. Not yet struck the bedrock. They gave up work & led the way down the hill-side into the valley to their cabin. Invited us to stay with them all night as it was already nearly dark, & too late to see the famous Hill diggings that night. We agreed, & they cooked us bacon & beans & with a small bottle of real 'H. B. Rum given us by John Ducie Cusheon at parting, we spent a very pleasant evening. Adam Ross one of the two, had been a very extensive explorer along Vancouver Island & this coast. Told us 24,000 of one tribe of Indians died last year of small-pox. Turned out into the bush when attacked by the disease, & the men shot themselves & the women hanged themselves; might be seen dead by hundreds; a continual fusillade; awful cold night & only one blanket apiece.

Saturday, October 31st.—Bade adieu to our miner friends & went on with Mathieson to view the Butcher & Discovery Claims on the hill; we found men at work on the Butcher, & some sinking a tunnel, others working out from the surface. Could pick out gold from the dirt about a yard below the surface; beautifully fine without quartz & deep yellow. Had all been worked by "hydraulicking", but now too cold, & sluicing used; 200 feet above creek. Old bed of a creek going at right angles into mountain; to be the great excitement next season. Lightning so termed from the Yankee expression, it being very difficult to work, & very uncertain. The lead is lost at every turn of the creek, where it passes round a point. Many claims thus found nothing. It is now supposed that the lead runs thro' the hill at these points, there having been slides which have covered over the original bed. The Hill diggings were discovered by their being at a claim below in the bed of present creek, & finding that the lead evidently did not come down the creek, but from the hill. They tunnelled into the hill to no purpose, but one day one of the boys went on to the top & scratching the earth with his knife saw gold, & on further investigating, it was found in plenty, sometimes 3 or 4 feet only below. Never more than 15 or 16; in Discovery Claim less. Went to Van Winkle for dinner, & then to Welsh Co., 2 miles on. Evans the manager not at home. His son very civil; if there is gold in the creek, they must have it, for they will prospect the whole bottom. Wheel burst with frost, stopping working of shaft; great drawback to Lightning is bed of quicksand which bursts in the limbers from its water; 25 Welshmen employed; backed by Manchester Capitalists.

Sunday, November 1st.—Bade goodbye to Mr. MacCaffrey & walked on to the Welsh Company's claim. Found Evans Senior at home keeping Sunday. A contrast to William's Creek. He told us that they were now prospecting in the mountains all round & had come upon what he expected would prove a valuable silver lead; no gold; expected to drop upon the "Last Chance" lead with their shaft. Provisions alone had cost $12,000, in 4 months. Had 4 pumps & were completely master of the water in the shaft, which he considered was the main point & which had been the great stumbling block to miners hitherto. Had taken up that claim on Lightning because as the mining laws at present stand the Government cannot grant a lease for a claim over 100 feet unless of ground already worked & abandoned by other miners; therefore he must either take up this large piece of abandoned ground or put himself in the hands of his men by taking up 100 feet in the name of each. But it appears there was enough vacant ground in William's Creek if the law had allowed him to lease it. We passed forward to Beaver Pass for Dinner, 10 miles from Van Winkle & from there 6 miles forward to Edward's. He has been a mate on board a merchant-man for 8 or 9 years, after that mining in Australia, came over here in '58. He is a thorough-going Englishman & gave us several amusing stories of the state of things on the first rush to this country. How he was quite alone amongst the Yankees at Boston Bar (or one of the Fraser River Bars); how they bullied him & he gave them tit for tat, they at last rolling him in a ditch & covering him with sand to make an American Citizen of him. We also heard the stories (I forget from whom) of

TRIP ACROSS CANADA

Abbot, the successful Cariboo miner, who shied a handful of 20 dollar pieces at a large pier-glass at Victoria worth some $200, and another who, having treated all the Company in the bar room & finding no more, had all the glasses of the Establishment filled up on the counter, & swept them off with his fist! Another who in the same way being unable to find enough people to treat opened a hamper of champagne & jumped into it, thereby cutting his shins considerably. Major Downie, formerly of Downieville, California, now on William's Creek, at the Christening of Downieville, set up champagne bottles in the ten pin alley & bowled at them! Most of these in fact all are in low water now. Edwards said altho' he hated Yankees, he had the greatest admiration of their energy; they opened out this country in '58 or '59, mostly Southerners; at Boston Bar some of the Yankees got up an excitement, which was agitated by the steamboat proprietor who brought such a report down to Victoria that the Governor sent up Col. Moody & a company of the Engineers in the steamer at once. Steamer stuck on the rapids & was detained a day or two, the owner drawing pay all the time; when they arrived at the place, there was a great laugh at the expense of the soldiers, the only disturbance which had occurred being between the notorious Ned McGowan & another, in which the former had blackened the eyes of the other. McGowan was fined $25, & the Officers went & had a champagne lunch with him afterwards! 2 Justices of the Peace, one at Yale & the other at Hope, each decided the cases according as he was paid & constant appeals from one to the other.

Monday, November 2nd.—A rough walk from Edward's to Cottonwood, 16 miles. Marten tracks every few yards. Milton & I treed one & fired 6 shots at him with our revolvers without effect. Dined at Smith & Ryder's, & then walked on in heavy snowstorm, to Ramsay's (Cottonwood) for the night. About 20 men there. Got plenty of blankets tho' not very clean. The same amount of snow as at William's Creek.

Tuesday, November 3rd.—Very muddy trail to 8-mile house, an Irishman's who gave us a very nice dinner. Chinaman cook. Trapping martens hard; had killed a dozen with a few wretched traps near the house. From there a long 12 miles in to Quesnel Mouth; where we arrived after dark; put up at Brown's where they made us very comfortable & gave us whiskey toddy as a nightcap. Milton not a bit knocked up, our gumboots serving us well (picked up on roadside going into Beaver Pass).

Wednesday, November 4th.—Steamer stopped & hauled on to the bank — row boat going down tomorrow to Yale which will take us to Soda Creek. Numerous Chinamen keep stores here. Chinese & English signs, "Kan See washing, ironing & Bakery "————", &c., &c. Called on Captain Done on the Steamer. Cocktails every 5 minutes, & champagne lunch afterwards. Happiest man I ever saw. Steward tells me he takes a cocktail every ten minutes when on board. Very jolly fellow. Had to give a keg of brandy to his men before they could haul the steamer on shore. Gave them a champagne dinner on being paid off today, & we heard them singing away below deck. Came in for many champagne drinks during the day. Paid $10 for passage in boat to Soda Creek, & found to our delight & surprise that we had still 3 oz. gold dust to take us forward. Talked with McBride who has been all the season up Peace River thro' the Rocky Mountains a little below Fort St. John. Gold all the way but not in paying quantities on the other side; 7 or 8 men wintering on Peace River. Coarse gold found on Nation River, one of its tributaries. An old Scotchman some 70 years old has found a fine paying claim on that branch. Describes the country as fine farming land. Mixed prairie & timber, lots of game, cariboo tracks like sheep walks, moose, mountain sheep & bears numerous. Immense quantities of fish. Fine salmon trout. Barley & potatoes grow well at Fort George. Also had long conversation with the discoverer of the Bentinck Arm route. He puts the distance from Fort Alexander to Coast at 190 miles, & brought a pack train thro' in 12 days. Lieut. Palmer followed the Indian trail & made it 270, & damned the route. This man however gives a favourable account of the country as being suitable for farming & somewhat resembling the land about Davidson's, &c. Deep Creek; bunch grass & meadow grass in abundance; 30 houses built at Bentinck Arm already. Packers have been running by that route all summer, & one man intends to get grant from Government to make a trail thro' next season.

— Here at Quesnel barley & potatoes grow well. The cultivated land has been 'reserved' by Government after being preempted by owners, & no compensation yet given for improvements. Quesnel is on a large flat surrounded by a semicircular range of low hills & on the river bank.

Thursday, November 5th.—"Captain" McBride got his boat, a large strongly built 6 oar, ready to start about 11 o'clock & we, together with some 40 other passengers, embarked; very crowded; no room to sit comfortably; like flock of penned sheep. He said he had taken 50 in the same boat last year, & ran thro' to Yale, where he intended to go this time if he could get sufficient passengers. It was a miserably cold, raw, cloudy November day just such as we have in England, & snowing fast, & we were dreadfully starved in spite of several whiskey bottles which came out very soon after we started, & were all emptied before we got very far. The river was unusually low, but we ran all the "riffles" successfully until we came to one below Alexandria, when McBride was induced to take the wrong side by the affirmation of a passenger that the steamer always took that course. Here we stuck fast in a tremendous stream, & could not get her off; there was therefore nothing for it but for some of the men to jump overboard & lighten the boat & help to push her off; several volunteered at once, & carried some of the passengers ashore on their backs, the water being only knee deep. One unfortunate little man got a gigantic miner on his back, & losing his footing, both fell overhead into the water & got thoroughly soused, the small fellow tumbling 3 or 4 times before he could get on his legs against the strong current. Water like ice & day cold enough. Milton & I in the most cowardly manner stuck to the ship & she was quickly lifted over the shallow & taking the drenched men on board again & wrapping them in blankets, we went on until it was almost dark, when the "Cap" suggested camping for the night. Several daredevils urged going forward, but as we were still 10 miles from Soda Creek, & the river so very dangerous, they were overruled by the more sensible, & we put ashore at a large pile of wood belonging to the steamer with which we made free to kindle some enormous fires which were kept going all night. The Captain produced plenty of bread & butter & a flitch of bacon, which with some tea went very well. Milton & I each had a blanket lent us in addition to our own one each, & he constructed a covering of pine boughs which with plenty of brush to lie on made very snug quarters for the night. I collected lots of small pine boughs, & with my feet to the fire, & a good stock of logs to replenish it, spent a very comfortable night.

Friday, November 6th.—Most of the men up before daybreak. Snowing heavily, & I kept my head under the blankets until dawn. We did not start until quite light & made Soda Creek in about an hour. There were several bad places in the river, rock sticking out in the rapids, which made us very thankful we did not try them in the dark. Had breakfast at Soda Creek, left our baggage there for the express to bring forward, & then walked quietly on to Frank Way's (Deep Creek) where we stayed the night. Found the engineer of steamer going down to winter. He told amusing story of the dodges he & Captain Thomas Wright used to work, when in a small underpowered steamer, one of the first on the Fraser. running up to Yale. Had a lot of Jew traders on board & heavy freight. Could not get up a riffle. "All passengers overboard to haul at the tow line," shouts Captain Wright. Not a man would stir. "How much steam on, engineer?" shouts the Captain. "175 lbs., sir, already," replies he with grea seriousness. "Then put on 25 lbs. more & blow her to h—ll," cries the Captain. "Aye, aye, Sir," responds engineer; this used to be quite enough for the Jew passengers; & overboard went every man like a shot & hauled up the steamer. Thus they made up for want of power.

Saturday, November 7th.—Walked forward to Davidson's (Lake Valley Farm) 14 miles. Met Todd the Canadian Horse keeper at Kamloops with a Company's pack train for Alexandria. Told us that Mr. & Mrs. Mackay had arrived at the Fort. Also Assiniboine & family who was now shepherd there. That *Martin* was all right, but *Burgess* had been blown up in the boat, only small pieces of either man or boat found; no one knew how it happened. Matches packed next to powder kegs & perhaps thus. Poor Burgess! quiet hard-working fellow.

Davidson down in Victoria but Hudson in charge, very kind; resolve to wait here a day or two for Express.

Sunday, November 8th.—Walk 3 miles down to head of William's Lake to see the farm. Only good land a bottom of perhaps a thousand acres. Some of barley sown late & small on account of drought. Earlier sown very fine. Farm only commenced in spring. Cabbages very fine; potatoes good. Wheat sown for experiment, but looked very small, weak, & yellow. These bottoms are the only land worth cultivation in British Columbia; all the rest rocky & dry, only producing bunch grass. And the alluvial valleys are not very numerous or of large extent. Pumpkins & squashes of large size. Cattle look very fat & well. Calves bred on the place particularly good.

Monday, November 9th.—Tried shooting but found no grouse; ducks too wild. Read newspapers by last Express.

Tuesday, November 10th.—Took walks & talked of music with Hudson,—Stenhouse, & Court in ....

Wednesday, November 11th.—Hear from men coming down that Express will be several days yet. Heigh ho; rather wearisome altho' first rate feed & cookery; nigger cook up to anything.

Thursday, November 12th.—Mulatto came in with nice specimen of gold from Horse Fly Creek about 35 miles from here; one of the tributaries into lower head of Quesnel lake. Coarse scaly gold of beautiful quality. Paid tolerably well, $2 to $10 to the pan. Not many men working there.

Friday, November 13th.—On Wednesday Frank Way came in for surgical assistance, having in a drunken row with an Irishman had his lower lip almost bitten off, & a finger to the bone. I stitched it up for him, making a very neat job. Foolishly refused any fee. The cause of quarrel was ludicrous; a bet, as to relative mishow payasgoniss, marka quatuck aenivu mistick iskootaoo ositou, aimen osharm. Nothing during the day. 80 acres under cultivation here.

Set to work & dried the barley still out, the weather being very fine & windy, the snow almost gone, quite hot in the sun, & slight frost at night. September or October weather of England.

Saturday, November 14th.—A number of men arrived on way down from William's Creek. Came down in canoes. One laden to water's edge with 14 men swamped in rough water of first riffle 2 miles below Quesnel; 7 men lost; of the others, 5 clung to canoe & got ashore, one was thrown on beach by an eddy, with money & blankets all safe. Another swam ashore, but obliged to drop his blankets containing the dust when within a few yards; 3 or 4,000 dollars lost; 5 belonging to Prince of Wales Claim. Adam Ross (in whose cabin we stopped on Lightning Creek) told us that his partner (whom we also met there) was one of those lost altho' a good swimmer. He delayed a day at the mouth in order to try & get a companion to go by Bentinck Arm & thus escaped. I remember the riffle well, a tremendous rush of water & very rough so that even our large boat shipped water. Frank Way came back to have his lip redressed. Went off into a fit of laughter the other night & sutures gave way. Milk punch instituted with great success.

Sunday, November 15th.—Milton & Hudson rode over to Briggs 6 miles towards Deep Creek where the latter had business. Came back seedy from bad claret. I mooned about the farm. Barley drying well.

Monday, November 16th.—Frank Way came over with horses for thrashing machine. Barley thrashed out altho' very wet. Express waggon came in to our great delight. Poole very sorry he had not met us, (being at Alexander when we passed in the boat) for he would have given us a waggon & pair to drive ourselves down to Yale, & we should have been in Victoria by this time. Bad luck; 18 inches snow on William's Creek; none at Quesnel Mouth.

Tuesday, November 17th.—Poole the Express man had to go down to William's Lake (Mimion Ranch) 11 miles, & came back this morning. Found Gompertz (who had charge of Post Office, & constable over 7 Indians, 3 of whom are under sentence of death, & the other 4 suspected of the crime) too drunk to read the letter. A Klootcheman with him as drunk as himself. Under constable equally drunk with Sywash & Klootcheman in company. Nice state of things, eh! Bid adieu to Hudson after dinner. One fellow passenger a Captain Harrison who told us he left England 20 years ago intending to return every year since & never been able. Been all over Coast of South America, Honolulu, Australia, New Zealand. Now interested in Cariboo, & partner in proposed bed rock flume.

Arrived at dark Blue Tent, 23 miles, after very cold drive. Hail storm & tremendous wind; heard trees falling all round like cannonade.

Wednesday, November 18th.—Off before day light; breakfast at Anderson's 10 miles on Lake La Hache. At Bridge Creek (27 miles) by dinner; from there, leaving the mixed & open country like Davidson's which extends from Bridge Creek to Frank Way's (Deep Creek), we pass up right on to the mountain of green timber at considerable elevation which lasts for 53 miles, nearly to Junction. The road here was covered with ice, & we had to walk up the hill. One horse came down, & we had to unlimber & help up the hill by pushing behind; took us till 8 to get to 84-mile house; we had hoped to reach 74 (Loch Lomond, the old Sergeant's); very severe for horses.

Thursday, November 19th.—Overslept & had breakfast before starting. Road a sheet of ice covered with a few inches of snow. Horses frequently down; had to help the waggon up the steep hills. Met Express coming up at 79-mile post & changed drivers, going forward to Loch Lomond, Sergeant McMurphy's, dined there, & afterwards only got to 59-mile house. Began to snow heavily before we got in. Man went out & shot wolf prowling round.

Friday, November 20th.—Up at 5.30, starting at daybreak to 47-mile House (Clinton Cut-Off Valley) for breakfast. Fearfully cold; 6 inches of snow during night. Arrived about 10. Horses done, & our feet almost frozen. A lot of teamsters & packers at the "Hotel", drinking & one proposed as a toast "The American Eagle which whipped Great Britain, spat on France, p — d on Spain & Portugal," & ——— with a brickbat afterwards. We were glad to get away from the noise. We did not get off until 3 o'clock, & then had 30 miles to do. We had fine moonlight & got to Cornwall's Ranch about 9 o'clock. They have 2 houses, one wayside kept by an employee & their own farm house some ½ mile distant.

The Chinaman cook had got to bed & turned out very sulky to provide us with beefsteaks — our fellow passenger Captain Harrison would have toast which added to his ill-temper. The younger Cornwall (the elder being down at Victoria for supplies) sent word down that he would be glad to see us at the other house, & Milton & I walked up there after supper. Found a tall regular First-Trinity man who received us very hospitably. Had evidently been much disappointed with the country & agriculture. He said some barley had turned out very well; the rest badly; irrigation required. Has got post holes dug for some 3 miles; land open, bunch grass country, either sand or gravel, & I feel certain will never pay for cultivation. They are now going in for Stock farming which will do well if bunch grass lasts. He took his degree in 1859; came out here April 1862.

During the day one of the waggon springs broke. The waggon a very light one. Pole tied on with rope from the first.

Saturday, November 21st.—Went off without disturbing our host & drove over to Cook's Ferry for dinner. The road for 3 or 4 miles some few miles before the ferry passes round some high rocky bluffs. The dangerous trail we rode over when coming down before, the road being then not finished. It is now only 12 feet wide professedly; in many parts really much less from sliding down of the steep sides above the road partially blocking it; the pole was loose, spring broken, waggon generally very loose, traces continually coming off, no brake, heavy load (170 lbs. gold, 4 passengers & luggage) 2 small horses very tired; road very steep up to point of bluff, & then ditto down, about width of waggon, sheer descent of 600 or 700 feet into rocky bed of Thompson, perpendicular side of mountain above; a restive horse or any breakage certain destruction. Part of the road last made by the Engineers (when L. Palmer was anxious to get away to be married) was a narrow strip of loose sand, built up at the edge by loose stones which had partly given way; an awful place. We crossed carefully & safely. Arrived at Cook's Ferry for dinner, after which drove within 10 miles of Lytton; similar road but wider; same precipices & steeps; waggon pole dropped loose, fortunately when we were on the level; tied him up again.

Sunday, November 22nd.—Arrived in Lytton to breakfast. Met Captain Ball again. Parson came up from Yale to hold service in the Court house, but no notice had been given, & no congregation could be got altho' vigorous efforts were made by sending a Sywash round as bellman. Nearly all French & French Canadians in Lytton. Great hopes from Shushwap country which is described as having $60 diggings and abounding in $20 ditto.

Went forward 15 miles for night horses being too tired to do more; leaving 47 miles to do tomorrow.

Monday, November 23rd.—Boston Bar to breakfast; 17 miles; quite a little town; same style of road. Had been well-to-do in river digging ore; now a miserable hole. Delayed a long time there feeding horses; reached bridge 14 miles above Yale a little after dark. On leaving here a few hundred yards the waggon completely broke down, the iron stanchions giving way and pole & cross bars tumbling to ground; on level road; wonderful luck; if this had happened on a precipice we should probably have been lost. Fortunately the other waggon belonging to Express was at the bridge with a splendid pair of horses, Smith's of Cottonwood who was taking some goods up in it. Humphreys, therefore went back for them, whilst we stayed to guard the treasure. We lighted a good fire in the road which served to amuse us until Humphreys returned with other waggon & extra horses which we hitched on in front. Humphreys had brought a bottle of brandy & was greatly exhilarated, had never driven 4 in hand before. Off we went, however we went rattling down hill along the edge of precipices at an awful pace. Humphreys holding reins, Smith sitting beside, whipping up & passing the brandy. Milton & I were in a funk at first, but seeing that the leaders took all the turns to perfection without guiding, felt relieved & half dozed into Yale where we arrived at ½ past 10, having come the 14 miles in about 2 hours. Had supper off tough old fowls, & then turned in about 1. Canyons above Yale very fine. Large rocks stand out in middle of river. La Porte d'Enfer suggests idea of river bursting thro' there.

Tuesday, November 24th.—On board Reliance, having borrowed $30 from Alard, H. B. Co.'s officer in charge there. Arrived at New Westminster about 6. Called on Captain Spalding, very demonstrative. Abused Colonel Moody & told very long wearisome yarns about tigers & serpents in India. Mrs. S. vainly endeavouring to break the spell. Went on board Enterprise for night in a pouring rain.

Wednesday, November 25th.—Not off till 12, full of passengers. Very rough thro' Gulf of Georgia; several sick; I had to retire & assume recumbent posture to quieten sundry qualms. After became still & dined in peace. No cash left. Purser refused to take our fare, the H. B. Co. magnificently granting free passage again. Captain Mowatt came to warn me against our travelling friend Captain Harrison whom he stated was rather disreputable; a kind of male pimp from what I could make out. We reached Victoria at 6.30 & went to St. George's where we were rapturously welcomed by Mrs. Bendixen. Had bath & went to Theatre where we saw tragedy of Camille, a version of Lady of Camellias, much overdone by Mrs. Dean Hayne. Milton then adjourned to the 'Fashion' & I to bed.

Thursday, November 26th.—Not up till noon! Spent day in reading papers & shopping as we required much refitting. Milton went to Lyceum, I remained to Journalise & read.

Friday, November 27th.—Called on Governor who kept us to dine. Begbie & Captain Martley also there. Begbie very fine, a fine tall fellow of 6 feet, well made & powerful, magnificent head, hair scanty & nearly white, with nearly black moustache & beard, full of wit. I was much taken with him. 'Sir James' was very kind, & Lady Douglas homely & good natured.

Saturday, November 28th.—Invited to St. Andrews Society's dinner on Monday. Dined with Good (Governor's son-in-law, & an Official of B. C.). Played Vingt-et-un till midnight.

Sunday, November 29th.—Called on the Mayor concerning steamer 'Emily Harris' for Nanaimo; to sail on Tuesday. Lascelles sent word we had better delay until the 'Forward' which he would take there when the next mail came in, & we decided to do so as being much pleasanter.

Monday November 30th.—Business all day with H. B. Company & our debts, &c., dining with St. Andrews Society in evening; hiring full dress from tailor. Very mild affair. Retired after set toasts & played whist soberly in Begbie's rooms till 4 a.m. Milton going round of town with Lascelles.

Tuesday, December 1st.—I wrote my journal & idled. Milton driving down to Esquimalt with Elwyn. Lascelles had not yet reappeared there. In evening were preparing to go to Mrs. Morse's when Milton was suddenly seized by one of his attacks without the usual premonitory symptoms & I had to wait on him all evening.

Wednesday, December 2nd.—Had arranged to go out to Race Rocks Lighthouse with Lascelles in gunboat but tremendous wind & rain in morning, & he sent word too rough. Milton very seedy of course & in bed, & I had to remain about.

Thursday, December 3rd.—Idled about, Milton being seedy & I looking after him. In evening went to dine with Dr. Walker who lives with a Mr. Passmores (any relation of Coventrys?) & young wife. Anstruther there, son of Sir Ralf. Tobey another baronet's son, Rushton of the bank, & a German name unknown; a quiet pleasant dinner; afterwards went to the 'Fashion' where Tobey got very screwed. Heard no more of Lascelles who seems to have subsided into private life again. He sent word he was waiting to take us out to the Race Rocks today but we, being not out of bed at the time, declined.

Friday, December 4th.—Dined with the Mayor, ("Madame Bendixen" inveighed against the degradation of dining with 'le gros boucher'); Harris is a butcher & commenced life here by borrowing 2 sheep from the H. B. Company & selling mutton retail in a tent. The Attorney General Cary was there & ended very drunk. We sat 5 hours & never joined the ladies. Walkem, a barrister, was great in stories of Cox & his "Rock Creek Justice". How he treated the thief at Hills Bar, cattle drive at Rock Creek & Mortgage case at William's Creek; he made us roar with laughter.

Saturday, December 5th.—Did nothing. Evening at home reading Lady Audley's Secret. Met William Beck & talked over old times. A Bar keep here.

Sunday, December 6th.—An awful storm of wind & rain all day; it was so severe that few people ventured out. We intended to go to Church in the evening, but Milton had some slight symptons, & we therefore did not venture. A house belonging to Kwong Lee was blown down, & innumerable signboards, flag poles & palings.

Monday, December 7th.—Storm considerably abated & we called on Kwong Lee, the China merchant here. He is one of the most wealthy merchants in the place. We had been introduced to him when first coming to Victoria on board the Enterprise, & he made us promise to call & see him. He treated us to champagne & very good cigars. His conversation principally turned upon teas (he is connected with large tea Factory at Canton). He told us that the most valuable kind grows on an inaccessible mountain (mohea?) & is only obtained by sending up monkeys trained to gather it in small baskets; this is therefore very scarce, & is worth in China 18 to 25 dollars per lb. The tea of European commerce is some of the inferior kind of a Farmer's produce, i.e. grown on cultivated trees; on each tree are 10 or 12 different kinds of tea, the most valuable being the young leaves at the end of the shoots & giving but little colour to water; this is worth $5 to $6 per lb. in China. Green tea is the younger shoots, coloured for European & American consumption by Prussian Blue. The use of copper is entirely false. Black tea is older leaves from same tree. Bottom leaves least valuable. Considerable adulteration of teas by mixing used tea dried over again. Every tea warehouse has a tea taster who has to brew & sip all the different samples. The only way to test teas being by the flavour, the appearance of even best teas being very variable & deceptive.

Kwong Lee is quite a gentleman of most polite manners, & very intelligent. Speaks English fluently in ordinary conversation, free from Yankee twang & slang. In explaining some subjects he became rather involved & obscure.

Tuesday, December 8th.—The mail steamer Oregon arrived having been exposed to the awful gale of Sunday between here & Portland. She had a hard time of it & was compelled to throw all upper deck cargo of fruits, eggs & fowls overboard. Walkem the Barrister & Hebbern the naturalist go in her. Hear from Mr. Morse that the gunboat will start tomorrow at 9 for Nanaimo.

Wednesday, December 9th.—Went on board H. M. S. Forward at 9, the other passengers being Mathew, (Judge Begbie's clerk) & Dr. Benson of Nanaimo, formerly in H. B. Company's Service. There was a strong breeze blowing which rapidly increased, & before we had finished breakfast & began to get off Trial Island, the rolling became so great, & the seas broke over the vessel so much that Lascelles decided to put back & wait till tomorrow. We had begun to feel rather squeamish & cast uncomfortable looks at one another over the breakfast table. We were all glad to be let off & returned to Victoria. Paid a few calls & promised to look in to Mrs. Neaves in the evening. Where we met Lascelles.

Thursday, December 10th.—Had a fair start on a beautiful clear morning with little wind, & just enough tossing round Trial island to make us feel uncertain. These gunboats roll tremendously & ship an awful lot of water; steer wonderfully, turning almost in their own length. We got to the Camp of the Royal Marines at St. Juan about 12 & were speedily introduced to Captain Bazalgette, in command, & Lieutenants Cooper & Sparshot & McBride the surgeon. Also surprised to meet Hoffmeister who travelled with us from the mouth of Quesnel in the boat & has the canteen here. The American camp is 12 miles from this at the Southern extremity of the Island. The camp is a beautiful little spot, with neat barracks

& officers' quarters. The men's quarters on a pebbly flat, the officers' do. on slope of hill. You enter the harbour by a narrow inlet, round a promontory, into a small bay.

Capt. Bazalgette has made bridle roads to American camp & various lakes & points in the island. The disputed Islands of which St. Juan is the chief are 14 in number, & bar the passage to New Westminster & all British Colonies by the Fraser. It is rather curious that no grouse are found on any of the disputed islands, altho' plentiful on all others. The island has a considerable number of settlers, consisting of white men who care not under which Government they may eventually be, & some Canakas & Indians. Bazalgette had just come in from shooting, having got some 200 ducks & geese in 3 days. Deer (small fallow) are common, & brought in frequently by officers. Sheep & cattle do well on island altho' it is rocky & herbage scanty in most places; some productive little farms. Fruit trees & strawberries flourish in an astonishing manner, as in all of this region.

Bazalgette is a merry fellow of rather affected manner, but his genial nature soon causes one to forget this. We had lunch soon after our arrival, & Captain Bazalgette regretted that the horses were away & we could not ride over to the Yankee camp. We however took a walk in the island; rocks & trees; fen & half open country; on the hills bare ground, or timber without underwood. Staying at the camp were 4 men who had been driven for refuge, having a small schooner which they had purchased to cruise about these islands in during the winter. Price, in command, was apparently a good naturalist, & had been all over the coast, up to Stikine River, & previously a good deal in the Rocky Mountains up north on the other side & in California & Oregon. Captain Lodge formerly in H. E. L. C. S., a very intelligent fellow. O'Grady also I believe a retired officer, & young Green who never spoke.

After dinner had grog & pipes & retired at 12.

Friday, December 11th.—Milton & I stayed night in Camp & were roused out at daybreak to go on board (7 o'clock), it being necessary to have the tide with us in passing thro' Dodds Narrows. Last night Lascelles after going on board beat to night quarters & fired 6 guns & a rocket, which was replied to by all the revolvers & guns in quarters, as a mock return of salute. Captain Bazalgette went with us to Nanaimo. We had a pleasant & picturesque voyage to Nanaimo thro' the islands which are all of a similar half rocky character tolerably well wooded, & then thro' the Narrows, a passage of not more than 100 feet wide, where the tides run with amazing force. These tides are of exceeding irregularity & Captain Richards of the Surveying-ship Hecate after long & careful observation was unable to reduce them to any certain rule. However when we passed the tide was slightly in our favour & we went thro' famously, about 5 miles from Nanaimo. The Town is situated in a small bay with *very* deep water & a tide in the harbour of 18 feet. The *Chameleon* which we expected to find there had gone day before to Comox. Arrived about 3 o'clock, went on shore & called on Captain Nicoll, manager of Coal Company here, & Captain Franklin the J. P. We brought Franklin back with us to dine on board. He is a very jolly fellow, having been a merchant Captain of high standing, commanding a transport in Crimea, & been much in China; he told many yarns. We played a rubber & then parted, Franklin having engaged us for dinner tomorrow.

Saturday, December 12th.—Went off with Dr. Benson according to agreement on an expedition thro' the woods to see an out-cropping of coal, the field of which he & Lascelles had engaged from Government under hope of forming a Company to work, Lascelles having made communications to his brother-in-law Mills the banker, with a view to get his assistance. A C. E. named Landaile was our guide, but he wandered thro' thick bush for an hour, when we brought up to close up the rear, Dr. Benson & the ship's boy with luncheon being far behind. Presently Dr. Benson who had lagged all the time, & kept up a continual halloaing to know where we were, arrived out of breath & very red in the face & assured us we were going wrong. We therefore lunched & piped, & then concluded, as our guides could not agree & it was getting rather late, it would be better to return rather than risk the almost certainty of being in the woods after dark & probably having to spend the night out.

Dined with Franklin & played whist in the evening. Mrs. Franklin a matronly body, Miss F—— or the "fair Polly", about 19, who played on a horribly tuneless piano & sang in a querulous voice, & was very shy. Two boys Harold & Sydney (nicknamed Mr. Pickles by Captain Bazalgette) & a very pretty little girl Edith.

Get on board about 11.

TRIP ACROSS CANADA

Sunday, December 13th.—Several passengers, including Mr. Landaile, & a prisoner for smuggling came on board in the morning, & we steamed out about 8, the Chameleon having left at daybreak. It snowed heavily & became very thick. Whilst Lascelles came down for a few moments to lunch, the man in command (Mr. Clarke being sick) lost landmarks & steered at random. Lascelles & Bazalgette who both knew the islands well were completely lost, and after cruising wildly about for 2 or 3 hours we came in sight of a beacon off Saltspring Island which they recognised, & we steered into Berford Harbour for the night.

Monday, December 14th.—Reached San Juan about noon & met the same hospitable reception as before. Played at skittles during the afternoon; in evening, whist, & then the subalterns gave us a musical entertainment, 'Gus' Hoffmeister with guitar, Sparshot with tambourine, & McBride with bones. Lieutenant Cooper had killed two deer whilst we had been away.

Tuesday, December 15th.—Reached Victoria about 12 & expect the steamer. In the evening stayed at home.

Wednesday, December 16th.—An awful day. Had been snowing all night & now raining in torrents, the streets so many rivers. Went to see Good about Milton's title deeds, & Young who was ill; in evening called & smoked a pipe with Mr. Morse.

Thursday, December 17th.—Milton went & rode out with the Governor, I staying behind to write up my journal & pack up my traps.

Friday, December 18th.—Lascelles sent an invitation to join him in his box at the theatre which we accepted & Mr. & Mrs. Morse also there. Saw Mrs. Julia Dean Hayne in Fazio & as Katherine in a short version of the Taming of the Shrew. The last piece was performed with great spirit & made us laugh. Afterwards had a pipe at Morse's. Promised to ride down to cottage tomorrow & lunch with Lascelles.

Saturday, December 19th.—Just about to get our horses when heard the gun intimating arrival of steamer. We therefore betook ourselves to adieux & preparation for departure. Governor very kind indeed and anxious for us to stay Xmas. Drove down to Esquimalt, put luggage on board "Pacific",

& finding she would not have finished coaling before midnight, we took a boat across the harbour to the Cottage & spent the evening with Lascelles. Saw the magnificent silver fox very tame, & the golden pheasant from Japan. Bazalgette there waiting to go back with gunboat on Monday. To return we hailed the Forward for a long time to bring a boat off for us, but the watch was I presume making merry below, & we should have been in an unpleasant fix, had not Dr. Wallace (who came out with Satellite, surveying ship, & is now in charge of Naval Hospital here) kindly volunteered to take us over in his boat; by the time we had got half way across the harbour, she was half full of water, & we arrived at the steps by dint of hard pulling just in time to save being swamped. Sprung a leak not known of. Met several friends, seeing others off, Mr. Flinn of Lilooet for one; and 'Johnny' the stage driver. Turned in to our berth about one a.m., & shall be under way before daylight.

Sunday, December 20th.—Having arrived on board last night, we turned in to our state room which contained 3 berths, the 3rd being occupied by Captain Elliott, U. S. A., going to San Francisco from Columbia river, at the mouth of which he is engaged in laying out fortifications.

We left Esquimalt about 4.30 a.m. & were well out in the Gulf before we awakened. Had a smooth passage until noon when the weather looked dirty, & the barometer went down so rapidly that the Captain put into Neagh Bay for the night. A tremendous storm broke over us during the night & we were very thankful in our safe position in this quiet little harbour. W. S. E.

Monday, December 21st.—A fearful night of rain, wind & hail, but this morning the barometer is going up, & wind decreasing. There is an Indian Reserve here (American), & the natives came off all day with articles for sale, mats of bark, baskets, models of canoes, &c., which met with very good sale at from [$0.50] to $2, Milton being the largest purchaser.

There is very miserable accommodation on board; about 50 passengers have to lie on cabin tables & floor; 3 tables set for each meal.

It is amusing to see the nigger stewards setting table & they march round in a string, one with plate, next with knife, next with fork, next with spoon, &c., & they each lay their article on the table at the same moment, with a clash, 6 arms all moving in time. When the table is laid & dishes on, a bell sounds. Each waiter lays each hand on a cover, & all stand in attitude until bell strikes again when off go all covers like magic; miserable grub underneath them. Tonight we got steam up & under way for about quarter of an hour when a slight explosion was heard, & all nigger & steerage passengers ran aft; we put back at once. It appeared one of the boiler pipes had given way, & we returned to our old anchorage for repair.

Tuesday, December 22nd.—Elliott seems a very intelligent, gentlemanly fellow, much disappointed at being now unable to reach 'Frisco' for Xmas with his family. Get up steam again this morning but other leaks in the boiler appeared & fresh repairs commenced. All calm now, & it is provoking not being able to go on.

Wednesday, December 23rd.—Ship got under way about 2 a.m., & we were bowling along when we awoke in morning. I felt squeamish as the sea was a little rough, & stayed in bed until dark. Thus escaped sickness. Milton got up, ate & c[h]atted & ate again as is his wont. Many ill.

Thursday, December 24th.—Felt pretty well this morning, & got up to breakfast after which played 3 hours at whist in close stinking cabin. I have a patient who has just come, brought by his brother from the Dalles with dysentery after mountain fever; a mere skeleton & will die. His brother been in Boisé river of which he gives favourable account as to gold, easy surface sand diggings & rich; unhealthy from water impregnated with copper & lead salts; scarcity of wood on way there. Salmon & Boisé river tributaries of Snake River which flows into Columbia. Boisé River about 500 miles from Portland, Idaho territory. Prices much same as in Cariboo. Hundreds of men killed there this summer; no laws; 2,000 men there once; now less. Xmas Eve! Alas I had hoped to spend it more pleasantly; my mother's birthday; is it? We are going along pleasantly with good North East breeze. Shall I ever spend another really Merry Xmas?

Friday, December 25th.—Xmas Day. Fine bright day with favourable breeze, expect to reach our port by 10 p.m. tomorrow. Played whist in afternoon with Hepburn, &c. In evening a dance was got up on deck, not very successful. Only a music on darkies' guitar. The bride, a little slender girl of 17 or 18, with nice figure & pretty face was the belle of the ball. She wished to be introduced to Milton, & he danced a quadrille with her. Very well to look at, but the moment she opens her mouth, oh! it is all over; a sharp shrewish voice, nasal twang, & quick manner. I did not see the fun of the dance. The bride is married to a sulky-looking Yankee, who takes as little notice of her as she of him; she chaffs & walks with any other gentleman in preference. One of the "American ladies" amused herself by chalking the backs of the gentlemen as they passed her seat. But this is quite in proper lady-like taste, even with strangers.

Saturday, December 26th.—Glorious bright warm sunny day, favouring breeze North-East. At 3.30 p.m. opposite Pointe del Re, & see lighthouse rocks in distance to the right, 35 miles from 'Frisco'. At the point see the commencement of rolling open [land] over which Wild Californian Cattle used to roam; killed out now in this neighbourhood. Plentiful in lower California. Entered San Francisco Bay between The Heads about 6.30, passing on the right a new hotel built close to some rocks where seals bask in the sunshine, undisturbed by common consent. Hence to city 7 miles. Through the "Golden Gate" (as the narrowing of the bay is called) to the *Golden City;* pass island of Alcatray where is strong fort, a mere rock in the middle of the channel; on the right shore is another fort. View of San Francisco by night very pretty, extends over two hills, Russian hill & Telegraph hill. Further to the East is the most important part; here were numerous sandhills which have been levelled away by steam levellers.

We arrived at the wharf by 8 & met with no detention from Customs officers, & took a cab, (or rather carriage) with Mr. Hepburn to the Union club. Driver charged $5 for less than a mile. Found rooms there & introduced to several members by their chaperon. Very nice quarters indeed, & a good supper. Played billiards with Milton afterwards, until 3 a.m.

Sunday, December 27th.—Up too late for Church, luxuriating in a comfortable bed once more, after our discomforts on board the Pacific. Hepburn introduced us to Booker the Consul, a very nice gentlemanly fellow who has been here 14 years. They then took us a walk over the town, & to a Mr. Bell's, a merchant here, who gave us very good claret which we enjoyed greatly after our walk, it being very warm; a beautiful day like the brightest of May in England, a fair specimen they said of Californian winter. In summer it is frequently cold & chilly from the strong westerly sea-breezes. In Bell's garden we saw the Oleander which blooms out, & in our club-balcony is a heliotrope in bloom. Roses all year round. Radishes do.; Green peas 9 months of year. Many German Jews & wealthy. Passing an undertaker's shop Booker told us of curious custom of having handsome polished coffins of rosewood & mahogany, (or some similar wood) & handsomely fitted with silvered rims, &c., over the head is a glass plate with a wooden slide over it, so that, after the body is fastened down, the face of the corpse may be viewed; and such is the morbid curiosity of people here that frequently when they see by crape on the door-knocker that death is in a house, strangers will walk in, gaze at the corpse & depart; considered as a compliment by friends of deceased. Walkem staying here, & engages to go tomorrow & see the big trees; about 6 days there & back, risking loss of next Panama Steamer. Dined at Club. At Bell's saw the smallest pony I ever came across, so small that Booker who is about my height could walk as well as ride when astride of his back. He rode round the garden to great amusement of 2 omnibus loads of people passing at time. Came from Hills of Java, a most absurd looking animal being very powerfully made like a strong little cob. Street railways almost universal here & seem to answer well. About 150 miles from here, cattle can be bought for 15 to 20 dollars a head, averaging 500 lbs. in weight. Beef wholesale not more than 5 cents per lb. (2 d).

Monday, December 28th.—Spent the morning in visiting the Custom House, & at last by the kindness of the Chief Collector being enabled to leave our boxes there unopened, & to have them out at a moment's notice. Officers very courteous, & Collector kindly presented us with a copy of New York Herald! Talked about the war. "The People of the North don't feel it, Sir; its nothing to us, we can carry an immense war like this without the least inconvenience, Sir," & so on, "gassing" tremendously. At 4 went on board Steamer Cornelia for Stockton on our way to Big Tree Valley, Booker having thoughtfully left written directions for us. Glorious weather, & pleasant little steamer on American plan. *Chrysopolis,* a magnificent boat for Sacramento, passed us going 14 or 15 knots, a floating palace. Dark soon after we entered the San Joachim River. Walkem who accompanied us told us the story of 'Bummer' & Lazarus, two dogs of Frisco, belonging to public, inseparable companions, wandering about from one of the Saloons so common in Frisco to another, & sharing in the 'Free Lunches' provided for the frequenters. 'Bummer', having unfortunately been run over by a buggy & his leg broken, was unable to accompany his friend; Lazarus fetched meat & fed him. 'Bummer' recovered, & their visits in company were resumed. 'Lazarus' poisoned by police, thro' mistake; stuffed at public expense (the project of a public funeral having been set on foot & abandoned), & placed in one of the principal saloons. Delight of Bummer on discovering his friend apparently alive again, tries all blandishments to induce him to accompany him in usual rambles. Visits him regularly. Emperor II, a man who made enormous fortune in mines here & lost it & his reason at one stroke. Under the idea that he is a bona-fide emperor, & publishes proclamations at intervals which are printed by all the papers. Dressed at expense of army tailors here in military costume, gold epaulettes, &c. 'Washington' a similar case, dressed by tailors also in cocked hat, embroidered military coat, silk stockings & pumps. A little drummer boy closes the list of 'bummers' who live on free lunches, &c. *Story by Captain Elliot*, U. S. E., illustrating intense heat in some of mining districts of California. Miner dies & goes below. Friends communicate with him thro' spiritual medium; only request he has to make is that they will send him his blankets!

Story by Walkem. In a box at Victoria Theatre with the Nutches. Adams, a miner worth $50,000 comes in. Walkem draws attention to portrait of Shakespeare above drop scene. "I don't think its at all like him," said Walkem. "Why? how do you know?" replies Adams. "Because I've seen him," says Walkem. "Why, I thought he was dead before your time," says Adams. "Where did you see him?" "Saw him in James Street, Dublin when I was 3 years old, he was then 45; had his portrait taken 2 years after; he was then 47, & died 3 months later. I've seen that portrait too, & it is not the least like this". "Well," said Adams, "I was mistaken altogether, I fancied he was before your time."

Notes on the visit to the Big Tree.
(Taken from small note book)

Monday, December 28th.—Leave San Francisco in Steamer

"Cornelia" for Stockton. Up the bay, & then up the San Joachim River; very comfortable little steamer on American plan; beautiful day; "Chrysopolis" magnificent steamer like Mississippi boats passes us at 11 or 12 miles an hour for Sacramento. Walkem accompanies us, tells us story of "Bummer" & Lazarus two dogs of Frisco who lived together wandering from saloon to saloon for food at free lunches. Bummer's leg broken, & Lazarus fetches meat for him. Lazarus poisoned by police thro' mistake, stuffed at public expense & placed in a saloon. Bummer visits him & tries to persuade him to follow him to usual haunts, &c. Emperor II a man who lives by "bumming" at free lunches dressed in military costume & epaulettes by tailors. Has made enormous fortune at mines & lost it, & now his head. Washington the same, lives in same manner, but dresses in cocked hat & white stockings to imitate his ideal. A little drummer boy the 3rd 'bummer' at San Francisco, (Story told me by Captain Elliot, U. S. E. of heat in some of California mining districts. Miner died & went below. Communication thro' "medium" to send his blankets.)

Tuesday, December 29th.—Steamer arrived in Stockton at 8. Milton late as usual, & stage to Murphy's Hotel. But Proprietor told us we ought to go by Crimea House, & Colterville; so took another stage. Found out on way from passengers that we must go on to Columbia City & thence to Murphy's & on to Big Tree Grove. Fine horses & bad roads; left at 8.30 & arrived at Columbia at 11. 72 miles. Recommended to stay at Morgan's House. He makes us very comfortable, & recommends us to take a buggy from here. (A Gloucestershire man.) We prefer saddle horses, but 3 are not to be got, therefore order buggy at 8 tomorrow.

Old & present gold diggings on flats & creeks.

Wednesday, December 30th.—Drive over to Murphy's to dinner, 13 miles; hilly road, one piece somewhat resembling rattlesnake grade on Pavilion Mountain.

Very rough after Murphy's, & we arrive at Big Tree Grove about dark. The (Murphy's to Big Tree, 16 miles) hotel proprietor there was introduced to us at Murphy's & rode back with us to show the wonders. (The country between Murphy's & half way to Stockton, by Sonora & Montezuma, has been very extensively mined. Old flumes & ditches all the way; & earth dug & washed out from rocks & boulders which now stand bare. Is now being extensively worked, deep workings in some places, & is paying up to $20 & $30; good in present cheap provisions, &c.) Much up hill; arrived just at dark; large hotel; pass between 2 large trees.

Thursday, December 31st.—Up at 7; & saw the trees after breakfast; much delighted with beauty of this little valley in the mountains & magnificent timber. The trees look much larger than I expected. Walked about in one fallen tree burnt out, room for man & horse! Collected cones; not very many young trees. Vandalism of Baptist minister, who actually cut down a young Wellington because he could not reach a branch to pluck & carry away! I should have liked to have kicked him. Most wonderful sight I ever saw; the pines also are enormous; sugar pine especially.

Walkem drove back, down hill, very fast, awful jolting, just reached Columbia by dark, take our places, & to be called for stage at 3 a.m. No chance of getting to Yosemite falls; 6 or 8 feet of snow, & road closed & impassable. Bought views of falls much frequented in summer by wedding parties; astonished by amount of mistletoe on evergreen oaks, some quite covered with it. Murphy's a pretty sight, lying in a basin with low rolling hills all round, covered with oak & pines.

Wheat grown here for hay, cut when in green ear; vines growing everywhere like gooseberry bushes. Delightful bright warm days; a little frost at night. Snow at Big Trees in shade; high up in mountains. Calaveras County.

Saw beautiful specimen of gold & gold quartz at saloon here, grotesquely shaped & frosted pure gold; finer than Griers specimen.

Walking round tree as near as roots permit, & stepping over those not too high, 35 paces (good). Standing at base can reach about 1/3 diameter, 7 paces from where cut down, just reach centre; the ball room summer house on stump 8 paces across gives wonderful idea of size.

Wonderful vitality of trees which have most of them been extensively burnt by forest fires, the bark now growing over & healing; wood of enormous tree cut down perfectly sound, so that it forms floor of summer house. Saw tree whence bark was taken for Crystal Palace; not largest, but scaffolding round & bare trunk make it look enormous.

Enterprise Claim Silver mine, $16,000 per foot paid for it; about 100 feet. The Plato 10,000 per foot, only 10 feet on surface, costing since erected over 10 Feet, & party buying at this enormous price *cleared* $13,200! and the lead may go to any depth; peculiarity of silver lead, which is also as steady & certain as gold is uncertain; this in Washoe. Numerous other claims similar. San Francisco Bulletin of Oct. 12th. /63.

Tuesday, December 29th.—Steamer arrived at Stockton at 8 this morning. Milton up too late, & miss the stage to Murphy's; therefore take one to Columbia City & thence to Murphy's. Fine horses, but rough, unmade roads & we have a very jolting ride of 14 hours to Columbia arriving there about 11. Recommended to stay at Morgan's house as proprietor is an Englishman. In the army 28th Infantry for 15 years, deserted in Australia during famine there, & according to his own account solely to obtain food; a very civil decent fellow; he advised us to take a buggy from here. We wanted saddle horses but none to be had; ordered buggy at 8. On our way here by stage we passed thro' varied country.

Stockton is situated on San Joachim, at commencement of immense plain of some 30 miles square. Surrounded by hills; fine farming country. No timber but scattered oaks. After that pass over bare range of sand hills, & come into mining country of Sonora, Chinese Camp, Montezuma, Columbia, & Murphy's. An immense deal of work has been done in the neighbourhood of these towns, where were formerly very rich placer diggings which are now principally worked by Chinamen. Also now many good quartz leads being worked (gold). Large flats & the beds of creeks; granite & quartz boulders. Saw quartz boulder at Morgan's weighing 2 cwt. & perfectly sound, found 14 feet below surface. Old flumes & ditches everywhere.

Wednesday, December 30th.—Drive over to Murphy's to dinner; 13 miles over hills, & road in one place resembles that on Pavilion Mountain on a small scale. Murphy's a place of perhaps 2000 or 3000 inhabitants now. In very pretty basin surrounded by low sparsely wooded hills, oak (evergreen principally), & pines, with bushes of arbutus & white Jessamine. The evergreen oaks covered with mistletoe; several bunches on almost every tree; some quite covered with it. Over hills forming commencement to Sierra Nevada to Big Tree Grove, 16 miles. The Hotel proprietor there, Graham, accompanied us from Murphy's & gave us much information. Nearly all up hill, & did not arrive until nearly dark, driving between "the sentinels," two of the smallest of the Large Trees.

Thursday, December 31st.—Up at 7 & breakfast, after which went round to see the trees.

Beautiful little valley, nice little farm cleared at one side of House. Favourite resort of wedding parties & lovers. Lady Franklin visited here, & two trees named by her Sir J[ohn] F[ranklin] & Dr. Kane. All the timber immense. Sugar pines 13 feet diameter. One of finest trees, the only very large one near the house, was cut down by former proprietor to make canes, &c., of wood; round ball room built on stump which is there 24 feet diameter standing opposite section of stump; I could just reach approximately 1/3 diameter with the tips of my fingers. 7 paces above I could just touch the heart. Saw the tree stripped of bark for Great Exhibition of 1851; scaffolding still up; bare trunk shews size off; fluting of bark making appear less. Walked about in largest tree which is on ground & burnt hollow. Man & horse can ride inside. Not many young trees. Vandalism of Baptist parson, who cut down a small tree to obtain a branch he wished to carry off. Stopped now. They are certainly the most astonishing sight I ever saw; only 3 places where they are found, viz, Big Tree Valley, Yosemite, & another. Started back at 11.30. Walkem driving at a tremendous pace, all down hill, steep; met several waggons in narrow road & much difficulty in passing; awful jolting. Hurried dinner at Murphy's; back to Columbia by dark. Inquire about possibility of getting into Yosemite falls; find there is probably 8 feet of snow there now & but little water coming down. Take our places in stage which ought to start at 3 a.m. After supper, Miss Morgan, a regular Yankee gal of 16, sang for us & accompanied herself on piano; very forward & chaffed us tremendously. Afterwards several people came in & various songs were sung. One man recited a wonderful speech of one Dennis McCarty (Mr. Clark, whom Walkem irritated by addressing him as Mr. McCarty). Then Walkem as a compliment to the Yankees asked if no one could give us "The Star of the Union", which was forthwith given. This melted the heart of one of them "Mr. B. F. Ryder" who immediately asked all hands & especially us to have a drink. Walkem & he got into conversation, & he invited us to go and see a collection of minerals which he had & we accompanied him to his house, & inspected his cabinets. He had some beautiful specimens of gold & silver quartz, peacock ore, copper & galena. The skeleton of a mastodon found near; silicified oak; asbestos, fluor spar. Told us horns of an ox 6 inches in diameter just found 12 feet below surface ½ mile from here & wished us to go over with him & see them tomorrow. Then in Coach office (a Saloon) saw more beautiful specimens. One of gold the most splendid I ever saw; grotesquely shaped, frosted, quartz decayed out. Told us several curious facts. Wheat is grown about here & cut when in green ear for hay. *Mining items.* The Enterprise Company at Washoe Silver mine $16,000 per foot paid for it; about 100 feet . The Plato claim $10,000 per foot, only 10 feet on surface, & the party buying it at this enormous price cleared already $13,000! and the lead may go to any depth. Peculiarity of silver lead, which is also as steady and certain as gold is uncertain. Numerous other claims similar.

(S. F. Bulletin, Oct. 12, 1863). It was getting late when we got back to Morgan's, but Walkem had so inflated Ryder, by his eulogiums on Americans & their qualities, institutions and Nation, that Ryder as he expressed it froze to him at once. Walkem related imaginary conversations between himself & me where we had resolved that they were the greatest nation on Earth & individually the noblest race. Ryder drew himself up, filled out his chest, cocked up his chin, & kept raising himself on his toes & smiling. "Well, you are a gentleman, I knew it when I first saw you. I froze to you at once. I should take you for an American. Come & have another drink." We had a great fun drawing out the man's conceit. A band came round to play the New Year in, & Walkem & Milton went out to treat the crowd. I slipped off & turned in to bed, expecting 2 hours, but in ½ an hour the landlord called me as the coach would start at 1; & I turned out growling. Milton & Walkem at the bar with their admirer Mr. Ryder. He walked down to Coach office & then bid us a reluctant farewell. I found out afterwards that Walkem & Milton were glad to be rid of him as he had told them with great pride how he had killed an Irishman who had quarrelled with him, stabbed him on the spot. Only cost him $1,000 to get off. Offered to take any fight we might get into off our hands.

Friday, January 1st, 1864.—A dull ride in stage. Cold

& sleepy; arrived at Stockton at 3 p.m. In steamer Paul Pry at 4. At San Francisco again about 12.30 a.m. & retire to Union Club.

Saturday, January 2nd.—Decide to postpone our departure for 10 days & go in crack steamer Constitution. The weather is so fine. Arrange to go with Captain Harris on to Ocean House tomorrow to see sea-lions & seals, & dine with him in evening. At night invited to Booker's room where they were playing Ecarté; 5, 10, & 20 dollar bets; Milton went in & lost $35. Played till 2 a.m.

Sunday, January 3rd.—Up too late for church. Call on Captain Elliot & Dr. Ringold. The latter has a beautiful sister; glorious smile & complexion & little twang. Both smitten. Another young lady, very jolly & pleasant, & very free. Can beat English ladies in conversational powers, so much more general information. His mother a fine old lady of 70 remembered Washington's funeral. Said she was a wonderful walker which she inherited from her English ancestors, could walk 5 miles a day in her prime; lamented general deficiency of American ladies in walking power. I astonished all when I told them my sisters could do 20 miles a day.

Dined with Harrison. Homely people; very slow.

Monday, January 4th.—Bought Chinese curiosities all day. Milton expending over $100, I only $25. Beautiful work. I did not believe the ladies' shoes, but the merchant was quite indignant. I bought ordinary ladies' size. In evening saw Miss Menken, Adah Isaacs Menken, once Mrs. Heenan; miserable piece only adapted to show her figure in scant costume. Saw cabinet of ores at California Alta office. Piece of quartz (Gould & Cu[rr]ie) $3,000 to the ton; average only $61 per ton. Ores of all kinds. Gold & silver quartz, copper pyrites & peacock ore; nearly pure specimen of sulphate of copper crystals mixed with carbonate & exactly like ore from Burra Burra in Australia; coal & petroleum; sulphur, salt; saltpetre, borax; cadmium, cinnabar; iron pyrites, ochres, sienna, molybdenite, &c., &c.

Tuesday, January 5th.—Wrote journal all day, copying hasty notes, &c. Go tomorrow to Almaden quicksilver mine. Play Loo with Walkem & Milton, lose only $1¼.

Wednesday, January 6th.—Left at 4 for San José by bus to Railway Station, & thence by rail to Santa Clara, 47 miles, a beautiful valley, level rich alluvial soil, dotted with evergreen oaks & bays.

From Santa Clara to San José, 3 miles by stage. Stayed at Crandell's Hotel. Santa Clara and San José two straggling towns, on the level plain in rich farming country, land of volunteer crops, &c.

Thursday, January 7th.—Left San José at 9 with pair of good horses & buggy for New Almaden, 12 miles of beautiful level road. The New Almaden *Works* are at the very end of the valley where it narrows into a gorge; the mines are 3 miles by road, 1 mile direct at an elevation of 1,200 feet. Mr. Brodie, a Scotchman & manager, was away; we gave however Booker's letter of introduction to Mr. Eldridge, the superintendent, who was very obliging, showing us first over the works where the ore is subjected to heat in brick furnaces or wood fires, & mercurial vapour condensed in lengthened flues, received into iron tanks, & then bottled up in the usual cast iron jars, a very simple process. It was found that the mercury escaped thro' the bottom of the old furnaces into the earth, sinking right down to the bedrock 20 or 30 feet. These old furnaces were removed, & the earth & gravel underneath washed thro' sluice boxes; $100,000 of mercury was obtained! Under the present furnaces sheet iron has been laid to prevent loss in this way. The system of working formerly was in retorts, causing considerable loss (from escape of vapour). The annual produce of the mine is about 40,000 jars, value $45 a piece, giving a total of $1,800,000 or about £350,000. The mine was formerly in the hands of the Barrons, a family of English descent settled in Mexico & one of the most important there. One of the sons formerly managed New Almaden. The American Government seized the mine as being on Government lands; retainers called out & resistance threatened by Barron. Lincoln repudiated, & eventually Barron sold out to American Company. Only 3 other mines in the world. The principal the Almaden mine in Spain which has been worked since 600 B. C.! The others in Germany, not now worked as not paying sufficient percentage, only 5 or 6 per cent of metal in ore. Here 30 per cent ore was only kind worked, now as low as 16 or 20. The richest quicksilver mine in world, & formerly, perhaps now, able to command monopoly, & swamp all others; sometimes a year's stock in hand. Cinnabar plentiful, but other mines cannot compete.

Drove 3 miles up to mine, passing numerous pretty cottages on our way up, the dwellings of the Cornish miners who form about ½ the men employed. On the top of hill is Mexican Village, for rest, Mexicans, about 600 in all. Donned villainous old coats & hats, & with candle stuck in end of a sort of hand-pike went thro' the mazes. Down ladders & inclines for 300 feet, very hot; rock very hard & all done by blasting; 20 barrels of powder per week; most uncertain & eccentric of all mining; found in no continuous lead, but in isolated masses & the mine is therefore worked in a series of irregular chambers, connected by galleries; 20 men always at work 'prospecting or discovering where the "pockets" are; 3 miles of mine; one old worked-out one, on top of hill; middle one we visited, & lower one commencing; all ore hauled up to top mine now by steam power; running a tunnel now to bottom of mine for last 5 years in order to shunt ore downwards, & easier carriage down to works; Mexican miners with villainous faces, working & smoking cigaritas. Enter mine by long tunnel for 100 yards, & thence descend into windings; spent about 2 hours. Ore found combined with limestone, sandstone, & green porphyry. Magnificent view from this hill; plain valley dotted with trees & houses, & bounded by amphitheatre of hills, with Frisco & bay in distance 50 miles off.

We tied the buggy wheel, there being no brakes, & no breech bands to harness, & drove quietly down the steep winding road to the manager's house, enjoying the magnificent weather; still the same May, & glorious view. Introduced to Mrs. Eldridge, superintendent's sister-in-law & a splendid champagne lunch. Mr. Eldridge very frank and pleasant tho' American. Drove Milton & Walkem round drive in a pretty little pony carriage drawn by tiny muletas. We strolled round garden & saw a little vineyard of less than ¼ acre 80 years old vines, producing 20 tons of grapes last year! Rotted on vines altho' given to every one who would take them. Cherry trees beginning to bloom. Strawberries gathered on Xmas day! Peaches, apples for ever in summer. Cherries as large as plums. Smoked a cigar & then bade good-bye to hospitable Mr. & Mrs. Eldridge & had a delightful drive back reaching San José by dark, having refused an invitation to spend the night with our hosts. Glorious sunset effect on distant hills in the clear light. Found some Burton (*draught*)

ale at an Englishman's in San José, & the effect was so ex-
hilarating, that a pillowing match took place in the bedroom,
to the great enjoyment of Milton, & we had to abstract his
pillows to keep him quiet.

Friday, January 8th.—Up at 5.30, taking revenge on Milton
by 'drawing' him out of bed; return by stage & cars to Frisco
by 10 a.m. Are introduced to Commodore Watkins, & engage
berths on board Constitution.

Saturday, January 9th.—Buy supplies for voyage & magnificent photographs of Yosemite by Walker's. In evening billiards.

Sunday, January 10th.—Introduced by Booker to his pew
in church. Differences between American & English ritual
slight. Verbal alterations such as in Te Deum, "didst humble
thyself to be born of a Virgin" instead of "didst not abhor the
Virgin's womb", "health & prosperity", for "health & wealth"
long to live. And for the "High & Mighty King of Kings &
Lord of Lords, the only ruler of Princes" is submitted the very
unequal "High & Mighty Ruler of the Universe". Afterwards
introduced by Booker to various families & pretty girls. The
Young family & sisters of Mrs. Young, 2 very nice half-Mex-
ican girls, tall & grand. Mrs. John Barron another sister. The
Barrons half English & Mexican, owners of the New Almaden
mine, living in a splendid house on top of hill commanding
view of whole city & harbour & country for 50 miles. House
most luxuriously furnished, corridors passing all round house
on each story, communicating with rooms in centre, & glass
all round outside, a most delightful arrangement for a warm
climate. "Buch & Breck", a champagne cocktail so called after
Buchanan & Breckenridge.

Monday, January 11th.—Were to have ridden out to Seal
Rocks with Booker, but it coming on very foggy & a little rain,
we postponed until tomorrow. Heard "Constitution" had
broken her shaft & could not go on Wednesday; & we were
strongly advised to delay another 10 days rather than sail in
the old "Orizato" which would take her place. I was reluctant,
but Milton wishful, induced by prospect of a grand ball at
Friedlanders on Thursday. Dined at Barron's in evening.
Beautiful dinner. Afterwards called on Mrs. John Young &
the Miss Walkenshaws who were delighted to see us, & told

us they had driven out to Seal Rocks in hopes of meeting us.

Tuesday, January 12th.—Rode out with Mr. Spiller who had been a surgeon in Rifle Brigade & afterwards in 14th Light Dragoons in India. Looks about 25, really 40! Is making a fortune now in Washoe mines.

Fog set in from Sea, but lifted when we were at Seal Rocks, & we had a fair view of the sea-lions with which the place was covered. A few isolated rocks some few 100 yards from shore, & large hotels built on cliff above. Rode home in time for dinner. Dr. Spiller gave most glowing account of richness of Washoe mines. Very good horses from livery stables, and a road like a boarded floor. In the evening went with Douglas, Captain of the police, round to some of the dens of San Francisco; round the Chinese quarter, & various houses of resort. The most curious sight was the Chinese Theatre, a kind of Opera was going on. The dresses were most magnificent, embroidered & brocaded silks. I could not make out the play. The orchestra was on the stage in a little recess in the centre, & consisted of a two-stringed fiddle of curious shape, a kettle drum, castanets, & a metal drum something like an iron pot, with a pipe which made a noise like bagpipes, & only brought in at "sensation" moments. The head-dresses were various, generally adorned with two long peacock's feathers hanging down behind. Continual music, & marching across stage behind scenes, & back again on other side; furious combat, the combatants waltzing round furiously between each blow, 2 persons apparently killed. Incessant clash of castanets & hammering of drum. Chinese song in most exceptionally nasal falsetto. Left early, there being a great monotony in the entertainment. Only Chinamen there; no scenery. Dirty hole. Douglas then would have taken us to some gambling houses, but said they had fallen off so much that $100 bets now were comparatively rare. He had seen in the "early days" $50,000 on the turning of a card; put down by only 2 men; great bags of gold dust staked & weighed afterwards. The Plays in Chinese Theatres continue for weeks, therefore playing every night. Hepburn told me of one which he went to see, a complete history of China, lasting for 6 weeks.

Wednesday, January 13th.—Idling about. Milton, Walkem & Spiller went for a ride, I stayed behind & wrote. All my

linen stolen from laundress, & I have to replace. Booker kindly
went around with me, & a walk afterwards. Showed me some
of General Halbeck's property. Made most of his money here.
Resigned his commission in the regular army & became lawyer,
speculated & made money. A quiet, retiring, rather repulsive
fellow. His wife rather good looking, but repelling. Hooker
also here a long time. Greatly given to drink & gambling.
Wanted to leave for East a long time. "What, here yet?"
says Booker. "Can't raise it yet, my boy, shall before long,"
says Hooker. Eventually his washerwoman lent him the
money. A very fine looking fellow; must have excitement;
devoted to poker; distinguished in Mexican war; Major Burton, the greatest blackguard. Booker anxious to give him a
dinner, but can't afford, persuades Major, now chief of Com-
missariat, to do it for him. Major "on the bust" & can't appear.
Burton annihilates a scientific swell asked to meet him by wonderful memory although very drunk; quotes any book you like
by the yard. Booker leaves Burton in care of Hooker, who
had capacity for any quantity of liquor without becoming incapable, & Burton having to sail by steamer at 9 next morning.
"Hooker's all right, my boy, I'll look after him." Booker
finds both next morning in a spoke, Weshgahaigun entre nees-
so usquaunk chac.

Thursday, January 14th.—Numerous difficulties about gar-
ments for the grand ball tonight at Mr. Friedlander's. Spiller
kindly supplied Milton, & Booker promised to do the same for
me. No dress coats to be found in the town. In afternoon
we called on Dr. Ringold, found him & all family laid up with
prevalent colds. Captain Elliot out. When preparing to dress
Booker discovered he had no trousers for me. I gave up the
idea of going, but Booker would not let me off & found an old
pair with a large rent behind which straightway patched up by
the tailor & answered admirably. At 10 we started for South
Neck & found the rooms crowded; not very large. 150 people
there, 250 invitations; given to Mrs. Joseph Barron the bride
(Miss Walkenshaw). After a time many of the older fogies
went off to the card room upstairs, & the dancing went on
furiously. I danced several quadrilles & lancers, all much
altered from English figures. A very pretty set of girls there,
elegant figures, exceedingly pretty faces, beautifully transparent,
delicate complexions, but nearly all with the usual failing of the
women of this continent, rather too flat chested & without that

lovely roundness of form & limb so characteristic of *our* girls at home. They are very friendly & free & easy at once. No difficulty in keeping up a conversation. Well informed, & many of them fresh from school. No affectation. Where the nasal twang was present, however, the sharp manner & boldness of a New York lady accompanied it. There were not many thoroughbred Yankee families there, mostly English. Friedlander is a German, formerly at New Orleans, a gigantic fellow of 6 feet 7. His daughter a fine handsome girl of 17. The dresses of the ladies were on the whole in very good taste, of silk, or muslin, expensive, & the jewellery costly. White silk with rose coloured bodice, &c. Two very handsome women appeared in powder, effect not pleasing. The men were very quietly dressed (not very many Americans there) & well behaved. What I expected would be a very snobbish assembly was really a very well-bred one. Several young officers there, like our own, furious dancers, but I thought contrasting very favourably by their quiet gentlemanly behaviour with many of our haw-haw'ing fellows. The supper was very good, champagne flowing like water. At the gaming table where they played Ecarté I only saw $120 each side. We left 2-3 a.m., very much pleased with our entertainment & half in love with several beauties. The time passed more quickly than I ever remember at a ball before.

Great closeness of rooms in San Francisco; windows never opened; perhaps from dust clouds in summer habit formed; thermometer about 65 in shade out of doors. People clothe up as if cold.

Friday, January 15th.—A wet day; billiards. Spiller told me of the Gould & Cu[rr]ie mine; $8,000,000 taken out last year. Cost of new mill $1,500,000. Shares $5,000. per foot.

Saturday, January 16th.—Milton, Spiller, & Booker out for a ride. I write, & Walkem draws.

Sunday, January 17th.—Very seedy. Church, & then calls after; Mrs. Scott from Cheltenham, Mrs. Col. Ransome, English lady, American husband & daughter, Friedlanders, Commodore Watkins, Barrons.

Monday, January 18th.—Very seedy all day, necessary to stop cigars. The club rule prohibiting pipes has brought me to this; very languid, nervous. Milton calls on Walkenshaw's & arranges ride with ladies on Wednesday.

TRIP ACROSS CANADA

Tuesday, January 19th.—Over to Mare Island U. S. Navy Yard, with Hepburn to see the Russian fleet. Admiral Papoff gone up to San Francisco; therefore disappointed. Russian sailors powerful looking fellows but dull, heavy & sullen looking. Midshipman in charge very civil, spoke English imperfectly. Drove thence to Benicia, & caught steamer which runs from Sacramento to San Francisco. Too seedy to enjoy the glorious weather.

Wednesday, January 20th.—Milton & Booker ride out with ladies. Spiller told me of his fortunes. Had £3,000 a year, spent most of it & capital, arrived in Frisco 4 years ago with $500. Spent all but $2 in mining; ordered men to roll over a large boulder in stream he was working. After much labour effected it with levers, found pocket of $7000 dollars there, done well ever since.

Thursday, January 21st.—Engaged in getting permit from Custom House for luggage left there, & in viewing the collection of minerals made by Mr. Donald Davidson, a merchant here, who ships ores for England. He was the first who encouraged the silver quartz mining by buying it when no one else would look at it, & shipping it home. Mount Davidson in Washoe named in honour of him. He is a stout, red faced old Scotchman who has been in India & China; formerly in Baring's house in London. He kindly promised to make up a little collection for us. In the evening engaged to go to a quiet little party at Col. Ransome's. I felt so very seedy; headache, fever, & giddiness that I begged to be excused & went to bed.

Friday, January 22nd.—Bothering at the Customs & buying light clothing for Panama. Milton & Walkem went off to call on Mrs. Young or rather Juanita Walkenshaw. I was too busy. Milton & I bought each a very handsome watchguard of Pure Washoe Silver. In evening packed & took a walk to bid goodbye to Juanita but rung the bell many times in vain & then were fain to retire! Would they not see us, or were they in bed? In the afternoon, I had a regular shivering fit, & then it dawned upon me that I was suffering from an attack of ague! I got quinine at once, & stodged it off completely with a dose that almost made my head blow off & have had no return. A complete change from languor & fever & headache to perfect health; quite magical.

Saturday, January 23rd.—On board by 9.30. Booker, Spiller, Hepburn & Walkem accompanying us to the boat. About 10.30 she got under way, & we bade a tender farewell to our friends Spiller & Walkem seemingly on the verge of weeping. I felt sorry to part with such pleasant friends, & dismally enough inclined. Milton's face was very lugubrious. Van Brunt, a very gentlemanly Bostonian accompanied us to Acapulco where he resides as agent for this company.

The *Golden City* is a splendid vessel of some 3,000 tons burthen, & most beautifully & conveniently fitted; she can carry about 300 first-cabin passengers, & as we have only 30 we have a fine time of it. The immense saloon, half the length of the ship, is the finest I ever saw, & the 30 passengers are quite lost in it. She has a hurricane deck over the upper deck, on which latter are the saloon & cabins, with the whole clear run of the ship aft. She has a most complete fire engine system. Has 3 engines specially for that purpose. Only one propelling engine (walking beam) of 12 feet stroke, &c. The most complete arrangement I have seen. We had a glorious day for our start & saw a large party at the Cliff House as we passed the Seal Rocks waving white handkerchiefs as a last adieu. Booker, the Barrons & Walkenshaws. Ship rolled a little over the bar & after in the night, but no one felt a qualm; bright & balmy.

Lights out at 10 a great nuisance, & ordered to be out of room & that tidied by 11 in morning for Captain to inspect as he goes round every day!

Sunday, January 24th.—276 miles by noon today; little wind. S. Coast in sight. Pass Santa Barbara. Drink whiskey punch with Van Brunt in evening. Fog came on in evening.

Monday, January 25th.—Bright again. Rebelled against regulations about turning out,—steward's boy frantic & awfully afraid of consequences to himself. We positively refuse to get out. He tells us that Mrs. Wilson had tried it on, but he made the stewardess have her out. Goes to Purser in despair who gives us leave to do as we like, & boy brings us tea & toast.

Another breakfast at noon; 268 miles.

Tuesday, January 26th.—Usual routine with whiskey punch at night. Conversation turns on horrible burning of the 2,000 in Cathedral at Santiago. Principally young girls, servants out of whom priests raise enormous sums, even in San Francisco.

Priest opened "Post office for Heaven," & the girls addressed the Virgin, &c. This vile fellow thus reading their secret thoughts & answering the letters. (Try & get newspaper account). The Captain is organising his Fire Brigade, & wants 30 volunteers from passengers. Milton & I intend to join. False alarms frequently given in middle of night, & all hands to engines. Hose always ready screwed on & everything handy; seems admirably arranged; but these boats with hurricane deck & top hamper [burn] like tinder. The *Golden Gate* burnt. No Fire Brigade. Captain Pearson last to leave ship. Captain Hudson burnt off the bobstay & tumbled in first, the rope charring thro'; both tossed on shore by breakers. Pearson finds he shall be thrown into debris of masts, &c., by next breaker; holds on to piece of mast, throws legs up into air as breaker comes, leaves go with hands, & is cast a complete summersault clear over the rigging & entanglements.

Wednesday, January 27th.—Passed Cape St. Luens about 1 p.m. Rough, craggy shore of no great height. Round the point lies San José, a garden spot of the greatest fertility; grapes, oranges, figs, &c., in enormous abundance. This Lower California barren & sterile as a rule, with isolated patches of great richness! Some deposits of natural salt on coast which are used. Whaling region. On previous voyage up, passed several whalers, boats out & a whale harpooned & killed close to steamer. Captain Pearson threw overside cases of mutton chops & sirloins of beef to boats which crowded round steamer for papers & news, &c.

—On passing the cape saw a good sized barque in full sail steering S. S. E., all telescopes to look if Alabama. Pronounced to be a whaler. A small boy, a bright youth of some 8 or 9 who was on board Ariel from New York to Aspinwall when overhauled by Alabama declared at first he was quite sure it was she. Afterwards that it was not like her. Made 290 miles today. Temperature 76° in shade. Steer across mouth of Gulf of California to Mansanita; thence coast of Acapulco. 291 miles.

Thursday, January 28th.—Temperature 78° in the shade which obliged us to resort to Linen Coats & trousers & straw hats, Milton & some others appearing in extraordinary contrivances much used on this coast, viz., hats made of pith, much larger than the head & with an inner ring of bamboo to fit the skull, thus allowing free ventilation. The crown also in sections of two different curves.

Towards 10 o'clock we passed the "White rock", a large white mass lying a little off the shore, between which & Manzanilla, & some 10 miles from the latter the *Golden Gate* was lost. Pearson praised the conduct of the women very highly; all heroes; jumped quickly overboard when their clothes took fire.

At 11 got into Port of Manzanita. I had gone to bed. Milton stayed up. Merely a line of houses on a sandspit below cliffs. The Port for Chiluma. Took 150 bales cotton on board & parted with some of our passengers, mostly Mexicans, one Yankee going to look after divers for treasure lost in Golden Gate, of which all has been recovered except 100,000 dollars, although Mexicans have made away with much that has been recaptured & there is no redress to be obtained from their law. They were in much disturbance from rumour that some schooners had been captured by French men-of-war said to be lying off the harbour; but we saw none; kept awake by rolling of kegs & Mexican jabbering.

Friday, January 29th.—Very hot indeed. The hysterical widow who laughs so heartily (who turns out to be only a "grass widow" or wife separated from her husband) has changed quarters to berth opposite ours. Has she a design upon us? Our other opposite neighbour is a hypochondriac who wraps himself in blankets with thermometer at 80° & dare not go out & comes out stealthily at intervals to shut the door leading out of passage between our staterooms. He has with great foresight brought his coffin on board with him. Thinks his food won't digest if he eats with his hat off, therefore has all meals in private! We are now going close to land. Hills covered with brush & low cliffs; 80° in the shade. Sea throughout like a lake. 225 miles.

Saturday, January 30th.—Had a farewell punch with Van Brunt, chairman of the society addicted to punch, & named by Pearson in consequence of the somnolent habits during the day of two of its most prominent members "The Owl Club" Mr. Wedderspoon the Valparaisan elected a member. Lord Milton, President. Called at 6 this morning by Van Brunt, the heads of the harbour of Acapulco being in sight. There are two entrances to it, one narrow one by which we entered, and a larger one. Across the latter lay a French frigate which quickly brought us to by a blank shot, & a boat put off, & the steamer still carrying way, another was fired. The French officer was very polite; said it was a mere matter of form to prevent arms being carried in; told us that they were only waiting the arrival of the Admiral to take the place; if there was a shot fired in opposition they would shell the town, &c. While we were in the town, we heard that they had mounted a few guns on the ruined old fort & would probably fire on the invaders. Altho' the Mexican in authority had promised repeatedly to the American inhabitants that they should be dismounted to prevent any firing.

Steered into little landlocked harbour, in which were lying two American coal ships, the Saginau, U. S. N., Admiral Bell, a tiny U. S. gunboat, and a Liverpool brig. A crowd of boats & canoes came off, the latter laden with oranges, yams, &c., stained corals & shells and a shoal of naked boys swimming from the shore, of all colours, from the darkness of a negro to the whiteness of the European; but all the bright eyes & pearly teeth; most of them showing a taint of nigger. These fellows swam about the ship untiringly & dived for dimes & quarters which they unfailingly caught before they got very far down. Captain Pearson, Milton & I then went ashore with Van Brunt in his gig, a beautiful boat manned by 6 dark-skinned Mexicans. The scene was new to us: cocoanuts with unripe fruit; oranges & mangoes; the former ripe. On the rocks lazy pelicans, numbers of which were also flapping lazily along in line. On one rock was stretched a hideous iguana sunning himself. Over the bay canoes & boats with awnings plying about. Everybody in white or light dresses, the Mexicans in the huge-brimmed sombreros. The town consists of a few irregular narrow streets & a plaza with a broken cross in the centre; & built on the flat below the hills which surround it. Houses of only a single story, & built of 'adobes', or of mud & bamboo, & roofed with reeds or loose tiles. Van Brunt's house consisted of several large rooms, very cool, airy & comfortable, built of same materials as rest. In his garden were oranges & mangoes, & amongst the flowers the Passion flower, oleander, heliotrope, phlox, trumpet honeysuckle. We went to the plaza & also into the church, a miserable old building with tawdry shrines & altar with tapers burning. A lot of Mexican boys came to us & called our attention to a tin money box with a paper print of the Virgin pasted on it, & we were fain to cast in half a dollar for their satisfaction. We found it is so hot in the sandy, shadeless streets that we were glad that the firing of the steamer's gun obliged us to return to Van Brunt's for Captain Pearson to go on board, & after an affectionate parting with Van Brunt we returned on board about 9. Really sorry to say goodbye. We heard that the French Admiral's ship was telegraphed in sight, & that the place would be taken in the afternoon or next day. There was not the slightest turmoil in the town about it. Everybody idling about listlessly with fruit baskets beside them or in their hands. 81° in the shade. On board found Admiral Bell, a fine old fellow with white hair. Steamed out, & soon after passed the "Golden Age" on her way back, close in to land, & we did not speak to her. 275 miles. Temperature 81°.

Sunday, January 31st.—Last night introduced by Mr. Bennett to the Western Girl, Miss Van Sickle of near Chicago, Illinois. And by her to the grass widow Mrs. Wetzner, a Canadian. I had a long talk with the former & found her good fun. A good-looking, buxom country lass, full of frolic & laughter, very good-natured & innocent as a baby. She had come over all the way from Illinois this summer to visit two brothers mining in Nevada; and was now on her way back to her parents, & travelling all alone. These long journeys by unprotected females are quite common. We have a Mrs. Merrit on board who left her husband & all her children but a nice little boy she has with her in the Eastern States in order to visit some relations in San Francisco & is now on her way back to her husband after 18 months absence. I got up a game of whist amongst the two ladies & Milton & myself; there was great fun & laughter; after this we induced them to go up into the Captain's room & drink champagne cup. where we all got very merry & happy, a great improvement upon our former dull evenings. At Acapulco a Mexican & his wife came on board, with several others of their countrymen. The former pair are about to travel in Europe. The lady is the best specimen of Spanish beauty I have seen, beautiful olive complexion, very transparent but too uniform in colour; eyes very black & languishing, beautifully pencilled eyebrows & long drooping lashes; delicate straight little nose & tiny mouth, with the reddest lips I have ever seen; oval face & delicate ears, figure pretty, rather too embonpoint in bust; graceful walk peculiar to Spanish women. 235 miles.

Monday, February 1st.—Last night had more fun with

the girls, giving them iced claret cup 'al fresco'. Captain & I had a very fierce argument at dinner which attracted notice of whole cabin; I attacked Henry W. Beecher, whom I find the Captain admires extremely & said he was the worst man his party could possibly have selected to advocate their views in England. He was down upon me like a shot & assured me he (Beecher) had produced a revolution in feeling in England, as proved by the change of action by the Government in case of Slaves. I assured him that Beecher most certainly would have rather induced the Government to turn the other way, &c. And this from a man of strong common sense in most things; the argument got very hot but neither of us lost temper; & I soothed him down all right at last. In the evening also the widow attacked Bennett on the Christian faith, founding her argument on the absurdity of an Immaculate & Supernatural Conception. And asked if she were to have a child, whether we should not at once infer that the conception was not immaculate or supernatural! certainly not. This floored Bennett, & Miss Van Sickle left in a hurry, pleasing all by her modesty. We were all disgusted with the strong-minded widow.

In the course of today passed three lofty peaks 2 of which are in Guatemala, all volcanic & some 12,000 to 18,000 feet. Weather delightful; same still sea & bright sun with slight breeze.

Crossed Gulf of Tehuantepec without a blow which is quite unusual; strong breeze sprang up.

Tuesday, February 2nd.—Played Old Maid & 'Muggins' a kind of complicated Patience with Miss Van Sickle, Bennett, Lord Milton & Wedderspoon & had great fun. The young lady having a wholesome terror of the dreadful card & screaming with laughter when she got it. Owl Club meeting & champagne cup by Mr. Wedderspoon in Saloon; very jolly evening. Fine breeze last night. Thermometer 88° in shade.

Wednesday, February 3rd.—The widow at her games; asked Milton yesterday to walk her about & pay her attention in order to rouse the jealousy of the Young Peruvian Consul, whom she says she is "regularly stuck after," & anxious evidently to carry on an intrigue with, having sent him poetry & met him in the quiet place at the stern, &c. Milton very properly intimated his dislike to being made a catspaw of & declined. She bullied him about it at our meeting of Owls when we played Muggins in the evening, & the laughter & chaff was as uproarious as ever. Not very refined but innocent enough; except that Mrs. Wetzner (the grass widow) sometimes brought out a "double entendre" of which no one took any notice. We all like the Western Girl, and all the gentlemen run after her to the great discomfiture of the widow. Mrs. Merrit & Mrs. Wilson appear dreadfully shocked by our boisterous conduct, & ignore all the gentlemen & Miss Van Sickle & the widow. Scandal is already rife concerning the widow & Mr. Kennedy, a most obstinate Yankee who denies that snow ever exists on mountains in the tropics! 88°. 207 miles.

Pass Cape Blanco about noon, Costa Rica.

Thursday, February 4th.—The anniversary of my Father's death. Will that sorrow never cease to be so very very painful? 190 miles. 88°.

Friday, February 5th.—Still keep up the fun with the Illinois infant & teaze her dreadfully. Everyone eats philopenas with her. The widow disconsolate. Peruvian Consul consoles her occasionally. At 12 noon reach the entrance of the bay, about 100 miles from the anchorage; very hot but I don't feel the weather disagreeably warm. Last meeting of the Owl club, & great fun over game of consequences; but several papers have to be suppressed, the objectionable passages being in the widow's handwriting. Turn in about 10, but unable to sleep much, expecting the stopping of the engines. Arrive at anchorage about 12.30.

Saturday, February 6th.—At an island, at two a.m. are roused out by the gong, have just time to eat a little breakfast before going on board the steam-trader, which takes us to a wharf on mainland, & close to station; quite dark & unable to see City of Panama which lies to the left & is, I hear, a fine old place with half ruined castle, churches & houses. But as small-pox & fever are rife there we regret the less our inability to visit it. Bennett, Milton & myself take Miss Van Sickle in tow with a basket of sandwiches from the steward, & a bottle of champagne & 1 of whisky from the Doctor (Dr. Treenor). The widow got the Reese River miner to look after her. We had to wait about an hour at the station or depot as the Yankees call it, the carriages unlighted except by the lanterns of numerous niggers in white who wandered about backwards & forwards the length of the train, vending all kinds of fruits, oranges, pineapples, bananas, alligator-pears, &c., and cakes, bottled ale, brandy, &c. Just as it was almost light the train moved off, (& 5 o'clock). There were a number of passengers from the Southern Pacific Coast, principally from Valparaiso going by Southampton. And now I saw for the first time the wonders of tropical vegetation, cocoanuts, orange trees, bananas in plenty. Coarse grass & large herbaceous plants, all tangled together by innumerable creepers. The vivid green of every shade was more brilliant than anything I have seen elsewhere. And there were beautiful flowers too, convolvoli of various colours, & flowers of brilliant red & yellow. One tree with cones of scarlet very bright. In the gardens, roses & oleanders. The railroad winds along between low hills, & principally thro' marshy country, frequently touching the banks of the Chagres river & eventually crossing it by a fine iron bridge. There were numerous tiny villages of bamboo & mud, with niggers of all shades & costumes, many of them the scantiest, the men generally lying basking in the sun, & the women nursing coppery babies. There is great variation in the colour, from the blackest nigger to the Spanish olive, all ugly; legs all shin bone; woman either skinny or very flabby. There are many sharp curves on the line, & some steep grades, and once or twice we had to have darkies running before the train to scatter sand on the rails; numerous cattle in the clearings, resembling Alderneys most completely in every way. About 8 we arrived at Aspinwall, a miserable place of two or three streets, & light white wooden houses, picked out with green, Yankee fashion. We found that we should not be allowed to go on board the steamer until she fired a gun, therefore had to turn into an hotel, where we ate our sandwiches & drank our bottle of champagne, then wandered about the streets, but found nothing to see but the same niggers of all shades, selling fruit, shells & corals. Milton anxious for curiosities but cannot find any. The steamer for St. Thomas had sailed at 6, although we arrived at 8, & the Golden City had been telegraphed as having arrived at Panama at midnight. The Southampton passengers had therefore no choice but to go by the 'Ariel' to New York, or wait a fortnight in Aspinwall for next English boat, & all (60) chose the former. Aspinwall is built almost in the sea, flat & marshy ground. *They say* that in building the Panama R. R. a man died for every sleeper laid, principally Irishmen, brought out in ignorance of the deadly nature of the climate. About 10.30

the gun fired, & we went on board the Ariel, which got under way about 11. A small ship of some 800 tons, but not so uncomfortable as I expected, altho' a miserable contrast to the Golden City. But our experience between Victoria & San Francisco on the 'Pacific' had made us look on even mediocrity as luxury. The cabins small, & the food only passable, but the officers, &c., very civil; and Captain Wilson a fine old Salt. There was a slight sea on, with a fine fresh breeze on from the N. E., & many of the passengers began to feel squeamish before evening when we got out into the Caribbean Sea.

Sunday, February 7th.—The breeze had increased & blew very fresh, the sea getting rather rough. Most of the passengers were down with sea-sickness. Milton had a slight turn, I felt squeamish but got over it by lying down a little, & had not to absent myself from a single meal. One poor lady with 8 children was completely prostrate; I never saw any one so awfully ill. Miss Van Sickle & Mr. Wedderspoon are both very bad & our fun vanished. Even the indomitable Bennett was almost mum. Several English ladies on board.

Monday, February 8th.—On getting out our luggage found that all our claret had been abstracted, but the brandy left. All our baggage was taken charge of on board the Golden City & redelivered to us here. I presumed the wine was taken on board the lighters which conveyed the baggage. Some one had derisively sketched a bottle on the side of the broken, open case. The breeze blew fresher & fresher, & the sea became higher & higher, the little Ariel pitching tremendously. I held out famously. Milton in bed nearly all day. Two old whaling Captains very unwell, the motion being so different from that of a sailing vessel. Towards evening the breeze abated a little. Poor Mrs. —— still prostrate on deck.

Tuesday, February 9th.—Quiet; very hot, passing close to San Domingo, between that island & Cuba — which we shall see this afternoon. Everyone up & lively. Last night I was fiercely attacked by a rabid Northerner, who abused England dreadfully for the Alabama & Slave affairs & because all the blockade runners carried the British Flag. I played with him, keeping quite cool, & making him almost mad. Assuring him Englishmen didn't care how the war went, & nonplussing him at last by comparing this "infernal, wicked, devilish rebellion" as he called it, with the American Revolution; it was good fun. We are very polite to one another this morning.

Wednesday, February 10th.—Yesterday afternoon passed within ½ mile of Cuba; very beautiful low bank with trees & grass of most vivid green. Last night after bed time it became rough; but before this in early evening we had some very nice duets from Mr. & Mrs. Robertson of Valparaiso who both sang very nicely, especially the lady who seemed a very talented woman, the mother of 8 children, the eldest only about 10. We persuaded Miss Van Sickle to give Annie Laurie which she did very well, & thus till quite late. I made the acquaintance of Dr. Birt, a Doctor of Valparaiso, in charge of Naval Hospital there. Had been in Crimea as a Civil Surgeon. Makes £2,000 a year in Valparaiso. An F. R. C. S. University College & Hospital man. Very jolly fellow.

Thursday, February 11th.—An awfully wet & windy morning. Rough sea. Ladies all down again. Our Star of attraction very sick, & all the satellites bereft of amusement on a dreary day; nowhere to sit; rain even coming in to our staterooms when door was open. In evening played whist with Wedderspoon, Robertson & a Frenchman. I won ½ dollar. Abused by Miss Van Sickle for neglect.

Friday, February 12th.—Another dreary, wet & windy day. We stayed in bed until noon to kill time. Then read, chaffed Miss Van Sickle & smoked. Calmed down towards night & stars came out.

Saturday, February 13th.—Fine bright morning & sea smooth. Sweepstakes on 3 days run, for two days no observation able to be taken. Wedderspoon won at 700 miles. (698 run).

Note. Story told me by Dr. Treenor of Golden City of Uncle Abe & the Homeopathists requesting him to appoint them to army.

Story told me by Dr. Birt of Ruggle the American Judge who came down to Chili concerning American vessel seized for carrying arms during Chilian Revolution. A Chilian at large dinner comparing Chili with United States, up jumped Ruggle "Wal, *good* damnation! You compare your little one-horse-power state with the great United States of America? I'd as soon compare a ———— with the Throne of God".

Expressions & Phrases 'dog goned', 'dogged', 'quit', 'kind o', 'didn't oughter', mean man, clever [equals] our "jolly", "recuperating".

The widow has cut us all dead.

Sunday, February 14th.—Last night played whist till 11.30, winning 5 dollars; the same party as before; very pleasant rubber. This morning, cold strong breeze. 263 miles. Saw land at 4.30. After dinner young Peruvian got into row with a German Jew (rather tight I fancy) who struck him & there was a scramble. They were separated by bystanders, & the Peruvian stamped, gnashed his teeth, struggled with his detainers, & escaping occasionally, making rushes at the other with a storm of invectives & gesticulating violently, — then tearing his hair & crying "Carramba", "carraco", &c.; generally conducting himself like a maniac. They both quietened down eventually. Very rough with N. W. breeze; expect to land about 10. Arrived off lights at entrance of Harbour about 8. Pilot came on board but in consequence of gale blowing he would not risk entering in dark; had therefore to lie off till morning.

Monday, February 15th.—Called up at 5.30 by mischievous fellow named Ryan who could not sleep himself & therefore roused all other passengers. Calling out, "All Ashore, Sir," like the steward. On turning out found we should be nearly 2 hours yet. Bitterly cold, strong North-East wind. No breakfast or even cup of coffee provided for passengers. A deal of waiting to get luggage, which was however passed without question being from California. Drove with Mr. Bennett to New York Hotel. The entrance to New York is pretty; nice houses, well wooded grounds on left; none of smoke & filth of Old Country; Broadway & 5th Avenue very fine broad streets with fine causeway; houses well built & lofty, but still an absence of magnificence or splendour. Nothing like Regent Street, altho' 10 times the length. Inquired for letters at 5th Avenue & Post Office. Milton got one at former, I none whatever. Met La Grange. Nothing but Greenbacks & small notes down to 5 cents. Went to Brady's & had carte de visite taken. Bennett also. After called on Miss Van Sickle at Astor House. In evening read papers, Milton going with La Grange to Music Hall. After, oyster supper at a Saloon. Looked at Robertson's tongue. Cancer; poor fellow with 8 children. Bade goodbye to Bennett; off by 6 a.m. tomorrow to Baltimore.

Tuesday, February 16th.—Like New York more, the more I see of it. The warehouses & hotels in Broadway are very fine. And the trees in the street, especially in 5th Avenue, make it look very like the West End of London rather than a business part of the town. The Anthracite coal burnt universally here makes no smoke, & the air is as clear as in the country. And on viewing the place from a distance, no cloud of smoke hanging over it. The small number of people in the streets, the only place where any are to be seen, being Broadway. Much disappointed with women, very few beautiful. Middle-aged ones yellow. Surprised that I have never yet heard the war discussed, or any political topic, at any of the bars, oyster saloons, or public places. Mourning worn by nearly half. Out of 30 hats outside dining room, 12 had crape on. Greenbacks cursed. Gold $60\frac{1}{2}$ per cent. On offering a bit to omnibus driver for fare, he burst out laughing, & everyone in bus followed. All paper except 1 cent pieces. I fancy only enthusiasm in favour of war is amongst shoddy contractors. Everyone seems extremely quiet & subdued, very unusual amongst Yankees. Snow falling most of the day, very cold. In evening went to say goodbye to Miss Van Sickle at Astor House, & found her glorious in a new set of furs. Mr. Hadgins the miner will escort her to Chicago. We went with them to the Station & then bid a fond farewell, the lady being really affected, & both Milton & myself very sorry to part with such an unsophisticated, natural, good-natured, buxom lass. In evening went to French Play at Academy of Music; benefit of a French Society. Crowded out & therefore we came away early. Fine House, as large as Covent Garden. Finished with oyster supper.

Wednesday, February 17th.—Fearfully cold, thermometer at 9° & strong wind; I was half frozen going down to Cunard's office to secure places on China. Spent afternoon at Brady's, Milton getting photographed.

Thursday, February 18th.—Bright clear morning, very very cold. Went off to Central Park & skated for 3 hours. About 1,000 people there, as many lady as gentleman skaters. Not many pretty faces. Ladies skate very well. Not much fancy skating. In evening went by 7.30 train to Washington. Cross river in steam ferry to Jersey & then Rail. Steam ferries large, flat-bottomed boats, taking horses & carriages. Pass Philadelphia & Baltimore in the dark. Train crosses a river between these 2 cities on gigantic ferry boats; hauled across by chains. No change, the cars being drawn thro' the streets of Baltimore by horses about 1 a.m.

Friday, February 19th.—Washington about 9. Willard's Hotel. Every place crammed full but as we had telegraphed, we got beds. Soldiers everywhere. Hotel bars & corridors crowded with officers & men; very slovenly looking soldiers in their light blue grey. I did not see one soldier-like fellow. Streets full of transport waggons with provisions & forage for the army. The Hotel a fine large building, but the floors filthy with tobacco juice squirted all over. After breakfast called on Lord Lyons who sent word by attaché that it was mail day & he was too busy to see Milton who must write if he wanted anything! We therefore retired discomfited, Milton much put out. Strolled down Pensylvania Avenue to the Capitol. It is a magnificent building in a magnificent situation, on an eminence which slopes away gradually on all sides, giving a very extensive view for many miles every way, & visible, I suppose, from a great distance. The building itself is marble, Grecian, dome in centre.

Inside, the decorations are not very extensive. Marble staircases. White painted wood, with some illuminated ceilings, &c. In the dome are pictures of Lord Cornwallis surrendering to Washington, General Burgoyne do. Landing of Columbus, Baptism of Pocahontas, Signing of Declaration of Independence, Washington resigning his commission back to Congress, & some others; a fine Equestrian portrait of General Scott, &c. The Senate Chamber & that of Representatives are lofty & convenient rooms, comfortably fitted without display. The speaker sits on an elevated chair with a desk before him, clerks, &c. below, & the stars & stripes with gilt American Eagle above him; arranged round in semicircular rows are the desks of the members, loose with chairs, a gallery round, separate portions for the ladies & gentlemen. Open to the public who are allowed to wander over the building at pleasure, except Chambers & Courts. In the House of Representatives, a Democrat was making a fierce attack on the Abolitionists & opposing a bill to provide a Bureau for administration & management of free niggers, animadverting severely on conduct of "Massachusets", in bringing negroes to present dreadful condition by abolition, viz. dying by hundreds on the Mississippi, & the same with those crowded round Washington, in hovels, & stricken by famine & disease (smallpox, fever, &c), & their being worked on confiscated plantations under military supervision, with wages too small even to buy food. In the Senate, a Senator was defending the President from an attack by the "Senator for Kentucky" who had called him a "viper", &c. The galleries were well filled. No applause except an occasional clap of one pair of hands in House of Representatives. In evening saw Edwin Booth in Coleman's "Iron Chest" & Taming of the Shrew. Gower's Theatre; very fair.

Saturday, February 20th.—Walked about having had but little sleep previous night, being unable to get a berth in sleeping car, we did not get up till noon. Treasury a fine Grecian building; nice grounds between it & White House, a very comfortable-looking place. Engaged sleeping cars beforehand. Dining room at Willard's the longest & best lighted room I ever saw, & filled with diners; nigger waiters; too crowded to get proper attendance. At ½ past 7 train for New York. Numbers of Soldiers going home on furlough.

Sunday, February 21st.—Arrived at Jersey City at 7.30 & across in steam-ferry. River full of ice. Back at Hotel by 8.30. In evening Mr. Page takes us to Lager beer place, where he drinks 10 glasses, I 6, & feel so sleepy I rush off to bed.

Monday, February 22nd.—In morning go down to Duncan & Sherman's (Bankers) with Milton to draw £150. Then pay passages at Cunard's. Afterwards Milton goes to Brady's, & look up Theodore Passavant whom I find at 44 Greene St. as Superintendent of a factory of Metallic Keg Co. Willy is a clerk in a machine shop. Theodore did not recognize me, but delighted when I introduced myself. Promised to bring his brother down to spend the evening with me at New York Hotel, which he accordingly did, & we had a social smoke, & pleasant talk of the good old times of Bingley. We were much delighted to meet, & I enjoyed the evening greatly.

Tuesday, February 23rd.—Sent all luggage down to China in afternoon, & then went to dine with Page. La Grange

accompanied us. Page is a Democratic lawyer, raised a regiment at beginning of war, & then on some dispute with authorities resigned. The dinner was plain but good, & the wine
also. A man named Evans connected with press, grandil-
oquent & pedantic, but well informed; Kent (nephew of Kent's
Commentaries), a very well informed clever fellow, who had
travelled in England & on the continent, pleased me very much.
He was a strong but not offensive Northerner. Complained
against prejudice against Yankees in England, was quite sure
all Englishmen were delighted that blustering U. S. were in
hot water & did not blame us. I agreed with that. Said most
Englishmen did not see the best part of American society, &
life, viz. that of the country gentlemen. Smoked & talked
till 12. Many playing poker when Evans insisted upon taking
us to a parting supper given by a Mr. Sandford to young
James Bennett, son of the notorious James Gardner, who
was going to England in the China.

Wednesday, February 24th.—We therefore drove down
to Delmonico's & were introduced to a lot of "Young New
Yorkers" & had a most magnificent supper. The supper was
on side-tables & handed, consisting of French dishes, & the
table at which we sat was literally covered with flowers,
camellias, orchids & rare exotics in epergnes & long baskets
worth $150. Wine of all kinds flowing incessantly. Toasts
& speeches. Milton's health & mine. Twaddle. Bennett &
others tight; 5 o'clock when all was over, therefore too late for
bed & sat up till light, then drove down to New York Hotel,
settled there, & went down to ship by 8.30, with Bennett's
friends, found all luggage right. Called into Bennett's cabin
where Sandford had sent a basket of champagne which we set
into. One in drunken folly shied his glass into the crowd &
wet me through. All getting very noisy & unmanageable
when the bell rang for all but passengers to go ashore & we
bade affectionate farewell, & were towed away from wharf
amid shouted adieus & waving of handkerchiefs at about 9.30.
Soon after Milton & I went to sleep till dinner time at 4.
Passed City of London from Liverpool.

Thursday, February 25th.—Fine weather with N. W.
breeze & doing 13 & 14 knots; 345 miles from New York.
Lord Abinger & bride on board. Miss Magruder, niece of
General M—— picked up in M[ountain]s, saw her at tea, little,

dark, nice figure, pretty face with marks of a very fierce temper. Passed Asia but did not speak her.

Friday, February 26th.—Breeze from South West, going well; 326 miles. Sea gone down.

Saturday, February 27th.—Breeze shifting more to South & blowing harder; fore & aft sails. Rolling & pitching. Many laid by. Milton sick occasionally, I uncomfortable.

Sunday, February 28th.—Heavy sea. Wind South. Uncomfortable, rolling hard.

Monday, February 29th.—Much the same. Sea higher. wind nearly dead ahead, few passengers visible.

Tuesday, March 1st.—Sea very rough. Wind dead ahead, pitching & rolling very great, & screw "racing" continually and almost shaking cabin to pieces. 211 miles. Played whist with Bennett, &c., in evening, & felt better. Bennett told us story of Captain ———, an Officer of U. S. Navy of Southern extraction, engaged off islands near Charleston; dug out with nigger, came off from mainland & alongside. Mrs. ———'s compliments (an old friend of the Captains), & she sent him a present for old acquaintance sake, something useful to an invader of the Southern Confederacy; he opened the parcel & there were 4 coffin handles. He sent a polite message in return & hung them as ornaments in his cabin!

Wednesday, March 2nd.—Sea much quieter. Wind dead ahead & likely to keep so. No hope of getting in now before Monday; only 140 miles!

Thursday, March 3rd.—Wind still East & very fresh. Sea running high, screw racing with the pitching & rolling, majority ill & invisible or only appearing at intervals.
Milton getting more & more seasick; I improve. 206 miles.

Friday, March 4th.—Sea very rough, water shipped over side occasionally. Wind a point North of East & fore & aft sails set to steady her. 199.

Saturday, March 5th.—Sea moderated & trying to go better, 246. Towards evening wind died away, going 12 knots to 13.

Sunday, March 6th.—Almost dead calm, only slight wind East; distance 296.

The day is beautifully bright & warm, & everyone appeared at meals; to reach Queenstown before midnight; passed Cape Clear at 7.30.

Monday, March 7th.—Off Queenstown at 1 a.m.; shortly before exchanged signals with Arabic on way out. Got papers but no news except that North American which ought to have gone by way of Londonderry passed Cape Clear at 4 yesterday.

At 11 passed North American steaming very slowly, probably disabled. At 2.45 passed Holyhead.

THE END.

NOTE ON THE ANNOTATORS OF THIS VOLUME

Lanctot, Gustave, B.L., LL.M., Dipl. Ox., D.Litt. (Paris), F.R.H.S., F.R.S.C., C.R. Chief French Archivist, Ottawa. Born at St. Constant, Que., Canada, son of Alphonse and Amelina (Riendeau) Lanctot. Married Marie Chauvin, daughter of Adolphe Chauvin. Educated: Public schools, St. Constant; Collège of Montreal; University of Montreal, Oxford University and Paris University. First engaged in newspaper work, took up law and was called to the Bar, 1907. Studied at London School of Economics, 1908; selected as Rhodes Scholar for Quebec, 1909. Studied at Oxford and later at Paris University specializing in historical work. Travelled extensively in Europe. Entered the Canadian Archives, 1912. Sent on special work to the United States, 1913. Enlisted, 1915, and went overseas. Later made a member of Canadian Special Mission to France, with rank of major, 1917. Assistant Director of War Trophies in C.E.F. 1918. One of Canada's representatives at International Congress, Rio-de-Janeiro, 1922, and International Congress, Brussels, 1923. Made a K. C. in 1925. Joint Secretary to Federal-Provincial Conference, Ottawa, 1927. Canadian Delegate to Historical Colonial Exhibition, Paris, 1929. Gold Medal in Confederation Jubilee Competition, 1927. David Prize for historical work, 1930.

Publications: Le dernier effort de la France au Canada, 1918; François Xavier Garneau, 1924; Les Archives du Canada, 1926; L'Administration de la Nouvelle-France, 1929; Editor: (with Dr. Kennedy) Reports on the Laws of Quebec, 1930; (with Dr. Doughty) Cheadle's Journal of Trip across Canada, 1931.

Association, Canadian Historical Review, La Revue trimestrielle, La Revue moderne, Le Canada-Français, etc.

Contributor to: Cambridge University History of British Empire, Encyclopaedia of Social Sciences, Royal Society of Canada, Journal of American Folk-Lore, Canadian Historical Societies: President Canadian Folk-Lore Society; Vicepresident Society of Authors, Ottawa; Joint-Secretary and Editor Canadian Historical Society; member: Royal Historical Society, England; American Historical Association; Société des Américanistes, Paris; Société historique de Montréal; Institut Canadien; Institute of International Affairs, France, Amérique and Alliance Française.

Dr. Doughty is Deputy-Minister of Public Archives, Dominion of Canada, Ottawa.

APPENDIX

1. Mgr. Charles Francois Baillargeon (1798-1870.)
2. Mgr. Edward J. Horan (1810-1875).
3. Bartholomew C. A. Gugy (1797-1876), a Quebec lawyer, once member of the Legislative Assembly and colonel of militia.
4. Quebec was taken only twice, in 1629 and 1759, by the British.
5. A sea-port in South Carolina, one of the Confederate States, was blockaded from April 6th 1863 and captured Feb. 18th 1865 by the Federal troops.
6. A prominent political man and member of the Legislative Council (1793-1860).
7. Fort Garry, at junction of Red and Assiniboine Rivers, where the city of Winnipeg now stands.
8. Louis La Ronde, a French half-breed who had accompanied O'Rae in his expedition in search of Sir John Franklin.
9. William McTavish was governor of Assiniboia for the Hudson's Bay Company from 1858 to 1870.
10. Dr. David Anderson (1814-1885) was bishop of Rupert's Land from 1849 to 1864.
11. Toussaint Vaudrie or Voudrie, a French half-breed.
12. Athanase Bruneau, a French half-breed engaged to go with the expeditition.
13. His name was Zear.
14. Fort Ellice of the Hudson's Bay Company on the Assiniboine, then in charge of Mr. Mackay.
15. This was Touchwood Hills House, a post of the Hudson's Bay Co. recently closed.
16. Carlton House, a fort of the Hudson's Bay Company on the south shore of the North Saskatchewan then in charge of Mr. Lillie.
17. In *the North-West Passage,* Cheadle calls it Belle Prairie.
18. The "Old Boy's" name was Kekwapkosis or, as in *The North-West Passage,* Kekekooarsis, the Child of the Hawk, in allusion to the beak-like form of his nose.
19. His name was Kinamontayoo or, as in *The North-West Passage* Keenamontiayoo, the Long Neck.
20. The Old boy's son-in-law, Kinamontayoo is referred to as the "Hunter" or the "Chasseur", the French equivalent.
21. Cheadle calls him Nashquamayoo, and later Misquamayoo and Mishoo for short. He was fourteen years old.
22. Nashquamayoo is indifferently referred to as "the young Indian", "the young Cree", & "the young one".
23. Sacreing, a word coined by Cheadle out of *sacrer* the popular French word for to swear.
24. His name was Mahaygun or the Wolf.

25. The house of Kekekooarsis.
26. This Indian was a Sauteux, whose name meant the Big Knife.
27. Kinnikinnick is the inner bark of the dog wood which is used as a poor substitute for tobacco.
28. An English half-breed in the service of the Hudson's Bay Company at Carlton.
29. Fort Pelly, a post of the Hudson's Bay Company on the Assiniboine.
30. Carlton House.
31. Fort Pitt of the Hudson's Bay Company then in charge of Mr. Chantelaine.
32. Louis Battenotte was the name of this French half-breed always called by the author "the Assiniboine."
33. For the rest of the Journal, the terms "the boy", and the "young one", used previously for Misquamayoo, now designate Assiniboine's young son.
34. A travaille is an Indian contrivance, consisting of two long poles joined together on the back of the horse, and fastened with cross bars. The lower ends of the poles drag on the ground and the baggage is tied on to the cross-bars.
35. B. stands for Baptiste Supernat.
36. Fort Edmonton of the Hudson's Bay Company then in charge of Mr. Hardisty.
36a. It was called St. Albans.
37. The priest was Father Lacombe (1827-1916) an Oblate missionary, who spent his life among the Indians and half-breeds. Through his great influence among them he rendered valuable help to the authorities, especially in 1885, in preventing a general uprising of the tribes.
38. Alexander Grant Dallas became governor of Rupert's Land for the Hudson's Bay Company in 1862.
39. Colin Fraser was an officer of the Hudson's Bay Company stationed at St. Ann's.
40. Dr (later Sir) James Hector was the geologist of the expedition sent by the British Government (1857-1860) to explore the Canadian North-West under John Palliser.
41. James Carnegie, Earl of Southesk, a well-known author visited Western Canada in 1859, accompanying Sir George Simpson (1792-1860) then Governor of the Hudson's Bay Company.
42. Jasper House, a post of the Hudson's Bay Company on the Athabaska then in charge of Mr. Macaulay.
43. Kamloops, a post of the Hudson's Bay Company on the Thompson River at the head of Lake Kamloops, on the other side of the Rockies in British Columbia.
44. Tete Juane Cache is at the western end of the Yellowhead Pass.
45. He was an Iroquois half-breed called Louis Caropontier.
46. Cariboo district where gold digging was carried on is in British Columbia situated inside the great bend of the Fraser River.
46a. For Mount Milton and Mount Cheadle, see the map at the end of the book.
47. Meaning the horse of that colour.
48. A dog belonging probably to the Assiniboine.

APPENDIX—*Continued*.

49. Prele, French for shave-grass.
50. The Fort at Kamloops now the goal of the expedition.
51. Rubaboo was made by boiling a piece of pemmican or dry meat the size of one's fist in a large quantity of water thickened with a single handful of flour.
52. O'Byrne afraid to venture on horseback crossed the river by holding to the tail of one of the horses and being towed over.
53. At Kamloops.
54. Joseph William Mackay (1829-1900) was then chief trader at Kamloops for the Hudson's Bay Company.
55. Roderick Finlayson (1818-1892) joined the Hudson's Bay Company in 1837 and became a chief factor in 1859. He is the author of a valuable narrative of the fur trade in British Columbia.
56. Richard Clements Moody (1813-1887) entered the army and was promoted lieutenant colonel in 1858, being appointed chief commissioner of lands and works in British Columbia. Founded New Westminster and built a number of provincial roads.
57. The Gold Escort was an escort provided by the Government for the protection of miners returning with their gold.
58. Sir James Douglas (1803-1877) joined in 1820 the North West Company merged the following year in the Hudson's Bay Company. He was promoted chief factor in 1840 and in 1847 built Fort Victoria on Vancouver Island. In 1851, was appointed governor of Vancouver Island and of the mainland in 1858. He showed great ability and resource in his administration.
59. The River Fraser excitement, took place in 1858, when gold was discovered in the bars of the Fraser river and a swarm of miners from everywhere invaded British Columbia.
60. San Juan island became the centre of a boundary dispute between Great Britain and the United States. To avoid conflict in 1859 it was decided that both nations would occupy the island. In 1872, arbitration decided in favour of America.
61. Sir Mathew Baillie Begbie (1819-1894) appointed judge of British Columbia in 1858, established a reputation during the days of the Gold Rush for fearlessness and impartial justice and became Chief Justice of the province in 1870.

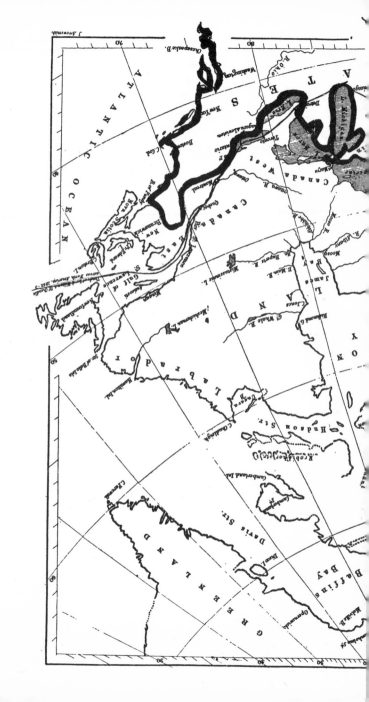

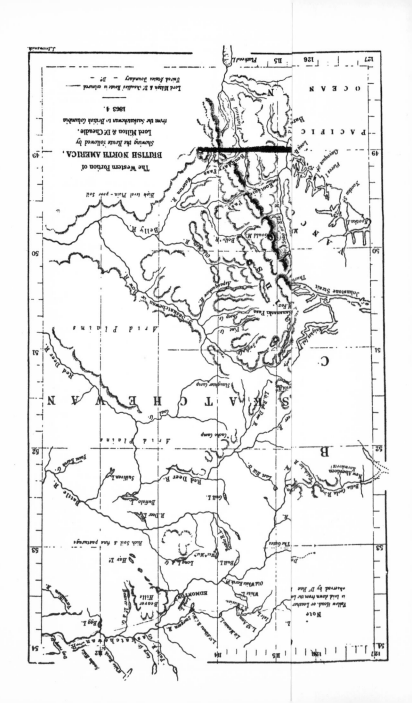

The Western Portion of
BRITISH NORTH AMERICA,
Showing the Route followed by
Lord Milton & D.ʳ Cheadle,
from the Saskatchewan to British Columbia
1863 4.

Lord Milton & D.ʳ Cheadles Route is coloured ───
United States Boundary ─ ─ D.º ─